ENGLISH RECUSANT LITERATURE
1558–1640

Selected and Edited by
D. M. ROGERS

Volume 279

ST. FRANCIS OF SALES
An Introduction to a Devoute Life
1613

ST. FRANCIS OF SALES
An Introduction to a Devoute Life
1613

The Scolar Press
1976

ISBN o 85967 28o 8

Published and printed in Great Britain by
The Scolar Press Limited, 59-61 East Parade,
Ilkley, Yorkshire and
39 Great Russell Street,
London WCi

NOTE

Reproduced (original size) from a copy in the possession of the Editor. In this copy the title-page is damaged and the second leaf (pp. 3–4) missing, and in the facsimile these pages are reproduced from a copy in the Plume Library, Maldon, by permission of the Trustees. Also, it should be noted that on page 11 the final word on the eighth line up from the foot of the page reads '*striving*'. This first edition is unrecorded in Allison and Rogers, where the second edition is no. 338 (STC 11317).

IHS

AN
INTRODVCTION
TO A DEVOVTE LIFE

COMPOSED IN
FRENCHE
By the R. Father in God,
FRANCIS SALES, Bishop
of Geneua.

AND TRANSLATED
INTO
ENGLISG. By I. Y.

william Duke̲s
& vvighāsing̲s

By IOHN.
HEIGHAM,
With Permission.
1613.

TO THE RIGHT
VIRTVOVS GENTLE-
WOMAN MISTRIS

ANNE ROPER,

DAVGHTER TO THE
RIGHT WORSHIPFVLL

SIR WILLIAM ROPER,
OF WELL-HALL IN ELTHAM.

THIS excellent fum-
marie of fpirituall life
(*Right worshipfull and
trulie Religious*) hath
gained fo great credit with all
deuout minds , for the excee-
ding· profit and delight which
they haue found by perufing
A 2   it:

it : that no booke whatsoeuer
hath been in so short a time, so
often, and in so manie places re-
printed; none by so manie men,
and those of so great iudgement,
and in such varietie of bookes
treating of the same subiect, so
much commended. Litle indeed
it is in quantitie, but in substance, and effect, (as I may say) infinite. Like the philosophers stone,
which being but small in bignes,
and not verie beautifull in shew,
conteineth in it the seedes of all
metalls, & with the onely touch,
changeth baser metalls into the
soueraignest of all, which is gold,
the sole gouernour now, of this
iron world. For euen so truly
not onely in my iudgement,
(which in these heauenly matters reacheth but low) but in the
iudgement of great diuines, and
very

very holy men, there hath not come out any abridgement of deuotion like this, conteining so copiouslie in few leaues, so plainlie in sweet language, so profitablie and aptlie for practize of all men, the rules and instruction of spirituall perfection, nor so pregnant in efficacie, to conuert the iron affections of our foules, into the golden virtue of charitie, and true deuotion the queene of virtues, that enamoureth God him self with her heauenlie beautie. This made me desirous to peruse it carefully, for the bettering of my owne soule; and to translate it painfully, for the benefit of manie soules in our poor distressed countrie: which more then any other countrie, standeth in need of such good bookes, for counter poisons against so manie vene-

A 3

venemous writings, as worldly
and fantasticall heads daylie publishe. This also made me so
bold, as to dedicate the booke,
and my labour, taken in transla-
ting of it, vnto your good selfe:
as a treatise likely to be most
pleasing to that excellent disposition which inclineth your mind
to all holie & virtuous exercises:
and an argument almost proper
and peculiar, to the feruent zeale
of Gods glorie, descending vnto
you, and all your worthy familie
by inheritance, and naturall affection receaued from your glorious progenitour, that excellent
true states-man, & learned coun-
cellour, englands honour, faithes
zealous champion, and Chrifts
conftant martyr, SIR THOMAS
MOORE, your great grand-father. His admirable virtues may
                              eafilie

eafilie perfuade any man , that
you neither would nor could degenerate from fo liuelie a pater-
ne : and your deuout and virtuous life, doth as eafilie proue
you to be defcended from that
faire roote, by fo goodly braunches as your worshipfull father
and grand-father; of whome as
you haue taken the worthines of
your bloud , fo haue you learned
their pietie and godlines , which
maketh you delight in nothing
fo much , as in the practize of
deuotion and Chriftian perfection. This I fay, makes me 'fo
hardie as to defire you to accept of this my labour, and not
onely to patronize it with your
title , as a thing vowed to your
feruice : but alfo at your beft leafure to read it,and practize it;that
fo I may be,not onely repayed by

your courteous acceptâce of my
good will, but likewife be partaker of thofe fpirituall ioyes , and
increafe of pietie , which I doubt
not but you will reap out of this
fertil field of deuotion : which is
the principall fruiĉt that in this
my poor labour, I defire to haue,
generally in all deuout foules that
shall read this book , and more
particularlie in yours; to whome
I dedicate it , and my felf, to remaine allwayes,

Your feruant in our Lord
and Sauiour Chriſt
Iefu ,   I. Y.

A

A DEDICATORY
prayer of the Authour.

O Svveet Iefu, *my Lord, my Sauiour, and my God: behold heere proflrate before thy diuine maieftie, I entitle and confecrate this vvriting vnto thy glory; giue fpirit and life vnto thofe lines by thy heauenly bleffing, that thofe foules for vvhome I vvrote them, may in reading thefe vvords, receaue the facred infpiratios,vvhich I vvishe thē: & particularlie may be moued to implore thy diuine mercie for me:that shevving vnto other the vvay of deuotion in this vvorlde,I become not a reprobate my felf in the vvorld to come; but*

together with all thy deuout soules,
vvho shall profit by this labour of
mine, I may ioyfully sing that triumphant song of the blessed Saints
in heauen , vvhich amidst the
daungers of this mortall life I pronounce from my hart as a testimo-
nie of my faith and fidelitie ; Life
and glorie to my Lord and Sauiour
Iesus; euen so svveete Iesu, liue and
raigne graciously and gloriously in
our soules for euer, and euer.
Amen.

MY

MY DEARE READER,
I befeeche thee to reade this Preface
for thy fatisfaction and myne.

I. **T**HE *Paynim hiftorians
report of a mayden called
Glycera, greatly delighted
in making of nofegayes,*
who could fo fitly and properly varie
and chaunge the difpofition and min-
gling of the fweet flowers in her pofies,
that with the felf fame flowers, she
would frame manie divers kinds of nofegayes ; in fo much that the painter
Paufias came short of his cunning, ftri-
uing as it were by emulation to expreffe the varietie of her flower-workes, for
he could not chaunge his colours into fo
many fashions in his pictures, but Glycera would find more by a new maner
of placing of her flowers in her nofegaies.
Euen fo doth the holy Ghoft difpofe and

orde.

order with enterchaungeable varietie
the instructions of deuotion which he
geueth by the tongues and pennes of his
seruaunts; that the doctrine which they
teache being one, and the self same : the
discourse notwithstanding which they
make, and in which they deliuer his doctrine do much differre, according to the
diuersitie of methods, & fashions (that
I may so say) in which they be couched
and composed. I cannot therfore, neither
ought I, or would I, in any sort write in
this introduction, any thing but that,
which hath been alreadie published by
our learned predecessours concerning this
matter; they be the self same flowers
that I present vnto thee (gentle reader)
which auters before me haue offered
vnto thy view · but the nosegay which
I haue framed of them, is of a different
fashion from theirs, as being handled
in another forme, and wrought after
another manner.

2. Those

2. *Those that haue treated of deuotion before me, haue allmoſt all attended onely to the inſtruction of perſons all-together retired from worldly conuerſation; or at the leaſt haue taught a forme of deuotion, which properly and principally directeth and tendeth to that retired ſtate of life. But my intention is particularly and principally to inſtruct ſuch as liue in cities and townes, buſied with the affaires of their houſ-hold, or forced by their place and calling to folow their princes court ; ſuch as by the obligation of their eſtate, are bound to take a common courſe of life in out-ward ſhew, and exteriour proceeding; Which kind of perſons for the moſt part of them, vnder colour of a ſee-ming, or pretended impoſsibilitie, will not ſo much as once thinke vpon the vndertaking of a deuout life : perſua-ding them ſelues, that as no beaſt (yf we may beleeue the naturaliſts) dare*

taſt

taſt of the ſeed of the hearbe called pal-
ma Chriſti, *ſo no man ought to endeuour to obtaine the palme of Chriſtian
pietie, ſo long as he liueth in the preſſe of
temporall occupations . To theſe men do
I demonſtrate: that as the mother pearles doe liue in the ſea , not taking one
drop of ſalt-water into their ſhelles; &
towards the* Chelidonian *Iſlands there
be fountaines of ſweet water in the
middeſt of the brackiſh ſea; and a ſmall
kind of flie called* Pycauſtes *borne and
bred in hot burning ouens and furnaces,
flies in the flames without ſcorching her
wings: ſo a vigourous and conſtant hart
may liue in the world, and yet not participate of the vaine humours of the
world; may find out freſh ſprings of
ſweete deuotion , in the midſt of the
briniſh waters of temporall affaires; &
may flie without harme among the flames of earthly occupations, and yet not
burne nor ſeare the wings of holy deſires*
                                        which

which lifte vp a deuout soule to heauen, although the bodie necessarily, tread
vpon earthen mould. True it is in deed,
that this is a thing of some difficultie:
but therfore would I desire that many
men would employ their cares in the
attaining of so high a thing with more
zeale then ordinarilie they doe, and
they should find it not so vneasie as they
imagine it. My self, weak and feeble
as I am, haue endeuoured by this worke, to cōtribute something of mine owne
cost, toward the helping of such, as with
a noble hart will vndertake this enterprize.

3. Yet not withstanding this present
desire of mine, it was neither by mine
owne choice nor liking, that this intro-
ductiō came to the publique Yew of the
world. A certaine frind of mine, endewed indeed with true honour and
virtue, hauing some good while receaued the grace of God, to aspire vnto a
                                    deuout

deuout life ; requested my particular ayde & afsistance in this kind: &
I being many wayes obliged vnto
him, and hauing long before noted
in him à singular good disposition for
this matter, easily suffered my self
to be ouer-intreated by him, and tooke great care in teaching him to my
power ; & hauing conducted him
through all the exercizes, which I
thought conuenient to his holy desire,
and agreeable to his estate, I left
him in writing for to help his memory
these few rules, that he might haue recourse to them when so euer he needed.
Since which time he communicated
them, vnto a great, learned, & deuout
person, who esteeming them so profitable
that many other might reape commoditie by them, did earnestly exhort me to
publishe thē:and easie was it for him to
persuade me, because his loue had great
power ouer my will, & his iudgem ent
had

had great authoritie ouer mine.

4. Wherfore, that it might be more acceptable, I haue tooke a review of it, enterlacing many things in diuers places, and adioyning some aduices and instructions, fit for the purpose which before I sayd that I entend: and all this haue I done, hauing almost no leasure at all to spare. For which cause look here for no exact or curious discources: but onely a plaine heape of good aduertisments, simplie and nakedly set downe and declared in easie and intelligible woords: at least wise I desired so to doe. As for the adorning of the stile and language, I could not so much as think of it, as hauing other things enough to doe.

5. All my words throughout the book are addressed to Philotheus. For my intention being to reduce to the common good many soules, that which I

had

had first writt for one onely: I think I
may fitly vse that name which is comō
to all such which wil be deuout and diligēt in gods seruice: for Philotheus is as
much to say as a louer of God.

6. Therfore in all the treatise, laying
before my consideration a soule which
by exercise of deuotion aspireth to the
loue of God: I haue deuided this introduction into fiue parts. In the first, I endeuour by persisasions and peculiar exercizes, to allure and winne the wille of
my Philotheus, to an entire and firme resolution of liuing well: which he
maketh at length after a generall confession, with a round and sound protestation, seconded by the receauing of the
holy communion, in which giuing vp
his soule vnto his sauiour, he receaues
his sauiour into his soule, and so entreth
happelie into the retreat and closet of his
heauenly loue. That done, to lead him
farther on, I shew him two speciall
                                    mea-

meanes how to vnite him self more & more euery day vnto his diuine maje-stie : the one, the vse of the sacramēts, by which our good God commeth vnto vs: the other, the exercize of holy prayer, wherby he draweth vs vnto him self: and in this I spend the second part. In the third, I set before his eyes, how he may exercise him selfe in such virtues as be fit and conuenient for his profit & aduancement: in which yet I onely bu-sie my penne, in laying together some particular aduices which I thought he could hardly haue had of another, or found out of him self. In the fourth part, I discouer the embushments and lur-king dennes of his enemies, shewing him how he may escape their snares, & deliuer him self frō their enticemēts, that so he may goe forward without hindraunce in his worthie enterprize. In the fift and last part, I teach him to with draw him self as it were from other

other ordinarie exercises to the cabinet
of his soule, to refreshe his weerie deuotions, and renew his holy purposes,
taking breath as it were, and repairing
his forces, that he may afterward cou-
rageously get ground & aduaunce him
self in his iourney to perfectiõ & deuotiõ.

7. Well do I see in this curious age
of ours, that many will say, it apper-
tainēth to religious votaries, to vndertake the particular guidaunce of soules,
Vnto this singular exercise of pietie,
which requireth more leasure then a
Bishop can well spare, charged with a
diocese so heauie as mine is; that these
deuout instructiõs too much distract the
Vnderstanding, which should be em-
ploied in affairs of greater importaunce.
But as for me, to speak what I think,
I say (deere reader) with great S. Denis
that it appertaineth principally to Bishops to conduct the soules committed to
their charge vnto perfection : since their
                                    ranck

ranck and order is supreme among men,
as is the order of Seraphins among the
quyres of Angels ; so that their leasure
cannot be better spent , then about such
busines. The aunciēt Bishops & fathers
of the church were at the least as much
affectioned to their charge , as wee : yet
letted they not for all that to vndertake
the particular care of guiding many sou-
les, which singulary had recourse vnto
their assistaūce , as it appeareth by their
epistles. And heerin they imitated the
Apostles them selues, who in the mid-
dest of the generall haruest of all the
world, gathered notwithstāding many
times with peculiar care and affection,
certaine notable scattered eares of corne ;
not onely contented to tye the vvhole
sheafes of wheat, but also not disdaining
euen to gleane, as they say , where they
perceiued any remarkable soule , that
in particular offered it self to their
care .　Who knovveth not that
　　　　　　　　　　　　　　　Timo-

*Timotheus , Philemon , Onesimus ,
Thecla , and Appia were the deare
children of the great S. Paule? as S.
Marck and S. Petronilla of S. Peter?
S. Petronilla I say , who (as Baronius
learnedly proueth , Gallonius folowing
him) was not the naturall daughter,
but onely the ghostly child of S. Peter.
And S. Iohn the beloued disciple of
our Lord, writeth he not one of his cano-
nicall epistles ʋnto a deuout Ladie ,
whome for her pietie he calleth* electa,
the elect , and chosen ladie?

8. *It is a painfull charge I confesse,
to take the particular care of soules, and
conduct them in such singular manner
in the way of perfection; but as painfull
as it is , it bringeth withall excessiue
comfort: much like ʋnto the painfull
toile of thriftie husbandmen in time
of haruest and vintage , who are neuer
more merry , then when their hands
are most full of such labours. It is a*
                                    burden

burden which recreateth and reuiueth
the hart of him that is loaden with it,
through the abundāce of delight which
floweth from it : as the bundles of Cin-
namom with sweet and recreatiue
odour comforteth those that carie them
through the boiling sands of Arabia.
They report of the Tygre, that hauing
recouered one of her whelpes (which
the craftie huntf-man leaueth in the
way, to busie her with all while he
caries away the rest of the litter) she
taketh it vp presently be it neuer so
great, and finds her self neuer a whit
the heauier or slower, but rather lighter
and swifter in her course, naturall loue
as it were lightening her with her
very loade. How much more willingly
then will a fatherly hart take vpon him
the charge of a soule, which he finds
all melting with desire of holy perfection? why should he not most carefully bear such a soule in his bosom (as I
may

*may say) like as a louing mother doth
her litle child , being neuer weary of
cariyng the burthen which she loueth
so entirely ? But it must be indeed a
fatherly hart that vndertakes so toil-
some a taske : and for that cause the
Apostles and Apostolique men, doe call
their disciples not only their children,
but with a terme of more tender affection , their litle children.*

*9. To conclude (gentle reader) I
confesse that I write of deuotion , being
my self without deuotion , yet truly
not without an earnest desire of attaining therunto. And this very desire
is that which hath giuen me courage
to vndertake to instruct thee in the way
to deuotion. For , as a great learned
man sayd, it is a good meanes to become
laarned , for a man to studie hard : a
better , to heare a learned maister : but
the best of all to teach another. And it
often commeth to passe (saith S. Aug.*

Wri-

writing to his deuout *Florentin*) that
the office of diftributing to o-
thers, ferueth vs as a merit to receaue the fame things our felues:
and the office of teaching, becomes a foundation of learning.
The great Alexander, caufed his louely
Compaspe to be pictured by the pencill
of the famous Appelles : who forced by
often reflexion to contemplate wifhfully
Compaspes perfection , as he drew the
lineaments of her faire bodie vpon his
table , fo imprinted he withall the loue
of her beautie in his hart, and became fo
paffionatly enamoured of her, that A-
lexander perceauing it , & pityng his
cafe , gaue him her in marriage , depri-
uing him felf for his fake , of the deareft
loue he had : shewing heerin (as Plinie
iudgeth) the greatnes of his hart more
plainly, then by any bloudie victory ouer
a puiffant enemie. I perfuade my felf
that it is the will of God , that I should

                    B   pro-

procure in the best colours that I am
able, to paint the formes of beautifull
virtues vpon the harts of those which
are committed to my charge, and especially the beautifull virtue of Deuotion,
most amiable and acceptable in his diuine eyes. And I vndertake the office
willingly, as well to obey, and performe my duty, as for the hope I haue,
that engrauing this louely virtue in the
minds of other men, mine owne perhaps
may wholly be enamoured of the sweetnes therof. And I doubt not, but yf
euer his diuine maiestie perceaue my
soule sincerely in loue with this beautifull virtue, he will bestowe her vpon
me, in a happie marriage for euer. The
faire and chast Rebecca watring Isaaks
camels with a readie good will, was
presently chosen to be his espouse, receauing out of hand in his name, pretious
earings and golden braceletts, as pledges
of his loue. So doe I persuade my self,
                                    through

through the boundlesse goodnes of my God, that carefully leading his beloued sheep to the wholsome waters of deuotion, he will make my poore soule his spouse, fastening in my eares the golden words of his holy loue, and binding on my wrists, force and vigour to practize them, in which consisteth the essence of true deuotion; which I humblie beseech his heauenly maiestie to bestow vpon me, and vpon all the obedient children of his holy church, To whose decrees & correction I do, and will, allway submitt my writings, my actions, my words, my wills, and my thoughts. At Necy, on S. Mary Magdalens day, 1609.

B 2   THE

THE FIRST PART

OF THE INTRODVCTION:

Conteyning aduices and exercises requisite for the conduct of a soule from her very first desire of a deuout life, vntill she be brought to a full resolution to embrace it stedfastly in all her actions.

What a deuout life is.

CHAPTER I.

1. YOv aspire to deuotion (my deere Philotheus) because being a good Christian you know that deuotiõ is a virtue most amiable and acceptable to Gods diuine maiestie. But for so much as small faults cõmitted in the beginning of any affaire, in the progresse therof grow infinite, and in the end, become almost irreparable, and past all amendement : it is necessary before all things, that

that you learne what kind of virtue Deuotion is ; for since there is but one
manner of true deuotion , and many
kindes of forged and false , yf you
know not which is the true and sincere
virtue that you seek after, you may very
easily be deceaued , and entertaine your
self with some impertinēt superstition,
insteed of true and profitable deuotion.

2. Aurelius, a Romane painter , was
wont to picture the faces of all the images which he made, to the likenes and
resemblance of the wemen whome he
loued : and so ordinarylie most men
paint their deuotion, according to the
passion or phantasie which predomina-
teth in them. He that is giuē to fasting,
holdeth him self for deuout enough , yf
he fast often, be his hart neuer so full of
rancour and malice: and not daring to
moiste his tongue in wine or water, for
feare of trāsgressing his affected sobrietie , makes no difficultie at all , to suck
the blood of his harmeles neighbour, by
slaunderous backbiting, and detracting
from his good name. Another will account him self full of deuotion for hud-
ling vp a multitude of prayers euery
                    B 3   mor-

morning, allthough all day after his
tongue neuer ceaſe throwing foorth
of way warde ſpeaches, or arrogant and
reproachefull taunts among his negh-
bours & familiars. Some there be, that
can very eaſilie pull an almes out of their
purſe to relieue a poore needie beggar, and therfore are eſteemed deuout
men, wheras they cannot find any ſweet
diſpoſition in their hart to forgiue their
enemies; or any readineſſe to ſatisfie
their creditours, vnleſſe the force of
law & the ſergeants maze do cóſtraine
them. And yet are all theſe men in the
deceiueable iudgemét of the common
people deemed deuout perſons: though
indeed they be very farre (God knowes)
from true deuotion. The ſeruaunts of
king Saule ſeeking for Dauid in his
houſe, Michol his wife layde an idol in
his bed, clothed in Dauids apparell, and
made them beleeue it was her husband
Dauid, ſicklie and ſleeping in his chamber: euen ſo do theſe men, couer them
ſelues with certanie externall actions
of ſeeming deuotió, wheras in deed they
are but vaine ſhadows, and idle Idols of
deuotion.

　　　　　　　　　　　　3. True

3. True and liuely deuotion (my Philotheus) presuppoſeth in our harts the
loue of God:nay rather it is nothing els
but a certain perfect and high degree of
the true loue of God:for whē we cōſider
the loue of God,as the thing that beau-
tifieth our ſoules , and maketh them
louely in the eyes of his maieſtie , then
do we call it heauēlygrace : and becauſe
this ſelf ſame loue of God, yf it be true
and vnfained loue , giueth vs ſtrength
& force to do good workes , it is called
charity : but when it growes to that degree of perfectiō,that it not only ſtrēg-
theneth vs to do well , but alſo vrgeth
vs vehemently to do good works diligently, frequently, and feruently, then
is it properly called deuotion. Auſtri-
ches becauſe of their monſtrous wai-
ghte,neuer flie in the ayre,but only run
vpon the ground by help of their wings:
Hennes flie ſometimes in the ayre, but
very ſeldom , and then alſo low and
ſlowlie : but doues, & eagles ſoare aloft
in the skies, with ſpeedines , and delight to ſee them ſelues farre from the
ground , and nigh to the element : In
like maner ſinfull men , loaden with
the

the burden of offences, flie not at all to
God-ward, but make al their courses vpő
earth, and for earthly delights : Good
honeſt men, that endeuour to abſtaine
from mortall ſinnes, but are not yet
arriued to the hight of deuotion, flie
to God with their actions and good
deeds, but ſlowlie, and rarely, and in
ordinarie things, as being hindred with
the waight of their imperfections, and
heauie winged thoughts frő higher exerciſes. But deuout ſoules flie to God
with ſwifte & nimble wings of holy affections, readilie, and feruourouſly, ſoa-
ring & mounting higher and higher to
the heauen of perfection. Briefly, deuotion, is nothing els but a ſpirituall ſwi-
ſtnes and nimblenes of loue, by which
charitie worketh our actions in vs, or
we by her, with readines of will, and
alacritie of mind ; And as it is the office
of charitie, in what degree ſoeuer it be,
to make vs keep the commandements
of God generally and vniuerſally : ſo is
it the proper function of deuotion, to
fullfill the commandemẽts with promptnes, feruour, and nimble vigour of
our minds, as it were delighting, and
reioy-

reioycing in doing our dutie towards,
God & man. Hence it is,that he which
keepeth not the commandements of
God, can neither be esteemed good,
nor deuout : since to be good, he must
be indued with charitie ; and to be deuout,it is not enough to haue any degree of charitie whatsoeuer, but besides
he must haue a quick and readie affe-
ctiõ and habit of exercising the highest
and perfectest actiós of charitie : which
readines of mind, is the true virtue of
deuotion.

4. Deuotion then consisteth in a certaine degree of excellent charitie, making vs prompt and readie, not onely
in the keeping of Gods commandements : but besides that,it prouoketh vs
to doe with ioy and delight all maner of
good works, although they be not in
any sort commanded by Gods law, but
onely commended vnto our free-will
by his counsells and holy inspirations.
For like as a man but newly recouered
from a long and daungerous sicknes,
walketh now and then as much as is
necessarie for his health, but yet slowly
and leasurely for want of strength and

B 5   vigour;

vigour : so a sinner but lately reclaimed
from the diseases of iniquitie, walketh
in the way of Gods commandements,
but yet slowly, and faintly, no more
then is necessarie for his saluatiō, vntill
such time as he gaine the strength of
deuotion, for then like a man in sound
& perfect health, he not onely walketh
lustely and cheerfully in the high way
of Gods commandements, but with exceeding courage, and earnest desire of
pleasing his Sauiour, runneth speedely,
as it were leaping & dancing for ioy and
exaltatiō of mind, in the pathes of Gods
councels and heauenly inspirations. To
conclude, charitie and deuotion doe
differ one from another, no more then
fire from flame : for charitie is a spirituall fire which God kindleth in our
harts, and when it breaketh out in to
flames, then is it called deuotion : So
that deuotion addeth nothing to the
fire of charitie, sauing a bright flame of
redines and promptnes of mind to exercise actiuely, speedily, with out delayes,
or difficulties, at all occasions, the commandements of God, and works of his
councells, and inspirations, which it
　　　　　　　　　　　　　pleaseth

pleaseth his diuine goodnes to infuse
into our harts.

The properties and excellency of Deuotion.

CHAPTER II.

1. **T**HEY that endeuoured to dif-
courage the Israëlits fró going
forward vnto the lád of promi-
se, told thē it was a countrie that deuoured the inhabitants therof, hauing an
ayre so contagious, that it were impof-
sible to liue long in health there, and
that on the other side, the inhabitants
of that land, were huge monstrous
giants, that did eate vp other men, as yf
they were but shrimpes or locusts. So
playes the world (my deer Philotheus)
it striuerh by all meanes possible to de-
fame holy deuotion, painting vs out
deuout persons with frowning, sad, and
griesly countenances, and publishing
maliciously that deuotion engendreth
melancholy humours, and vnsufferable

B 6   con-

conditions. But as Iosua and Caleb, constantly protested, not onely that the countrie was beautifull & fruitfull, but also that the winning & possessiõ therof would both be easie, and agreable to their wishes: so doth the holy Ghost by the mouthes of all his saints, and our Sauiour Christ him self by his owne blessed mouth assure vs, that a deuout life is sweete, happie, and full of vnspeakeable delights and comforts.

2. The world sees that the louers of saintlike deuotiõ, fast, pray, watch, serue the sick, giue to the poore, bridle their anger, restranie their passions, depriue them selues of sensuall pleasures, and do other such acts as are of them selues both sharpe & rigorous. But the world sees not the inward cordiall affection which rendreth all these actions most pleasaunt, sweete, and easie to performe. Looke but on the litle Bees, busilie beset vpon the thime, the iuyce wherof euery man knowes to be bitter: and yet no sooner haue they sucked it from the herbe, but presently they conuert it into honny. Deuout soules (ô you worldlings) feele (no doubt) the bitternes

ternes of thefe mortifications: yet fuch
is the nature of deuotion, that euen in
the verie exercife of thefe aufterities,
it transformes them into pleafaunt and
fweete delights. The fiers, and flames,
the racks, and tortures, fwords, and
fcourges, feemed flowers, and perfumes
to the valiaunt martyrs, becaufe they
were deuout: yf then deuotion can giue
fo fweet a taft to the moft cruell torments, yea euen to death it felf: how
daintie and diuine a taft will it giue
vnto virtuous actes and exercifes? Sugar
fweetneth fower and vnripened fruit,
and correcteth the cruditie thereof whē
it is ouer-ripe: and deuotion is the fpirituall fugar, which taketh away all
fowernes from mortification, and mendeth the furfeting fweetnes of confolation. It taketh away difcontentement
from the poore man, and the difordinat
appetit and defire of riches: defpaire
from the oppreffed, and infolence from
the fauourifed: fadnes from the folita-
rie, and diffolution from him that keepeth companie. It ferueth for fire in
the winter of aduerfitie, and for morning dew in the fummer of profperitie.
Deuo-

Deuotion knowes how to abound in
plentie , and how to be patient in pouertie : deuotiõ maketh equall efteeme
of honour and difgrace , and receaueth
pleafure and paine,almoft,with one and
the fame vnchaungeable mind ; and finally filleth our foules brim-full of ineftimable delights.

3. The myfterious ladder which Iacob faw in his happie dreame,(the true
pourtraiƈt of the deuout life) the two
fides wherof , fignifie prayer which obtaineth the loue of almightie God, and
the holy facramẽts which cõfer it vnto
vs,when we duly receaue them : The
ftaues, or fteps faftned to the fides,be-
token diuers degrees of charitie , by
which deuout foules do goe frõ virtue
to virtue: either defcending by aƈion
to fuccour and help their neighbours,
or afcending by contemplation vp to
the happie vnion with almightie God.
Now looke (my Philotheus) vpon
thofe which be on this ladder , and you
shall find them men that haue Angels
harts, or Angels, that haue mens bodies; They feeme young though indeed
they be not,becaufe they be full of force
                                    and

& fpirituall vigour in all theire actiós:
They haue golden wings,to foare vp to
the very throne of God , and to datt
them felues into him by feruent prayer,
but they haue feet alfo to walke among
men, by an holy,amiable,and exemplar
conuerfation;faire and goodly are their
faces , for they receaue all things with
ioy and fweetnes. Their legges , their
armes,& their heads ar alwayes vncoue-
red,for as much as their thoughts, affections and actions are voide of all other
motiue or defignement,fauing onely a
pure and naked intentió to pleafe God :
The reft of their bodie,is couered with
a faire and light robe , becaufe though
they vfe the felf fame world that worldlings doe , yet take they but fparingly
of worldly things, no more then is requifite for their eftate. Such Angels as
thefe, be deuout perfons. Beleeue (me
louing · Philotheus) deuotion is the
fweet of all fweetes, the queene of virtues ,for it is the ornament and perfection of charitie : for yf charitie be
milke to feed our faint foules, deuotion is the creame ; yf charitie be
the plante, deuotion is the floure ;
y²

yf charitie be the precious gemme,
deuotion is the luftre of it ; yf charitie
be a healthfull baulme , deuotion is the
côfortable odour therof,which recreateth men and refresheth the Angels.

That deuotion is an inftrument, and an
ornament befitting all voca-
tions, and profeſsions.

CHAPTER III.

1. **G**OD commaunded the plants
in their creation , to beare
frute, euery one according to
his kind : euen ſo commandeth he all
Chriſtians, (who are the liuing plants
of his Church) to fructifie and bring
foorth the workes of deuotion , euery
one according to his kinde and qualitie. For deuotion ought to be exerciſed differently by the gentleman,by
the artificer , by the ſeruant , by the
Prince, by the widdow, by the maid,
and by the married. And the practiſe of
deuotion is not onely diuers in diuers
esta-

estates, but euen in the self same estate
must it be accomodated, to the forces,
affaires, leafure, and dutie of euery one
in particular. For I pray thee, would it
doe well yf the Bishop should be foli-
tarie like the Carthusian ? or the married man should lay vp no more in store
for the maintenance of his familie, then
the Capuchin ? or that the Artificer
should be all day in the church like
the monk : and the monke busie him
self in all kindes of occurrents, for the
seruice of his neighbour, as doth the
Bishop ? Were not such deuotion ridiculous, disorderly, and intolerable ? And
yet is this preposterous manner of proceeding now a dayes most vsuall : and
the world either not able, or not willing
to discerne deuotion, from indiscretion, murmureth & blameth deuotion,
which not-withstanding , can nether
helpe, nor redresse these disorders.

2. No (my Philotheus) true deuotion neuer marreth any thing , but
rather maketh and perfecteth : and deuotion that is contrarie to the lawfull
calling of any man, is vndoubtedly forged and false deuotion. The Bee (saith
the

the philofopher) fucketh hony from
heatbes and flowers without hurting
or endamageing them , but leauing the
as whole & as freshe as she found them:
but true deuotiõ doth more then fo:for
it not onely hurteth no ftate , vocation
or affaire, but contrariwife bettereth &
adorneth it. All kind of pearles and pretious gẽmes being fteeped in hony, become more glittering , euery one after
its natiue colour:and fo euery chriftian
becommeth more perfeᴄt , & excellent
in his vocation, ioyning the fame with
true deuotion : the care of familie by it
is made more quiet and peaceable ; the
loue of man and wife more fincere and
durable ; the feruice of fubieᴄts to their
prince more loyal and acceptable ; and
all kind of occupations become more
eafie and tolerable.

3. It were an errour, nay an herefie,
to go about to banishe deuotion from
the companies of foldiours , out of the
shops of artificers,the courts of princes,
and from the houshold or familie of
maried folk. True it is , that the deuotion , altogether contemplatiue, mo-
nafticall,and religious,cannot be exercifed

cifed in thefe vocations : yet are there
many other degrees and exercifes of deuotion , which fufficiently and eafilie
lead fecular perfons to perfection ; A-
braham, Ifaak, Iacob, Dauid, Iob, Tobias, Sara , Rebecca , and Iudith , are
witneffes heerof in the ancient law:and
as touching the new, *S.* Iofeph, *S.* Lydia,
and *S.* Crifpin, were perfectly deuout in
their open fhops ; *S.* Anne, *S.* Martha,
S. Monica, amonghft their families · *S.*
Cornelius , *S.* Sebaftian , *S.* Maurice,
amidft the armies : and Conftantin, *S.*
Helen , *S.* Lewis, *S.* Amé, and *S.* Edward
in their royall throanes & duke-domes.
Nay it hath oftentimes happened, that
many haue loft their perfection in folitude (which notwithftading is fo much
defired to perfection) and haue conferued it amidft the multitude, which fee-
meth litle fauourable to perfectió. Lott,
(faith *S.* Gregory) that was fo chaft
in the citie, defiled himfelf in folitude :
wherfoeuer we be, or of whatfoeuer calling we are, we may and ought to afpire
to perfection.

The

*The necessitie of a guide to enter and go
forward in exercises of deuotion.*

CHAPTER IIII.

1. YOVNG Tobias, commanded by
his father to goe to the citie of
Rages, said, I know no whit of
the way : goe then (replied his father)
and seeke out some faithfull guide to
conduct thee. The same say I to thee
(my beloued Philotheus) desirest thou
in good earnest to walk to the citie of
deuotion ? seek some skilfull man to
direct and lead thee. This is the rule of
rules : and the aduertisment of aduertisments : for albeit thou search neuer
so curiously (sayth the deuout Auila)
thou shalt neuer so securely and certainly finde out the will of God, as by
this safe way of humble obedience, so
much recommended and practized by
all his deuout and faithfull seruants in
former times. The blessed Mother Te-
resa, foundresse of the reformed Car-
melits,

melits, seeing the straunge and extraordinarie penances, which the great Ladie
Catherin of Cardoua, exercised in a caue, in a wildernes of Spanie, was much
moued in hart to imitate her therein,
cõtrarie to the aduice of her confessour,
who had forbid her such kind of auste-
rities: yet was she tempted not to obay
him in that behalfe: but God (who
many times familiarly talked with her)
sayd vnto her: my daughter thou hast
alreadie begunne a very safe and assured
way: seest thou the penaunce of that
good ladie? but I doe make more ac-
compt of thy obedience. And therfore
this blessed woman euer after so loued
this vîrtue, that beside the ordinarie
obedience due vnto her superiours, she
made one vowe in particular, to a certaine learned & excellent man, to folow
in all things his direction, by which she
found inestimable comfort and profit;
as both before, and after her, many deuout soules haue done the like, who to
subiect them selues more perfectly to
the will of God, submitted their owne
willes to the disposition of his seruants:
a thing which holy S. Catherin of Siena
highly

highly commendeth in her spirituall
dialogues. The most virtuous princesse
S. Elizabeth, submitted her selfe most
extraordinarilie to the direction of her
ghostly confessour Conradus. And one
of the last aduices that great S. Lewis
gaue to his sonne before his death , was
in this in kind: confesse often & choose
a confessour of learning, and discretion,
that can, and dare aduertise thee, to do
such things as are necessary for thy
saluation.

2. *A faithfull frind* (saith the holy scripture) *is a strong protection: he that hath
found him hath found a treasure. A faithfull
frind is a medicin of life and immortallitie:
such as feare God doe finde such a frind.*
These sacred wordes, as you may see, are
principallie spoken of immortallitie ,
for the obtayning whereof, it is neede-
full aboue all thinges to haue this faithfull frind , who may guide our actions
by his prudentiall councell , and coun-
tergard vs , against the ambushments
and slightes of our ghostly enemie.
Such an one shall be vnto vs, as a treasure of wisdome in all our afflictions,
desolations, and falles : he shall serue vs

as a

as a medicine to eafe and comfort our hartes in our ghoftlie difeafes : he will keepe vs from euill, and make what is good in vs, agreat deale better : and if any infirmities chance to befall vs, his carefull afiftance will procure, that it shall not be mortall, for he will lift vs vp againe from our downefall.

3. But who is he (fay you) that shall be fo happie as to finde fuch a frind? The wife man in the fame place tells vs, fayi) g. *They that feare God,* they that with an humble minde, affectuoufly defire their aduacement in pietie, and in the feruice and worship of their Creator. Seeing then that it importeth thee fo much (my Philotheus) to goe accompanied wirh a good guide in this holy voyage of deuotion, pray vnto God with very great inftance, that he will furnish thee with one according to his hart, and dout not, albeit it were needfull for this end, to fend an Angell from heauen, as he did to young Tobias, but that he will giue thee a good one, and a faithfull.

4. And in verie deed, in place of an Angel ought he to be vnto thee, when
thou

thou haſt once found him. Regard him
not ſimplie as a man, nether truſt in
him, nor in his humaine prudence, but
in the prouidence of almightie God,
who wil no dout fauour thy indeuours,
and ſpeake vnto thee by the meanes and
interpoſition of this man : putting into
his minde, and into his mouthe, that
which ſhall be moſt expedient for thy
ſpiritual aduancement : ſo that thou
oughteſt to hearken vnto him, as vnto
an Angell deſcended from heauen, to
conduct and leade thee thither. Treate
with him freely, and with an open hart,
manifeſting without al diſſimulation or
fayninge, the good and euil which thou
findeſt in thy ſoule : and by this meanes, thy good ſhall be more examined
and aſſured, and thy euil corrected and
amended : thou ſhalt be both eaſed and
fortified in thy afflictions, and moderated and ordered in thy conſolations.
Place then an exceeding confidence in
him, ioyned with a religious and reſpe-
ctiue reuerence : yet ſo, that the reuerence diminiſhe not thy confidence in
him, nor thy confidence hinder the
reuerence due vnto him : but truſt
in him

in him with trembling, as a chaft mayden doth refpect his feuere, but louing
father: and refpect him with an affured
truft in his loue and care, as an obedict
fonne, would doe his deare and tender
harted mother. In a woord, the frindship betwixt thee and thy ghoftly in-
ftructor, muft be ftronge and fweete,
al holie, al facred, and all celeftial.

5. For this caufe, choofe one amoge
a thoufand, faith Auilla, but I fay vnto
thee, one amonge ten thoufand, for
there are fewer to be found then men
imagin, who are fit and capable of fuch
an office. He muft be replenished with
charitie, knowledg, and with prudence,
for if but one of thefe three partes be
wanting in him, it wil be dangerous for
thy foule. Therfore once againe I aduife thee, to demaund him inftantly at
the handes of almightie God, and hauing once obtayned him, bleffe his diuine maieftie for fo great a benefit.
Stand firme and ftedfaft vnder his conduct, and change him not lightly for
any other, but goe to him fimply, humbly, and confidently: and fo shalt thou
make a profperous voyage.

C   *That*

*That the begining of a deuout life, muſt
be taken from the purgation
of the ſoule.*

CHAPTER V.

1. FLowers *appeare in our ground,*
(ſayeth the ſpouſe in the Canticles) *the time of pruning our
vines is come* . What be the flowers
of our hartes (ô Philotheus) but
our good deſires? *So* ſoone then as
they appeare, we muſt lay hand to the
hooke, and cut from our conſcience,
all withered, dead , and ſuperfluous
workes. In the law of Moyſes, the
ſtranger woman taken priſoner , that
would marrie with an Iſralite, was to
put of the robe of hir captiuitie, to
pare hir nayles, and to cut away the
treſſes of hir hayre : in like maner , the
ſoule that aſpireth to the honour to be
the eſpouſe of the Sonne of God, muſt
firſt put of the old man, and put on the
new, caſt away and forſake ſinne , and
then pare and ſhaue of all kind of impediments, which doe diuert from the
loue of almightie God. It is the firſt
be-

begining of our health , to purge our corrupt and peccant humors. S. Paul euen in an instant , was purged and cleansed with a perfect purgation. So was S. Marie Magdalen , S. Pelagia, S. Catharin of Genua , and certaine others. But this kinde of purgation, is altogether miraculous and extraordinary in grace , as is the resurrection of the dead in nature , and therfore we must not pretend therunto . The ordinary manner of purging and healing ether body or minde , is not wrought but by litle and litle, and by proceeding from degree to degree,with paine, leasure, and expectation.

2. The Angels had winges, vpon the mysterious ladder of the Patriarche Iacob , yet they flew not therfore , but ascended, and descended by order from one step to another. The soule which ariseth from sinne to deuotion , is fitly compared to the morning starre , which in rising expelleth not the darknes in a trice or moment , but gradatim and by degrees. That cure (saith the Physiciens Aphorisme) which is done faire and softly, is alwayes most assured.

G 2　　　　The

The diseases of the soule, as wel as those of the body, come to vs, as a man may say, in post, or a horse back, but they depart from vs on foote, and faire and softly. We must then be courageous (ô Philotheus) in vndertaking this enterprise. Alas, what pittie is it of these soules, which seeing them selues subiect to sundrie imperfections, after they haue bene exercised some few monthes in deuotion, begin to trouble, disquiete, and discourage them selues, suffering their hartes almost to be borne away vnto the temptation of leauing of all, and returning back? But now on the other part, is it not an exceeding peril vnto those soules, which by a contrary temptation, perswade them selues to be purged from their imperfections, the first day, as it were, of their purgation, reputing them selues to be made perfect, before, in a manner, they be scarcely made, and presuming to flye, before they haue winges. O Philotheus, in what great danger are they, of falling againe into their former diseases, for taking them selues to timely out of the handes of the phisicien? *It is in vaine to*

rise

rise before the light (saith the kingly Prophet) *rise after you haue sitten.* And he
him selfe putting the same lesson in
practise, hauing bene washed & cleansed from his sinne, yet humbly deman-
deth to be washed againe.

3. The exercise of purging soules,
can not, nor may not end, but with our
life. Let vs neuer therfore afflict our
selues about our imperfections, for
our perfection cheifly consisteth in resisting against them, and we can not
resist them vnles we doe see them, nor
can we vanquish them, vnles we encounter them. Our victorie consisteth
not, in not feeling them, but in not
consenting nor yeelding vnto them: for
to receaue vexation and trouble from
them, is not to consent vnto them:
nay it is necessarie for the exercise of
our humilitie, that we sometime receaue some smale blowes or foiles in this
spiritual battaile: but we are neuer to
be accounted for ouercome, but only
when we leese ether life or courage.
Now certaine it is, that imperfections
and venial sinnes, can not take from vs
the life of grace, for that is neuer lost

C 3   but

but by deadly sinne. The only care then
that remayneth is, that these imperfections doe not daunt our courage. *De-*
liuer me ô Lord, said Dauid, *from cowardli-*
nes, and faintnes of hart. For this is the
happie condition and aduantage which
we haue in this ghostly warre, that we
shal euer be conquerors, prouided
alwayes that we wil combat.

Of the first Purgation: which is, from mortall sinnes.

CHAPTER VI.

1. THE first purgation then which
we must minister to our soule,
is, to cleanse and voide away
the filth of sinne: and the meanes to
make this purgation, is the holy Sacrament of Pennance. For the due receauing whereof, thou must seeke out
the best confessar that can be found.
Then take in hand some litle treatise,
that hath bene set forth; to helpe consciences to confesse well, as Granada,
Bruno, Arias, Augerius, or such like.
Read it with good attention, and marke
from point to point, in what thou hast
offen-

offended, beginirg from the time in
which thou hadſt firſt the vſe of reaſon,
vntil this preſent houre of thy conuerſion. And if thou dooſt diſtruſt thy
memorie, ſet downe in writinge what
thou haſt obſerued : and hauing in this
ſort prepared and gathered together
the peccant humors of thy guiltie conſcience, deteſt them, and reiect them
by Contrition and diſpleaſure, euen as
great and as profound as euer thy hart
is able to ſuffer, dilligently pondering
theſe four pointes. That by ſinne thou
haſt loſt the grace of God. Forſaken
thy part of heauen. Accepted of the
perpetual paynes of hell. And renounced the viſion, and euerlaſting loue of
almightie God.

2. Thou perceiueſt, Philotheus, that
I ſpeake in this place of a generall Confeſſion of all thy life, the which truly,
although I graunt that it is not alwayes
abſolutely neceſſarie, yet doe I côſider,
that it will be exceeding profitable vnto
thee in this begining: and for this cauſe
I doe moſt earneſtly exhort therunto.
It happneth oft times, that the ordinary
Confeſſions of ſuch as liue a vuigar life,

are full of great and grosse defaultes:
one while they prepare not them selues
any whit at all, or at the least very litle:
another while they come, but not with
that Contrition and sorrowe that is requisite for their sinnes: nay, somtimes
it happeneth that they goe to Confession, with a secret purpose to returne to
sinne, namely when they doe not shunne
and auoide the occasions, nor vse the
necessarie dispatches, which are meete
and proper for the amendment of life:
and in all these cases, a general Confession is véry requisite to assure our soules. But besides this, a generall Confession, recalleth vs to the knowledg of
our selues: prouoketh vs to a wholsome confusion for our life past: and
moueth vs to admire the mercie of
God, who hath expected vs with such
incredible and exceeding patience: fur-
thermore, it pacifieth our consciences:
easeth our spirits: exciteth good purposes: ministreth matter to our ghostly
father, to prescribe vs aduises, fit and
conuenient for our condition: and
openeth our hart, that we may with
more confidence manifest our Con-
                                fessions

feſſions that be to come.

3. Being then in this Introduction, to diſcourſe of a general renewing and reforming of our hartes, and of an vniuerſal conuerſion of our ſoules vnto God, by the enterpriſe of a deuout life, I haue great reaſon, as it ſeemeth to me, Philotheus, to counſayle thee to make this generall Confeſſion.

The ſecond Purgation : which is from the affections of ſinne.

CHAPTER VII.

1. ALL the Iſraelites departed in effect out of the Land of Egipt, but they departed not all in hart and affection ; which was euident to be ſeene, in that many of them in the deſert repined, for that they had not the onyons & fleſh potts of Egipt: euen ſo there are certaine penitents, who in effect goe foorth of ſinne, but neuertheles doe not vtterly leaue nor forſake the affection: that is to ſay, they purpoſe indeed to ſinne no more, but it

is

is with a certaine harts-breake which
they haue , to depriue them selues,
and to abstaine from the accursed delightes and contentments of sinne.
Their hart renounceth sinne and standeth a loofe of, but they leaue not for
all that, often times to looke that way,
as Lotts wife looked back towardes
Sodom. They abstaine from sinne, as
sick men doe from millons , which
they forbeare , becaufe the phisicien
threatens them death if that they eate
them : but not withstanding this con-
strayned abstinence , their fancie stil
longeth after those forbidden meates,
they speake of them , cheapen them,
and would likewise buy of them , if it
were lawfull , at the least they wil smel
to them , and account them happie
that are not bound to forbeare them:
euen so these feeble and faint harted
penitents, refraine them selues from sinne for awhile , but to their griefe, they
wish to God, that they might sinne,
and not be damned: they talke with a
kind of tast and sauour of sinne, and account the coteted that doe comit them.

   2. A man resolued to be reuenged,
                                   wil

wil change his wil when he comes to
Confeſſion , but immediatly after, one
may finde him amongſt his frindes,
taking pleaſure and contentment in
recounting his quarrel , ſaying , that
had it not bene for the feare of God,
he had done this , or he had done that:
and that the deuine law , in this point
of pardoning is very hard , and wiſheth
to God that it were lawful for him to
be reuenged. Alas, who ſeeth not,that
although this poore man be gotten
faintly out of ſinne, yet that he is altogether incenſed to the affectió of ſinne?
that being foorth of Egipt in effect, he
is yet there ſtil in wil and appetite ,
greedely deſiring the ruſtick fare of
the onyons and garlick , which he was
wont to eate: euen as a wanton woman , that hath newly deteſted hir
lewed loues , findes ſtil a delight to be
courted and inuironed with hir fond
wooers : alas what exceeding danger
are ſuch people in ?

3. O Philotheus,ſeing thou reſolueſt
to vndertake a deuout courſe of life,
thou muſt not only forſake ſinne , but
withall, wholy purge thy hart from all

C 6   affe-

affections, which any way depend or fauour of sinne. For besides the danger
that there is of relapse, these miserable
affections wil cōtinually tyre thy spirit,
and wil make it become so heauie and
lumpishe, that it shall not doe any good
workes promptly, dilligently, and frequently, wherin not withstanding consisteth the true essence of deuotion.
Such soules as hauing gotten out of
the estate of sinne, and retayne notwithstanding these bad affections and
languishinges, resemble in my opinion, the maydens that haue the greene
sicknes, who are not sick, and yet all
their actions are sick: they eate without relishe, sleepe without repose,
laughe without ioy, and dragge them
selues, rather then goe or walke: euen
so these soules doe wel, but with a spirituall wearisomnes, and that so great,
that it takes away all the grace from
their good exercises: which are but
few in number, and smale in effect.

Of

Of the meanes of applying this second Purgation.

CHAPTER VIII.

1. NOw the foundation of this second purgation, is a liuely and stronge apprehention of the greate harme which sinne bringeth vnto vs, by meanes whereof, we enter into a profound and vehement Contrition. For as neuer so litle Contrition (if it be true and vnfeined) especially conioyned with the vertu of the Sacraments, doth purge vs sufficiently from the guilt of sinne, so also when it is great and vehement, it purgeth vs from all the affections depending of sinne. A hatred or rancour which is feeble and weake, causeth our hart to rise at the very sight of him whom we doe hate, and maketh vs to flie his companie, but if it be a violent and deadly hatred, it maketh vs not only to flye his company, but euen to be disgusted, and not to endure the conuersation of any

any of his kinred , parents , or frindes,
no , not so much as his picture it selfe,
or of any thinge else appertayninge
vnto him , but is abhominable and
odious vnto vs : euen so when the penitent hateth his sinne , only with a
weake and cold, though true Contrition , he resolueth fully and truly indeed,neuer to offend nor sinne any more , but when he hateth it with a Contrition vigorous and forcible , he not
only hateth and detesteth the sinne, but
likewise all the affections,dependances,
and pathes of sinne.

2. We must then endeuour feruently, Philotheus, to augment as much as
is possible for vs, our sorrow , contrition, and inward repentance,to the end
that it may stretch and extend , to the
least appurtenance and sparke of sinne.
So blessed Marie Magdalen in hir conuersion,lost so perfectly all tast of sinne,
and of the pleasures she had taken therin , that she neuer afterwardes thought
more vpon them. And holy Dauid pro-
testeth , that he not only hated sinne,
but also all the wayes a nd pathes of the
same. And in this resolution, consisteth
the

the renouation of the soule, wherby she returnes by innocencie to hir youthfull dayes; which the same prophet compareth to the renewing of the eagle.

3. Now to attaine this apprehention and Contrition, thou must exercise thy selfe dilligently in these meditations following, which being duly practised, will (by the helpe of Gods heauenly grace) roote out of thy hart all sinne, as also the principall affections to the same : to this end haue I principally ordayned them. Thou shalt practise them therfore in order as I haue placed them, taking but one for euery day, and that in the morning, if it be possible, which is the time most proper for all the actions of the spirit : and the rest of the day following, ruminate and chew that which thou hast meditated in the morning. If thou be not yet accustomed to meditation, see that which afterwardes shal be said in the second part.

The

The first Meditation; of our Creation. Chap. 9.

Preparation.

1. Place thy selfe with reuerence before God.
2. Pray him to inspire thee with his grace.

Considerations.

1. C Onsider that there are but so many yeares past, when thou wast now yet come into the world, & thy being was a iust nothinge. Where were we (ô my soule) in that time? The world had then lasted so many ages, and yet there was no newes of vs.

2. God hath caused thee to be hatcht of this nothing, to be this somethinge which now thou art : without hauing any maner of neede of thee, but moued therunto by his only bountie.

3. Consider the being that God hath giuen thee, for it is the chiefest and most excellentst in this visible worlde:

capa-

capable to liue eternally : and to vnite thy selfe perfectly vnto his diuine maiestie.

Affections and resolutions.

1. *Humble thy self profoundly before the presence of God, saying from the bottom of thy hart with the Psalmist :* O Lord before thee, and in comparison of thy maiesty, I am iust nothing ? and how wast thou then mindfull of me to create me? Alas my soule, thou wast hidden (as it were) in the abisse of nothing : and in this abysse of nothing shouldst thou haue remained vntil this present, yf God had not drawne thee foorth from thence. And what couldst thou haue done, within this nothing?

2. *Giue thancks to God.* O my great and good Creatour, how infinitly am I indebted vnto thee, for that thou hast taken me out of this nothing, to make me by thy mercie that somthing which I am ? What shall I euer be able to doe worthelie, to blesse and magnifie thy name ? and to render thancks to thyne exceeding bountie ?

3. *Confound thy selfe.* But alas my Creatour, instead of vniting my self vnto thee

thee by pure loue and loyall seruice, I
haue alwayes been rebellious by my
vnruly affections: separating and with-
drawing my selfe from thee, to ioine
and vnite my selfe vnto sinne and iniquitie ; doing no more honour to thy
goodnes, then yf thou hadst not been
my Creatour.

4. *Prostrate and debase thy selfe before
God.* O my soule, knowe that our Lord
is thy God : it is he that hath made
thee, and not thou thy selfe. O God,
I am the work of thy hands. I will then
no more henceforth take pleasure in
my selfe, since in my selfe, and of my
self I am truly nothing. Wherof doost
thou bragge and boast, ô dust and ashes?
whereof doest thou extolle thy selfe,
ô meere nothing? Wherfore to humble my selfe I will doe such or such a
thinge, I will support such or such contempt, I will change my life, and
heerafter folow my Creatour, and doe
my selfe honour with the condition
and being which he hath giuen me,
employing it wholly in the obedience
of his blessed will, by such meanes as
shalbe taught me, and as I shall be in-
formed.

formed of by my ghoſtly father.
Concluſion.

1. *Giue thancks to God.* Bleſſe thy God (ô my ſoule) and let all my bowells praiſe his holy name, for his boûtie hath drawne me forth of the abiſſe of nothing, and his mercie hath created me.

2. *Offer.* O my God, I offer vnto thee with all my hart, the eſſence and being, which thou of thy bountie haſt beſtowed vpon me : with all my hart do I dedicate & conſecrate the ſame vnto thee.

3. *Pray.* O my God, ſtrengthen me in theſe affections and reſolutions. O holy virgin mother of our Lord, commend them by thy bleſſed interceſſion vnto thy mercifull Sonne, together with all thoſe for whom I ought to praye &c. *Pater. Aue. Credo.*

After thou haſt ended thy exerciſe, walke a while, and of theſe conſiderations which thou haſt made, gather and bind together a litle noſegay of deuotion to ſmell vnto, and to recreate the ſent of thy ſoule all the day followinge.

The second Meditation, of the end,
for the which were created.
Chap. 10.

Preparation.

1. Place thy self with reuerence before God.

2. Pray him to inspire thee with his
grace.

Considerations.

1. GOD did not place thee in this
world for any need that he had
of thee, who art altogether vnprofitable to him, but only to exercise
& declare his bountie in thee, in besto-
wing vpō thee, his grace & glorie. And
therfore hath he enriched thee, with vnderstanding to know him, remēbrance
to be mindful of him, will to loue him,
imagination to represent his benefits
vnto thy thoughts, eyes to behold the
wonders of his works, & a tongue to
praise him, and so foorth of others.

2. Being created, and sett in the
world for this intention, all actions
con-

contrarie to this end, muſt be reiected
and caſt away : and ſuch as ſerue not to
obtaine this end , ought to be deſpiſed
as vaine and ſuperfluous.

3. Conſider then the miſerable caſe
of moſt men in the world, who neuer
thinck of this end, but liue as yf they
beleeued that they were not made , but
onely to build faire houſes , to plant
pleaſaunt orchards , and to heape together riches , and ſuch like fooleries.

Affections and reſolutions.

1. *Confound thy ſelf , reproaching and
obiecting to thy ſoule her miſery ; which hath
beene ſo greate heretofore that ſhe hath ſeldom
or neuer thought of any of all this.* Alas
what did I buſie my thoughts vpon (ô
my God) when I placed them not vpon
thee ? what was I mindfull of, when I
forgot thee ? what did I loue , when I
did not loue thee? Ay me, I ſhould haue
fed my ſoule with thy veritie, and I haue
fild it with vanitie , and haue ſerued the
world,which was not made but to ſerue
me.

2. *Deteſt thy life paſt.* I defie you vtterly ô vaine cogitations , and vnprofitable fancies : I abhorre , and abiure
you,

you , ô deteftable and friuoulous ima-
ginatiôs : I renounce you vnfaithfull
and difloyall loues , miferable and loft
feruices, vngratfull gratifications, com-
berfome and vnpleafing pleafures.

3. *Turne thy felfe to God.* And thou,
ô my God, and my Lord , thou shalt
bee for the time to come the onely
obiect of my thoughts: no, I will neuer
more applie my fpirit to any cogitations , which may be offenfiue or difli-
kinge to thee. My memorie all the
dayes of my life,shall be filled with confideration of thy exceffiue goodnes , fo
louingly declared in my behalf: thou
shalt be the delicioufnes of my hart,and
the fweetnes of my affections.

4. Hence therfore from my fight for
euer , fuch and fuch toyes and trifles,
wherunto I haue vainely applied my
mind: fuch and fuch idle exercifes, in
which I fondly fpent my dayes ; fuch &
fuch affectiôs which entangled my hart,
shall henceforth be a horrour vnto my
thoughts: and to this end I will vfe fuch
and fuch remedies.

Conclufion.

1. *Thanck God that it pleafed him to create*
thee

thee for so excellent an end. Thou hast made
me ô Lord for thy selfe , to enioy euer-
lastingly the immensitie of thy glorie:
ô when shall it be that I shall be worthie, and when shall I praise thee according to my dutie ?

2. *Offer.* I offer vnto thee (ô my deare
Creatour) all these good affections and
holy resolutions , with all my hart & all
my soule.

3. *Pray.* I beseech thee (ô God) to
accept these my desires and vowes, and
to giue my soule thy holy blessing, that
she may faithfully accomplishe them ,
through the merits of the bloud of thy
blessed Sonne , shedd for me vpon the
crosse &c. *Pater. Aue. Credo.*

*Remember to make a litle nosegay of deuo-
tion as aforesaid.*

---

*The third meditation : of the Bene-
fits of God.* CHAP. II.
Preparation.

1. Place thy self with reuerence before God.

2. Pray him to inspire thee with his
grace.

Consi-

Confiderations.

1. C ONSIDER the corporall graces
which God hath giue thee: what
a bodie, what commodities to maintaine it, what health, and lawfull confolations to entertaine it, what frinds,
what helpes, and what affiftaunce. But
thou shalt confider all this, with comparifon of many other perfons in the
world, which are farre better and wor-
thier then thou, who notwithftanding
are deftitute of all thefe benefits; fome
fpoild in their bodies, health, and members: other abandoned to the mercie
of reproaches, contempts and difho-
nours: other oppreffed and ouerwhelmed with pouertie: And God would
not fuffer thee to become fo miferable.

2. Confider the benefits and gifts of
mind; How manie are there in the
world, fencelefle, foolish, and befides
them felues? and why art not thou one
of the number? God vouchfafed to fauour thee: How manie are there whofe
education hath been rude, brutish, and
barbarous, who haue been nourished
and bred vp in groffe ignoraunce, and
clownish behaueour? wheras the prouidence

uidence of God hath fo prouided, that
thou haft been brought vp ciuilie, and
in honour.

3. Confider the fupernaturall benefits of heuenly grace. O Philotheus,
thou art a childe of the Catholique
churche. God hath taught thee the
knowledge of his true religion, euen
from thy infancie and youth. How
manie times hath he giuen thee his
holy facraments ? how manie times
infpirations, internal illuminations, &
for thy amendment gratious reprehen-
fions? how often hath he pardoned
thee thy faults ? how often hath he deliuered thee from occafions of cafting
away thy felf, when thou waft in danger? And thefe laft yeares of thy life,
which he hath fo liberally lent thee, did
they not affored thee leafure enough,
to aduaunce thy felfe in the fpirituall
profit and good of thy foule ? Confider
at the leaft how fweet & gracious God
hath beene vnto thee.

Affections and refolutions.

1. *Admire the goodnes of God.* O how
good and how mercifull is my God in
my behalf ! O how gratious is he ! O
D   how

how rich is his hart in mercie, and liberall in bountie ? O my foule, let vs
recount for euer how manie fauours
he hath done vnto vs.

2. *Admire thy ingratitude.* But who
am I (ô Lord) that thou haſt been ſo
mindfull of me ? Ah how great is my
vnworthines, how intolerable is my
vnthanckfulnes ? Alas I haue troden
vnder foote theſe benefits, I haue
dishonoured thy fauours, turning them
into abuſes, and contempt, of thy
foueraigne bountie : againſt the infinit
depth of thy graces, haue I oppoſed
the bottomleſſe depth of my ingratitude.

3. *Sturre thy ſelf vp to acknowledgement
of his benefits.* Vp then my hart, be no
more vnfaithfull, vnthanckfull, and
deſloyal vnto thy great and gracious
benefactour. And how shall not my
foule, be ſubiect wholie vnto God,
who hath wrought ſo manie wonders
and graces both in me, and for me?

4. Goe to then, Philotheus, from
hence forward withdraw thy bodie frô
ſuch and ſuch voluptuous pleaſures ;
ſubiect it entirely, to the ſeruice of
God,

God, who hath done so much for it. Applie thy soule how to know and acknowledge the goodnes of thy God, by such and such like exercises, which be requisit for that end. Employ diligently the meanes which are in holy Church, to saue thy soule, and to profit in the loue and worship of God. Yea, ô my God, I will frequent the exercise of prayer, and the vse of thy sacraments: I will heare thy holy word, I will practize thy holy inspirations and thy counsails, &c.

Conclusion.

1. Giue God thancks for the knowledge he hath giuen thee at this present of thy bounden dutie, and of the benefits heretofore receaued.

2. Offer him thy hart with all thy good purposes and resolutions.

3. Pray vnto him to fortifie thee, that thou maist practize them faithfully, through the merits of the death and passion of his Sonne our deere Sauiour. Implore the intercession of the blessed Virgin, and of the Saints, &c.
Remember to make a litle nosegay of deuotion, as aforesaid.

The

The fourth meditation : of sinne.
CHAPTER 12.

Preparation.

1. Place thy self with reuerence before God.
2. Pray him to inspire thee with his
   grace.

Considerations.

1. CALL to mind how long it is
   since thou beganst to sinne, &
   examin how much from that
beginning, sinnes haue bene multiplied
in thy hart : how euery day thou hast
encreased them, against God, against
thy selfe, and against thy neighbour :
by worke, by worde, by desire and
thought.

2. Consider thy naughtie inclinations, & how much thou hast folowed
them. And by this meanes thou shalt
plainly see, that thy sinnes are greater in
number then the haires of thy head, yea
then the sands of the sea.

3. Consider and ponder in particular
the sinne of ingratitude against God:
which

which is a generall sinne, and extendeth it self aboue all the rest, & maketh the infinitly more enorme and hainous. Behold then how manie benefits God hath bestowed vpon thee, and how thou hast abused them all against the giuers goodnes : in particular consider how many good inspiratiõs thou hast despised, how many good motions thou hast vnprofitablie neglected. But aboue all, how manie times hast thou receaued the holy sacraments, and where are the frutes therof? what are become of all those pretious Iewells wherwith thy deare spouse adorned thee ? all these haue been hid and couered vnder the filth of thy iniquities. With what preparation hast thou receaued them ? Thinck I pray thee vpon this ingratitude : that God hauing runne so after thee, and that to saue thee, thou hast out-runne him, and that to destroye thee.

Affections and resolutions.

1. *Be confounded, and ashamed of this thy misery.* O my God, how dare I appeare before thine eyes ? Alas I am but an aposteme of the world, and a verie

D 3   sincke

fincke of finne and ingratitude. Is it
poffible, that I haue been fo difloyall,
that I haue not left any one of my
fences, nor any one of the powers of
my foule, which I haue not polluted,
violated, and defiled? and that not fo
much as one day of my life hath paffed,
in which I haue not brought foorth
fuch naughtie effects? Is it thus that I
ought to recompenfe the benefits of
my Creatour, and the pretious bloud
of my redeemer?

2. *Craue pardon for thyne offences*. O my
Lord, I caft my felf dowe before thy
feete, like the prodigall child, like another Magdalen, like a woman conuin-
ced to haue dishonoured her mariage
bed with all kind of adulterie O pittifull
Lord, mercie on this poore finfull wretche. Alas ô liuely and neuer-ceafing
wellfpring of compaffion, haue pittie
vpon this miferable fuppliant.

3. *Purpofe to liue better heerafter*. O my
bleffed Lorde, no; neuer any more with
the helpe of thy grace; no, neuer any
more will I abandon my felf to finne.
Alas I haue loued it but too too much:
but now I deteft it, & embrace thee. O
father

father of mercie, I wil liue & die in thee.

4. To blott out my sinnes past , I will accuse my self couragiouslie · I will not leaue one, but thrust it head long out of my hart.

5. I will do all that I can to pull vp by the verie rootes, all the plants of sinne frō my hart : & in particular, such and such which doe most annoy me.

6. To accomplish this , I will con-stātly embrace the meanes which shall be aduited me: and neuer thinck I haue done euough, to repaire the ruines of so great offences.

Conclusion.

1. Giue God thanks , for expecting thy amendment , vntill this houre : and blesse him that he hath giuen thee these good affections.

2. Offer him vp thy soule franckly and freely, that thou maist putt them in execution by the helpe of his grace.

3. Desire him to strengthen thee with his heauenly ayde , for his deere Sonns pretious death: for our blessed Ladies in-tercessiō, & the prayers of all his Saints, &c. *Pater. Aue. Credo. Remember to make a litle nosegay of deuotion as aforesaid.*

The

The fifte meditation : of Death.
CHAPTER 13.

Preparation.

1. Place thy self reuerently in the presence of God.
2. Pray him to inspire thee with his grace.
3. Imagine thy self to be extremly sick, liyng vpõ thy death-bedd, without any hope at all of euer escaping.

Considerations.

1. CONSIDER the vncertaintie of the day of thy death. O my poore soule, thou must out of this body one day : but when shall that day be ? Will it be in winter, or in summer ? In citie, or contrie ? By day, or by night ? Shall it be vnawares , or with aduertisment ? by sicknes , or by casuallity ? Shalt thou haue leasure to confesse thee , or not ? Shalt thou haue the asistance of thy ghostly father, or not ? Alas , ô my soule , of all these thinges we knowe not one , only certaine

taine it is that dye we muſt, and alwayes
ſooner then we imagin.

2. Conſider that at that time the
whole world ſhall haue an end, ſo far
foorth as concerneth thee, that is, there
ſhall be no more world for thee, yea, it
will turne vpſide downe before thyne
eyes : for then the pleaſures, the vanities, the worldly ioyes, the fond affections of our life, will ſeeme vnto vs
like flying ſhadowes, and fadinge cloudes. Ah wretched caytiue that I am,
for what trifles, and bables haue I offended almightie God? Thou ſhalt then
euidently ſee, that we haue offended
him for iuſt nothing. Contrary-wiſe,
at that houre, al deuotion, pietie, and
other good workes, will ſeeme vnto
thee the greateſt and ſweeteſt treaſure
in the world. O wherfore did I not
follow this faire and pleaſant path ? At
that ſorrowfull time, thy ſinnes, which
before ſeemed vnto thee but litle mou-
le-hilles, will appeare biggar then huge
mountaines : and thy deuotion ſo litle,
that thou wilt ſcarcely be able to per-
ceiue it.

3. Conſider the longe & languiſhing

D 5　　far-

farwells , that thy diſtreſſed ſoule wil
then giue to this world : how ſorrow-
fully ſhee will bid adieu to riches , to
honours, to vanities, to vaine company,
to pleaſures, to paſtimes, to frindes , to
neighbours, to parents, to kinsfolke, to
husband , to wife , to children , and in
a word to all creatures , and finally to
hir owne bodie , which ſhe muſt likewiſe leaue , al pale , wrinckled , hideous , loathſome , and moſt deteſta-
bly ſtinking.

4. Conſider the impreſſiõs that one
ſhall haue , to lift vp , or lay hand on
this thy body : the great haſt, that euen
thy beſt frindes will make , to carrie
thy carcaſſe out of doores, and to hide
the ſame full deepe vnder the ground,
far inough from their ſight & behoulding : and this done , how ſeeldome
afterwardes the world will thinke vpon
thee, ſurely no more then thou thy ſelfe
haſt thought vpon other men , who
haue deceaſed before thee. God haue
mercie on his ſoule, ſay they, and there
is all. O death how art thou to be pondered ? How art thou terrible , pitti-
les , and without compaſſion ?

                    5. That

5. That at this departure from the body, the foule ta keth his way on the right hand, or the left. Alas, alas, wither then shall thine goe, what way shall it take? furely no other then that, which it hath heretofore begunne in this world.

Affections and refolutions.

1. *Pray earneftly to God, and caft thy felfe with trembling loue betwixt his armes.* Alas ô my Lord, receaue me into thy protection at that dreadfull day: make that laft houre happie and fauourable vnto me, and let rather all the reft of my life be nothing elfe but dayes of forrowe, affliction, and calamitie.

2. *Defpife the world.* Seeing I know not the houre wherein I muft leaue thee, ô wretched world, I will no more fet my loue vpon thee. O you my deare frindes, knisfolkes, and allies, fuffer me to beare you only that affection, which is compatible with an holie amitie, and may therfore laft eternallie: for why should I vnite my felfe vnto you in fuch fort, as that afterwardes we should

D 6 be

be forced to breake the knot of amitie
betwixt vs?

3. I will therfore from this very instant, prepare my selfe for that peril-
lous houre, and take that care which is
requisite, to end this iorney happelie:
I wil secure the estate of my conscience, to the vtmost of my abilitie,
and take present order for the refor-
mation and amendment, of such and
such defaultes.

Conclusion.

Giue thankes vnto God for these
resolutions which he hath infused and
giuen vnto thee: and offer them againe
thankfully, louingly, and lowly vnto
his majestie. Entreat him a new to giue
thee a happie death, for the death of
his dearly beloued Sonne, our Lord
and Sauiour. Implore the asistance of
the B. Virgin, thy Angel gardian, and
all the Saintes in heauen. *Pater. Aue.*
Credo. And bind vp a sweete posie of
myrhe, to recreate thy soule the day
following.

The

The Sixt Meditation, of Iudgment.
CHAPTER 14.

1. Place thy selfe in the presence of God.
2. Pray him to asist thee with his grace.

Considerations.

1.   **A**FTER the time that God hath ordayned for the continnance of the world, and after a number of dreadfull signes and horrible presages, the terrour wherof shall make men wither for feare and anguish, a cosuming fire, comming like a flood, shall burne and reduce to ashes, euery thinge that is vpon the face of the earth, nothing which we see excepted, nothinge to be priueledged from this fiery deluge.

2. After this flood of flames and lightninges, all men shall arise from their graues (excepting such as already be risen) and at the summoning of the Archangels voice, they shall appeare
before

before the iudgment throane, in the
valley of Iosaphat. But alas with what
difference? For the one sort shall arise
with glorifed bodies, casting foorth
rayes of exceeding light, and the other
in bodies, or rather in carrions, most
hideous and loathsome to behould.

3. Consider the maiestie wherwith
the soueraigne Iudge will appeare,
enuironed with all the armies of his
Angells and Saintes. Before him shall
be borne triumphantly his sacred Crosse, shining much more brighter then
the sunne: a standart of grace to the
good, and of rigour and terrour to the
wicked.

4. This soueraigne Iudge by his re-
douted commandemēt, and which shall
sodainly and in a moment be put in
execution, shall seperate the good from
the bad, placing the one at his right
hand, and the other at his left: euerlasting seperation, after the which these
to bandes shall neuer any more meete
againe together.

5. This seperation being made, and
the bookes of consciences being layd
open, all men shall see clearly the malice
of

of the wicked, and the contempt which they haue borne to the maiestie of God: and on the other side, the penance of the good, and the effectes of the grace of God which they haue receaued, and nothing at all shall be hidden or kept secret in that great consistorie. O good God, what a shamefull confusion will this be for the one, and what a glorious consolation for the other ?

6. Consider the last sentence pronoūced against the wicked. *Goe you cursed into euerlasting fire, prepared for the diuel and his Angels* Waigh wel these wordes which are so waightie. *Goe*, saith he, a word of eternal reiection and abandoning of those vnfortunate wretches, bānishing them eternally from his glorious face. Next he tearmeth them *accursed*: ô my soule how dreadfull a curse? how generall a curse? a curse cōprising in it all maner of mischiefe and miserie; an irreuocable curse, comprehendinge all times and eternitie. He addeth , *into euerlasting fyre*. Behould, ô my hart, the grieuous horrour of this eternitie; O eternal eternitie, and boundles infinitie of paines, how dreadful art th ou ?

7. Con-

7. Confider the contrary fentence giuen and pronounced in fauour of the good. *Come* , faith the Iudge; O fweete word , and beginning of faluation , by which God draweth vs vp vnto him felfe, and receaueth vs into the bofome of reft and glorie. *The bleffed of my Father.* O deare bleffing , treafure of bliffe. *Poffeffe the kingdome which is prepared for you from the begining of the world.* O good God what exceffe of fauour : for this kingdome hath no end.

Affections and refolutions.

1. *Tremble, ô my foule , at the remembrance hereof.* O my God , who can fecure me at that difmall day , in which the pillars of heauen fhall tremble for feare ?

2. Deteft and abhorre thy finnes, for only they can caft thee away at that dreadfull houre.

3. *Ah wretched hart of myne refolue to mend all.* O Lord I will iudge my felfe now with all care and ftricktnes , left I be then iudged far more rigoroufly. I will examine and condemne my felfe, accufe and chaftice my felfe , that the eternall Iudge condemne me not in
that

that latter day. I wil with al forrowe
and humblenes, frequent the Sacrament of Confeffion, and will accept
all neceffarie penances and aduices.
&c.

Conclufion.

1. Thanke the goodnes of God, that
hath giuen thee meanes to prouide for
that day, and time and opportunitie to
doe pennance.

2. Offer him thy hart to performe it.

3. Pray him to giue thee grace, well
and truly to accomplish it. *Pater. Aue.
Credo*. And prouide a pofie for all the
day.

The feuenth Meditation, of Hell.
CHAPTER If.

1. Place thy felfe in the prefence of
   God.
2. Pray him to afift thee with his
   grace.
3. Imagin to thy felfe a darke citie, al
   on fire with pitch and brimftone,
   and thronged with miferable citizens, which cannot get out.

Confi-

1. CONSIDER that the damned are within this bottomles pit of hell, as with in this vnfortunate citie, where they suffer vnspeakable torments in all their sences, and in all their members : because as they haue employed all their sences and members to commit sinne, so shall they suffer in all their sences and members, the paines and torments due vnto sinne. There the wanton eies and lasciuious lookes, shall be afflicted with the horrible vision of diuels, and hellish spectacles. The eares for delighting in vitious discourses, detractions, and slaunders, shall heare nothing but lamentable outcries, and desperate howlinges : and so of others.

2. Consider that ouer and aboue all these bitter torments, there is yet another greater then they all, which is the losse and priuatiõ of the glorie of God, from whose most amiable face & fruition, they are for euer irreuocably debarred. Now if Absalon found, that the priuation of the face of his father Dauid, was more grieuous vnto him,

then

then his very exile, ô merciful Lord,
what an infinite griefe will it be, to
be for euer depriued from behoulding,
of thy moſt delightfull and louely
face.

3. Conſider withall, the eternitie of
theſe paines, which only thinge maketh hell intollerable Alas if a flea in
our eare, or if the heate of a litle fe-
uer, make one short night ſo long
and tedious, how tedious and terrible
shall the night of eternitie be, accompanied with ſo many vnſpeakable torments? Of this eternitie groweth in
the damned, an eternall deſperation,
infinitie rage, and moſt abhominable
blaſphemie. &c.

Affections and reſolutions.

1. *Certifie thy ſoule, and ſtir thy ſelfe
vp to feare with the wordes of holy Iob.* O
my ſoule, art thou able to liue for euer
with euerlaſting flames, and amidſt
this deuouring fire? Wilt thou willingly forſake the ſight of thy God
for euer?

2. *Confeſſe that thou haſt deſerued it.* And
wretch that I am, how often? O my deare Lord, from hencefoorth I will take a
new

new courſe, and tread a contrary way, for why ſhould I deſcend into this bottomles pit of hell ? I will therfore doe this or that indeuour to auoide ſinne, which only can giue this immortal death.

Giue thankes, Offer, Pray. Pater. Aue. Credo.

The eight Meditation *, of* Paradice.
CHAPTER 16.

Preparation.

1. Place thy ſelfe in the preſence of God.
2. Pray him to aſiſt thee with his grace.

Conſiderations.

1. CONSIDER a faire and a cleare night, and thinke how pleſant a thinge it is to behould the skie all ſpangled with an innumerable multitude and varietie of ſtarres. Then againe in thy imagination, ioyne all this nightes goodly beautie, with the beautie of a faire ſunne-ſhine day, ſuch an one, that the brightnes of the ſunne

bea-

beames, should not hinder the fight of
the goulden ftarres, nor the filuer rayes
of the moone : and after all this, fay
bouldly, that all this is nothing in regard of the excellent beautie of that
great Paradife. O how this place is to
be defired,and to be loued ! O how pretious is this noble citie !

2. Confider the nobilitie, beautie,
and multitude of the inhabitants, and
citizens of this bleffed contrie, thofe
millions of millions of Angels, and
Archangells, of Cherubins and Seraphins : thofe troupes of Apoftles, Pro-
phets, Martyrs, Confeffors, Virgins,
and holie Matrons. O how bleffed is
this bleffed companie ? The loweft and
meaneft whereof, is more beautifull
to behould, then all this vifible world:
what a fight wil it then be, to fee them
altogether ? But ô my God, how happie are they ? They finge continually
melodious fonges of eternal loue,they
alwayes enioy, a conftant and ftedfaft
eftate of gladnes,they enterchange one
to another,vnfpeakable contentments,
and liue in the comfort of endles and
indiffoluble amitie.

3. In

3. In a word, confider what good they all haue to enioy God, who grati-fieth them foreuer with his amiable countenance, and by the fame, powreth into their hartes an abiffe of delightes. What a good is it, to be vnited euerla-ftingly to their begining? They are the-re iike happie birdes, which flye, chir-ping & finging perpetually in the hea-uen of the diuinitie, which encompaf-feth them on all fides with vnfpeakable pleafures: there euery one ftriueth with an holie emulation, who may doe beft, and without any enuy, finge the praifes of their Creator. Bleffed be thou, ô fweete lord and foueraigne maker, who art fo bountiful vnto vs, & dooft com-municate vnto vs fo liberally, the euer-lafting treafures of thy glory. And God on the other fide, bleffeth them all with an eternall benediction. Bleffed be you for euer, faith he, my beloued creatures who haue fo faithfully ferued me, and who shall laude me euerlaftingly with fo great loue, courage, and content-ment.

Affections and refolutions.

1. *Admire and praife this heauenly coun-*
                                        trie,

trie. O how beautifull art thou, my deare Hierusalem?

2. *Reproache vnto thy hart the litle courage which it hath had vnto this present, for hauing gone so much awrye from the way of this glorious habitation.* O wherfore haue I so much estranged my selfe from my soueraigne good? Ah wretch that I am, for these pleasures, so displeasant and pight, haue I a thousand, and a thousand times, left the eternall and infinit delightes. Where was my wit and vnderstanding, to despise such goods so desireable, for desires so vaine and contemptible:

3. *Aspire notwithstanding with vehement resolution to this delicious & desired aboade.* O my gratious God, since it hath pleased thee at the lenght to recall my wandering steppes, and to direct them into the right way, neuer hereafter will I tnrne back to those by-wayes, neuer hereafter wil I stray from the true path. Let vs goe with courage, my deare soule, let vs runne towardes this blessed countrie, which is promised vs in the kingdome of heauen: what make we so longe in this beggarly coun-

countrie of Egipt? I will therfore difpatch my felfe from all fuch things
as may put me out of the way, or hinder me in fo happie a iorney. I will performe fuch and fuch thinges, as may
bringe me fafely and fpeedely to my
iornyes end. *Giue thankes. Offer. Pray.*
Pater. Aue. Credo.

The ninth Meditation; by way of
election or choife of Paradife.
Chapter 17.

Preparation.

1. Place thy felfe in the prefence of
   God.
2. Humble thy felfe before his maieftie, praying him to infpire thee
   with his grace.
3. Imagin thy felfe to be in a plaine
   field, all alone in companie of thy
   good Angell, as younge Toby
   going to Rages: and that he caufeth thee to fee aboue thee, Pari-
   dife open, with all the pleafures
   reprefented in the former meditation of Paradife : and beneathe,
                                    that

that he makes thee see the pitt of hell wide open, with all the torments described in the meditation of hell. Thou being thus placed vpon thy knees before thy good Angel,

Considerations.

1. CONSIDER that it is most certaine, that thou art in very deede in the midway to Paradise and hell, and that the one, and the other, is open to receaue thee, according to the choise which thou shalt make.

2. Consider that the choice which now thou makest, of the one, or the other place in this world, shall last for all eternitie in the world to come.

3. Consider that although both the one, and the other, be open to receaue thee, according to thy choice, yet that God who is readie to giue thee, ether the one by his iustice, or the other by his mercie, desireth not with standing, with an incomperable desire, that thou wouldest make choice of Paradise : and thy good Angel also, vrgeth and presseth thee with all his power, offering

E   thee

thee on Gods behalfe, a thoufand fuc-
cours, and a thoufand graces, to helpe
thee to afcend and mount vp thither.

4. Confider that Iefus Chrift from
heauen aboue , louingly behouldeth
thee,and inuiteth thee fweetly,fayinge.
Come ô my deare foule to euerlafting
repofe betweene the armes of my goodnes , where I haue prepared immortall
delightes for thee , in the multitude of
my loue. Behould likewife with thy inward eies , the holy Virgin, who with a
mothers tender loue exhorteth thee,
faying. Take hart & courage my child,
defpife not the defires of my Sonne,nor
the manifould fighes which I haue caft
foorth for thee,earneftly together with
my Sonne,tendering thy eternall faluation. Behould the Saintes alfo which
exhort thee, and a milllon of holy foules courteoufly alluring thee,and wishing nothing elfe , but that one day thy
hart may be ioyned with theirs in that
happie companie , there to prayfe God
for euer and euer, affuring thee that the
way to heauen , is not fo vneafie as the
world would make it. Come bouldly
deare foule,fay they,forward with cou-
                                        rage,

rage, for he that shal ponder dilligently the way of deuotion, by which we haue ascended hither, shall perceaue, that we arriued to these eternall ioyes, thorough pleasures, without comparison more pleasant, then all the delightes, and pleasures of the world.

Election.

1. O hell I detest thee now and for euermore, I detest thy torments and paines, I detest thy vnfortunat and accursed eternitie, and aboue all, I detest those eternall blasphemies and execrations, which thou vomitest out eternally against my God. And turning my soule to thee, ô beautifull paradice, euerlasting glorie, and endles felicitie, I make choice for euer and irreuocably, of my dwelling & habitation within thy faire and beautiful buyldinges, within thy holy and most louely tabernacles. I blesse thy mercie, ô my God, and accept the offer which it pleaseth thee to make me. O sweete Sauiour Iesus, I likewise embrace thy euerlasting loue, and agree to the purchase which thou hast made for me, of a happie lodging in this blessed Ierusalem;

E 2   not

not so much for any thinge else, as to loue and blesse thee for euer and euer.

2.   In like maner accept the fauours which the Virgin, and all the B. Saintes, present vnto thee. Promise them that thou wilt walke towardes them; and giue thy hand to thy good Angell, that he may guide thee thither, and encourage thy soule to make this choice. *Pater. Aue. Credo.*

The tenth Meditation; by way of election and choice which the soule maketh of the deuout life.

CHAPTER 18.

Preparation.

1.   Place thy selfe before God.
2.   Prostrate thy selfe before him, and craue the asistance of his grace.

Considerations.

1.   IMAGIN thy selfe once againe to be in a plaine field, all alone with thy good Angel, & that thou seest on thy left hand, the diuel seated vpon a great highe throne, with many infernall fiendes by him; & round about

him,

him , a great troupe of worldlinges, which all bareheaded, acknowledg him for their Lord , and doe him homage, fome by one finne, & fome by another. Behould the countenances of all thefe vnfortunate courtyers of this abhomi-nable kinge Behould fome of them fu-rious, and madde with hatred, enuie, and choller: others killing one another with fpite and rácour : others withered away, penfiue & bufie only to heape vp riches: others attéding only to vanitie, led away with pleafures, altogether fond and vn-profitable: others filthie, ougly, rotté, & putrified, in their brutish affectións. Be-hould how they are all without any re-pofe, wihout order, and without cótent-mét. Behould how they defpife one ano-ther, & loue but only fró the theeth out-ward. In a word , thou shat fee a pittifull cómon wealth, miferable tyrannized by this accurfed kinge , which may iuftly moue thy hart to compaffion.

2. On the right fide , behould Iefus Chrift crucified , who with moft hartie loue , prayeth for thefe poo-re people pofeffed of the diuel , that they may be freed and deliuered from

that

that tirannical thraldome, and calling
them meekly and curteoufly vnto him.
Behould roũd about him, a greát troupe
of deuout perfons, euery one in company of his holy Angel. Behould the
beautie of this kingdome of deuotion.
O what a goodly fight is it, to fee this
troupe of virgins, of men, and women,
whiter then the lillies, that affemblie of
widdowes ful of holie mortification
and humilitie. Behould the rancks of
diuers marryed folke, liuing fo fweetly
together with mutuall comfort, which
can not proceede but from heauenly
charitie. Confider how thefe deuout
foules, accommodate the care of theire
exteriour houfe, with the care of the
interiour : and the honeft loue of the
husband, with that of the celeftiall bri-
degrome. Behould them all vniuerfally,
and thou shalt fee in them all, a fweete,
holy, and amiable countenance, all of
them reuerently giuing eare to our bleffed Lord, whom euery one would willingly plant in the midft of his hart.
They are all full of ioy, but their ioy is
gratious, charitable, and well ordered : they abound in loue one towardes
ano-

another ; but their loue is sacred , pure,
and vnspotted. Such as suffer afflictions
amongst this deuout company , nether
torment nor trouble them selues , nor
leese their courage. Lastly , behould
those louely eies of our Lord and Sauiour , which sweetly are cast vpon
them all to comfort them , and how
they altogether aspire vnto him.

3. Thou hast alredie cast of Sathan,
with all his woful and execrable troupe,
by the good affections and resolutions
which through Gods grace thou hast
cōceaued: notwithstāding thou art not
yet arriued to the palace of thy king,
our Lord Iesus ,' nor ioyned with his
blessed court of deuout soules : but hetherto thou hast alwayes remained, between the one and the other.

4 The blessed Virgin,with S. Ioseph,
S.Lewis, S. Monica,& a hundred thousand other Saints,which are in the squa-
dron of those that liued deuoutly in the
middest of the world, doe inuite and
encourage thee.

5. The crucified king of glorie him
selfe, calleth thee courteously by thyne
owne name : Come my welbeloud,

E 4　　　come

come hither that I may crowne thee.

Election.

1. O vaine world , ô aʼbhominable troupe,no; you shall neuer more see me vnder your báner. I haue for euer left of your fooleries and vanities.O execrable king of pride , ô cursed kinge , fiend of hell,I renounce thee with all thy vaine pompes,I detest and defie thee, with all thy works.

2. And humblie turning my self vnto thee my deer Lord Iesus,king of felici-tie and eternall glorie , I embrace thee with all the forces of my soule , I adore thee with all my hart:I choose thee now and euer for my king , and for my only prince:I offer vp vnto thee my inuiola-ble fidelitie : I do homage irreuocably vnto thy diuine maiestie, and submitt my self wholly to the obedience of thy holy lawes,and ordinances.

3. O sacred Virgin my dread and deer ladie, I choose thee for my aduocate & my guide:I render my self vnder thy co-lours:I offer frô hencefoorth,a particu-lar respect &reuerêce vnto thy memorie.

4. O my good Angel , present me vnto this glorious and sacred assemblie,
and

and abandō me not vntil I arriue to the
societie of this blessed companie : with
whome I say frō my hart, & will say for
euer. Liue for euer my Lord Iesus, liue
for euer my Lord Iesus. *Pater.Aue.Credo.*

How to make a generall Confession.
CHAPTER 19.

1. HETHERTO (my deer Philotheus)
haue I set downe the meditatiōs
which I thought requisite for
our purpose: and when thou hast passed
them ouer with diligence and deuotiō,
then goe with an hūble, but yet courageous spirit, to make thy generall Con-
fessiō. But I pray thee suffer not thy self
to be troubled with any kinde of apprehension. The Scorpion is venemous in
the wound which ariseth frō his sting:
but him self being reduced into oyle,
becomes a singular remedie against his
owne stinging : so sinne is not shamefull, but when it is cōmitted : but being
cōuerted into cōfession & penaunce, becometh wholsome & honorable. Contrition and Confession are so precious,
and of so sweet a smell, that they blott
out the filthe, and disperse the stinche

of sinne. Simon the leaper, iudged
Mary Magdalen to be a sinner, and
called her so : but our mercifull Sauiour denied it, and spake no more of
her sinnes, but of the sweet perfumes
which she poured foorth, and of the
greatnes, and odoriferous sent, of her
inflamed charitie.

2. O my Philotheus, yf we be trulie
humble in our owne eyes and in the sight of God : our sinnes will displease vs
aboue all things, because God is highly
offended with thē: but the accusatiō of
our sinnes wilbe sweet and pleasaūt vnto
vs, because God is greatly honored with
it. A kind of hart ease, and an asswaging
of paine it is, to haue declared plainly &
sufficiētly, the disease that tormēteth vs,
to a skillfull physician, that can cure vs.

.3 When thou comest before thy
ghostly father, imagin thy selfe to be on
the mount of Caluary, kneeling right
vnder the feete of Iesus Christ crucified,
frō whome distilleth his most pretious
blood on al sides, to bathe & washe thee
from thy iniquitie For although it be
not the verie bloud of our Sauiour, yet
it is the merit and valor of his bloud,
                                    shed

shed for vs vpō the croſſe, which waſh-
eth & watereth abundantly,the ſoules of
the penitents , in euery confeſſionarie.
Open then thy hart well , to expell thy
ſinnes by virtue of Confeſſion , for according to that meaſure, in which they
goe out of thy ſoule , will the grace of
God enter in their rome , to fill thee
brim-full with his bleſſing.

4. But be ſure to declare the ſtate of
thy ſoule , and all thy ſinnes , ſimply,
plainly,and fully: ſatisfie thy confcience
in this , once for all thy life after : and
that done , hearken to the aduertiſmēts
and ordonances of the ſeruant of God,
to whome thou confeſſeſt, and ſay with
holy Samuel in thy hart : *Speak Lord, for
thy ſeruant hearkneth vnto thee.* Yea (my
Philotheus) it is God whoſe voice thou
heareſt in that place: for ſo ſayd he vnto
his vicars, *he that heareth you, heareth me.*

5. After that, take in hand this proteſtation folowing , which ſerueth for
a concluſion of all thy Contrition :
ponder it well from the begining to
the ending , and read it attentiuely , and
with the greateſt feeling that poſſible
thou canſt.

E 6   *An*

An authenticall protestation, seruing to en-
graue in thy soule a firme resolution to
serue God, and to conclude the actes of
Penaunce.   CHAP. 20.

1. I wretched sinner heere personally
appeering & standing in the presence of God euerlasting, and of
all the court of heauen ; hauing considered the exceeding mercie of his diuine goodnes towards me, most vnworthie and miserable caytife , whome he
hath created of nothing, preserued, su-
steined , and deliuered from so manie
dangers, & endowed with so manie benefits. But aboue all considering the in-
comprehensible sweetnes & clemency
wherwith this most good God hath so
bountifully tollerated me in my iniquities, so often , and so louingly inspired
me inuiting me to amendment , and so
patiently expected my penance & conuersion vntill this N. yeare of my age:
notwithstāding all my vnthanckfulnes,
disloyaltie, and infidelitie, wherby dif-
ferring my conuersion , & despising his
graces , I haue so impudently offended
him ; Hauing moreouer cōsidered that
at the

at the day of my Chriftening , I was fo
happely & holily vowed and dedicated
vnto my God to be his childe, and that
contrary to the profeffion, which then
was made in my name , I haue fo many
and fundrie times, fo execrably and de-
teftably profaned & violated my foule,
imploying it, & oppofing it againft his
diuine maieftie; At length recalling my
felf , & proftrating my felf in hart and
mind before the throne of his diuine
iuftice, I acknowledge, confeffe, and
yeald my felf lawfully attached & con-
uicted of high treafon againfte his diuine maieftie, & guiltie of the death &
paffion of Iefus Chrift, by reafon of the
hainous finnes which I haue cõmitted,
for which he died , and fuffered the torment of the croffe: fo that confequently, I am worthie to be caft away , and
damned for euer.

2. But turning my felf towards the
throne of the infinit mercie, of the felf
fame eternall God ; hauing detefted
from the bottom of my hart, & with all
my force.the iniquities of my life fore-
paffed, I moft humbly require & craue
pardon , grace , and mercie with entire
abfo-

abfolution from my crime, through
virtue of the paſſion and death of the
fame Saueour & redeemer of my ſoule,
vpon whome relying, as vpon the
only foundation of my hope, I confirme againe, advowe, and renew, the ſacred profeſſion of loyall ſeruice and fidelitie, made in my name & behalfe, vnto my God at my Baptiſing: renoun-
cing the diuel, the fleſh, and the world,
abhorring their execrable ſuggeſtions,
vanities, and concupiſcences for all the
time of this preſent life, and for all eternitie; And conuerting my ſelf vnto my
moſt gracious and mercifull God, I deſire, deliberate, purpoſe, and fully reſolue irreuocablie, to honour him, ſerue
him, and loue him, now and for euer:
giuing him for this end, and dedica-
ting, and conſecrating, my ſpirit with
all his faculties, my ſoule with all her
funĉtiōs, my hart with al his affeĉtiōs, &
my bodie with all his ſences: proteſting
neuer more to abuſe any one part of my
being or nature, againſt his diuine will
and ſoueraigne maieſtie: to whom I
offer vp and ſacrifice my ſelf in ſpirit, to
be to him a loyall, obedient, & faithfull
crea-

creature for euer, without euer vnſaying reuoking or repēting me of my promiſe.

3. But yf alas, through ſuggeſtion of myne enemie, or through humane frailtie, I chaunce at any time to tranſgreſſe in any thing whatſoeuer, this my purpoſe and reſolution, I proteſt and determin frō this verie houre, through the grace and ayde of the holy Ghoſt, to ariſe againe ſo ſoone as I ſhall perceaue my fall, & ſo to returne a new to the diuine mercie, without any ſtay or delay whatſoeuer. This is my will, intention, and reſolution irreuocable & inuiolable, which I aduowe, and confirme without reſeruation or exception in the ſame ſacred preſence of my God, and in the ſight of the triumphāt churche, and in the face of the churche militant my mother, who vnderſtandeth & regiſtreth this my declaration in perſō of him, who as her officer hearth me & taketh my confeſſion in this action.

4. Let it pleaſe thee ô my eternall God, allmightie and all good Father, Sonne, and holy Ghoſt, to confirme & ſtrengthen me in this reſolution, and to accept this my cordiall and inward ſacrifice,

crifice, in the odour of fweetnes . And
as it pleafed thee to lightē me with thy
holy infpiration, & to giue me the will
to purpofe fully, fo graunt me alfo force and grace to performe it perfectly.
O my God, thou art my God : God of
my hart, God of my foule, and God of
my fpirit: and for fuch do I reuerently,
thanckfully, and louingly acknowledge, honour, and adore thee, now, and
for euer. Liue ô Iefus.

A deuoute manner to receaue
abfolution. CHAP. 21.

1. THIS proteftation ended, be
verie attentiue, and open the
eares of thy hart, to heare the
wordes of thy abfolution, which the
Sauiour of thy foule him felf, fitting
vpon the throne of his mercie, will pronounce from aboue in heauen, before
all his Angells and Saints, at the fame
time, that the prieft in his name doth
abfolue thee heere beneath vpō earthe.
So that all that glorious troupe of the
bleffed citizens of heauen, reioicing at
this happie fucceffe of thine, will fing
a fpirituall canticle with incomparable
ioye,

ioye, and all giue the kisse of peace &
felowship vnto thy hart, now sanctified
and reestablished in grace.

2. Behold here (my Philotheus) an
admirable contract, which passeth between thee and thy God, by which thou
makest so happie a peace with his diuine maiestie, for as much as giuing thy
selfe to him, thou gainest him & thy self
also, for life euerlasting. It remaineth
onely to take penne in had, & subscribe
with a ioyfull hart to the act of thy protestation, and afterward, thou shalt goe
to the sacred Altar, where God on the
other side will reciprocallie, signe and
seale thy absolution, and the promise
which he makes vnto thee of the kingdome of heauen, putting him self by his
venerable sacrament, as a sacred seale &
signet vpon thy renewed hart.

3. Thus I trowe (Philotheus) thy soule
wilbe wholly purged from sinne, and all
sinfull affectiós. Yet because these affectiós are easilie bredd & borne a new in
the soule, through our failtie, & our rebellious cócupiscéce, which may well be
mortified, but neuer wholie extiguished
while we liue in this mortall life : I will
giue

giue thee some instructions, which
being well practized, may preserue thee
hereafter from mortall sinne, and from
all inclination or affection therof, so
that it may neuer hencefoorth find place in thy hart . And for so much as the
self same instructions, serue also for a
more perfect and higher purification
of the soule , before I deliuer them , I
will say a word or two of this absolute
and perfect puritie of mind, whervnto I
would so willinglie conduct thee.

That we must purifie our selues from
the affections which we haue to
veniall sinnes .

CHAPTER 22.

1. **A**S the day light encreasing,
we see by degrees more cleerly in a looking glasse, the spot-
tes and blemishes of our countenance:
euen so as the inward light of the holy
Ghost illustrates our consciences, we
see more plainly and distinctly, the sinnes, inclinations , and imperfections,
which may hinder vs to attaine vnto
true

true deuotion. And the very same light which causeth vs to discouer those spotts and deformities, enflameth vs likewise with desire to clense and purge vs from them.

2. Thou shalt discouer in thy self (my deare Philotheus) that besides mortall sinns & the affection to them, from which by the afore mentioned exercises, thou hast bene purged, there remaine yet in thy soule, diuerse inclinations and affections to veniall sinnes. I do not say thou shalt discouer veniall sinnes, but inclinations to them : now the one is farre differēt from the other: for we can neuer be alltogether free from veniall sinnes in this mortall life, at least so to continue in that puritie for any long time , but we may be well without all affection vnto veniall sinns: for (to giue an example of this difference) it is one thinge to lie once or twice merrilie, in things of small importance , and another thing to take pleasure in lying , and to beare an affection to this kind of sinne.

3. I say then, that one must purge his soule from all the affections and inclinations

nations that he feeleth to venial finnes, that is to fay, that he muſt not nouriſhe, voluntarilie a will to continue and per-feuer, in any kind of veniall finne: for it would be too too great a negligence, to keepe wittingly and aware vnto vs in our confcience, a thing fo difplea-fing vnto God, as is the will to be wil-linge to difpleaſe him: for a venial finne be it neuer fo litle, difpleaſeth almigh-tie God, though not fo hainouſly, that he will damne vs, or caſt vs away for e-uer for the fame. Yf then veniall finne difpleaſe him, the will and affection which one hath to venial finne, is no other thing, but a refolution and pur-poſe to difpleaſe his diuine maieſtie. And how is it poſſible, that a gene-rous and noble foule, should indu-re, not onely to difpleaſe his God, but to beare an affection to difplea-fe him.

4. Such affections (my Philotheus) are directly contrarie to deuotion, as affection and delight in morrall finnes, are oppoſite to charitie: They wearie and weaken the forces of the fpirit, hin-der the courſe of diuine confolations,

open

open wide a gate to tentations: and allthough they kil not the soule outright,
yet they make it exceeding sick and
feeble . *Dead flies* (saith the wiseman)
marre the sweetnes of an ointment : but
those which eate thereof in passing ,
spoyle nothing but that which they take , leauing the rest vntainted : but
when they linger long and die in the
ointment , they marre both the virtue and valew of it , and leaue it nothing worth but to be cast away . So
veniall sinnes , chauncing to fall in a
deuout soule , and not staying there any time , do not much harme vnto it : but yf the same sinnes dwell
in the soule , through the affection
& delight wherwith she entertaineth
them , they make hir without doubt,
to leese the sweetnes of the ointment , which is the grace of holie deuotion .

5. Spiders kill not the bees in
theire hiues , but they spoile and corrupt their honie , and entangle their
honniecombs with theire cobweb-
bes , so that the bees can not goe forward in theire worke. This is to be
vnder-

vnderſtood, when ſpiders get into the hiues ſo that they make their aboade in them. So venial ſinnes kill not our ſoules, but yet marre the honnie of our deuotion, and intangle the powers of our ſoule ſo ſtronglie with naughtie cuſtomes & bad inclinatiõs, that it can no more exerciſe charitie with promptnes and alacritie, in which deuotion conſiſteth: but this is to be vnderſtood when veniall ſinnes do dwell in our conſcience, by the affection & delight which we beare vnto them.

6. It is no hainous ſinne (my Philotheus) to tell ſóme litle lie in paſtime, to exceed ſomwhat in needleſſe talk, in careleſſe lookes, in apparel, in myrthe, in play, in dancing, and ſuch like toyes, ſo that as ſoone as we perceaue theſe ghoſtly ſpiders entered into our ſoules, we chaſe them and driue them preſently away, as the Bees driue away the corporal ſpiders: but if we permit them to ſtay in our hartes, and not only this, but if we bend our affections to retaine and multiplie them, we ſhal ſoone find our honnie deſtroyed, and made bitter, and the hiue of our conſcience peſtered

and

and spoiled. But I say once againe :
what likelyhood is there, that a noble
and virtuous soule, would take pleasure
in displeasing God : and delight her
self in becoming disagreable vnto him,
and to retaine a desire and will to do
that, which she knoweth to be grieueous vnto him.

That we ought to purifie our selues from
affection and delight of vnprofita-
ble and dangerous things.

CHAPTER 23.

1. Gaming, dancing, feasting,
brauerie, maskes, comedies &
such like pastimes, of them selues are not hurtfull at all, but indifferent, and may be well and ill vsed : yet
notwithstanding, these things be dangerous : and for one to beare an affection vnto them, is yet more dangerous. I say then Philotheus, that allthough it be no sinne at all, but lawfull
to play, to daunce, to deck and adorne
thy self, according to thy estate and the
custome of times, to heare honest comedies,

medies, to banquet with fober companie: yet to delight in fuch things, is
exceeding dangerous, and alltogether
contrarie to the exercife of deuotion.
It is no finne to do fuch things: but it is
very ill to fett thy affection that way. It
is pittie to fow fuch vaine and foolish
thoughts in the fertil field of our hart,
which take vp the roome of virtuous
impreffions, and hinder the iuice of
the foule from nourishing good and
wholfome inclinations.

2. The auncient Nazarits abftained
not onely from all that which might
inebriate or make them dronck, but
from grapes allfo, and the veriuce of
grapes: not that the grape of veriuce
maketh drûke, but becaufe it was to be
feared leaft tafting the veriuce, they
should be tempted to eate the grapes,
and by eating grapes they should ftirre
vp an appetite of drincking wine. I
denie not but we may fomtimes vfe
thefe dangerous thinges, but I auouch
abfolutely, that we can neuer fetle our
affection and delight on them, without
detriment to deuotion. The *Stagges*
when they feele themfelues ouerfatt,
retire

retire to the bushes and thickets of the
foreſts , becauſe they perceaue that
being loaden with their owne waight,
they should not be able to runne , yf
they should chaunce to be hunted. In
like manner the hart of man ſurcharged
with theſe ſuperfluous,vnprofitable,and
perillous affeƈtions, cannot runne after
his God with promptnes , facilitie, and
willingneſſe of mind, which is the true
point of deuotion.

3. Litle children ſweat and tyre them
ſelues to catche butterflies , and no
bodie thincks it ill in them , becauſe
they be litle children : but is it not a
ridiculous thing , nay rather is it not
lamentable, to ſee men of vnderſtanding and yeares, to be beſotted with
the delight of ſuch fond toyes, and baſe
trifles, as theſe of which we ſpeake ?
which beſides that they be alltogether
vnprofitable,put vs likewiſe in euident
danger of erring , and diſordering our
ſelues, in the purſute of holineſſe and
pietie. For this cauſe (my deer Philotheus) I ſay that we muſt neceſſarilie
purifie and cleanſe our ſelues frō theſe
affeƈtions : for though the aƈts them
F   ſelues

selues be not alwaies cōtrarie to deuotion, the inclination & delight in such actions is alwaies damageable vnto it.

That we must purge our selues, from bad inclinations.   CHAP. 24.

1. BESIDES these vitious inclinatiōs, we haue (my Philotheus) certaine naturall inclinations to some kind of acts: which inclinatiōs, because they proceed not in vs frō our particular sinnes, are not properlie sinnes, neither mortall nor veniall, but are onely imperfections, & defects; for exāple the holie matron S. Paula, according to the relation of S Hierom, had a great inclinatiō to griefe and sadnes, so that at the death of her children and husband, she was allwaies like to die for sorow: this was an imperfection in this blessed woman, but no sinne at all, since she had it against her will, for no doubt she took no pleasure in this kind of sorow.

2. There be some that naturallie are light of behaueour, others stubborne & sullen, others hard to receaue & admitt another mās coūcell, other some prone to indignatiō, others to choller, others

to

to loue:&to be brief,few shalt thou find,
in whome some such imperfection may
not be noted. Which allthough they be
as it were proper & natural to euery one,
yet by a care & contrarie affection, they
may be moderated & corrected,yea & be
altogether purged & deliuered of them.

3. And I tel thee (ô Philothee) that it
is necessarie that thou endeuour so to
doe. Men haue found the meanes to
change bitter almond-trees into sweet,
only by percing thē close by the root,
to lett out the bitter iuice of thē: why
may we not thē, let foorth our peruerse
inclinations,frō the root of our hart to
become better ? There is not so good a
nature,but may be corrupted by vitious
customs:nor so badd & stubborne a cō-
ditiō but may first by the grace of God
& next by good industrie & diligēce,be
corrected,and surmounted. To this end
therfore wil I now set thee downe some
instructions & exercises,by which thou
mayst purge thy soule frō all affectiōs to
veniall sinnes,& from these naturall im-
perfectiōs & withall fortifie & arme thy
self against all mortall sinne. God giue
thee grace to practize them well & effe-
ctually.   F 2   THE

THE SECOND PART

OF THIS INTRODVCTION,
Containing diuers aduices for
the lifting vp of the foule to
God by prayer, and by vfe of
the Sacraments.

Of the necefity of prayer.
CHAPTER I.

 H E exercife of prayer placeth our vnderſtanding in
the cleernes of the diuine
light, and expoſeth our
cold affection, to be war-
med by the heate of heauenly loue:
there is nothing that ſo much purgeth
our vnderſtanding from ignorance, and
our will frō depraued affections. Prayer
is the water of benedictiō which being
ſprinckled vpon our foule, maketh the
plants

plants of our good desires to flourishe,
washeth our minds from imperfectiós,
and tempereth the inflamed alteration,
which passions produce in our harts.

2. All prayer hath these good effects,
but aboue all I counsel thee to applie
thy self to mentall and cordiall prayer,
and especially that which hath for its
matter or subiect, the life and passion of
our Lord : for beholding him often by
meditation , thy soule wilbe filled with
him , thou wilt learne his cariage, as it
were and gestures, and conforme all thy
actions according to the measure and
model of his. He is the light of the
world: it is in him then, by him, and for
him, that we must be cleered and illumi-
nated , he is the louely tree of life: vnder
his shadow then , must we refresh our
selues; he is the liuing well of Iacob, to
washe away all the ordure and staines
of our soule. To be short , we see that
litle children by hearing their mothers
speak and pratling often with them, do
come to learne their language : and so
we continually conuersing with our Sauiour by meditation , obseruing and
pondering reuerently , his words , his

workes, & his affections, shal soone, by
the helpe of his grace, learne to speak,
to work, to will & desire as he did. We
must rest vpó this resolution my Philotheus, & beleeue me we can not come
vnto God the father by any other gate
but this: & euē as the glasse of a mirrour
cannot stay or retaine the rayes of our
ey-sight, vnlesse the back be seeled with
tinne or leade: so the deitie cannot well
be cótemplated by vs in this world, yf it
were not ioyned to the sacred humanitie of our Sauiour, whose life & death is
the most proportionable, delicious,
sweet and profitable obiect, that we can
choose for our ordinary meditatió Our
Sauiour, not for nothing caled him self
the bread of heuen: for as bread is to be
eaten with all sorts of meats: so our Sauiours life must be meditated, considered, and sought after, in all our prayers
& actions. This life & death, hath been
disposed and distributed, into diuers
points and passages to serue for meditation, by many authours: those whom
I councell thee to vse, are S. Bonauenture, Bellitán, Bruno, and Capilia.

3. Employ in it euery day an houre, &
that

that before dinner , yf it may be, beti-
mes at the beginning of the morning:
for then shalt thou find thy spirit lesse
troubled and distracted, & more freshe
& disposed after the repose of the night.
But spend no more then an houre, vnlesse
thy spiritual father expressely comad it.

4. Yf thou canst performe this exercise in the church , and find leasure and
tranquilitie there, it would be a place
most commodious: for no bodie , nether father nor mother , nor wife nor
husband , nor any other whosoeuer,
can with any reason hinder thee to stay
at the least one houre in the church :
wheras being subiect by any obligation
or dutie to such parties as I haue named
in thy owne house , thou wilt not be
able peraduenture , to promise thy self
an houre so free and quiet.

5. Begin all thy deuotions , be they
mentall or vocal, with the presence of
God : keep this rule without faile, and
without exception : and in short time
thou shalt perceaue, what inestimable
profit thou shalt reape by it.

6. If thou wilt beleeue my councell,
accustom thy self to say thy *Pater*, *Aue*,

and

and Creed in Latin : but learne likewiſe
to vnderſtand well the words contained
in them, and what they ſignifie in thyne
owne lauguage : to the end that ſaying
them in the common language of
the church , thou maiſt iointly taſt and
reliſh, the admirable and delicious ſence of thoſe holy prayers : which thou
muſt vſe to ſay, fixing profoundly thy
thoughts vpon euery word of them, and
procuring to folow the ſence of them
with an enfl.med affectiō : not making
poſt haſt , or ſtriuing to ſay a great
many ; but rather ſtudying and endeuouring to ſay thoſe which thou ſayeſt,
from thy hart : for one onely *Pater no-*
ſter , ſayd with feeling and heedfull attention of mind and deſire , is better
worth by farre, thē many recited haſtely
and with litle ponderation of the meaning of them.

7   The beades or roſary of our ladie,
is a very profitable kind of prayer , yf it
be vſed as it ought : which that thou
mayſt practize, prouide thy ſelf of ſome
litle treatiſe or other , of many which
be ſett ſoorth for that purpoſe. It is
good alſo to ſay the letanies of our Ladie,

die, of the Saints, of our Sauiour, and
other such vocall prayers, as are in ap-
proued manualls & primers allowed of
by the church : with this item, that yf
God haue bestowed vpon thee the gift
of metall prayer, thou reserue alwais the
principall place and time for it. So that
yf after thy mentall exercise, either for
multitude of thy affaires, or for any
other respect, thou be not able to say
thy accustomed vocall prayers : be not
therfore troubled or disquieted, but rest
content to say before, or after thy meditations, the Pater noster, Aue, and
Creed of the Apostles.

8.   Yf in making thy vocall prayers,
thou feele thy hart drawen and inuited
to inward mentall prayer, refuse not to
go where this good motion inuiteth
thee, but let thy spirit decline faire and
softly on that side : and care not much
for missing thy vocal prayers, which
thou didst intend ; for the mentall
prayer which thou hast made insteed
therof, is much more pleasing to God,
and more profitable for thy soule. I
except from this rule, the ecclesiasticall office ; for yf thou be bound to say

F 5   it

it by obligation of order, or ſtate of
life, that duty muſt firſt of all be payed
and performed.

9. Yf it should ſo happen, that all the
whole morning should paſſe away, without performance of this ſacred exerciſe of mentall prayer, either for the
multitude of thy affaires, or any other
cauſe (yet procure by all meanes poſſible that ſuch cauſes happē but ſeldom)
endeuour to repaire this loſſe after dinner, in ſome houre furtheſt after meate:
for doing it preſently after repaſt, before degeſtion be well made, thy health
would be much impaired, and thou
shouldſt find thy ſelf ouercharged with
drouſines. But yf all the day long, thou
canſt not recouer this loſſe, recompence it at leaſt by multiplying iaculatorie prayers, and by reading of ſome
book of deuotion, with ſome penaunce
or other for committing this fault: and
therwithall make a ſtrong reſolution,
to ſett thy ſelf in good order all the
day folowing.

A breef

*A breef method of meditation. And
first of the presence of God, which is
the first point of Preparation.*

CHAPTER 2.

1. BVT perhaps (Philotheus) thou
knowest not, how thou shouldst
make this mentall prayer, which
wee so much comend vnto thee: for it is
a thing that in this our vnhappie age,
verie few are acquainted withall. For
this cause I present thee a breef & simple method to that end: vntill such time
as by reading of many good bookes
that haue been copofed vpon this fubiect, and aboue all by often vfe & exercife, thou be more amplie inftructed.
And firft I fett thee downe the Preparation, which confifteth in two points:
wherof the firft is to place thy felf in the
prefence of God; and the fecond, to inuoke his ayde and affiftance. To place
thy felf in the prefence of God, I propound vnto thee the four principall
meanes folowing, wherwith thou maift
help thy felf in this thy beginning.

2. The firft confifteth in a liuelie &

F 6   fee-

feeling apprehension of the omnipre-
sence of God, that is to say, to conceaue and acknowledge, that God is in all,
and euery where, and that there is nether place nor thing in the world, wherin he is not most assuredly & certaine-
ly present: so that as the birds, whersoeuer they flie, encounter always with the
ayre, wherwith they ar alway compassed:
in like máner, where euer we be, we find
God still present. Euery one knoweth
this veritie , but euery one is not attentiue to apprehend, and ponder it. Blind
men that see not a Prince who is present with them, omitt not to respect &
honour him , when they are admoni-
shed of his presence: but because they
see him not with their eyes, they easily
forgett that he is present , and forget-
ting him , more easily omit their due
respect and reuerence. Alas we see not
God (my Philotheus) who is present
allway with vs , though faith do aduertise vs of his presence : yet not seeing
him with our eyes, we often forgett
our selues , and therfore comport and
carie out selues , as though God were
very farre from vs . For allthough we
knowe

knowe well enough that he is prefent
in all things ; yet not pondering, nor
waying this prefence, it is euen as much
as yf we knew it not . Therefore euer
before prayer, we muft prouoke our
foule , to an attentiue fight (as it were)
and confideration of Gods prefence: fo
did holy Dauid, when he cried out : *If
I mount into heauen , O my God , thou art
there: yf I defcend into hell thou art there prefent:*we muft thē vfe the words of Iacob,
who after he had feene the myftery of
the facred ladder , he fayd : *O how holy
and dreadfull is this place ! verely God is in
this place , and I knew it not:* that is., he
thought not of it : for he was not ignorant, that God was in all , and euery
where. Whē thou comeft thē to prayer
(Philotheus) fay inwardly to thy owne
hart: O my hart, my hart, God almightie is heer prefent in very deed.

3.   The fecond meane to place thy
felf in this facred prefence is, to thinck,
and confider , that God is not only in
the place where thou art : but that he is
by a moft particular and peculiar manner in thy hart, and in the very bottom
of thy fpirit , which he quickeneth and
ani-

animateth with his diuine presence, being there as the hart of thy hart, and the spirit of thy spirit. For as thy soule is as it were spread through all thy bodie, and in euery part and parcell therof, and yet is in a more speciall and remarkeable manner present in the hart: so likewise God being verily present in all things , assisteth notwithstanding with a more particular & notable presence in our spirit. For this cause Dauid calleth God, the *God of his hart*, and *S.* Paul sayeth, that, we *liue, we moue, and wee are in God*. In consideration then of this veritie , stirre vp in thy hart, a great reuerence towards thy God , who is so inwardly present in thy soule.

4. The third manner of presence is, to consider and behold our blessed Sauiour, who in his sacred humanitie, beholdeth from heauen all persons in the world, but especially all Christians, who are his children , and most particularly such as be in prayer : whose actions and behauiour, he marketh most louingly. And this is not a simple imagination of our phantasie , but an infallible veritie: for allthough we see not him , yet he
from

frō thence aboue cōsidereth & looketh
vpō vs. S. Stephen saw him in such sort,
viewing & marking his comportmēt in
his martyrdom . So that we may truly
say with the espouse: *Behold him there be-*
hind the wal, look where he is looking through
the windowes, seeing through the lettise.

5. The fourth manner of presence,
consisteth in helping our selues with a
simple imagination, by representing to
our thoughts, our Sauiour in his sacred
humanitie, as yf he were hard by vs, according as we are accustomed to represent our frinds to our fancie, and to say,
me thincks I see such a one doing this
or that, it seemes vnto me that I behold
him thus or thus attired , and such like.
But yf the venerable sacrament of the
altar were present , then this presence
were reall , & not by meere imgina-
tion, for the forces and appeerance of
bread should be as a tapistrie , behind
which our Lord being really present,
seeth & marketh our actions, although
we see not him in his owne likenes.

6. Vse then, (my Philotheus) these
fower manners of placing thy soule in
the presence of God before prayer: but
they

they muſt not be all employed at once;
one only at one time will ſuffice, and
that briefly and ſimplie, not ſtaying
long, or ſpending much time in calling this preſence to thy mind.

Of Inuocation, the ſecond point of Preparation.
CHAPTER 3.

1. INVOCATION, is made in
this manner. Thy ſoule remembring and conceauing, her ſelf to
be in the preſence of God, proſtrate
before his diuine maieſtie with all reuerence, acknowledgeth her ſelf moſt
vnworthy to abide before ſo ſoueraigne
and glorious an excellency : yet knowing notwithſtanding, that his goodnes will haue it ſo, ſhe humbly demaun-
deth grace of him, to ſerue him well,
and adore him purely in this her meditation.

2. Yf thou wilt, to this end thou
mayſt vſe ſome ſhort and inflamed
words, ſuch as be theſe of holy Dauid.
Caſt me not (ò God) *from thy face : take*
not

not from me the fauour of thy holy spirit. Suf-
fer thy face to shine vpon thy seruant ; and
I will consider thy meruailes . Giue me vn-
derstanding, and I will ponder thy law : and
keep it with all my hart. I am thy seruant,
giue me vnderstanding : and such like as
these.

3. It would be good also to call vpon
thy good Angel, and vpon the sacred
persons which were present at the mysterie that thou doest meditate on . As
for example ; in the meditation of the
death of our Lord, thou maist inuocate
our blessed Lady , *S. Iohn, S. Mary*
Magdalen, the good thieefe : that the
inward feelings , and motions, which
they receiued in their soules at that time, may be likewise at this instant
communicated vnto thee . So in the
meditation of thine owne death , thou
mayst inuoke thy good Angel gardian,
(who will be present at thy departure)
desiring him to inspire thee with conuenient considerations . And the like
may be done in other like mysteries.

Of the

*Of the third point of preparation, consi-
sting in proposing the mystery which
we meane to meditate.*

CHAPTER 4.

1.   AFTER these two ordinarie
pointes of preparation, there
is a third, which is not com-
mon vnto all sorts of meditatiõs, which
some call, the forming or figuring of
the place, or an interiour lecture, or
reading of the passage to be meditated
on. And this is nothing els, but to represent vnto thy imagination, the summe
and substance of the mysterie which
thou wilt meditate, and to paint it out
in thy thoughts so liuelie, as though it
passed reallie & verylie in thy presence.
For example sake: yf thou wouldest meditate our Lord vpon the crosse, imagin
thy self to be present vpon the mount
of Caluary; and that there thou behol-
dest and hearest, all that is done or sayd
in the passion of our Lord; or yf thou
wilt (for it cometh all to one end) imagin

gin to the felf,that in thy very fame place where thou art,they crucifie our Sauiour,in fuch māner, as the holy Euan-
gelifts doe defcribe.

2. The like may be done,when thou
wilt meditate of death , as I haue noted
in the meditation therof : and likewife
in the meditation of hell:and in all fuch
myfteries , in which vifible and fenfible
things are hādled;for as touching other
forts of myfteries, of the greatnes of
God; of the excellencie of virtue;of the
end for which we were created,and fuch
like,which be inuifible things, and not
fubiect to the apprehenfion of our fences;in thefe queftionleffe, we cānot vfe
this kind of imaginatiō. True it is,that
we may vfe fome fimilitude or comparifon, to help our confideration withall
in fuch inuifible myfteries, but thofe fi-
militudes are hard to be mett with; and
my meaning is to deale with thee but
plainly , fo that thy fpirit be not weeried , and ouerlaboured in fearching
out curious inuentions.

3. By the meanes of this imagination,we lock vp our fpirit as it were,wi-
thin the clofet of the myfterie which
we

we meane to meditate : to the end it
range not idly hether, and thether; euen
as we shutt vp a bird in a cage, that she
flie not away ; or as we tye a hauke by
her leash , that so she be forced to tarie
quietly vpon the hand.

4. *Some* cunninger maisters will
perchaunce councell thee, that it is better to vse only a simple thought or act
of faith, in beleeuing the mysterie, and a
brief apprehension altogether mentall
and spirituall, therof ; Others that we
frame within our selues the place, and
maner , or the historie proposed to meditate , and not considering it as yf it
passed in some other place without
thee , or farr distant from thee : But
these wayes are to subtil and hard for
young beginners ; and therfore vntill
such time as Gods grace do lifte thee
higher , I councell thee (ô Philotheus)
to keep thee in this low valley, which I
haue shewed vnto thee.

Of the

Of the considerations and discources of our vnderstanding; which are the second part of meditation.

CHAPTER 5.

1. **A**FTER the acts of imaginatiō, which we haue described in the former chapters, folow the acte of our vnderstanding, which we call properly meditation: and is no other thing, but one, or many considerations made by our reason, to stirre vp our affections to God, and Godly things. For in this is meditation different from studie, and discourcing, which are not vndertaken to obtaine vertue, or the loue of God, but for other respects, and intentions, as to become learned, to write, dispute, or talke intelligiblie, of such like matters.

2. Hauing then shutt vp thy mind and thought (as I said before) within the bounds, and limits of the subiect, which thou wilt meditate on, either by imaginarie representation, yf the mat-

ter

ter may be fubiect to the fences ; or by
a fimple propofing and conceit of it, yf
it be a matter aboue fence , and wholly
fpirituall : begin to make confiderations, and difcourfes therof , according
to the exaples which thou maift fee redy
made in the meditatiõs aboue written.

3. And yf fo be thy foule find taft,
fruite , and light enough in any one of
the confideratiõs or points which thou
haft difcourced vpon: ftay there without going any further to any other
point ; doing in this as the thriftie bees
do , which neuer leaue the flower they
once light on, fo long as they find any
honny to .be fucked out of it. But; if
thou find not taft enough according to
thy defire in any point , after thou haft
tried a litle by difcourcing on it, & like
a good merchant , hauing as it were
cheapned a while in that point , for to
gaine fome fwetnes of deuotion , then
paffe on faire and foftly to fome other
poinct or confideration, and all without
forcing thy thoughts to much, making
to fpeedie haft , to runne ouer all the
points of thy meditation. For one point
well pondered, is enough for once , and
the

the other points may serue thee for
another time.

Of the affects and resolutions of our
will, the third part of meditation.
CHAPTER 6.

1.   MEDITATION poureth out
abundance of good motions
in our will, or the affectiue
part of our soule: such as are, the loue of
God & of our neighbour; the desire of
Paradise, and eternall glory; zeale of the
saluatiō of soules; imitatiō of the life of
our Lord; cōpassiō, ioye, feare of iudgement, of hell, of being in the disgrace of
God; hatred of sinne; confidence in the
goodnes, and mercy of God; shame and
confusiō for our naughty life passed; In
these and such like affections, our spirit
must burst out, and extend and stretche
it self, as much as is possible And yf thou
desire to learne an easie method how to
do so, reade the preface of the meditations of Andrew Capillia, where he
sheweth plainly the maner and trace of
dilating and amplifiyng, and exten-
ding these affects of our soule : and
more

more largely doth Arias declare the same in his treatise of prayer.

2. Now thou must not content thy self with these generall affections, be they neuer so feruourous and holie, nor stand onlie vpon them, but descend to speciall and particular resolutions, for thy correction and amendment. For example ; the first word that our Lord spake vpon the crosse, will doubtlesse stirre vp in thy soule a good affect of imitation, and a desire to pardon thy enemies, and to loue them for thy Saueours sake and example: but this generall affect and desire is to small purpose, yf thou adde not to it a particular resolution, in this manner ; Well since my blessed redeemer so louingly did pardon these obstinate enemies of his, hanging vpon the bitter crosse, I will not heerafter be troubled or vexed whē I heare my neighbour; or my seruant, or felow N. vse such or such tanting words against me: I will not be aggrieued at this or that despite, or contemptuous trick, that he, or she doth vse against me: but rather I will endeuour to say & doe such and such a thing, to gaine his

good

good will , and to mollifie his anger or
indignation cōceaued againſt me. And
the like deſcent to particular purpoſes
of amendment, muſt be made in all
other generall affections. By this meanes (Philotheus) thou ſhalt correct and
amend thy defects in very ſhort time:
wheras otherwiſe , by only generall affects and deſires , amendment will be
made but hardly and ſlowly.

Of the concluſion of the exerciſe ,
and ſpirituall poſy to be ga-
thered out of it.

CHAPTER 7.

I. **L**AST· of all , we muſt conclude
our meditation by three acts,
which muſt be done with the
greateſt humilitie that we can. The firſt
act is, Thanks-giuing vnto God for the
holy affections, and reſolutions, or purpoſes, which he hath inſpired into vs :
and for his goodnes, and mercy, which
we haue diſcouered in the diſcourſe of
our meditation.

G   2. The

2. The second acte, is an oblation, wherin we present and offer vnto God, the self same goodnes,& mercie of his, which we haue tasted in meditating; the death also, and passion, virtues, and merits of his only Sonne our redeemer; and consequently with them, all the affections and resolutions which by his holy grace,we made in our exercise.

3. The third acte,is a petitió or supplication ; in which we demaund of God, and earnestly coniure him (as it were) to communicate and impart vnto vs,the graces, virtues , and merits of his deer Sonne; and to blesse the affections and resolutions which we haue made in his honour, and name, to the end we may faithfully put them in execution. After these three acts, we must pray for the whole churche of God , for our countrie,pastours,parents , and frinds: imploying and imploring to that end, the intercession of our blessed Ladie, of the glorious Angels, & holy Saints of heauen. Lastly I haue aduised that thou shouldst say a Pater,an Aue,and a Creed;which is the generall and necessarie prayer of all the faithfull.

4. To

4. To all thefe acts I haue added, that thou shouldft gather a litle nofe-gay of deuotion ; my meaning in this may be vnderftood by this example. Such as haue delighted them felues walking in a pleafant garden , go not ordinarily from thence,without taking in their hands , four or fiue flowers to fmell on, and keepe in theire hands all the daye after. Euen fo , when our mind hath fpirituallie recreated it felf, by affectiue difcourcing and medita-tion of fome facred myfterie , we should cull out , one or two points which we haue found moft pleafing to our taft , and moft agreeable to our vnderftanding, vpon which we might bufie our mind , and as it were mentally fmell theron all the reft of the day.And this muft be done immediatlie in the felf fame place, where we made our meditation , walking alone a turne or two , and binding thofe points in our memorie, as we would do flowers in a litle nofegay.

G 2   *Some*

Some profitable instructions and aduices for meditation.

CHAPTER 8.

1. **A** BOVE all things Philotheus, when thou arisest frō thy meditation, remēber carefully the resolutions & purposes which thou hast deliberated, and made : endeuouring to put them in practize that very day. This is the chiefest fruict of meditatiō, without which oft times, it is not onely vnprofitable, but hurtfull ; for virtues meditated, and not practized , do puffe vp the mind, and make vs ouerboldlie presume that we be such in deed, as we resolued , and purposed to be : which doubtlesse is true, when our resolutions be liuelie & solid: but they are not such, but rather they are vaine and dāgerous, yf they be not brought to practize and exercise. We must therfore vse all meanes , and searche out all occasions of executing our good purposes: so that, yf in my meditation I resolued by Gods grace, tò winne the minds of such as haue

haue offended me, by faire meanes, and
sweet behaueour: I must cast this verie
day how to meet with them, to salute
them courteouslie; or yf I cannot meet
with them, to speak well of them, and
to pray vnto God for them.

2. At the end of thy exercise, take
heede thou giue not thy hart scope to
raunge and wander: least thou spill the
delicious balme of good thoughts, and
holie desires which thou hast receaued
by prayer. My meaning is, that for some
time after, thou keep thy self silent and
quiet, & not presentlie with hastinesse,
but fair & softlie, remoue thy hart from
thy prayers, to thy affaires: and in the
verie entraunce into other busines, endeuour to keep as long as is possible,
the feeling and tast of those good affects, which thou hast receaued in meditation. Any man that had receaued
some pretious liquor in a faire porcel-
lan, or china platter, to carie home to
his house, would go with it, faire and
softly, neuer almost looking aside,
but always either before him, for feare
that by stumbling he should marre
all; or else vppon his vessel, to see

G 3   that

that he spill not the liquor which he so much esteemeth: Euen so must thou doe when thou hast ended thy meditation; not distract thy self all at once, but looking simplie before thee; as for example. If thou chance to meet with any whome thou art bound to heare or entertain, so that there is no remedie but thou must needs accommodate thy self to his conuersation, yet look oftentimes also vpon thy hart, that the pretious liquor of holie prayer, be not poured out, but the lest that may be.

3. Accustom thy self to passe with facilitie and easines, from prayer to all kind of businesse, which thy vocation and profession justly and lawfully requireth of thee, be they neuer so different from the affections which thou receauest in prayer: So let the aduocate learne to passe from prayer to pleading, the merchant to his traffick, the maried woman to her houswifrie, and care of her familie, with that sweetnes and tranquillitie, that their minds be neuer a whit troubled or vexed therwith: for since the one and the other, that is, prayer and our necessarie oc-

cupa-

cupations, are according to the will
of God, we muſt learne to go from
the one to the other, with an humble
and deuout ſpirit, and folow the will,
and ordonance of God, both in the
one and the other.

4. Many times immediatly after
preparation, thy affection wilbe altogether fired, and inflamed, with deuotion to God: and then Philotheus, thou
muſt lett go the bridle to thy affectiós:
that they may runne freely after the
inuiting of Gods ſpirit, without keeping that method which I haue ſet
downe. For although ordinarilie, conſiderations ought to goe before affections and reſolutions: yet neuertheleſſe, when the holy Ghoſt poureth
foorth deuout affections, and holy
motions in to thy ſoule without diſcource and conſideration, thou muſt
not then ſpend time in diſcourcing the
points of thy exerciſe; for thoſe diſcources ſerue for no other end, but to
ſture vp good affections, which in this
caſe the holy Ghoſt graciouſly ſtirreth
vp, and therfore need no diſcource at
all. In a woorde, when ſo euer good

affects, and deuout motions offer them
selues vnto thee, receaue them presently, and make them roome in thy
hart , whether they come before, or
after, all the considerations proposed
in thy exercise. Though I haue placed
in the aboue-written examples of meditation , the affections in order after
all the considerations and points of
discource : I did it only to distinguish
more plainlie and intelligiblie the parts
and acts to be vsed in prayer : so that
notwithstanding that order there sett
downe, take this for a generall rule,
neuer to restrain , or with-hold thy
affections once inflamed with any deuout motion , but let them haue their
free course : And this is to be vnderstood, not only of the affections folowing the considerations , but also
of the three acts of thanks giuing,
oblation, and petition, which may likewise be vsed amid the considerations
when they offer them selues feruently:
although afterward, for the conclusion
of the meditation , thou must repeat
them againe.

5. As for resolutions and particular
                                   pur-

purpoſes drawne from thoſe generall
affeƈtions, make them alway after the
affeƈtions them ſelues, and about the
end of thy exerciſe, before the concluſion of it : for yf we should preſent vnto our thoughts particular and
familiar obieƈts, in the heat of our
meditation and affeƈtion, they would
put vs in danger of cooling our deuotion, and to enter into diſtra-
ƈtions.

6. Amid theſe affeƈtions and reſolutions, it is good to vſe collo-
quies, or familiar talke, as it were
ſomtime with God our Lord, ſomtime with our bleſſed Ladie, with the
Angels, and perſons repreſented in the
myſterie which we meditate, with
the Saints of heauen, with our ſelues,
with our owne hart, with ſinners,
yea and with inſenſible creatures : as
we ſee that holy Dauid doth in his
pſalmes, and other deuout Saints in
their prayers and meditations.

Of the

Of the drynesse of affection, which often happeneth in meditating.

CHAPTER 9.

1. IF it chaunce thee to find no taſt
or comfort in thy meditation : I
charge thee Philotheus notwithſtanding, to be in no ſort troubled or
vexed therfore, but in ſuch occaſions
ſomtimes open the dore to vocall prayers, and with deuout words in the beſt
manner thou canſt, complaine of thy
ſelf vnto our Lord, confeſſe thy vnwor-
thynes, deſire him to be thy helper ;
ſomtme kiſſe reuerently ſome image of
his, and ſay vnto him theſe words of
Iacob: *I will not leaue thee Lord, vntill thou
giue me thy bleſſing*. Or thoſe of the Ca-
nanæan woman: *yes in deed Lord, I am a
dogge, but yett dogges eate the crummes that
fall from their maiſters table*. Other times
take ſome ſpirituall book in thy hand,
read it with heed and attention, vntill
ſuch time as thy ſpirit be awakned, and
reeſtabliſhed in it ſelf againe; ſtirre vp
thy

thy hart other times with corporall geftures of outward deuotion, proftrating
thy felf vpon the ground, laying thy armes a croffe before thy breft, embracing a crucifix ; which exteriour acts
are onely to be vfed when thou art retired alone into fome fecret clofet.

2. But yf after all this, thou obtaine
no comfort, be the drineffe and baren-
neffe neuer fo great, afflict not thy felf
with it, but perfeuer conftantly in as deuout a manner as thou canft, before al-
mighty God . How many courtyers be
there, that goe a hundred times in the
yeare into the Princes chamber, with
out hope of once fpeaking vnto him :
only to be feene of him, & that he may
take notice of the, that they endeuour
to fhew their dutie to him ? So muft
we (my deare Philotheus) come to the
exercife of prayer, which is as it were
Gods chamber of prefence, purely and
meerly to do our duty, and teftifie our
fidelitie . Yf it will pleafe his diuine
maieftie to talk with vs, to entertaine
him felf with vs by his holy infpirations
and interiour confolations, it wilbe
doubtleffe an ineftimable honor to vs,

and a pleafure aboue all pleafures : but
yf it pleafe him not to do vs this fauour, leauing vs without once fpeaking vnto vs , no otherwife then yf
he faw vs not , or yf we were not in
his prefence : we muft not for all
that go our way grumbling , or melancholie , but continew ftill patiently and with deuout behaueour, in the
prefence of his foueraigne goodnes ;
And then without faile our perfeuerance will be acceptable vnto him, he
will take notice of our conftancy
and diligence , fo that another time
when we shall come before him , he
will fauour vs , and paffe his time (as
we may fay) with vs in heauenly confolations , and make vs fee and taft
the beautie and delicioufneffe of holy
prayer . And allthough he should not
shew vs this fauour , let vs content
our felues Philotheus , it is an ouer-
great honour for fuch filly earth-
wormes as we are, to be in his fight and
prefence.

A mor-

A morning exercise.
CHAPTER 10.

BESIDES this maine exercise of mentall prayer and vocall, which thou oughft to performe once euery day, there be fiue other forts of shorter prayers, which be as it were helpps, and braunches of the other principall exercife: amongft which the firft is, that which we vfe to make euery morning, as a generall preparation to all the works and actions of the day : which thou muft make in this wife.

1. Giue thancks and adore God profoundly from thy hart, for the fauour that he hath done thee, in preferuing thee the night paffed, from all kind of daungers: and yf in that time thou haue committed any finne, craue pardon of him humblie for it.

2. Confider that this prefent day enfwing, is lent vnto thee, that in it thou mayeft by liuing wel, gaine the day that is to come, of eternitie in heauen: and make a ftedfaft purpofe to employ euery part of this day to this intention.

3. Fo-

3. Forecaſt with thy ſelf what affaires, what occupations, and what occaſions thou shalt encounter withall this day, to ſerue God ; and what tentations may befall thee to offend him, either by anger, or by vanity and lightnes, or by any other kinde of diſorder: and prepare thy ſelf with a holy reſolution , to employ diligently thoſe meanes and occaſions, which shall occurre to ſerue God, and profit in deuotion; as alſo on the other ſide, diſpoſe and arme thy ſelf carefully, to eſchew, reſiſt, & vanquish that which may preſent it ſelf againſt thy ſaluation, & againſt Gods honour, and glorie . Now it is not enough to make this reſolution , but thou muſt withall prepare the particular meanes, to put this purpoſe in execution ; for example : yf I foreſee that I am to treat of ſome buſines with one that is ſubiect to paſſion, and prompt to choler, I will not onely reſolue my ſelf to offend him in no wiſe, or fall at variance with him, but I will likewiſe prepare courteous words to preuent him ſweetly with all; or the aſſiſtance and companie of ſome perſon , that may ſtay and temper his condi.

condition. If I forefee that I meane to
vifit fome fick bodie , I will difpofe of
the hower, the affiftance, & the côfort,
which I am to do him: and fo foorth of
all other occafions.

4. This done , humble thy felf reuerently before God , acknowledging
that of thy felf thou canft do no one
thing of thofe which thou haft deliberated, be it to auoid euil, or to do good.
And therfore , as yf thou heldeſt thy
hart in thy hands., offer it withall thy
good defignements vnto the diuine
maieftie, intreating him to take it into
his protection, and to ftrengthen it, &
to bleffe thee with good fucceffe in his
feruice , vfing thefe or the like interior
words . O my Lord and God , behold
heere I offer into thy hands , this my
poor miferable hart , that through thy
goodnes , hath conceaued many pious
affections. But alas, it is of it felf to caytife and feeble , to exequute the good,
which it defireth , vnleffe thou impart
vnto it thy heauenly bleffing : which
for this end I humbly craue of thee , ô
Father of goodnes, by the merit of the
paffion of thy Sonne ; vnto whofe honour,

nour I confecrate this day folowing, &
all the refidue of my life. Then call vpon
our bleffed Ladie, vpõ thy good Angel,
and the Saints thy protectours, to the
end they may all affift thee this day with
their interceffion.

5. All thefe fpirituall acts and affections, muft be done brieflie , and fee-
linglie, before thou fteppe out of thy
chamber, yf it be poffible : that by this
holie preuention , all that thou art to
doe the whole day folowing , may be
bedewed, and watered with the bleffing
of God : and I pray thee my Philotheus, neuer omitt this exercife.

*An exercife for Euening. And of the
examination of our confcience before
bed time.* CHAP. II.

1. AS before thy corporail dinner
in the morning, thou muft make a fpirituall dinner for thy
foule by meditation : fo likewife before
thou giue thy bodie his fupper, prouide
a litle fupper, or at leaft wife a fpirituall
collation for thy foule. Gaine then fo
much time from other affaires , a litle
before

before supper time,as may sufficeto prostrate thy self before God, and to recol-
lect thy spirit, before thy Lord Iesus
Christ crucified (whome thou mayst
represent vnto thy selfe,by a simple cōsi-
deration & an inward view of thy mind)
kindle againe the fire of thy morning
meditation , by a dozen of liuelie aspirations, humiliatiōs, & louing glaunces
vpon this beautifull Lord and Saueour
of thy soule : Or els by repeating the
points of thy meditation,in which thou
feltest most sauour ; or by sturing vp
thy deuotion by some new spirituall
obiect , according to that which thou
best likest.

2. Touching the examinatiō of our cō-
science,which must allway be done im-
mediarlie before thou goe to bed:euery
one knoweth how it is to be performed.

1. We giue thancks to God , for hauing preserued vs the day past.

2. We examin carefullie how we haue
behaued our selfs in euerie houre of the
day:and to do this more easilie,we must
consider where,with whome,in what,&
how long we haue beene employed.

3. Yf we find by our examinatiō, that
we

we haue done any good , we muſt giue
God thancks therfore , by whoſe grace
we did it: and contrariwiſe , yf we find
our ſelues guilty of any euil,in thoughts
words , or deeds ; we muſt aske pardon
of his infinit mercie , with a true reſolution and purpoſe, to confeſſe it at
the firſt occaſion,and to amend it carefully.

4. After this, we commend vnto his
diuine prouidence,our ſoule and bodie,
the holy churche, our parents, frendes,
and countrie : we pray vnto our Ladie,
our Angel gardian, the Saints our protectours , that they would watche
ouer vs , and for vs : and ſo with the
bleiſing of God we go to take that
corporall reſt , which he hath ordained
requiſite for vs.

This exerciſe muſt neuer be forgetten , no more then the other morning
exerciſe before mentionned ;- for by
that of the morning,thou openeſt the
windowes of thy ſoule to the ſunne of
iuſtice : and by this of the euening ,
thou shutteſt them warilie,againſt infernall darknes .

                                            The

Of the spirituall retyring of the soule.
CHAPTER 12.

IT is in this place (my deer Philotheus) that I most affectuously desire thee to folow my councell: for in this article consisteth one of the most assured meanes of thy perpetuall profit.

1. As often as thou canst in the day time, recall thy soule home to her with-drawing chamber, there to appeer in the presence of God, by one of those fower meanes which we set downe in the 2. chapter of this 2. part ; and consider what God doeth, and what thou doest: and thou shalt find his eies turnd to thee wardes, and perpetuallie fastned vpon thee, by an incomparable loue. O my God (mayest thou say) wherfore do not I look alwayes vpon thee , as thou alwayes lookeest vpon me ? wherfore thinckest thou so much vpon me, ô my Lord? and wherfore thinck I so litle vpô thee? where be wee, whether wander wee ô my soule ? Our proper place is God himself, and whether do we straggle, and runne abroade ?

2. As

2. As birds haue their nests vpó trees, to retire thē selues vnto, whē they stand in need;& deers haue bushes& thickets to hide & shroude thē selues, & to take the coolenes and shadowe in the summers heat: euē so, my Philotheus, should our harts choose out euery day some place, either vpó the mount of Caluary, or in the wounds of our redeemer, there to make our spirituall retreat at euery occasion; there to recreate & refreshe our selues amidst the turmoile of exterior affaires; thereto be as in a fortresse, to defend our selues against the poursuit of ghostly tentatiós. Blessed is that soule that can truly & vnfainedly say to God: *Tou art my house of refuge, my secure ramper, my couert against raine and tempest, & my shadow & shelter against heat.*

3. Remember then Philotheus, to make euery day sondrie retreats and retirings into the solitary closet of thy hart whiles thou art outwardly busied in tēporall affaires & conuersations: for this mental or spiritual solitarinesse, cannot be hindered by the cōpanie of such as are about thee, for they are not about thy hart, but about thy bodie : thy hart
for

for all their prefence, remaineth alone
by it felf in the prefence of God. This
is the retreat that king Dauid made oftentimes admift fo many occupatiōs as
the cares of a kingdom bringeth withit:
fo he fignifieth in a thoufand places of
his pfalmes : *O lord, for me , I am alwayes
with theee. I behold God alwayes before me. I
haue lifted vp mine eyes vnto thee, ō my God
that dwelleft in heaué: Myne eyes be alwayes
toward God.* And againe it is certain, this
inward retreat is not fo hard to make
many times a daye, fince our conuerfa-
tions ordinarily are not fo importāt, but
one may fomtimes break thē of, & with
draw his hart to retire it into this fpiri-
tual folitude. Whē the father & mother
of S. Catherin of Siena, had takē frō her
all cōmoditie of place, & opportunitie
of leafure, to pray & meditate: our Lord
infpired her how to make a litle interior
oratorie within her hart , within the
which retyring her felf mentally , she
might amiddes thefe exteriour affaires,
attēd to this holy folitude of hart: & whē
the world affaulted her , then receaued
shee no hurt nor incōueniēce , becaufe
she had shut vp her thoughts & affectiōs
in her

in her interiour closet, where she comforted and solaced her self with her heauenly spouse. From experience of this exercise, she afterwards councelled her ghostly children, to build them a closet and chappel in their hart , and to dwell there alone in presence of their Lord.

5. Accustome thy self then to withdraw thy self often into thy self , where sequestred frō all men, thou maist, hart to hart, deal in thy soule with allmighty God, and say with Dauid : _I haue beene made like the Pelican in the wildernesse : like the night-rauen or screech-owle within the house: I haue watched, & been like the solitary sparrow in the roofe of the house_ . Which words (beside their literall sence, which telleth vs that this great king took some houres from other affaires, to spēd in the solitaire contemplation of spirituall things,) do moreouer shew vs in their mysticall sence, three excellent retreats , and as it were three deuout eremitages , wherin we may exercise our solitarines ; imitating our Lord and Sauiour , who vpon the mount of Caluary was like a Pelican in the desart, that quickeneth her dead chickens with
her

her owne bloud: In his natiuitie in the forsaken stable, he was like the screech-owle in a ruinous howse, weeping and bewailing our sinnes and offences; And at the day of his ascension, he was like to the sparrow, retiring him self, and flying vp to heauen, which is as it were the roof of the world. And in all these three places may we make our spiritual retreat, euen amidst the labours and turmoiles of our exteriour occupations.

6. Holy Elzear Count of Arian, in Prouence, hauing beene long absent from his deuout and chast Delphina: she sent expresselie a messenger vnto him, to know of his health: and the blessed Count made her this aunswer. I am verie well, my deere wife, but yf thou desirest to see me, seek me in the wide wound of my blessed *Saueours* side, for there dwell I, and there thou shalt find me: otherwise thou wilt search for me but in vaine. This was a right Christian knight in deede.

Of. aspirations, iaculatory prayers, and good thoughts. CHAP. 13.

1. WE retire our selues into God, because we aspire vnto him : and we aspire vnto him, to retire vs into him ; so that the aspiring of the soule vnto god, and the spirituall retreat, do mutuallie entertaine one another, and both of them proceed and issue from holy thoughts.

2. Aspire then verie often from the bottom of thy hart vnto God (ô my Philotheus) through brief and short, yet burning & inflamed desires, darted from thy soule : admire his beautie; call vpon him for his assistance ; cast thy self in spirit at the foote of the crosse; adore his goodnes ; question with him often about thy saluatiõ; giue thy soule vnto him a thousand times a day; fasten the inward view of thy soule vpon his inestimable sweetnes ; stretch foorth thy hand vnto him, as a litle child doth to his Father, that he may côduct thee : place him in thy bosome like a sweet-

smel-

smelling posie ; plant him in thy soule like an encouraging standart : finally make a thousand sorts and diuersities of motions in thy hart, to enkindle the loue of God within thee, and to engender in thy soule a passionate and tender affection of this diuine spouse. Thus are iaculatory prayers made , which that great S. Austen so carefully councelled the deuout ladie Proba to vse. O Philotheus, our spirit once giuing it self entirelie to the companie, hant, and familiaritie of his God , must needs be all perfumed, with the odoriferous ayre of his perfections.

3. This exercise is nothing hard or vneasie : it may be enterlaced with all our occupations, without any hindrance of them at all : for whether we retire our selues spirituallie, or whether we vse onlie these feruorous desires & darts of deuout loue ; we do no other thing, but make certain short digressions, as it were stepping a litle from our busines in hand , to talke a word or two with our God : which cannot hinder, but rather help forward, the prosequuting and performance

H   of

of the affaires which we were about.
The weerie Pilgrim that taketh a litle
wine to comfort his hart , and refreshe
his mouth, allthough he make some litle stay in drinking , breaketh not off
his iourney for all that stay, but gaineth
more force to end it more speedilie, he
only resting, to trauaile afterwards so
much the better.

4. Many authours haue gathered together abundantly, store of vocal aspirations , which out of all dout are very
profitable : but in my iudgement , it is
better not to bind thy self to any sort
of words, but only pronounce either in
hart , or by mouth , those words that
feruent and holy loue shall by the way
suggest vnto thee, for true loue will furnish thee, with as many as thou canst
desire . True it is that there are certain
words, with haue a particular force and
efficacie to content and satisfie the hart
in this behalf: such are the daintie si-
ghes , and passionate complaints , and
louing exclamations that are sowed so
thick in the psalmes of Dauid ; the often inuocation of the sweet & delightfull name of I ᴇ s v s ; the louely passages

ges which be expressed in the Canticle
of Canticles ; and spirituall songs also
do serue for this ende , when they be
song with attention.

5. To conclude , as they that be enamoured with humane and natural loue,
haue almost alway their thoughts fixed
vpon the parson beloued, their hart full
of affection towards hir , their mouth
flowing with hir praises; when their beloued is absent they leese no occasion
to testifie their passions by kind letters,
and not a tree do they meet with all ,
but in the barck of it, they engraue the
name of their darling : euen so such as
loue God feruently , can neuer cease
thincking vpon him , they draw their
breath only for him , they sigh and sorow for their absence from him , all
their talk is of him: and yf it were possible , they would graue the sacred name
of our Lord I e s v s, vpon the brests of
all the men in the world.

6. And certainly all creatures do inuite them to this , and not one but in
its kind, declareth vnto them the praises of their beloued: and as *S.* Augustin
sayth (taking it from *S.* Anthony) all

things in this world speak vnto vs with a
kind of láguage, which though dumbe,
in that it is not expressed in words, yet
intelligiblie enough in regard of their
loue: for all things prouoke vs and giue
vs occasió of good & godlie thoughts,
from whence afterward do arise many
motions and aspirations of our soule to
God. Behold a noble exáple of this veritie. *S.* Gregorie Bishop of Naziázen,
(as he him self related to this people,)
walking vpó the sea-shore, & cósidering
how the waues floting vpó the sands, left
behind them manie litle cockle-shells,
perewinkles, stalkes of hearbes, litle oy-
sters, and such like stuffe which the sea
cast vp, & spit as it were vpó the shore:
& the returning with other waues, swept
them away & swallowed the vp againe,
while in the mean time the rocks round
about him continued firme and immoueable, though the billowes neuer so
rudelie beat & battered vpon the: out of
this sight & cósideratió (I say) S. Gregory deduced this goodly cogitation: that
feeble & weak minded men, like cockle
shelles, & stalkes of rushes, suffer them
selues to be tossed vp & downe, & caried
som-

fomtime by affliction , fomtime by có-
folation, liuing allways at the mercy of
the vnconftant waues of chaunce and
fortune,but that great & well grounded
courages,perfeuered ftable,& vnmoued
againft all kinde of ftormes & tempefts:
And then prefently out of this thought,
he drew & deriued thofe afpirations &
affections of holy Dauid: *Saue me ô Lord,*
for the waters haue pearced euen to my very
foule. O Lord deliuer me from the deapth of
thefe waters. I am plunged in the deapth of the
fea,and the tempeft hath ouerwhelmed mee.
For at that time this glorious Saint was
in great trouble, by the wicked vfurpa-
tion which Maximus intended ouer his
bishoprick. S. Fulgētius Bishop of Ruf-
pa, being prefent at a generall affemblie
of the nobilitie of Rome , to whome
Theodoricus king of the Gothes made
an oratiô,& marking the fplēdour of fo
many worthy lords , gathered together,
& rancked each one according to their
ftate & qualitie. O God (fayd he) how beautifull & gorgeous is the heauēly Hie-
rufalem aboue,fince that earthly Rome
heare below, is fo glorious in her pôpe
& maieftie ? if in this tranfitorie world

H 3   the

the louers of vanitie be permitted to shine in such prosperitie: what glorie, what felicitie is reserued and layde vp in the world to come for the true louers of virtue and veritie? S. Anselme Arch-bishop of Canterburie, whose birth hath highly honoured these mountai-nes of ours, was admirable in the pra-ctise of these good thoughts. A Leue-ret, started, and sore pressed by hounds, as this holy prelat went on a iourney, ran vnder his horse, as to the best place of refuge that the imminent danger of death suggested; and the hounds bar-king & baying round about, durst not presume to violate the sanctuarie, to which their prey had taken recourse: a sight truly very extraordinarie; wherat when all the traine laughed, great S. Anselme, answered weeping & sighing: Ah (sayd he) you laugh at the matter, but the poor beast laugheth not; the enemies of the soule (combatted & ill-handled on all sides by multitudes of tentations & sinnes) do expect & besie-ge her at the narrow passage of death:& she wholly affrighted, seeketh succour and refuge on euery side, which yf she find

find not, then do her ghoſtly enemies
laugh and mock at her: which when
the good biſhop had ſayd, he went on
forward in his iourney. *S.* Francis on a
time ſeeing a ſheep all alone amidſt a
heard of goates: behold (ſayd he to his
companions) how meek is this litle
poor ſheep among thoſe wanton kids:
our bleſſed Lord went in ſuch meek
manner among the proud Phariſeys.
And at anothet time, ſeeing a litle lamb
deuoured by a hogge: ah litle ſeely Lā-
bkin (ſayd he weeping for compaſſion)
how liuely doſt thou expreſſe the death
of my Saueour? That great and excellent perſonage of our dayes, Francis
Borgia, while he was yet duke of Gan-
dia, going a hunting, made to him ſelf a
thouſand of theſe deuout conceipts. **I**
was wont to admire (ſayd he, recounting it afterward) how the faulcons come to hand, ſuffring their eyes to be
hood-winckd, and their talents to be
bound to the pearch: & that men are ſo
ſtubborne & rebellious to the voice &
cal of almightie God. *S.* Baſil the great
ſayth, that the roſe among the thornes
& briers, ſeemeth to make this exhorta-

tion to men. *Whatsoeuer is most pleasant
in this world,ó mortal men , is entermingled
with sorow: nothing is pure and vnmixed:
griefs be always companions of myrth , and
widdowhead of mariage , and care of education is ioined with fertilty & aboundance of
children,shame folowes glory , expences waite
vpon honours, disgust is the sauce of delicate
dishes,and sicknes pue-felow of health. A fair
flower is the rose (*sayth this holy man*) *but
yet it filleth me with sadnes , putting me in
mind of my sinne , for which the earth hath
been condemned to bring foorth thornes and
bryers.* Adeuout soule beholding the skie
and the starres in a faire moon-shine
night, represented in a cleer fountaine ,
O my God (sayd shee) these self same
starres shall one day be vnder my feet,
when thou shalt vouchsafe to lodge me
in thy holy tabernacle,and as the starres
of heauen are represented in this fountaine vpó earth: Euen so all men of this
earth are liuenly represented in heauen
in the liuing well of the diuine charitie.
A nother soule seeing a riuer swiftly flowing,cried out in this manner:my soule
shall neuer take rest , vntill she be swallowed vp in the boundlesse sea of the
deitie,

deitie, from whence she had her beginning. S. Frãcisca considering & viewing
attentiuely a pleasant brooke, vpon the
banck wherof she kneeled to pour
foorth her prayers, was rapt into an ex-
tasie, repeating oft times to her self these words : thus sweetly , & plesantly floweth the grace of my God vnto our
harts, as this riuerett danceth downe his
channell. Another looking vpon the
fruittrees of an orchard, which were all
bedecked with their timely blossoms,
sighed & sayd , ay me wretch that I am,
wherfore am I alone without blossom
or budd in the orchard of holy churche?
Another seeing litle chickens gathered
together vnder their mothers wings,
that sat louingly couring ouer them :
O Lord (sayd he) preserue vs vnder the wings of thy diuine prouidence . Another looking vpon the
heliotropium , that openeth and shutteth his leaues with the rising and setting of the sunne : when shall the time
be (sayd he) O my God, that my
soule in this manner shall wholly
folow the inuitement of thy goodnes , and attraction of thy holy spirit?
H 5   Ano-

A nother feeing the flowers which we call panfies, faire to the eye, but without any fweet odour. Ah (fayd he) fuch are my thoughts, fuch are my deeds, faire in conceipt and shew, but in effect fruitleffe, and vnprofitable.

See my Philotheus, how eafilie and redilie a man may draw good thoughts and holy infpirations, from all things great and fmall that are prefented to our fences and vnderftanding in the varietie of this mortal life. Moft vnhappy be they which do turne afide the creatures from their creatour, to chaunge & apply them to finne: And happie are they that turne all the creatures to the glorie of their creatour, and do employ their fading vanitie, to the honour of the euerlafting veritie. My cuftom (fayth S. Gregory Nazianzen) hath been allways, to accommodate and applie all things to my fpirituall profit. Read the Epitaphe or funeral fermon, which S. Hierom hath made in honour of holy Paula, for it is worthy the reading to fee how it is all as it were poudered with facred affects, afpirations, and deuout conceipts, which that blef-

fed

sed matron was wont to draw from all
occasions and occurrences whatsoeuer.

Well then, in this exercise of spirituall retyring, iaculatorie prayers, feruently darted from an enflamed desire,
consisteth the great work of deuotion;
this exercise may supplie the want of
al other prayers: but the want of it, can
not almost be repayred by any other
exercise: without it, we cannot well
lead a contemplatiue life, and but bad-
ly performe the actiue life; without it,
repose is but idlenes, and labour is but
drudgerie: therfore I charge and coniure thee of all loue, to embrace this exercise from thy hart, & neuer to omitt
it, or leaue it of.

How we ought to heare the holy
Masse. CHAP. 14.

1. HETHERTO I haue not spoken any thing of the bright
Sunne of all spiritual exercises,
I meane the most holy, dreadful, & soueraigne sacrifice and sacrament of the
masse, the verie center of Christian reli-

gion,the hart of deuotion,and foule of pietie, an vnfpeakeable myfterie,which comprehendeth in it the bottomleffe depth of Gods charitie, and by which God vniting him felf reallie vnto vs, doth moft liberallie communicate his graces and fauours to our foules.

2.   The prayer made in vnion of this diuine facrifice , hath an vnfpeakable force and efficacie : fo that the foule (my Philotheus) by the ayde heerof, aboundeth with heauenly fauours , as leaning and repofing vpon her welbe-loued , who filleth her hart brim full of odours and fpirituall fweetnes;that shee may be rightlie refembled to a pillar of fmoak proceeding from aromaticall wood , from myrrhe, and incenfe , and all the pouders of fweeteft perfumes ; as it is fayd in the canticles.

3.   Vfe then all diligéce to affift euerie day at the holie maffe, that thou maift iointlie with the prieft offer vp thy Re-deemer vnto God his Father, for thy felf,and for all the churche; The Angels of heauen (as S Iohn Chryfoftom fayth) be always prefent in great nóber,to ho-nour this facred myfterie : & we being
pre-

prefent with them , & affifting with the
fame intétion, cannot but receaue many
excellét influéces by fuch a focietie, the
two quiers of the triumphant and militant church ioine thé felues to our Lord
in this diuine actió, with him, in him, &
by him to rauishe the hart of God the
father, & to make vs owners of his mercie. O what felicitie enioyeth that foule
that withTo glorious a companie con-
tributeth her deuout affections , for fo
pretious and defired a good.

4. Yf vpon fome vrgét neceffitie thou
be forced to be ablét fró the celebrating
of this foueraigne facrifice ; at the leaft,
though thou canft not be really prefent,
yet fend thy hart and defire thether , to
affift there with a fpirituall prefence. At
fome time then of the morning , when
thou forfeeft any impedimét of hearing
maffe, goe in fpirit , (if otherwife thou
canft not) into the church, & there vnite
thy intentió with the intétió of all faithfull Chriftians: & vfe the fame interiour
actions in the place where thou haft
thus retired thy felf, which thou wouldft
vfe yf thou wert really prefent in fome
church at the office of the holy maffe.

                                    1. Now

1. Now to heare either reallie or mentallie the holie maſſe as we ought: firſt frō the beginning, vntill the prieſt go vp to the altar, prepare thy ſelf with him : which preparation conſiſteth in placing thy ſelf reuerentlie in the preſence of God, in acknowledging thine owne vnworthines, and crauing pardon for thy ſinnes and offences.

2. From the time that the prieſt aſcendeth to the altar, vntill the ghoſpell : conſider the aduent, or coming of our Saueour into this world, and his life amongſt vs, by a ſimple and generall apprehenſion therof.

3. From the ghoſpell to the end of the Creede: conſider the preaching of our Lord, and proteſt that thou doeſt purpoſe by his good grace, to liue and die in the faith, and obedience of his holie word, and in the vnitie of his Catholique church.

4. From the creed vnto the *Paternoſter*, applie thy conſideration hartelie to the death and paſſion of our Redeemer, which are actuallie and eſſentiallie repreſented in this holie ſacrifice: which with the prieſt, and the reſt of the faith-

full

full people thou shalt offer vp vnto
God the Father, for his eternall honour, and thyne owne saluation.

5. From the *Pater noster*, vnto the
Communion, endeuour to produce a
thousand feruent desires from thy hart,
wishing ardentlie to be for euer ioyned,
& vnited to thy Saueour, through euerlasting loue.

6. From the Communion vntill the
end, giue thancks vnto his diuine maiestie for his incarnation, life, death and
passion : and for the infinite loue which
he abundantlie witnesseth vnto vs in
this holie sacrifice : suppliantlie besee-
ching him, for his owne selfs sake, to
be mercifull vnto thee, to thy parents,
and frinds, & to all the whole churche :
and humbling thy self from the bottom of thy hart, receaue with deuotion the heauenlie blessing, which our
Lord giueth vnto thee, by the means
of the priest his lieutenant in this sacrifice.

But yf thou purpose during the
masse, to make thy meditation vpon
the mysteries, which thou prosequutest
from day to day; it will not then be
need-

needfull that thou diuert to make all
these particular actions and considerations; but it will suffise, that at the begining thou rectifie thy intention, to
adore and offer vp this heauenly sacrifice, by the exercise of thy meditation; for in all meditations are
found the aforesayd actions, either
expresselie, or els virtuallie and equi-
ualentlie.

---

*Of other publique and common exer-
cises.* CHAP. 15.

1. **B**ESIDES all these exercises, Philotheus, on holy days and sun-
dayes thou must be present at the
ecclesiasticall office of the morning
howers, and euensong: so farr foorth
as thy state and opportunitie will permitte. For these dayes be dedicated vnto
God peculiarlie, therfore in them thou
must performe many more actes of his
honour and worship, then vpon other
dayes. So dooing thou shalt feel a thousand diuersities of pleasures in thy deuotions, as S. Austen did; who confess-
seth

feth of him felf, that when he affifted
at the churche-feruice in the beginning of his conuerfion, his hart did
melt in fweet content, and his eyes
ouer-flowed with teares of deuotion.
And (to fay the veritie once for all)
there is euer more comfort and merit
to be gained at the publique feruice
of the churche, then in our other
particular actions. God hauing fo
ordained, that the communitie be
preferred before all kind of particu-
laritie.

2. Enter thy felf willinglie into the
deuout confraternities which are inftituted in the place where thou dwelleft : principallie in thofe whofe exercifes be of moft fruict and edification : fo thou fhalt exercife a kind
of obedience, verie acceptable vnto
almightie God. For though thefe
confraternities be not commanded,
yet are they commended by hollie
church : which to witnes how much
fhe defireth that many fhould enroll
them felues in fuch fodalities, giueth large indulgences and priuiledges vnto all fuch as enter into them.
                                    And

And besides these indulgences of the church which are gained by them, it is a deed of excellent charitie in it self, to concurre with many in welldoing, and to cooperate with others in their good works and designements. And although it may so happen, that one doth as good exercises alone, as in the confraternitie with others ; and perchaunce feeleth more spirituall delight and comfort by performing them alone in particular : yet is God much more glorified by the vnion and contribution which we make with our bretheren and neighbours, in good works and deuout exercises.

3. The like doe I say of all other kind of publique prayers, and acts of religion : which (as much as is possible) we should honour , and grace with our example , for the edification of our neighbour, and our owne soule, and for the glorie of God , and for the common intention, both of the churche and all the faithfull.

Of ho-

Of honour and inuocation of the Sainɛts.

CHAPTER 16.

1. SINCE God doth oftentimes send downe to vs his holie inspirations by ministerie of his Angels : we should likewise be diligent , to send vp vnto him our deuout aspirations by the self same heauenlie messengers. The holie soules of the dead , which are in Paradise , in companie of the blessed Angels , and are (as our Saueour sayth) equall and felowes of the Angels , do likewise doe vs the same good office of inspiring vs, and aspiring for vs by their sacred interceffions.

2. My Philotheus, let vs ioine our harts vnto these heauenlie spirits and happie soules : for as the litle young nightingales, learne to sing by chirping in companie of the old ones , so by the holie affociation which wee frequent with the Sainɛts and Angels of heauen, we shall learne farre better to pray and sing Gods diuine prayses : *I will sing to thee ô Lord* (sayth Dauid) *in the sight*
and

3. Honour, reuerence and respect the sacred and glorious virgin Mary, with an especiall loue : she is the mother of our foueraigne Father, & consequently our Grand mother. Let vs runne then vnto her, and like her litle nephewes, cast our felues about her, & in her lappe with perfect confidence, in all affayres, and occurrences. Let vs call vpon this sweet mother of ours, let vs inuoke her motherlie affection towards vs : and endeuouring to imitate her excellent virtues, let vs beare a true filiall hart and affection toward her.

4. Make thy self very familiar with the holy Angels, behold them often times in spirit and in thought, as yf they were visiblie present with thee : aboue all, loue and reuerence the Angel of the Dioces where thou dwellest, and the Angels of those persons with whom thou liuest, but especiallie thy owne Angel gardian : befeech them often, praife them ordinarilie, request their assistance and succour in all thy affaires, spirituall, or temporall, that they may cooperate with
thy

thy intentions.

5. That great perſonage, Peter Faber, the firſt prieſt, firſt preacher, firſt diuinitie-reader of the holie companie of the name of I ᴇ s v s, and firſt companion of B. Ignatius, the founder of that inſtitute ; coming on a day out of Germanie, where he had done great good ſeruice to the glorie of our Lord, and going through this dioces (the place of his natiuitie) related, that hauing paſſed many hereticall places, he had receaued thouſands of conſolations by ſaluting at the entrie of euerie pariſh, the Angels protectours of the ſame ; and that he ſenſiblie perceaued them to haue been fauourable vnto him ; both ·by preſeruing him from the ambuſhments of the hereticks, as allſo in mollifiyng many ſoules, and making them ſupple and docil, to receaue from him the doctrine of ſaluation. This did he tell with ſo liuelie an affection, that a gentle-woman, then verie young, hearing it from his owne mouth, told me it but fower yeares
paſ.

passed, (to wit aboue threefcore years
after he had told it him felf) with an
extraordinarie feeling of deuotion. I
my felf had the comfort this laft yeare,
to confecrate an altar in the place, on
which God appointed this bleffed man
to be borne , at a litle village called
Villaret , among thefe craggie mountaines of our countrie.

6. Choofe fome particular *Sainéts*
among the reft whofe liues thou mayft
more peculiarlie read, taft, and imitate : and in whofe interceffions thou
mayeft place an efpeciall truft and confidence : the *Sainét* , whofe name thou
beareft, is alredie affigned to be thy
deuote interceffor euen from thy Chriftening.

---

*How we ought to heare and read Gods
holy word.* C H A P. 17.

1. **B** E A R E always an efpeciall deuotion to the word of God :
whether thou heare it in familiar
difcourfe, among thy fpirituall frinds,
or at a publique fermon in the churche:
                                    heare

heare it alway with attention , and reuerence,and make thy profit and commoditie of it , to thy vttermoft power:
fuffer it not to fall vpon the grounde,
but receaue it thanckfullie into thy hart
as a foueraigne baulme ; imitating in
this the bleſſed Virgin our Ladie , who
kept carefullie in the treafure houfe of
her hart, all the words which she heard
fpoken in praife of her Sonne. Remember , that our Lord efteemeth of the
words which we fpeak to him in our
prayers , accordinge as we efteeme of
thofe which he fpeaketh vnto vs in
holie fermons.

2. Haue ftill lying by thee, fome
good booke of deuotion, as fome work
of *S. Bonauenture* , *of Gerſon* , *of Denis the
Charterhouſe monk* , *of Lewes Bloſius monk*
of S.Benet, of Grenada, Stella, Arias, Pinelli,
Auila , the fpirituall Conſiliat , S. Auguſtins
confeſſions , *S. Hieroms epiſtles ,* and fuch
like. Read euerie day a litle, in fome
one of them,with great deuotion, as yf
it were a letter miſſiue , which fome
Saint in heauen had fent vnto thee , to
shew thee the way thether , and to encourage thee in thy iourney.

3. Reed

3. Reed alſo the liues of the Sainčts, in which as in a mirrour, thou mayſt ſee the pourtraicture of Chriſtian perfe-čtion : and accommodate all their actions, to thy owne profit , accor-ding to thy vocation. For allthough very many actions of the Saints be not abſolutely imitable by ſuch as liue in the world ; yet all of them may be in ſome degree folowed, either neere or farr of: ſo the ſolitarieneſſe of S. Paul the firſt heremite , is imitated in ſome ſort, by the ſpirituall retreats of which we haue ſpoken : and the extreme po-uertie of S. Francis, may be imitated by theſe practiſes or exerciſes of ſpirituall pouertie which wee will heerafter ſet downe.

4. True it is , that there be ſome Saints liues, which more directly ſerue to guide and order our liues, then other doe : as the life of the bleſſed Mother Tereſa, which is moſt admirable for that purpoſe: as alſo the liues of the firſt Ieſuits , of the holy cardinall Borrom-eus, S. Lewes, S. Bernard , the chroni-cles of S. Francis , of S. Dominck, of S. Benet, and ſuch like. Other Saints
liues

liues there are which containe more
matter of admiration, then of imitation : as the life of *S.* Mary of Egypt,
of *S.* Simeon Shilites, of the two Saint
Catherines of Siena , and of Genua , of
S. Angela , and such like : which neuerthelesse, do minister vnto vs great occasions, to tast the sweetnes of the loue
of God.

How to receaue inspirations.
CHAPTER 18.

1. VV E call inspiratiōs , all those
inward alluremēts, motiōs,
reproches, remorses, lights,
and knowledges , which God worketh
in vs, preuenting our hart with his bles-
sings, through his fatherly care and loue
of vs , to the end he might awake vs,
stirre vs vp, driue and drawe vs to virtue,
to heauenly loue , to good resolutions,
and in a word, to all those things which
lead and direct vs to our euerlasting
good. These inspirations in the scripture, the bridegroome calleth , knocking
at the gate, and speaking to the hart

I   of

of his efpoufe ; to wake her when she fleepeth ; to crie and call after her, when she abfenteth her felf : to inuite her to his honnie , and to gather apples in his orcharde , and flowers in his garden ; to fing , and caufe to found her fweete voice to delight his eares.

2. I need a comparifon to declare my meaning . Three things are required to the matching, or ftriking vp of a marriage , on the maidens behalfe that muft be married . Firft , the partie is propounded vnto her : fecondly, she likes of the propofition: thirdly, she giueth her confent. So likewife God , intending to work in vs, by vs , and with vs, fome acte of charitie , firft of all he propofeth it vnto vs by infpiration ; fecondly, we accept it with delight ; and thirdly, we giue our full confent vnto it. For as to defcend vnto finne , there are three fteppes or degrees , tentation, delight , and confent : fo there are three other ftaires to afcend vnto grace and virtue : infpiration, which is oppofit to tentation ; the delight felt in the

infpi-

infpiration , contrarie to the delight
taken in dallying with the tentation ;
and confent to the infpiration, contrarie to the confent giuen to the tentation.

3. For,though the infpiration should
endure all our life long, yet should we
not be acceptable vnto God,if we took
no delight nor contentment in it , nay
contrarywife,his diuine maieftie would
be highly offended with vs , as he was
with the Ifraelits, with whom he had
beene labouring , forty yeares (as he
fayth him felf) and foliciting their conuerfion , in all which time they would
not giue eare vnto him: wherupon he
fware againft them in his wrath, that
they should neuer enter into his reft.
So likewife , the gentleman that had
long time ferued his miftris, should
be much difobliged, if after al this she
would in no cafe hearken to the marriage which he defired.

4. The pleafure which one taketh
in infpirations, is a great aduancement
to the glorie of God , and by it
one beginneth alreadie to pleafe
his diuine maieftie . For although

this delight be not as yet a perfect and
resolute consent, yet is it an assured and
certain disposition thereto; And if it be
accounted a good signe, to take pleasure in hearing the word of God preached, which is as it were an exteriour
inspiration : it is also no doubt an acceptable thinge in the sight of God, to
feele a delight in his internall inspiration. Such was that pleasure wherof the
espouse speaketh, when she sayeth : *my*
soule was melted with pleasure, so soone as
my beloued spake. And so the gentleman
is highly content with his mistresse
whome he serueth, and taketh it for a
great fauour, when he seeth that she
takes delight in his seruice.

5. But to conclude, the consent is
that which bringeth the virtuous act to
its full perfection : for if after the inspiration of God receaued, and delight
taken in the inspiration ; we refuse notwithstanding to giue our consent vnto
God, wee are extremely vngratefull,
and offend excessiuely his diuine maiestie : for in so dooing manifestly there
appeers a more disdainfull contempt in
our refusall. So happened it to the
espouse

espouse in the canticles , for though
the delicate voice of her beloued,
had touched her with harts-ease , and
holy delight : yet she would not open
him the doore , but excused her self
with a friuoulous reason , wherat her
louer iustly displeased , went his
way and left her alone. So the gentleman after long sute to his mistresse,
and seruice accepted , if he should
not with standing be shaken of and
despised , should haue much more occasion of discontent , then if his seruice had not at all beene accepted or
fauoured.

6. Resolue then (my Philotheus) to
accept with all thy hart the inspirations, that it shall please God to send
thee , and when they arriue at the
doore of thy hart , admitt them as
ambassadours from the king of heauen , who desireth to make a contract of mariage with thee : make
much of their embassage , ponder
well the loue of him that vouchsa-
feth to inspire thee, and esteeme of
the inspiration , as a message from
so great a kinge as God him selfe.
I 3   Con-

Confent to the motion which he in-
fpireth and propoundeth , but with a
perfect , conftant, and refolut confent,
that admitteth no wauering or doub-
ting : For fo God almightie , whome
thou canft not oblig' with all thy forces, will not with ftanding louingly
hold him felf obliged vnto thee for thy
affection.

7. Before thou giue plenarie confent
to thofe infpirations , which propound
vnto thee importāt matters, or extraordinarie motiōs, leaft thou be deceaued,
aske councell of thy guide & fpirituall
maifter , that he may warilie examin,
whether the infpiration be true or falfe:
for oftentimes the enemie perceuing a
foule prompt and willing to confent to
good infpirations, propofeth traiterou-
fly of his part, as if thy came from God,
falfe infpirations , to deceaue her : but
he can neuer compaffe his drifte , fo
long as fhe with humilitie obeyeth her
conductour.

8. Thy cōfent being giuen, thou muft
procure with all good endeuour the effect, for which thou gaueft confent , &
go about diligētly to put the infpiratiō
in exe-

in execution : which is the hight & perfection of true virtue : for to haue consented in hart , and not to attaine to the
effect & fruict therof, would be euen as
if one should plant a vine,and not desire
that it should fructifie. To all this the
morning exercise, and spirituall retreat
which I haue described , doe serue exceedingly : for by those meanes as by
ordinarie forecasts,and preuentions,we
prepare our selues not onely in generall,but in particular also, to execute all
the good we can.

Of holy Confession.
CHAPTER 19.

1. OVr Saueour hath left in his
church the holy sacrament of
Confession,or Penaunce , that
in it we may washe our selues from all
our sinnes, when soeuer we be defiled
with them.Suffer not thy hart (my Philotheus)any long time to continue soi-
led with the ordure of sinne , since thou
hast so easie a remedie to cleanse thee
with all.

I 4   2. The

2. The Lionesse hauing layen with the leopard , goeth presently to some brook to washe away the stinche which that disloyall fact of hers leaues in her bodie , least her Lion finding it by the smell, should be offended ther with. The soule which hath consented to sinne , should feele a horrour and abomination of her selfe , and procure to washe away that filth , for reuerence and respect of the eyes of Gods diuine maiestie, which behold her. And what should make vs to die this ghostly death , hauing so soueraigne a remedie to reuiue vs ?

3. Confesse thy selfe humbly, and deuoutly once euery seuenight , and euer before thou communicatest , if it be possible : allthough thou feele not thy conscience charged with guilt of any mortall sinne. For by confession, thou doest not onely receaue absolution of thy veniall sinnes , which thou mayst then confesse : but also iointly great force and vigour to avoide them heerafter , and a cleere light and knowledge to iudge and discerne them , and abundance of heuenly

heuenly grace , to repaire all the damage which' thou haſt incurred by
them. By confeſſion thou practizeſt
the noble virtues of humilitie , obedience , ſimplicitie , and charitie : in a
word , in this only act of confeſſion ,
thou exerciſeſt more virtues , then in
any other whatſoeuer.

4. Procure alway to bring with thee
to confeſſion a true ſorow and abhomi-
nation of the ſinnes which thou wilt
confeſſe , be they neuer ſo litle : and a
firme ſetled reſolution to amend them
heerafter. Many of cuſtom confeſſe
their veniall ſinnes in a kind of brauerie , not purpoſing at all to amend
them , continewing therfore all their
life charged with the burden of them,
and looſe by that meanes infinit benefits and graces of the ſpirit. Yf then
thou confeſſe to haue lyed in matter
of ſmall importance, without harming
any man , to haue ſpoken ſome inordinate or idle word , or to haue played
ouermuch : repent thy ſelf hartely for
theſe ſinnes , and purpoſe in very deed
to amend. For it is a great abuſe of the
ſacrament,to côfeſſe any kind of ſinne,

I 5   be it

be it mortall, or be it venial, without
any will or defire to be purged and
cleanfed from it ; fince Confeffion, was
inftituted for no other end, but to purifie vs from finne.

5. Make not thofe fuperfluous accufations which many doe of cuftome : I
haue not loued God fo well as I ought:
I haue not prayed with fo great deuotió
as I should. I haue not made much of
my neighbour as I ought to haue done:
I haue not receaued the facrament
with fo great reuerence as I ought,
and fuch like. For faying fuch like
accufations, thou bringeft nothing
in particular, that may make thy
confeffour vnderftand the eftate of thy
confcience : for all the men vpon
earth, and all the *Sainɛts* of paradife,
may fay the felfe fame with all truth,
if they should come to Confeffion.
Confider therfore what particular
fubieɛt or caufe thou haft to accufe
thy felf in that generall manner, and
when thou haft difcouered it, then
accufe thy felf of that default fimplie and plainly. For example, when
thou accufeft thy felf not to haue
che-

cherished thy neighbour as thou
oughteſt to haue done , peraduenture , becauſe hauing ſeene ſome poore
body in great neceſſitie , whome
thou mighteſt eaſily haue ſuccoured
and comforted , thou didſt neglect
that good occaſion of doing that
worke of mercie. Well then in this
caſe, accuſe thy ſelf thus in particular. Hauing ſeene a poore man in
neceſſitie , I did not aſſiſt him as I
could well haue done , through my
meere negligence , or hardnes of hart,
or contempt , or ill will borne to the
partie ; or according as thou knoweſt
the occaſion of that default. So likewiſe accuſe not thy ſelfe that thou haſt
not prayed vnto God with ſuch deuotion,as thou oughteſt ; but if thou haſt
admitted any voluntary diſtractions, or
neglected to take conuenient place,due
time,and leaſure requiſite for attention
in prayer, accuſe thy ſelf with all plain-
neſſe and ſimplicitie of that particular cauſe of thy default , not alledging thoſe generall tearmes , which
make the confeſſion neither hot nor
cold.

I 6   6. Thinck

6. Thinck it not enough to confesse thy veniall sinnes, but accuse thy self also of the motiue which induced thee to committe them. For example, be not content to say that thou hast lyed without endamaging any person: but declare whether it was for vainglorie to praise, or to excuse thy self: or for vaine myrthe, or for willfull stubbornesse. Yf thou haue sinned in gaming, expresse whether it were for greedines of lucre, or for conuersation and companie sake: and so foorth of other sinnes. Manifest likewise how long thou hast perseuered in the sinne which thou confessest; for continuance of time, is a circumstance noteablie encreasing and aggrauating the guilt of the sinne. Becaufe there is great difference betwixt a light vanitie or foolerie, that presentlie is giuen ouer, and layd a side, or which slippeth into our spirit for some quarter of an houre: and one wherin our hart hath beene steeped and souced for two or three dayes. We must then confesse the particular fact, the motiue, and the continuance of our sinnes. For
though

though ordinarilie we are not bound to be so punctuall in explicating our veniall sinnes, nay we are not absolutelie bound to confesse them at all: yet they that desire to cleanse and purifie their soules in good sort, the better to attaine to the perfection of true deuotion, must be carefull to manifest and lay open to their spirituall Physician, the disease wherof they wishe to be healed, be it neuer so litle.

7. Spare not to tell plainlie what soeuer is requisite to declare purelie the qualitie of thy offence, as the cause, subiect, or occasion which thou hast taken to be angrie, or to support and maintaine one in his faulte. For example : A certaine personage to whome I beare no liking at all, by chaunce speaketh to me some merrie word in iest., and I construe it in the worsse part, rising into cholar for it : wheras yf an other man that had been more agreable and acceptable to me, had spoken a shrodder worde, I should haue taken it in good part. In such a case, I will

not

not omitt to fay : I haue vfed cholerick
and angrie fpeeches againft a certaine
parfon, taking in ill part at his hands
fome words which he fpake to me,
not fo much for the qualitie of the
wordes in themfelues, as for the litle
good will or liking I had of the partie that fpake them. And yf it were
moreouer needfull to expreffe the verie angrie termes, vfed againft that
partie, to declare thy felf the better,
I will thinck it were good to expreffe them : for accufing thy felf fo
plainly and cleerly, thou doeft not
onely difcouer the fault committed,
but with all the naughtie inclinations,
cuftoms, and habits and other roots
of finne : fo that by this meanes thy
ghoftly father cometh to haue a perfecter knowledge of the confcience
which he dealeth with, and of the
remedies moft conuenient to be applied vnto it. Yet muft thou allways
procure to conceale the third perfons, who haue been partakers with
thee in the offence, as much as is
poffible.

8. Take diligent heede of manie
cou-

couuert finnes which raigne fo fe-
cretly and infenfiblie in our confcien-
ces, that we fcarcely perceaue or difcouer them : And that thou maift
find them out, and know them when
thou meeteft with them, read atten-
tiuelie the 6. 27. 28. 29. 33. & 36. chapters of the third part, and the 8. th.
chapter of the 4. th. part.

9. Chaunge not lightly nor eafilie
thy Confeffour, but hauing made
choice of a fufficient one, continew
conftantlie, rendring him account
of thy confcience on the dayes and
times appointed, opening to him
freely and plainly, the finnes thou
haft committed from time to time:
and monthly, or from two months,
to two months, tell him likewife
the eftate of thy inclinations, though
thou haue not finned by them : as
whether thou be tormented with fadnes, or with peeuishnes : whether
thou be giuen to ouer much myrthe,
or defirous of gaine, or fuch like
inclinations.

Offre

Of frequenting the holie Communion.

Chapter 20.

1. IT is faid, that Mithridates king of Pontus, hauing inuented the Mithridate, fo ftrengthened his bodie by the meanes of the fame, that endeuouring afterward to poifon him felfe, fo to auoide the feruitude of the Romans, he could not poffiblie do it. Our bleffed Sauiour hath inftituted the venerable Sacrament of the Eucharift, which containeth really and verilie his flesh and his bloud, to the end that he that eateth it, should liue eternallie. Who fo euer then shall vfe it often with fincere deuotion, fo confirmeth his health, and fecureth the life of his foule: that it is all moft impoffible he should be empoifoned with any kind of naughtie affection. One cannot be nourished with this flesh of life, and yet liue in affections of death. Man dwelling in the terreftriall paradife, could neuer haue died corporally, through virtue of

the

the tree of life, which God had planted there: fo cannot good Chriſtians in the church of God die ſpirituallie, through the efficacie of this Sacrament of life. Yf the tendreſt fruits that be, and moſt ſubiect to corruption, as cherries, ſtrawberries, and apricocks, be preſerued eaſilie all the yeare long, being confited in ſugar or honnie : it is no wonder that our harts, though neuer ſo fraile and feeble, be preſerued from the rott of ſinne, when they be candied and ſugred with the incorruptiblie fleſhe and bloud of the Sonne of God. O Philotheus, thoſe Chriſtians that muſt be damned for their naughtines, will be without replie, when the iuſt iudge ſhall make them ſee the wrong that they did them ſelues, to incurre ſpirituall death: ſeeing it was ſo facil a thing for them to maintaine them ſelues in life and health, by the ſacramentall manducation or eating of his bodie, which he had left vnto them, for that end. Miſerable wretches (will he ſay) why would you needs dye, hauing, the fruit and foode of life at your commandement.

2. To

2. *To receaue the communion of the eucha-*
rist euery day, neither do I commend, nor dif-
commend:but to communicate euery funday,
I would wishe it,and would exhort euery one
fo to do,yf his foule be without any affection
to finne. Thefe be the very words of S.
Auguftin, with whome I likewife, neither blame, nor prayfe abfolutely thofe
that communicate euery day : but I
leaue that poinct to the difcretion of
the ghoftly father of him , that would
be refolued ther vpon. For the difpofition requifite for fuch frequent vfe of
the holy communion requiring fuch
exactnes ; it is not good to councell it
generally or commonly to all. And
becaufe euen this exquifite and exact
difpofition , may be found in many
good foules , it were not well done to
diuert or diffuade generally all mē from
it ; but this muft be handled and ordered by confideration and knowledge
of the inward eftate of euery one in
particular.It were no wifdome to councell euery one without any diftin-
ction , to frequent the communion
euery day : and it were impudencie on
the other fide, to blame any one for
it,

it, especially yf he folow therin the aduice of any worthy and difcreet dire-
ctor. S. Catherin of Sienes anfwer was
commendable and gracious in this cafe : when it was obiected againft her
often communicating, that Saint Auftin did neither approue nor difallowe
communicating euery day : well (quoth
shee) fince Saint Auftin difalloweth
it not , do not you difpraife it , and
I am content.

4. But Saint Auguftin , as thou haft
heard (my Philotheus) exhorteth and
councelleth verie earneftlie to communicate, euery funday : folowe his
councell then , and doe fo as neare
as it is poffible : for I prefuppofe thou
haft no kind of affection at all to
mortall finne , nor any delight or affection to veniall finnes , and therfore
thou art in the true difpofition which
S. Auftin thincketh fufficient ; yea,
and in a more excellent, becaufe thou
haft not fo much as an affection to
finne venially : fo that yf it pleafe
thy ghoftly father, thou mayft pro-
fitably communicate more often then
euery funday.

4. Yet

4. Yet many lawfull impediments may befall thee not of thine owne part, but of theirs with whome thou liueſt, which may giue occaſion to a ſage and diſcreet conductour, to forbid thee to communicate ſo often. As for example, yf thou liue in any kind of ſubiection, and thoſe to whome thou oweſt this ſubiection, reuerence, or obedience, be ſo ill inſtructed in affaires of the ſoule, or ſo wayward, that they be troubled, or diſquieted to ſee thee communicate ſo often : peraduenture, all things well conſidered, it would be good to condiſcend to theſe mens infirmitie, and ſo to communicate but once euerie fifteen dayes; when thou canſt by no meanes ouercome this difficultie of theſe mens opinion. In a word it is hard to giue a generall rule in this caſe : the ſureſt is to remitt it allways to our ghoſtlie fathers aduiſe; though I thinck I may boldlie ſay, that the greateſt diſtance between the times of communicating, among ſuch as deſire to ſerue God deuoutlie, is from month to month.

5. A

5. A difcreet and prudent perfon should not be hindred, neither by father, nor mother, husband, nor wife, from often communicating : for fince the daye of communion, takes not from thee that care and fore-caft of affaires which are conuenient to thy calling ; nor makes thee leffe mild, fweet, and amiable toward them, nor forceth thee to denie them any kind of dutifull office or refpeſt ; there is no likelyhood, that they should feek to withdraw thee from this exercife, with any profit or pleafure of their owne ; vnleffe they be of a fpirit exceeding froward and intraſtable : for then perhaps thy ghoftlie father would councell thee, to condifcend fomewhat to their frailtie.

6. A word or two for married folke. In the ancient law, God would not haue the creditours exaſt that which was owing vnto them, vpon feafts and holydayes, but he forbad not debtours to pay and reftore that which they ought, to fuch as demaunded it. It is an vndecencie, though no great
finne

sinne, to sollicit the payment of the mariage due, the day that one hath communicated, but it is no indecency at all,
nay it is meritorious, to render it being
demaunded. Therfore for rendring this
nuptiall debt, none should be debarred
from the cōmunion, yf on the other side
their deuotiō vrgeth thē to desire it. Certainly in the primitiue church, all Chri-
stiās did cōmunicate euery day, were thy
vnmarried, or married, and blessed with
manie childrē. For this cause I sayd right
now, that often cōmunicating, bringeth
not any incōuenience at all, to father or
mother, husband or wife: so that the partie communicating be indued with discretion and wisdome, to know what be-
longs to his estate and dutie.

7. As for bodelie diseases, none are
lawfull impedimēts from participation
of this holy Sacrament, saue only those
which prouoke much vomiting.

8. To cōmunicate euery eight dayes, it
is requisit, neither to be guiltie of mortall sinne, nor of anie affection to veniall
sinne, and to haue a feruēt desire of comming to this heauenly banquet; But to
communicate euery day, it behoueth
                                    mo-

moreouer to haue surmouted and mortified the greatest part of our naughtie
inclinations, and to come so often not
of our owne head, but by leaue and aduise of our spirituall father.

How we ought to Communicate.
CHAPTER 21.

1. **B**EGINNE to prepare thy self to
the Communiõ, the euening before, by manie aspirations and
throwes of loue : retire thy self frõ exteriour labours somwhat earlier, that thou
maist rise sooner in the morning. Yf
thou chãce to awake in the night time,
by & by fill thy hart , & thy mouth with
some deuout wordes, which like sweet
odours, may perfume thy soule, as it were, to receaue thy spouse: who watching
whilst thou sleepest , prepareth him
self , to bring thee a thousand gracious
fauours, yf on thy part thou dispose thy
self to receaue them.

2. In the morning get vp with great
ioye, for the happinesse which thou ho-
pest to participate: and being cõfest, go
with great confidence, accõpanied with
great

great humilitie, to receaue this heauenly food, which nourisheth thee to immortall life. After thou haſt recited the
ſacred words, *O Lord I am not worthy* ,
moue not thy head or lippes any more,
neither to pray, nor yet to ſighe, but
opening thy mouth handſomly, and
lifting vp thy head as much as is needfull, that the prieſt may ſee what he
doth, full of hope, faith, and charitie,
receaue him, in whome, by whome,
and for whome, thou beleeueſt, hopéſt,
and loueſt.

3. O Philotheee, thinck with thy
ſelf, that as the Bee gathering from
flowers the dew of heauen, and choi-
ceſt iuice vpon the earth, conuerteth
it into honny, and carieth it into her
hiue : iuſt ſo the prieſt, taking the Saueour of the world from the altar, true
Sonne of God, as dewe come from
heauen, and true Sonne of the Virgin,
like a flower ſprong from the earth of
our humanitie, conuerteth him into
delightfull meate, in thy mouth, and
in thy bodie. Hauing thus receaued
him, ſummon all thy thoughts and deſires, to come and doe homage to this
                                        king

king of saluation : treat with him of thy
inward affaires and necessities:conferre
with him , as a noble guest now lodged
within thee for thy soules good.. To
cōclude, doe him all reuerence possible,
and carie thy self with such behaueour,
that men way iudge by thy actions,that
God is within thee.

4. When thou canst not haue the
benefit and commoditie, of communicating reallie and indeed at the holy sacrifice of the masse, cōmunicate at least
in hart and spirit : vniting thy self with
an ardent desire , to this life-bringing
flesh of our B. Sauiour.

5. Thy principall intent in communicating must be,to aduance, comfort,
and strengthen thy self in the loue of
God.Thou must receaue only for loues
sake , that which only loue hath caused
to be giuen.Thou canst not cōsider our
Sauiour in any action more amiable,
more tender harted towards thee , then
in this sacrament : in which he annihi-
lateth him self,in a manner,and turneth
him self into meat, that so he might penetrate our soules,& vnite him self most
straightly and intrinsicallie , with the

K   harts

harts & bodies of his faithfull seruants.

6. Yf worldlings demaund of thee, why thou communicatest so often ? tell the thou doest it, to learne to loue God, to be purified from thy imperfections, to be deliuered from thy miseries, to be comforted in thy afflictions, and to find rest, repose, and ease in thy weaknes. Tell them, that two sortes of persons, should comunicate very often : the perfect, becauſe being well diſpoſed, they should do thē ſelues wrong, in not approaching to the wellſpring and ſource it ſelf of perfection : the imperfect, that they might with better reaſon and title aſpire to perfection ; the ſtrong leaſt they become feeble, and the feeble to become ſtrong ; the ſick to be healed, and the healthie, leaſt they fall into ſicknes. Tell them, that for thy owne part, as óne very vnperfect, feeble, and ſick, thou haſt great need to communicate often with him, who is thy only perfection, ſtrength, and health. Tell them, ſuch as haue not many worldlie affaires, ſhould communicate often, becauſe they haue good leaſure : and ſuch as haue many temporall occupations, should

should likewise so do, because they haue
need: and that he that laboureth much,
and taketh great paines, must vse often
to eate, and strengthen him selfe with
hartie meat. Tell them, that thou receauest the blessed Sacrament, to learne
to receaue it well: for no man can do an
action well, which he hath not often
practized.

7. Communicate often Philotheus,
and as often as thou canst, with counsell
and aduice of thy ghostly father; for beleeue me, the Leuererres in these mountaines of ours, become all white, because
they neither see nor eate any thing but
driuen snowe: so by adoring and eating
beautie, goodnes, and puritie it selfe in
this diuine sacrament, thou wilt become alltogether, virtuous, pure, and
beautifull.

K 1   THE

THE THIRD PART
OF THE INTRODVCTION,
Containing sundrie rules and aduiçes , concerning the exercise of virtues.

Of the choice which we must make in the exercise of virtue.

CHAPTER I.

1. T H E king of the Bees neuer goeth a progresse into the fields, but enuironned with all his litle people: and charitie neuer entreth into the hart of man , but she lodgeth with her, all the whole traine of other virtues , exercising and setting them a worke , as a

Captaine

Captaine doth his foldiours. But she
fetteth them a worke, neither all at
once, nor all alike, nor in all feafons,
nor in euery place : for the iuſt man
is like a tree planted vpon the water
fide, which bringeth foorth fruit in due
feafon : and charitie as it were watring
the foule, bringeth foorth in her the
actions and workes of virtue, euery
one in their proper time. *Muſick, being
fo pleaſaunt a thing in it felf, is trouble-
fom in time of mourning,* faith the prouerb.
It is a great fault in manie, who vndertaking the exercife of fome particular
virtue, enforce them felues to practife
the acts therof, at euery encounter and
in all occurences; imitating the ancient
philofophers Democritus and Heracly-
tus, alway laughing, or alway weeping;
and (which is yet worfe) blaming and
cenfuring fuch, as do not always exercife the felf fame virtues. One muſt
reioice with the ioyfull, and weep with
the forowfull, fayth the Apoſtle : and
charitie is patient, bountifull, liberall,
difcreet, and condefcending or accommodating it felfe, to all occafions, and
exigences of our brethren.

2. There are notwithstanding some virtues, whose vse is almost vniuersall, and must not worke their actions only seuerally and a part, but must spread and extend them amid the qualities and operations of all other virtues. Occasions are seldome presented to exercise the virtues of fortitude, magnanimitie and magnificence: but meeknes, mildnes, temperance, modestie, and humilitie, are virtues, with which all the actions of our life, should be died and coloured. Many virtues may be more excellent then this one, but the vse of this one may be more necessarie. Sugar is of more exeellence then salt, but salt is more often and generallie vsed. We must allways therfore haue good store, and readie prouision of these generall and common virtues, since the vse of them is so ordinarie.

3. Among the virtues which we would exercise, we must preferre that, which is most conformable to our calling, not that which is most agreeable to our owne tast and will. Sainct Paula delighted in the exercise of asperities, and corporall mortifications,

that

that so she might more easilie enioy
the sweet tranquillitie of the spirit:
but she had more obligation to obey
her superiours, then to seeke her owne
contentment ; and therefore S. Hierom
amid her commendations sayth , that
in this she was to be reprehended , that
she vsed immoderate abstineces,againſt
her Bishops aduice. The Apoſtles on
the other side , appointed by God to
preach the ghospel , and diſtriбute the
bread of heauen to hungrie soules , iudged exceeding well,that they should do
wrong to this great function of theirs,
yf they should employ their time,in ſeruing & looking to the poore,although
to do so , were the act of an excellent
virtue.Euery calling and vocation ſtan-
deth in neede of the practiſe of some
peculiar virtue. Difference is there,
betweene the vertue of a Prelat , and
of a prince , or a soldiour : the virtue
of a married man , is different from
the virtues of a widow : and although
euery man should be endowed with
all virtues , euery one notwithſtanding , is not bound to practiſe them
alike, but each one muſt giue him selfe

K 4   in

in more particular manner, to those
virtues that belong to that kind of life
where vnto he is called.

4. Of the virtues which appertaine
not peculiarly to our particular estate,
and dutie, we must preferre those which
are most excellent in deed, not those
which excell only in apparéce. Blazing
starres ordinarilie, seeme greater and
goodlier thē the verie starres of heauen,
and occupie much more place, at least
wise in our eyes; wheras in deed they are
neither in greatnes, nor in qualitie, and
influence, comparable to the starres of
the skie; neither seeme they great for
any other reason, but because they are
neerer vnto vs, and in a more grosse subiect in respect of the starres. There are
likewise certaine virtues, which because
they are neerer to our senses, and (yf I
may say so) somwhat material, are highly
esteemed by the vulgar people: for so
cōmonly they preferre corporall almes,
before the spirituall workes of mercy:
haircloth fasting, nakednes, disciplins,
and other such bodilie mortifications,
before meekenes, courtesie, modestie,
and other mortifications of the mind,
which

which notwithstanding in true iudgements censure, are much more excellent. Choose then, Philotheus, those
virtues which are best, not those which
are only esteemed so by the vnskilfull
vulgar;those which are more excellent,
not those which are more apparent;the
substantial'st,not the brauest.

5. It is exceeding profitable, that
euery man should make choice of some
particular virtue, not neglecting or
abandoning the rest, but procuring to
be most conuersant, in the exercise of
some one peculiar virtue, to which he
thincks him self most apte, all things
well considered.

6. A beautifull damosell shining like
the sunne, royally adorned, and crow-
ned wth a garland of oliues, appee-
red in a vision to S. Iohn Bishop of
Alexandria, and sayd vnto him : I am
the kings eldest daughter, yf thou
canst gaine my good will, I will conduct thee to his presence. He perceaued that this was Mercy, towards
the poore, which God commanded
vnto him by this vision : and therfore
euer after, he gaue him selfe in such

K 5   fort

sort to the exercise of the workes of mercie, that he is now commonlie called amongst all S. Iohn the Almner.

7. Eulogius of Alexandria, desiring to do some peculiar seruice, to the honour of God, and being not able to embrace a solitary eremiticall life, or to resigne him self vp to the obedience of of an other, took vnto him in his house a miserable person, all infected with leaprosy, to exercise his charitie and mortification vpon him; and to performe this with more perfection, he made a vow to entertaine him, honour, and serue him, as any seruant doth his Lord and maister. Now vpon some tentation happening, as well to the lazar, as to Eulogius, to depart one from the other, they went vnto greate Saint Anthony for his councell. Who sayd vnto them. Beware my children, that you separate not your selues one from the other, for both of you, approaching nigh to your end, yf the Angels find you not together, you are in great dauger of leesing your crownes.

8. The holy king Lewes, visited the hospitals, and serued the sick, with his owne

owne hãds, as yf he had been a hireling,
that for wages & gaine had been induced to that feruice. *S.* Francis aboue all
things loued pouertie, which he was
wont to terme, his ladie and miftreffe :
S. Dominick moft affectioned to preaching to the ignorant, wherof his order
takes the name. *S.* Gregory the great,
took pleafure in entertaining pilgrims
and ftrangers, folowing the example of
Abraham, and had the fame grace granted him, that Abraham had, to receaue
the king of glorie in formé of a pilgrim.
Tobias exercifed his charitie in bu-
riyng the dead : *S.* Elifabeth, as great a
princeffe as fhe was, delighted fo much
in nothing, as in the abiecting and aba-
fing of her felfe. *S.* Catherin of Genua in
her widowhood, dedicated her felfe to
ferue an hofpitall. Caffianus recounteth,
that a deuoute gentlewomã defirous to
exercife the virtue of patience, came to
S. Athanafius, who at her requeft, placed
a poore widow with her, fo wayward,
cholerick, troublefome, & intolerable,
that fhe gaue the deuout dame, matter
and occafion enough, to practize the
virtue of meeknes and fufferaunce.

9. Finally among the feruãts of God, fome applie them felues principallie to attend and vifit the fick ; others with almes and fauour, fuccour the needie and poore ; others procure to inftruct litle children, in the neceffary know-ledge of Chriftian doctrine ; others endeuour to recall home to God and his church, foules that are loft and gone aftray ; others folace them felues in adorning churches, and decking the holy altars ; others to make peace and agreement, amongft fuch as are fallen at ftrife and variaunce. Wherein they imitate skilfull imbroderers, who vpon diuers grounds, with admirable varie-tie, entermingle filk, filuer, and gold twifts, wherof they drawe fondrie forts of flowers: and fo thefe godly foules, vndertaking fome particular exercife of deuotion, do make it ferue them, as a groundwork of their fpirituall im-broyderie, vpon which they work the varietie of all other virtues: holding by that meanes all their actions and affe-ctions, better vnited and ordered, by the carefull application of them to their principall exercife, and in this, ende-

endeuour to shew their excellent art,
and fingular cuning.

Her garments bordered all with flowers of
gold.

And curious needlework fair to behold.
Saith the pfalmift, defcribing the coftly
apparell of the fpoufe of God, which is
the foule exercifed in varietie of virtues.

6. When we are afflicted and combatted by any kind of vice, it behoueth
vs, as much as it lieth in vs, to giue our
felues wholly to the practize of the cōtrarie virtue, and to order and applie all
other virtues, to the perfecting of that
particular virtue. For fo we shall ouercome the enemie againft which we
fight, & aduance our felues likewife in
other virtues. If I feel my felf impugned
with pride, or choler, in all my actiōs
I will bend my felf to the contrarie fide,
that is to humilitie, and meeknes : and
to obtaine that virtue I will applie all
my other exercifes of prayer, receauing
the facraments, of prudence, of con-
ftancie, fobrietie and the reft. For as
the wild Boares to sharpē their tuskes,
do fcoure and whet them with their
other teeth, fo that all of them do
reci-

reciprocallie become sharpe , and piercing : so a virtuous man , propounding to perfect him self in one virtue, of which he findeth most neede, doth as it were whet it and sharpen it, by the exercise of other virtues , which confirming and strengthening that one , which he particularly seeketh , become all of them more polished and excellēt. So it happned vnto holy Iob , who exercising him selfe peculiarly in patience, against so many vehement tentations wherwith he was assalted : became perfect in all kinde of virtues and holinesse. Yea oft times it happeneth (as S. Gregory Nazianzen sayth) that by one onely act of some virtue, well and perfectly performed, a man may attaine to the hight of virtue : and he alleadgeth in proofe of this saying , the example of Rahab , who hauing exactly practized the virtue of hospitalitie , attained vnto a glorious soueraignty in holines. Which is to be vnderstood , when such acts are practized, with excellent feruour of charitie.

An addition to the former difcource,
about choice in the exercife of vir-
tues. CHAPT. 2.

1. SAINT Auguftin fayth excellently well, that young beginners in deuotion, doe committ
certaine faults, which according to the
rigour of perfect lawes, are in very deed
blame worthy, and yet in thefe beginners are very commendable, as tokens
and prefages of a future excellencie in
godlines, to which thefe pettie-faults,
do ferue as a kind of difpofition. That
bafe and feruil feare, which engendreth
exceffiue fcruples, in the foules of
thofe that are newlie efcaped from the
cuftome and thraldom of finne, is a
commendable virtue in beginners, and
a fure and certaine figne, of a future puritie of confcience in them : but the
felf fame feare would be verie reprehen-
fible in thofe, that haue profited in
good life and deuotion, in whofe harts
that perfect loue should raigne and
predominate, that by litle and litle,
driueth this feruil feare out of doores.

2. Holy

2. Holy S. Bernard in his beginnings, was full of rigour and austeritie towards them, that rancked them selues vnder his conduct, and gouernement, whome he commanded euen at their first entrance, that they should leaue their bodies behind them, and come to him only with their soules; When he heard their confessions, he detested with an extraordinarie seueritie, all kind of faults, were they neuer so small, and so pressed and vrged the poore prentises or nouices in perfectiō, that in steed of thrusting them forward, he drew them backward, for they lost hart and courage, becoming altogether out of breath, to see them selues so instantly and eagerly, thrust and forced so hastely to mount so high and craggie a mountaine. This all proceeded from an ardent zeale (my Philotheus) and a most perfect puritie of conscience which was in this glorious Saint, and made him folowe this method of proceeding with his religious: and this zeale was a great virtue in him, yet a virtue which had something annexed that was reprehensible, and to be
amen-

amended : and God him felf in a holy
apparition , did correct and amend
him , powring into his foule a meeke,
mild , fweet , amiable,and tender fpirit,
fo that now turnd cleane into another
man , he accufed him felf very much of
his former exact feueritie ; and became
fo fauourable and appliable to euery
one,that he accommodated him felf to
all, to gaine all.

3. Saint Hierom hauing recounted
of holy Paula , (that was his ghoftly
child) that she was not only exceffiue,
but as it were felf-willed in the exercife
of bodily mortifications , in fo much
that she would not giue eare, to the
contrarie aduices and councels which
S. Epiphanius her bishop , had giuen
her in that refpect : and moreouer that
she fuffered her felf to be borne away
in fuch fort, by grief and forow for the
death of her frinds,that she was allways
in danger of death , by her extremes in
fuch occafions : in the end he conclu-
deth in this fort. Some man will fay ,
that in fteed of writing the praifes of
this holy Saint-like ladie , I make a ca-
talogue of her faults and imperfectiõs,
                                    but

but I call Iesus to witnes, whome she serued, and whome I defire to serue, that I lye not, either on the one fide, or on the other : but do fett downe cleerly what she was, as a Chriftian, writing of a Chriftian : that is, that write an hiftorie, and not a panegyricall oration of her life, and that her vices, be the virtues of others. His meaning is, that the defeds and imperfedions of S. Paula, would haue borne the name and nature of virtues, in a foule of leffe perfedion; As in very deed, there are adions which are deemed imperfedions, in fuch as be perfed, which not with ftanding, would be efteemed great perfedions, in thofe which yet are imperfed. It is a good figne in a fick man, when at the end of his ficknes, his legges do fwell, for it shewes that nature now ftrengthened, cafteth out her fuperfluous humours : but the very fame figne, is bad and ominous in him, that were not fick at all, for it betokeneth the weakneffe of nature, not hauing force enough, to diffolue and diffipate thofe corrupt and naughtie humours.

4. My

4. My Philotheus, we muſt haue alway a good opinion and eſtimation of them, in whome we ſee the practize of virtues, although exerciſed with ſome defects and imperfections, ſince the great Saints them ſelues, haue often times exerciſed them in ſuch manner. But for our owne parts, we muſt procure to exerciſe our ſelues in them, not only diligently, but diſcreetly, and for that end, obſerue carefullie and faithfullie the aduiſe and councell of wiſe men, not leaning to our owne prudence, but to the skill and wiſdom of ſuch, whome God hath giuen vs for our conductours.

5. There are certaine other perfections which many eſteeme and account virtues, though in deed they be no virtues at all: of which it is needfull to ſpeake a worde or two. I meane thoſe perfections, which are called extaſies, rauiſhments in ſpirit, inſenſibilities, languiſhments, or impoſſibilitie of exteriour actions, deificall vnions, eleuations, transformations of the ſoule, and ſuch like; of which
ſome

some bookes do treat, promising to
eleuate and promote the soule to contemplation, purely intellectual, to the
essentiall application of the spirit, and
of the supereminent life of the soule.
Mark me well what I say, my Philotheus, these perfections, be not virtues,
but rather rewardes and recompences,
that God giueth his seruants in this
life for their virtues : or as it were
scantlings, and listes, of the happines of
the life to come, which somtime are
presented vnto men, to make them desire to buy the whole peeces them selues, which are aboue in Paradise. We
must not pretend to come vnto such
high fauours and graces, since they
are not any wise necessarie to serue
and loue God well and truly, which
should be our chief and only pretence :
Neither are they graces which may
ordinarilie be obtained, by our owne
trauell or industrie, since they are rather passions, then actions, which
therfore we may well receaue, but
worke them or produce them in vs,
we can not. I adde moreouer that we
haue not vndertooke any higher
matter

matter, then to make our felues virtuous, deuout, and good men and good
wemen : and therfore it behoueth vs to
beftow all our endeuour to that end ;
and if it pleafe God to eleuate & extoll
vs to thefe Angelicall perfections, we
fhalbe then alfo good Angels : but in
the meane time , let vs exercife our
felues fimply, humbly, and deuoutly
in thefe lower humane virtues , the
conqueft and gaining of which, our
Saueour hath left to our owne power
and diligence; fuch as are the virtues
of patience , courtefie, meeknes , mortification of our harts, and willes, humilitie , obedience , pouertie, chaftyty ,
compaffion towards our neighbours,
and bearing with their imperfections,
diligence, and holy feruour in fulfilling
the will of God. Let vs leaue thefe fu-
pereminences, for fuperexcellent foules , we merit not fo high a place in
Gods feruice ; it wilbe happines for vs,
to ferue our God , in his kitchin (as
they fay) or in his pantrie, to be lackies,
porters, torche-bearers, groomes of the
chamber , in his houfe. It is his mercy
and ineftimable goodnes only , if afterwards

wards he pleafe to remoue vs higher to
his clofet, and priuie chamber, or to
be of his councell. Yea, my Philotheus, this muft be the refignation
of our hart; for this king of glory,
doth recompence his feruants, not
according to the dignitie of the offices which they beare vnder him,
but according to the meafure of the
loue and humilitie, with which they
execute them. Saul feeking after his
fathers Affes, found the crowne and
kingdome of Ifrael. Rebecca by watring Abrahams Camels, became the
efpoufe of his fonne Ifaac. Ruth,
the Moabiteffe, gleaning after the
harueft men of Boos, and lying at his
feete, was exalted to lie by his fide,
and made his wedded wife. Surely the
pretentions and defires of fuch loftie,
extraordinary, and admirable things,
are obnoxious and fubiect vnto il-
lufions, deceipts, and errours; and
it chaunceth oft times, that thefe
fublimated perfons, that thinck them
felues Angels, are fcantly fo much
as good men, and that there is more
excellence and fublimitie in theire
words,

wordes, and rare termes, then feeling, and fubftance, in theire workes
and actions. Yet muft we not lightly
difpraife, or rashly cenfure any thing,
but bleffing God for the fuperemi-
nence of other men, reft our felues
humbly in this low, plaine, and
eafie way, which is indeed more
plaine, but yet more fecure; leffe
excellent, but yet more futeable to
our infufficiency and weaknes: wherin if we conuerfe humbly and faithfully, God will lift vs vp to greatnes, great enough for our foules
good.

Of Patience.

CHAPTER 3.

1. **P**ATIENCE *is neceffary for you,*
that performing the will of God,
you may obtaine the promife, fayth
the Apoftle: yea, for as our Lord him
felf pronounced, *In your patience you shall*
poffeffe your foules. It is the happieft thing
that cã befall to mã (Philotheus) to haue
his

his owne foule in fure and fecure poffeffion : and the more perfect that our
patience is, the more fecure is the poffeffion of our foules: we muft endeuour
then to perfect this virtue in vs , to the
vttermoft of our power. Call to mind
continually, that our bleffed Redeemer
faued vs , by fuffering and enduring :
and that we therfore in like manner ,
muft work our faluation , by fuffering
afflictions , and enduring iniuries, and
bearing contradictions, and difpleafu-
res, with the greateft meeknes that
poffible we can.

2. Limit not thy patience , to fuch
and fuch kind of iniuries, and afflictiõs:
but extend it magnanimoufly and vniuerfally, to all thofe that God fhal fend,
and fuffer to befall thee. There be fome
men that will fuffer no tribulations, but
fuch as be honourable: As for example,
to be wounded in battaile , to be taken
prifoner in warre , to be perfequuted,
and ill handled, for religion fake, to be
impouerished by fome fute or proceffe,
in which they haue gott the vpper
hand : thefe men loue not tribulation,
but the honour which the tribulation
                                   bringeth.

bringeth. He that is patient in deed,
and a true seruant of God. Suffereth in-
differently those tribulations, that are
coupled with infamie and shame , as
well as those that be honourable. To
be reprehended , accused , slandered by
naughtie and wicked men, is a pleasure
to a man of courage: but to suffer these
accusations and persequutions at the
hands of our parents and frinds, and of
such as are good and virtuous , and
esteemed so, there is the right triall of
true patience , there it is in deed , that
we must play the men. I esteeme more
of the meeknes , wherwith the blessed
Cardinal Borromæus , suffered a long
time the publique reprehensions, which
a great preacher of an order , exceedinglie well reformed , thundered against
him out of the pulpit : the of all the co-
bats which he had with any other. For
like as the stinging of a Bee , is farre
forer and fulle of ache, then the byting
of a flye : so the euil that one receaueth
of good men, and the contradictions
that they raise against one , are much
more vnsupportable then others ; and
yet it chanceth very often , that two
L   good

good and virtuous men, hauing both of them right intentions, through diuersitie of opinions, do ftirre vp great perfequutions & contradictions, one againft the other.

3. Be patient, not onely in the great, and principall afflictions which arriue vnto thee, but allfo in the acceffories and accidents which depend thereon. Many could be content to haue afflictions happen vnto them, fo that they might not be hurt, troubled or vexed by them. I am not grieued fayth one, that I am fallen into pouertie, but that by that meanes I canot pleafure my frinds, nor bring vp my children in fuch honorable education as I defire. I care not (fayth another) were it not that the world will thinck, that this is befallen me by mine owne fault. Another would be cotent fome should fpeak ill of him, and would fuffer it patiently, fo that no man would beleeue the detractour. Others there are, that could willingly away with fome part of the tribulation, as they fuppofe, but not with the whole. They are not impatient, or vexed (fay they) that they are fick: but that they

want

want mony to cure them selues of
their sicknes, or that they that be about
them, are too importunat and troublesome to them. But I say (my Philotheus) that we must haue patience,
not only to be sick, but euen to be visited with that disease that God will
lay vpon vs, what euer it be, and in that
place whersoeuer he will haue it happen
to vs, and amongst such persons, and
with those wants and incommodities,
which he will; and the like is to be vnderstood of all other tribulatiõs. When
any damage or harme shall chaunce vnto thee, oppose against it a Gods name,
those remedies which thou cãst applie,
for to do otherwise, were to tempt God
almightie: but hauing done thy diligẽ-
ce in the matter, attend with an entire
resignatiõ, that successe & euent, which
it shall please God to send: if he permitt the remedies to ouercome thy
harmes, giue him thancks with reuerence, if it please him that thy harmes
surmount the remedies, blesse him with
patience.

4. I am of the aduice of Saint Gregory. When thou art iustly accused

for any fault which thou haſt committed, humble thy ſelf for it, and confeſſe
vnfainedlie, that thou deſerueſt more
then the accuſation that is layd againſt
thee. But yf thou be accuſed falſly, excuſe thy ſelf with all meeknes, denying
thy ſelf to be guiltie of that which is
layd to thy charge, for thou oweſt that
dutie to the truth, and to the edification of thy neighbour; But withall, yf
after thy true and lawfull diſcharge,
men cõtinue notwithſtanding their accuſation againſt thee, ſtriue not much
to make thy excuſe be admitted and beleeued, for hauing complied with the
dutie thou oweſt vnto the truth, thou
muſt render alſo the dutie thou oweſt
to humilitie. Thus thou ſhalt neither
offend, againſt the care that thou
oughteſt to haue of thy good renowne,
nor againſt the loue and affection,
which thou ſhouldſt haue to tranquillitie of hart, meeknes, and humilitie.

5. Complaine as litle as thou canſt
of the wrongs that be done thee; for
ordinarilie he that cõplaineth of them,
ſinneth: becauſe ſelf loue alway maketh

V

vs beleeue the iniuries offered vs, to be worſe then indeed they be. But aboue all things complaine not to ſuch perſons , as are apt to take indignation, and to turne all to the worſt. Yf it be expedient to make thy mone to any, either to get the offence remedied, or thy mind eaſed, let it be done to quiet & peaceable ſoules , that loue God ſincerelie ; for otherwiſe , inſteed of eaſirg aud diſcharging thy griefs , they will prouoke thee to greater diſquiet : in ſteed of pulling out the thorne that pricketh thee, they will faſten and ſtick it deeper into thy foote.

6.   Manie being ſick , afflicted , or moleſted, refraine them ſelues frō complaining , or ſhewing any delicatenes, iudging (& that rightlie) that it would euidentlie teſtifie want of courage and generoſitie in them : but for all that, they deſire exceedingly , and by ſlights and ſubtilities procure, that other men bemone them, take cōpaſſion of them, and eſteeme them to be not onlie afflicted , but patient, yea , and courageous alſo in their afflictions . This is a kind of patience indeed , but a falſe

one, which in effect, is nothing elſe but a fine ſubtil and ſecret pride and vanitie : *They haue glorie* (ſaith the Apoſtle) *but not before God.* The true patient man, neither complaineth of his griefs and harmes, nor deſireth to be pittied and bemoned:he ſpeaketh of his caſe cleerly, truly, and ſimplie, without lamentations, or aggtauations : yf he be pittied, he thancketh God for the charitie and comfort ſhewed him, and patientlie ſuffereth him ſelf to be pittied, vnleſſe they bemone the harme or euil, which he hath not : for then will he modeſtly declare, that he ſuffereth no ſuch grief, as they imagin; and in this ſort continueth peaceably, betwixt truth and patience, confeſſing, nor complaining of his afflictions.

7. In the contradictions which befall thee in the exerciſe of deuotion, (for they will not be lacking one time or other) remember the words of our Sauiour Ieſus Chriſt : *A woman when ſhe is in trauail, hath anguiſh becauſe her hour is come : but when ſhe hath brought foorth her child, then ſhe remembreth not the*

the anguishe , for ioy that a man is borne into the world. Thou conceiuest spirituallie in thy soule the noblest child in
the world , to wit , Iesus Christ ; vntill
he be brought foorth altogether, thou
canst not choose but suffer excessiue
pangs : but be of a good hart , these
dolours once past, thou shalt find euerlasting ioye, for hauing brought foorth
such a child to the world. And he
shalbe whollie brought foorth and borne in thee, when thou framest , and
conformest thy hart and thy actions, to
the imitation of his life.

8. When thou art sick offer vp all thy
griefs, paines, aches, & languishments,
to the honour and seruice of our Lord:
and beseech him to ioine & vnite them
with the torments which he suffered for
thee. Obey thy physician , take those
medicines , meats and remedies which
he prescribeth, for the loue of God, calling to mind the gall which he tasted
for our sakes: desire to amend, that thou
mayst serue him; refuse not to laguishe,
that thou mayst obey him : and dispose
thy self to die (yf so it please him) that
thou mayst prayse and enioy him. Con-
si-

sider that the Bees whē they make their
hunny, do liue and eate of a bitter prouision : and that we in like manner, can
neuer exercise sweeter acts of patience,
nor compose more excellent hunny of
true virtues, thē when we eate the bread
of bitternes, and liue in the middest of
afflictions. And as the hunny which is
gathered frō thyme, a litle bitter herbe,
is the best that is : so virtue exercised in
the bitternes of vile, base, and most abiect tribulations, is the finest and excel-
lentest of all.

9. Reflect often times the inward
eyes of thy soule, vpon Christ Iesus crucified, naked, blasphemed, slandred, forsaken for thy loue, and in a word, ouerwhelmed with all sortes of sorowes,
griefs, and persequutions. Consider that
all thy sufferings, neither in qualitie, nor
quantitie, are in any sort comparable
vnto his: and that thou cāst neuer suffer
any thing for his sweet sake, in comparison of that which he hath endured
for thine.

10. Consider the pangs and tormēts,
which in old time the martyrs suffered;
and the dolours and griefs which at
                                    this

this time many endure, more grieuous
without all proportion , then thofe
which thou endureſt , and ſay to thy
ſelf : Alas , my paines be conſolations,
and my briers be roſes in compariſon
of them, which without all ſuccour,at-
tendaunce, or relief, do liue in a perpetuall death , ouercharged with afflictiós
infinitlie heauier then mine are.

Of exteriour Humilitie.

CHAPTER 4.

1. **B**ORROW *and take many empty
veſſels* (ſayd Elizæus vnto the
poore Widowe) *and powre oyle
into them.* To receaue abundance of
the grace of God into our harts , they
muſt be voide of ſelf-pride and vain-
glorie.The Keſterell criyng & looking
conſtantly vpon the haukes , and other
birds of preye, doth terrifie thē by a ſecret proprietie or virtue which it hath
by nature, therfor the fearfull Doues,
do loue it aboue all other birds, and
liue in ſecuritie in companie of it : ſo

humi-

humilitie rebutteth the eager onfett of
Satan, and conferueth the graces and
guiftes of the holy Ghoft in vs, and
therefore all the Saints of heauen,
but efpecially Chrift the king of Saints
and his bleffed mother, made more
efteeme of this virtue, then of any other
amongft all the morall virtues.

2. We call that glorie vaine, which
one taketh of himfelf, either for that
which is not in him, or for that which
is in him, but is none of his; or for that
which is in him, and is his owne, but
deferues not that one should glorie of
it. Nobilitie of race, fauour with great
potentates, popular honour, be things
that are not in vs, but in our progeni-
tours, or in the eftimation of other
men. Some men there be, that shew
them felues fierce and ftout, becaufe
they be mounted on a lufty courfer, or
for a great goodly fether in their cap,
or for their coftly and fumptuous apparel: but who feeth not this to be follie?
For yf there be any glorie at all in thefe cafes, it is glorie for the horfe, for
the bird, and for the tailer : and what
great want of witt is it, to borrow credit

dit and eſtimation from a horſe, from
a bird , from a new faſhiond ruffe?
Others bragge, and behold themſelues with great ſatisfaction, for a good-
lye long mouſtaches , or a trimme
beard, for their curled lockes , and ſoft
hands: or for skill in dauncing, ſinging,
playing : but are not thoſe hartleſſe,
and baſe minded men , who fetch their
eſtimation and reputation , from ſuch
friuolous and fond trifles? Others for
a litle knowledge and learning, would
be honoured & reſpected in the worlde,
as yf euerybody ſhould come to ſchoo-
le to learne of them, and account them
their maiſters, for which cauſe they are
rightly termed pedantical companions.
Others carie the ſelues like peacocks,
proud of their beautie , and thinck all
the world is fond of them . All theſe
humours are vaine, fooliſh, and impertinent: and glorie grounded vpon ſuch
weak and feeble foundations , is vaine
and friuolous.

3.   A man may know true virtue like
true baulme : for baulme is tried by
dipping it into the water ; yf it ſinck
to the bottom , it is counted the moſt
L 6   excel-

excellent and pretious. Euen fo to
know whether a man be in deed wife,
learned, generous, noble, mark whether
thefe good gifts and qualities tend in
him to humilitie, modeftie, and fub-
miffion, for then they be true in deed:
but if they fwimme aboue water, if
they ftriue to appeare and shew them
felues, they are fo much the leffe fub-
ftantiall, and more fuperficiall, by how
much more apparent they are, or
would be. Pearles that be conceaued
and grow in the wind, or in time of
thunder, haue nothing but the barke,
or shell of a pearle, and are voide of
fubftance: fo thefe virtues and good
qualities bred and nourished in pride,
boafting, and vanitie, haue nothing
but a fimple shew and appearance of
good, without iuice, without marrow,
without foliditie and fubftance. Honours, eftates, and dignities, are like to
faffron, which is beft, & groweth moft
plentifully, whē it is trodden ꝟnder feet.
It is no honour to be faire in a mans
owne eyes: beautie, to haue a good
grace in deed, should be fomwhat neglected: knowledge dishonours vs,
                                when

when it puffeth vs vp, and degenerateth
then to plaine pedanterie.

4. If we ſtand curiouſly vpon our
points, touching precedence and pre-
eminence in place and titles, beſides the
expoſing of our ſelues to the danger of
hauing our qualities too narowly ſif-
ted, examined, and contradicted, we
make them vile and contemptible: for
honour, which is indeed honourable,
when it is freely giuen and granted, becomes foule, infamous, and shamefull
when it is affected, ſought after, and in
a manner begged, and wreſted, from
them in whole companie we are. When
the Peacock bruſtles vp his gay ſtarrie
wheele, lifting vp his goodly painted
feathers to be looked vpon, he forget-
teth him ſelf, that in the meane while he
sheweth other parts, which are moſt ill
fauoured in him. Flowers that be beautifull, growing vpon the ground, or in
the garden-beds, wither away with
much handling. The ſweet ſmell of the
Mandragora taken a farre of, & but for
a short time, is moſt pleaſaunt: but they
that ſmell to it very neere, and a long
time, become altogether drowſie, faint,

and

and languishing ; Euen so honour and
courteous respects confortablie smell
a farre of, being taken lightly, and not
standing much vpon them , or placing
his phantasie , in depainting them according to our vainglorious desire: but
to such as affect them ouergreedily,
and do in a manner feed vpon them ,
they are reprehensible, and full of contempt and follie.

5. The pursute and loue of virtue,
maketh vs virtuous : but the pursuite
and loue of titles , honours , and pre-
eminences , make vs abiect and contemptible. Minds that are well-borne
and well-brought vp , busie not them
selues about these toyes of places,
rancks, complements, and salutations,
they haue other things to employ their
time in ; for to spend time in these
things, is the propertie of idle and vnprofitable braines. He that may loade
him self with pearles , will neuer ouercharge him self with cocle shelles : and
such as aspire to true virtue , neuer trouble them selues with complements. Euery one may in compai-
ne, take the ranck and the place that
                                    is due

is due vnto him, without preiudice
of humilitie, so that it be done as it
were carelesselie, not with affectation,
or strife, or as yf he counted it a matter of much importance. For as they
that come from Peru, besides store of
gold and siluer which they bring from
thence, do many times bring with
them Apes and Parrets, becaule they
neither cost much, nor are burdenlom
or chargeable to their ship : so the true
folowers of virtue, need not omitt or
neglect their ranck and place due vnto
them, so that it cost them not much
care or attention, and that the same
be done without trouble, dilquiet, cauills, or contentions. Yet speak I not
heere of them whose dignitie redoun-
deth to the common good, nor of certain particular occasions, vpon which
great confequents depend : for in such
euery one may keep his due and right
with prudence and dilcretion, accom-
pained with charitie and courtesie.

Of his

Of Humility more internall then the
former. CHAP. 5.

1. **B**VT thou defireſt I ſee Philotheus, to be farther endoctrined
in humilitie : for that which we
haue hetherto ſayd, is rather wiſdome
and good manners, then humilitie : let
vs therfore paſſe on farther.

2. Many there are, that will not, and
dare not ponder and conſider, the graces that God hath giuen them in particular, fearing leaſt they ſhould therby
fall into vaine glorie, & ſelf conceipted
loue, whereas in deed they deceaue thē
ſelues : for ſince the true direct meanes
to attaine to the loue of God (as S.
Thomas the Angelicall doctour teacheth) is the conſideration of his benefits, the more we conſider them, the
more we ſhall loue him; and as particular benefits do more efficaciouſly moue
and winne affection, then ſuch as are
common to other: ſo ought they to be
pondered and wayed more attentiuely.
Certain it is, that nothing can humble
vs ſo much before the mercie of God,
                                    as the

as the knowledge of the infinite multitude of his benefits, neither can any thing so much humble vs before his iustice, as the multitude of our offences. Let vs then consider what he hath done for vs, and what we haue done against him: and as we consider and way our sinnes one by one, so let vs acknowledge & suruay his graces one by one. Neuer feare that the knowledge which he giues vs of his graces, will puffe vs vp in pride, so long as we be attentiue to this knowne and acknowledged veritie, that whatsoeuer is good in vs, is altogether from God, and not from our selues. Alas, Mules and Camels, cease they to be lumpishe and brute beasts, though they be neuer so loaded with the pretious and perfumed moueables of the prince? *What hast thou which thou hast not receaued?* sayth the Apostle; *and yf thou hast receaued it, why doest thou glorye?* Nay contratiwise, the liuelie and feeling consideration, of the fauours receaued from Gods hand, humbleth vs; because knowledge engendreth acknowledgement.

3. But yf in this reuiew and accounting

ting (as it were) of the graces of God, any kind of vanitie should tickle vs: the infallible, and easie remedie is, to passe by and by, to the consideration of our ingratitude, of our imperfections, and of our miseries; Yf we consider what we haue done, when God was not with vs, we shall soone acknowledge, that all which we haue done, since he hath been with vs; is not our handy woik, nor is not of our owne stock; we shall enioy them, and reioice that we haue them, but we shall glorifie God alone, for being the sole authour and giuer of them. So the blessed virgin, confessed and professed, that God had wrought great and admirable things in her, and for her, but she confessed it for no other cause, then for to humble her self, and to glorifie God: *My soule* (sayth she) *doth magnify our Lord, because he hath done great things to me.*

4. We vse to say manie times, that we are nothing, that we are miserie it self, that we are the skumme and out-casts of the world: but we would be loath any man should take vs at our word, and publish vs abroad to be such
as we

as we say we are : Nay we make as if
we would hide our selues , to the end
men may runne after vs , and searche vs
out; we make show as yf we would indeed be the last , & sitt at the louest end
of the table : but we do soe that with
more credit we may be set at the vpper-
end of all. True humilitie neuer sheweth her self , nor vseth many words
of humble sound , because she intendeth not onely to hide other virtues,
but withall and aboue all , to hide her
owne self. And y fit were lawfull for her
to lie , to dissemble , or scandalize her
neighbour , she would vse manie an
action of arrogancie, and brauerie that
vnder them she might hide her selfe , &
so be altogether couered & vnknowne.
My aduice therfore is this Philotheus,
either let vs vse no words of humilitie
at all , or let vs vse them with an inward
feeling , meaning in our hart, as we
pronoúce with our mouth. Let vs neuer
cast our eyes downe to the ground, but
humbling our harts with all : let vs not
seeme to desire the lowest roome, vnlesse
we desire it frő our hart. And I hold this
rule so general, that I bring no exceptiő
only

only I adde, that courtesie requireth,
that we present the aduantage somtime
to those, whome we know manifestly
will refuse it : for this is no double dealing, nor false humilitie, for in this case
the only proffer of the aduantage in
place, or precedence, or such like, is an
honouring of them to whome we proffer it · and since then, one cannot giue
them entirely that which in hart we
would, we do not ill to giue it them in
part. The like I vnderstand of some termes of honour, and respect, which (to
examin them in rigour) seeme not to
be true, & yet are in deed true enough,
yf the hart of him that pronounceth
them, haue a true intention, to honour,
and respect him, for whose sake he
vseth those tearmes. For although the
words doe signifie with some excesse,
that which we would say: yet it is not ill
done to vse them, when common cu-
stom of ciuilitie requireth it. I wishe
that our wordes, were always ioined to
our intention and affection, as neer as
it is possible, so to follow in all, and
through all, the pure and naked simplicitie of a virtuous hart:

s. A.

5. A man that is truly humble, would rather that another should say of him that he is a miserable wretche, that he is nothing, nor worth nothing, then to say so much him self : at least, if he know that any man say so of him, he doth not gainsay it, but agreeth to it with all his hart : for since he beleeueth firmely & vnfainedly, that he is in deed worth nothing, he is right glad to haue others of his mind and opinion.

6. Manie say that they leaue mentall prayer, for those that are perfect, that they themselues are not worthie to frequent such an exercise. Others protest they dare not communicate often, because they feele not them selues pure enough. Others that verely they feare least they should disgrace deuotion, if they should entermedle with it, by reason of their great miserie and frailtie : Others refuse to employ their talent in the seruice of God, and of their neighbour, because (say they) they knowe theire owne weaknes, and feeblenes : and that they feare to become proude, if they should be instruments of any good : & that in giuing light to others,
                                          they

they should consume them selues. All this is an artificiall kind of humilitie, not only false, but also malignant, wherby one seeketh secretly and subtilly, to blame the guifts of God, or at the least with the cloke of humilitie, to couer the loue of his owne humour and slothfulnes. *Demaund of God a signe, either, from heauen aboue, or from the depth of the sea below* : sayd the prophet to vnhappie Achaz, and he answerd : *I will demaund none, neither will I tempt God.* O wicked man, he would seeme to beare great reuerence to God, and vnder colour of humilitie, excuseth him self from aspiring to the grace which Gods goodnes offereth vnto him : but he vnderstood not, that when our Lord offereth vs his graces, it is pride to refuse them ; that the guifts of God, oblige vs to receaue them, and that true humilitie, is to obey and folow his will and desire the neerest we can. But Gods desire is, that we become perfect, vniting our selues vnto him, and imitating him the best we can. The proud man which trusteth in him self, hath iust occasion (if he knew it) to vnder-

take

take nothing : but he that is humble,
is so much more courageous, by how
much more vnable he acknowledgeth him selfe : and according to
the measure that he measureth his
owne frailtie, his boldnes in God in-
creaseth ; for all his trust is in God,
and God (he knowes) delighteth to
exalt his omnipotencie, in our infirmitie, and to magnifie his mercie, by
our miserie. We must then humbly
and holily dare and vndertake, what
soeuer is iudged fit and conuenient
to our spirituall aduancement , by
them that haue the guiding of our
soules.

7. To thinck one knoweth that,
which he knoweth not, is an expresse
follie : to play the learned man in that,
in which it is manifest we haue no
skill nor experience , is an intolerable vanitie . For my part , I would
not take vpon me a learned mans person , euen in things which I were
certaine that I knew wel enough : as
cōtrariewise, I would not counterfet my
self altogether ignorant. When charitie
requireth, we must readilie and sweetlie

com-

communicate to our neighbour, not
only that, which is neceſſarie for his
inſtruction, but withall, that which is
profitable for his conſolation : for humilitie, which hideth and concealeth
virtues, to conſerue them in their puritie, doth neuertheles diſcouer them,
and make them shew them ſelues,
when charitie commandeth,to increaſe
and perfect them. Wherin she reſem-
bleth a tree in the Iſles of Tylos, which
all night long, locketh and encloſeth
vp her faire carnation flowers, and
doth not open them, but at the riſing
of the ſunne, ſo that the inhabitants of
the countrie do ſay, that theſe flowers
do ſleep by night : for euen ſo humilitie, couereth and hideth all our virtues
and humane perfections, and letteth
them not be ſeene abroad, but when
charitie commandeth : and charitie
being a virtue not humane, but heauenly,not moral but diuine,is the verie true
ſunne of all other virtues, vpon which
she muſt therfore euer predominate :
ſo that humilitie which is preiudicious
to charitie, is without all doubt falſe
humilitie.

S. I

8. I would neither coūterfeit a foole, nor a wifeman : for yf humilitie forbid me to counterfeit my felf wife, fimplicitie and plainnes forbid me likewife, to coūterfeit my felf a foole : for as vanitie and pride are contrarie to humilitie ; fo are affectation and diffembling cōtrarie to fimplicitie, and plaine-dealing. And yf fome great feruāts of God haue made as yf they had been fooles, to render them felues more abiect in the eyes of the worlde , we muft admire them, and not imitate them: for they had motiues that induced them to this exceffe, which were fo peculiar vnto them , & extraordinarie , that no man ought from thence to inferre any confequence for him felf. As for Dauid , when he daunced before the arke of the teftament , with fome more demonftration of myrth, then feemed to befeeme the maieftie of a king, he did it not as counterfaiting any foolish myrthe , but fimplie and plainlie vfed he thefe exteriour motions, conformable to the extraordinarie gladnes which he felt in his hart. True it is , that when Michol his wife vpbraided him for this fact , as to bafe

and fond for a king , he was neuer a
whit forrie to fee himfelfe defpifed , but
perfeuering in the true and fincere re-
prefentation of the ioye which he had
conceiued in his foule , he protefted
that he was likewife glad to receaue a
litle shame for the loue of his God.
And confequently I fay , that yf for
acts of true and profound deuotion ,
thou be efteemed fimple , abiect , and
bafe-minded , humilitie will make thee
reioyce at this happie shame, the caufe
wherof is not in thee, but in them that
lay it vpon thee.

That humilitie maketh vs loue
our owne debafement
and abiection.

CHAPTER 6.

1.   I PASSE farther Philothee, to tel
thee, that aboue all things thou
loue thy owne abiection . But
thou wilt aske me, what it is to loue our
owne abiection. In latin abiection is all
one with humilitie , and humilitie with
                                    abie-

abiection: for so when our Ladie in her
sacred hymne, sayth, that all generations should tearme her blessed, because God had seene the humilitie of his
hādmaide:her meaning is,that our Lord
beheld with great loue her abiection,
her basenes, and lownesse, to endowe
her with fauours & inestimable graces.
Yet there is great difference between
the virtue of humilitie, and abiection:
for abiection is the litlenes, basenes,
poornes, & the nothing that is in vs of
our owne selues, we not knowing nor
considering it: but as for the virtue of
humilitie, it is a true feeling knowledge, and voluntarie acknowledgement
of our abiection and vilenesse.

2. But the principall point of humilitie consisteth not only in this willing
acknowledgement of our abiection,
but to loue it, and take a delight and
contentment in it: not for want of
courage or magnanimitie, but to
extoll so much the more the diuine
maiestie, and to esteeme much better
of our neighbour in comparison of
our selues. This point is that which
I exhort thee to insist in most of al:

and that thou mayft the better vnderftand and conceiue it. Confider that
amongft the afflictions and troubles
which we fuffer in this life , fome of
them be bafe,contemptible,and abiect,
other be honourable , and glorious,
and many applie them felues willinglie
to honourable tribulations , but fcarce
any at all will abide thofe that be abiect
& ignominious. So a deuout hermit all
ragged , and fhiuering for cold, euerie
bodie honoureth his torne habit , taking compaffion of that which he en-
dureth:but yf a poore tradefeman,a de-
cayed gentleman, or a poore gentlewo-
man be in the fame cafe , men defpife
and mock them : and fo thou feeft
how their pouertie is abiect , and ignominious. A religious man receaueth deuoutly a rigorous reprehenfió of his fuperiour, and a child of his father , and
all men count it and call it mortification,obedience, and good manners:but
let a knight , or fome great ladie, fuffer
the like of another , and although they
do it for the loue of God , men will call
it cowardlineffe , pufillanimitie, & lack
of courage : behold heere is another
ab-

abiect euil. One hath a cancker on his
arme , and another vpon his face : the
firft hath only the difeafe , which is
bad enough;but this other iointly with
the difeafe, hath contempt , fhame,
and abiection in all companie. What
fay I then of louing abiection ? I fay,
that we muft not only loue the harme
it felf, which we do by the virtue of patience : but we muft alfo loue the contempt, the shame, the vilenes, bafenes,
and abiection therof, which we doe by
the virtue of humilitie.

3. Againe there be fome virtues,that
feeme abiect and contemptible , other
that are honorable and refpected by all
men. Patience, meeknes, plaindealing,
fimplicitie,& humility it felf, are of the
number of thofe virtues, which worldly
men hold as vile , and abiect : contrariwife they make great eftimation of
wifdome , fortitude , and liberalitie.
There be alfo diuerfe actions of the
felf fame virtue , wherof fome be contemptible , and others honorable ; to
giue almes , and to pardon iniuries
and offences , are both of them acts
proceeding from charitie : and the
M 3   firft

firſt is honoured of all men, the laſt
moſt baſe in the eyes of the blind
world. A young gentleman or gentle-
woman, that will not diſorder them
ſelues, with a companie of diſſolute
mates in prating, dauncing, drincking,
ſuperfluous pompe, and curioſitie of
apparell, ſhalbe ſcoffed at and cenſu-
red by others, and their laudable modeſtie, termed hypocriſie or affected
ſanctitie: To loue theſe cenſures, to
reioyce in that the world hath this
opinion of vs, is to loue our owne
abiection. Behold againe another
ſort of abiection which we muſt loue.
We goe to viſit the ſick, many of vs
together: if I be ſent to the moſt
miſerable, that is to me an abiection
in the iudgement of the world, and
for that cauſe will I embrace it more
willingly: but if I be ſent to viſit a
perſon of more qualitie, it is an
abiection according to iudgement of
the ſpirit, for there is not in it ſo much
virtue nor merit, and therefore I
will loue this abiection likewiſe. One
falleth in the midſt of the ſtreet,
and not only receaueth damage therby,

by, but is alfo shamfully laughed at : this is an abiection which we muft make much of.

4. There are fome defects alfo, which haue no other harme in them, but only the shame that they bring with them: and humilitie, though it require not that one should committ them of fett purpofe ; yet it requireth that one difquiet not him felf, for hauing fallen into fome fuch defect. Thefe defects which I now fpeak of, be certaine fooleries, inciuilities, inconfiderate acts, or words, which as we ought to efchew before they be committed, to obay ciuilitie and prudence : fo when they are once committed, we muft be content with the reproache that commeth therby, and accept it willingly, that fo we may folow the rule of holie humilitie. I fay yet more : yf I chaunce to difordre my felf through paffion, or diffolution, or to fpeak fome vndecent words, wherwith God and my neighbour are offended : I will repent my felf hartelie, with true forowe for the finne

M 4   com-

committed, and procure to repare the
harme or offence done to my neighbour the beſt that poſſible I can : but I
will be content, and right glad, with
the ſhame, contempt, and abiection
which therby I haue incurred ; and if
the one could poſſibly be ſeparated
from the other, I would ſincerely caſt
away the ſinne, and earneſtly retaine
the abiection.

5. But though we loue the abiection
and contempt, which foloweth ſome
euel or defect of ours : we muſt not neglect the redreſſe of the ill (that cauſed
it) by conuenient and lawfull meanes,
eſpecially, when the euil is of ſome
conſequence and importance. As if I
haue ſome deformed loathſome diſeaſe
vpon my face, I will procure to haue it
cured, but not to haue men forget the
deformitie which it cauſed. Yf I haue
committed ſome foolery, which is of-
fenſiue to no man, I will not excuſe
my ſelf at all : becauſe although it was
a defect, and a fault, it is not permanent, and therfore it needeth no excuſe
but onely for the abiection, ſhame, or
contempt which befalls me for it,
                                    and

and to excuse that, is against humilitie.
But if through my vnaduisednesse and
follie, I haue offended, or scandalized
any man : I will make amends for the
offence by some probable excuse, because it containeth a permanent ill ;
and that charitie obligeth me to blot
out and deface if I can.

6. To conclude it happeneth some
times, that charitie commandeth vs to
remedie and wipe away, the abiection
& contempt which we incurre, because
our reputation & good name, is necessarie for the edification of our neighbours. And in that case, though we remoue abiection & contempt, from our
neighbours eyes , least he should be
scandalized or troubled therby : yet
must we carefully lock it vp like a pretious Iewell in our hart, that we our
selues may be edified therby.

7. Perchaunce thou wouldst learne
of me , Philotheus, which abiections
amongst all are to be esteemed best ?
and I tell thee plainly in one word, that
those are most profitable to our soules,
and most acceptable to God , which
happen to vs as it were by chaunce, or

M 5   by

by the course , condition and estate
of our life , because we choose thē not,
but receaue them only from the hands
of God , that sends them , whose election and choice we know , is always
better for vs , then our owne . But yf
we were to choose them our selues ,
then the greatest are the best for vs:
and those are to be esteemed greatest,
which are most contrarie to our inclinations, (so that they be conformable
to our vocation) for to speak the truth
once for all , our owne choice spoileth
in a manner , and bringeth to naught
all our virtues . O who will giue vs the
grace , to say from our hart in all sinceritie with that great king : *I haue made
choice to be an abiect in the house of God, rather then to dwell in the tabernacles of sinners?* None certainly can giue vs this
grace (deare Philotheē) but he that to
exalt vs, liued and died for vs in such
manner , that he was esteemed the out-
cast of men, and the most abiect of the
people.

I haue told thee many things Philotheus , which no doubt will seeme somwhat hard vnto thee when thou consi-
derest

dereft them : but beleeue me, they
will be fweeter then fugar or hunny to
thee, when thon doft put them in
practize.

---

*How to keep our good renowne
in the practize of
humility.*

Chapter 7.

1. **H**ONOVR, praife, and glorie
are not giuen to men for euerie ordinarie virtue, but for
fome excellent and notable virtue : for
by prayfe we feek to perfwade others
to efteeme the excellency of fome man
in whome fuch a virtue excelleth : by
honour we proteft that we our felues do
efteeme him therfore : & glorie in my
iudgemēt, is nothing els, but a certaine
luftre, fplendour, or fhining brightnes of reputation, which arifeth frō the
concourfe of many praifes & honours.
So that honours and prayfes, are as it
were pretious ftones and pearles, from

whence glorie produceth his luftre, and varnish, like to enamel. Now humilitie, not being able to endure, that we should haue any opinion, of our owne excellence or precedence before others, cannot likewife fuffer, that we should hunt after praife, honour, nor glorie, which be due only to fome kind of excellencie: but yet she confenteth to the aduertifement of the wifeman, who admonisheth vs, to haue care of our credit: becaufe good renowne is an eftimation, not of any excellencie, but abfolutly, of an ordinarie prudence, and integritie of a well-gouerned life, which humilitie forbiddeth not to acknowledge in our felues, and fo confequently willeth vs to defire this reputation. True it is that humilitie would likewife cōtemne this renowne, if charitie ftoode not in need of it: but becaufe it is one of the foundatiōs of humane focietie, and without it, we are not only vnprofitable, but alfo damageable to the communitie in which we liue, through the fcandall which it receaueth by our ill name, there charitie requireth, and humilitie accordeth, that wo
                    procure

procure and most carefully conserue
our good renowne.

2. Againe, as the leaues of trees, though
in them selues of no great valew, yet
serue for very much, not onely to beau-
tifie the trees, but also for the conseruation of their fruicts, whilst they be yet
young and tender: so good renowne, of
it self not much to be desired, is not
with stading exceeding profitable, both
for the ornament of our life, as also for
the garde and conseruation of our virtues, especially while they be yet tender
and feeble, as being but newlie habitua-
ted in vs. The obligatió of maintaining
our reputation, and of procuring to be
such in deed, as men thinck vs to be,
forceth a noble courage, in a manner,
with a sweet king of violence. Let vs
conserue our virtues my Philotheus, as
iewels very acceptable to God, the chief
and soueraigne obiect of all our actiós;
But as they that would keep fruict very
long, are not cotitent to stew, confit,
and conserue them with sugar, but with
all put them into vessels, fit and commodious for the preseruation of them : so
albeit the loue of God be the principall
pre-

preseruer of our virtues, yet may we with all imploye our good name and renowne, as a thing most conuenient to keep them in vigour.

3. Yet must we not be ouer-punctuall, nor too curious and exact in conseruation of our reputation : for such as be so tender and ticklish in their good name, are like vnto them, that for euerie slight infirmitie do take physick. For as these imagining by such extraordinarie care, to conserue their health, do vtterly ouerthrow it : so these iealous defenders of their reputation, do altogether loose it by standing so much vpon it, becoming therfore phantasticall, murmurours, pickquarrells, and prouoke the malice of bad tongues against them. To dissemble an iniurie offered, or to contemne it, is ordinarily a farre better remedie, then the reuenging or quarrelling vpon it, for contempt of calumniations, maketh them vanishe away : wheras yf we be moued and angred with them, we seeme to confesse and aduow them as deseruedly offered vs. Crocodiles hurt none but those that do feare them : nether

ther doth detraction endamage anie,
but such as are aggrieued therwith. Excessiue feare of loosing our estimation,
argueth great distrust of the true foundation therof, which is the sinceritie
and vnfained vprightnes of a virtuous
life, and good conscience. Townes
that haue woodden bridges ouer great
riuers, doe feare least they should
be borne downe by euerie flood, or
encrease of waters: but they that haue
bridges built of stone, do not care
but only for extraordinarie inundations: So they that haue a soule well
grounded in Christian perfection,
doe contemne the ordinarie excesse
and ouerflowing of iniurious tongues; but such as knowe them selues
weake in perfection, are disquieted
with euery blast of broad-mouthed
companions. And indeed (Philotheus)
he that will haue the good opinion
of all men, looseth it with all men,
since it is impossible to please all men
with one manner of carriage; and he
deserueth to loose his reputation, that
seeks to keep it, or haue it among the,
whose vices make them infamous.

4. Re-

4. Reputation and good renowne, is but a figne wherby we may vnderftand where virtue is lodged, it is virtue then that muft be preferred before all. Wherfore yf any call and count thee an hypocrite, becaufe thou giueft thy felf to deuotion; or hold thee for a coward, and bafe-minded perfon, becaufe thou haft put vp an iniurie for Gods fake: laugh at fuch mens words and opinions; for befide that fuch iudgements are only made by fooles, contemptible ideots, or vanie braggars, a man muft not forfake virtue, nor ftirre out of the path of true pietie, although he should loofe his reputation and fame; we muft make more efteeme of fruict, then of leaues, and preferre interiour and fpirituall virtues, before externall and corporall goods. It is lawfull to be zelous, but not to be idolaters of our credit; as we muft not offend the eyes of the good, fo muft we not feeke to content the opinion of the malitious. The beard is an ornament to the face of euerie man, and large treffes of haire grace wemens heads: yf one pull away by the rootes (as it vere) the beard from

the

the chinne, or the heare from the head,
it will very hardly grow againe : but if
it be onely cut and polled , nay though
it should be shaued away all together,
it would so one growe againe , and wax
as copious as it was before . So although our credit and reputation be
cut and shauen, as a man may say , by a
detracting tongue (which Dauid saith
is like to a *sharpe razour*) we must not
therfore be disquieted, for by and by it
will spring foorth againe, not only as
faire as euer it was , but much more
sound and beautifull . But yf our vices,
dissolute manners,and wicked life, take
our reputation from vs , it will scarce
grow againe , or be restored entirely,
because it is so in a manner pulled vp
by the roote. For the roote of true reputation, is virtue and good life,and therfore, as long as that is aliue in vs , our
fame and credit will allways sprout and
growe , and bring foorth fruit of honour and estimation , due to virtue.
When vaine conuersation , vnprofitable familiarity, fond frindship,& haun-
ting of idle companie,hurt our reputation : we must presently renounce and
for-

forsake them, for a good name is of
more price and valew then all vaine contentments and passe times ; But yf for
the exercise of pietie, for profit and encrease in virtue and deuotion, for mar-
ching cheerfullie towards eternall happinesse, men grumble, repine, murmur,
and cauill at vs : then suffer these ma-
stiues to bark against the moone, for
though they may be able for a time, or
among sone men, to raise an ill opinion against our good name, and by
that meanes as it were shaue and polle
away that ornament of our virtues;they
will notwithstanding spring vp againe
as abundantly as before, and the razour
of these malicious back biting tongues,
wilbe to our credit, as the gardeners
hook to the vine, which by cutting
of leaues, and pruning some super-
fluous braches, makes it become more
fructifull.

5. Let vs fixe our eyes alway vpon
our *Sauiour Iesus Christ* crucified for
vs, and marche on confidently in his
seruice, simplie and plainlie, yet prudentlie and discreetlie : and he wilbe
the protectour of our reputation ; yf
he

he fuffer it to be taken from vs ; it is
either to honour vs with a farre more
glorious renowne, or at leaft wife to
make vs profit in the exercife of holy
humilitie, wherof one onely ounce,
is better then a thoufand pounds of
honours and eftimations. Yf we be
vniuftlie defamed, let vs meekly and
quietly oppofe the plaine truth againft
falfe calummation : yf then neuer
the lefle cauills perfeuer, let vs likewife perfeuer in humbling our felues;
refigning our reputation, together
with our foule into Gods hands, we
cannot place it in better fecuritie;
Let vs ferue God in infamie or good
fame, according to faint Paules example, that we may fay to God with
Dauid, for thee (ô Lord) haue I
fuffered fhame, and confufion hath
couered my face. I except neuerthe-
lefle certaine enormious crimes, fo
infamous, that no man ought to fuf-
ferre him felfe to be falfelie charged
with them : when he can lawfullie
difprooue the defamers ; and certaine perfons likewife, vpon whofe
reputation and credit the edification
of

of manie foules dependeth : for in thefe cafes we muft with tranquillitie and difcreet moderation , ftand vpon the defence of our honour and good name, according to the doctrine of al diuines.

Of meeknes and gentlenes towardes our neighbours; and remedies againft anger.   CHAP. 8.

1. THE holy Chrifme which by apoftolicall tradition we vfe in the churche of God for confirmations and confecrations , is compofed of oile of Oliues, mingled with Baulme: which befide other things, reprefenteth vnto vs, the two deere and louely virtues which fhined in the facred perfon of our Lord , and which he moft particularly did commend vnto vs, as yf by them our hart were efpecially to be confecrated to his feruice, and applied to his imitation : *Learne of me* (fayth he) *for I am meek & humble of hart.* Humilitie perfecteth vs to Godward, and mildnes , or meeknes towards our neighbour. The Baulme which (as I fayde

fayde before) finketh to the loweft place in all other liquors, reprefenteth humilitie : and the oyle of Oliues, which
fwimmeth always aboue other liquors,
fignifieth mildnes and affabilitie,which
among all virtues is moft excellent and
of delightfulleft appeerance , as being
the flower of charitie : for charitie (according to *S.* Bernard) is then moft
perfect , when it is not onely patient,
but mild alfo and courteous.

2. But take heede, Philotheus, that
this myfticall Chrifme, compofed of
meekenes & humilitie be indeed with
in thy hart , for it is one of the greateft
fubtilities of the deuil , to make many
a man verie cnrioufly ftudie, to make a
fhew of thefe two virtues in words and
exteriour complements , who not exa-
ming throughly their inward affections
efteeme them felues humble and meek,
where as in deed they be nothing foe;
which we may well perceaue , becaufe
for all their ceremonious mildnes and
humilitie , at the leaft croffe word giuen them,at the verie leaft iniurie prof-
fered them , they puffe and fwell like
toades,with meruailous arrogancie and
                                                    impa-

impatience. They fay, that thofe who
haue taken the preferuatiue, com-
monlie called, the grace of S. Paul,
fwell not at all by the bityng and ftinging of vipers, prouided that the preferuatiue be not counterfeit : in like
manner, when humilitie and mildnes
are true and vnfained, they preferue vs
from the burning foares and fwelling
humours, which iniuries are wont to
raife in mens harts. But yf being ftung
and bitt by the flanderous and malicious tongues of our enemies, we fwell
with fiercenes, fpite, and rage : it is
an euident figne, that our humilitie and
meeknes, is not franck and free, but
artificiallie counterfetted.

3   That holie and illuftrious patriarche Iofeph, fending back his brethren from Egypte to his father, gaue
them this only aduice : *Be not angrie by
the way.* I fay the felf fame to thee, Philotheus, this wretched life, is but a
waye to the happie life of heauen : let
vs not be angrie one with another in
this waye, but marche with the troupe
of our brethren and companions fweetlie, peaceably, and louingly : and I
meane

meane we should do so roundly without all exception. Be not angrie at all, yf it be possible, take no occasion or pretext what soeuer be offered, to open the gate of your hart to anger, for. *S.* Iames tells vs very brieflie, and without any distinction or reseruation : *the anger of man worketh not the iustice of God.*

4. We must indeed resist the euil, and suppresse the vices of them that are vnder our charge, constantly and stoutly : but yet mildly, and peaceablie. Nothing so soone tameth the Elephant being angred, then the sight of a litle lambe : nothing breaketh so easilie the force of canon shott, as soft wooll : we esteeme not so much the correctió that proceeds from passion, though it be accópained with neuer so much reason, as that which hath no other cause or beginning but reason. For the soule of má being naturallie subiect to the rule of reason, is neuer subiect to passió but tyrannicallie : and therfore when reason is accópained with passion she maketh her self odious, her iust gouernement being abased & vilyfied, by the felowship of the tyrát passió. Princes do honour & cófort
their

their people exceedinglie when they
viſit them with a peaceable traine: but
when they come garded with armed troupes, though it be for the good
of the commonwealth, their coming is
allwaies diſpleaſing and dammageable;
for let them keepe militarie diſcipline
neuer ſo rigorouſly among their ſoldiours, yet they can neuer bring it ſo to
paſſe, but ſome diſorder will alway
chaunce, whereby the good poore man
is iniuried. Euen ſo, as long as reaſon
ruleth, and exerciſeth ſweetly and mildly the chaſtiſſements, corrections, and
reprehenſions due to offences, although
they be inflicted exactly and with rigour, euerie man loueth and liketh of
it: but when ſhe brings with her thoſe
armed paſſions of wrath, choler, ſpite,
and rage, taunts, and frownings (which
S. Auſtin calleth the ſoldiours of reaſon) ſhe maketh her ſelf more drea-
ded then loued, and euen her owne
hart becomes therby afflicted, and ill
handled.

5. Better it is (ſayth the ſame glorious Saint writing to his frind Profu-
turus) to denie the entrie to anger, be it
neuer

neuer vpon so iust & reasonable a cause, then to receaue it, be it neuer so litle
into our harts : for being once admitted, it is hardly gott out adores againe:
for it entreth like a litle braunche , and
in a moment waxeth a great tree : and
yf it can but gaine the night of vs, that
the sunne do but sett vpon our anger
(which the Apostle forbiddeth) conuerting it selfe into hatred and rancour,
there is almost no remedie to be freed
from it : for it nourisheth it self with a
thousand surmises and false persuasions:
because neuer was there yet any angrie
man, that thought his anger to be cau-
selesse , or vniust . It is better then and
easier, to learne and accustom our selues, to liue without choler , then to vse
our choler and anger moderatly , and
discreetly. But yf through imperfection
and frailtie, we find our selues surprised
and ouertaken therwith , it is better to
chace it away speedelie, then to stand
dalliyng and as it were copning with it.
For giue it neuer so litle leaue, and it
wilbe mistresse of the fort, and like the
serpent, which can easilie draw in his
whole bodie , where he can once get

N   in his

in his head.

6. But thou wilt fay, how shall I re-
preffe and refraine my anger once hea-
ted and inflamed? Thou muft Philotheus, at the firft affault of choler, fpee-
dilie affemble thy forces together, re-
flecting vpon that which thou haft in
hand, not rudely nor violently, but mildly and gentlie, though ferioufly and in
all earneft. For as wee fee in the audien-
ces & affemblies of the fenats or courts,
the vshers, with criyng of peace, make more noife a great deale, then thofe
whome they bid to be filent: fo it happeneth manie times, that endeuouring
with impetuofitie and manie force to
affwage our choler, we ftirre vp more
perturbation and trouble in our felues,
then the motion it felf of choler had
done before, fo that the hart being thus
troubled, is no more maifter of it felf.

7 Secondly after this foft and fweet
ftraining of thy powers, to reflect vpon
them felues, practize the aduice which
S. Auftin being now old, gaue vnto
the young bishop Auxilius. Doe (faith
he) that which a mã should doe. Yf that
bechaunce thee, which the mã of God
                                    fayd

fayd, in the pſalme. *My eye is troubled for anger*, haue recourſe vnto God criyng, *haue mercy vpon me ô Lord*, that he may ſtretche foorth his right hand to repreſſe thy choller. I meane, that we ſhould inuoke the aſſiſtance of God, when we perceaue our ſelues ſhaken with choler; imitating the Apoſtles, when they were toſſed with winds and tempeſt vpon the waters, for he wil cõmãd our paſſiõsto ceaſe, & cauſe a quiet calme to enſew. But I admoniſhe thee, that alwaythe praier which thou makeſt againſtthis paſſiõof ãgerwhich thẽpoſſeſſeth & preſſeth thee, be exerciſed meeklie, leaſurly, & calmely, not violẽtly, haſtely, or turbulẽtly, & this ſelf ſame rule muſt be obſerued in all remedies which are applied againſt this paſſiõ of anger.

8. Thirdly, ſo ſoone as thou perceaueſt, that thou haſt done ſome act of choler, repare and redreſſe the fault immediatly, with another contrarie act of mildnes, exerciſed promptly and ſweetly towards the ſame perſon, againſt whoime thou waſt angrie. For as it is a ſoueraigne remedie againſt liyng, to vnſay it, and goe back from the lie, euen

in the verie place where thou toldeſt it:
ſo is it an excellent ſalue againſt anger,
to applie ſodainly, and out of hand, a
contrarie act of mildnes and courteſie:
for greene wounds (they ſay) are eaſieſt
to be cured.

9. Fourthely, when thou art at repoſe and tranquillitie, and whithout any
occaſion or ſubiect of choler, make
great ſtore and prouiſion (as they ſay)
of meeknes, and gentlenes, ſpeaking all
thy words, and working al thy actions,
and vſing all thy behaueour, in the ſweeteſt, ſofteſt, and mildeſt manner thou
canſt: calling to mind that the ſpouſe
in the canticles, had hunnie, not only in
her lippes, but alſo vnder her tongue,
that is in her breſt: nor hunnie only, but
milk too; for ſo we muſt not only haue
ſweete and courteous wordes to our
neighbour, but they muſt proceed alſo
from the bottom of our hart. Neither
muſt we haue this hunnie-ſweet mildnes, which is pleaſaunt and odoriferous,
in our conuerſation with ſtrangers, &
forreners abroade, but with all the
milk ſweet behaueour, and fatherly, or
brotherly cariage alſo within doores,
                                    amongſt

amongſt our domeſticall frinds , and
neere neighbours:wherin they are greatly to ſeek , who in the ſtreet be like
Angels, and within theire houſe, ſeeme
almoſt deuils.

Of ſweetnes and gentlenes towardes
our ſelues.

Chapter 9.

1. **O**N e of the beſt exerciſes of
meeknes,is that which we may
practize towards our owne ſel-
ues:neuer deſpightfully fretting againſt
our owne imperfections . For though
reaſon command,that we ſhould be di-
ſpleaſed & ſorrie when we committ any
faults , yet we muſt allway eſchew all
melancholie, deſpightfull, & bitter diſpleaſure: wherin manie do egregiouſly
offend, who ſtirred vp a litle to choler
and anger , are angrie that they be angrie, & frett & chafe, to ſee themſelues
chafe ; for by this manner of proceeding , their hart is (as a man may ſay)
ſoaked in choler ; and though it ſeemes
to rhem , that the ſecond anger, con-
quers and bannishes away the firſt,

yet notwithstanding it openeth an entrance and a passage, for a new choler at the first occasion that shalbe offered. Besides that these angers, frettings, and bitter chafing against our selues, tend to pride, and haue no other roote nor beginninge but self loue, which troubleth and vnquieteth the soule to see it self vnperfect.

2. The dislike then which we must haue of our faults, must be a sober, quiet and setled dislike. For as a iudge, punisheth much better any malefactour, when he giueth sentence; his reason being vntroubled with passion, and his spirit in calme, then yf he should pronounce the sentence with a passionate minde, because iudginge in passion, he chastiseth not the faults according as they are, but according as he himself is: so we correct our selues much better, by calme & setled repentance, then by sower, fretting, and fuming dislike; for repentance done with violence of passion, is neuer according to the heauinesse of our fault, but according to the sway of our inclinations. For example, he that much affecteth chastitie, will

vex

vex himſelf with an vnſpeakeable bitter-
neſſe, for the leaſt fault that he ſhould
committ againſt it: and will but laugh
at a groſſe ſclander and detraction proceeding from him. On the other ſide, he
that hateth the ſinne of detraction, will
afflict his ſoule for murmuring a litle,
and make no reckening of a grieuous
fault committed againſt chaſtitie: & ſo of
others. And this ſpringeth frõ no other
fountaine, thẽ that they iudge not their
conſcience by reaſon, but by paſſion.

3. Beleeue me Philotheus, as the good
aduiſes of a father, giuen ſweetly & hartely to his child, haue farre more opera-
tion to correct him, thẽ choler & indi-
gnatiõ: ſo whẽ our ſoule ſhal haue done
any fault, yf we reprehẽd it with a quiet
& ſweet reprehenſiõ, more by cõpaſſiõ,
thẽ by paſſiõ, & gẽtlie encouraging our
ſelues to amendment, the repentance
conceaued thervpon, will penetrate farther, and ſinck deeper in vs, then a frett-
full, angrie and ſtorming repentance.

4. For my part, yf (for example) I
had a great affection and deſire, not to
fall into the ſinne of vaine-glorie,
and yet notwithſtanding ſhould haue
N 4　　　　　fallen

fallen grieuously into the self same vice:
I would not reprehend my soule in this
manner : Art thou not a miserable and
abominable caytife , that after so many
resolutions , hast suffered thy self to be
caried after this vanitie ? fie for shame ,
lift not vp thy eyes to heauen , blind,
impudent , traitorous , and disloyall to
thy God ; and such like chasing fumes
of reprehension; but I would reprehend
it rather with reason , and compassiuely
in this sort. Ah my poore hart , we are
now fallen into the ditche , which we,
had so resolutely determined to escape.
Well , let vs out againe , and forsake it
heerafter for euer. Let vs yet againe call
vpon the mercie of God, and trust in it,
and hope that he will louingly assist vs,
to make vs hence forward more constant, and so let vs turne into the plaine
way of humilitie. Courage my soule,
from this day we will stand vpon our
watch and garde , God will ayde vs , we
shall prosper by his grace. And vpō this
gentle reprehension , would I build a
sound and firme resolution ,neuer to fall
againe into that fault,vsing to that end,
the meanes conuenient , and especially
the

the aduice of my directour.

5. But yf notwithstanding, one finds, that his hart is not sufficientlie moued with this sweet manner of reprehensio: he may reproache the fault to him self, & check his soule somwhat roughly, to raise a virtuous shame in it : prouided that after he hath thus roundely rated & reuiled his hart , he end sweetly and meekly, concluding all his chiding, with a mild quiet confidence in God, imitating that great penitent, who seeing his soule afflicted , eased it in this manner: *Why art thou sad, ô my soule, and why doest thou trouble me? Hope in God, for I will cofesse vnto him , the saueing health of my countenance , and my God.*

6. Raise vp againe thy hart therfore frō his fall, with all reposed quiet, humble thy self hartelie before God , acknowledginge thine owne miserie , not much wondring at thy fall ; for it is not straunge, that weakenes should be feeble, or miserie wretched. Yet for all that, detest from thy hart , that thou hast so often offended God, and with cheerfull courage, and humble confidence in his mercie , returne to the path of virtue

N 5   from

from which thou haſt ſwarued.

That we muſt handle our affaires with
diligence , but not with too much
eagrenes , and ſolicitude.

CHAPTER 10.

1. THE care & diligence which we
ought to haue in our buſines,
are things much different from
ſollicitude , carke , and ouermuch earneſtnes. The Angels haue care of our
ſaluatiō, & do procure it diligently:but
for all that they take no thought, they
are not ſolicitous therfore, for care and
diligence in our cauſe belonge to their
charitie:ſolicitous,& vexinge thoughts,
be cleane contrarie to their felicitie:for
care & diligēce may be accōpanied with
tranquillitie & peace of mind, but ſolicitude is allways ioyned with trouble of
ſpirit.

2. Be carefull then and diligent in all
thy affaires,for ſince God hath cōmēded
them to thy truſte and charge , it is his
will that thou take care of them:but yf
it be poſſible,be not ſolicitous, take no
thought for them, vndertake them not
with anxietie , and too much feruour:

force

force not thy felf in the matter, for all
violent impreſſions trouble the iudgement and blind reaſon, and hinder vs
from doing well, that which we defire
to do ouer earneſtly.

3. When our Lord reprehēded S. Mar-
tha, he fayd: *Martha, Martha, thou art ſolici-*
tous, and troubleſt thy felf about, many things.
Where thou feeſt, yf ſhe had been onely
carefull, ſhe had not been troubled, but
becaufe ſhe was full of folicitous thoughts, & vnquietneſſe, ſhe vexed & troubled her felf, and for that caufe did our
Lord reprehend her. Riuers which glide
fmoothely through the dale, beare great
boates, & rich merchandife, & the raine
which falleth gentlie in the champion
countrie, maketh the ground to abound
in graſſe & corne; but brookes &rilles,
which runne with violent downe-falles,
or great ouerflowings, ruine the borde-
ring villages, and are vnprofitable for
traffique; as likewife tempeſtuous and
ſtormie ſhewers, fpoile both fields and
meadowes : Neuer came work to be
well donne that was folowed with too
much earneſtnes. We muſt difpatche
with leaſure, and foft fire, maketh fweet
N 6   malt

malt (as the old prouerbe fayth :) he
that maketh too much haft , (fayth
Salomon) is in danger of ftumbling,
or hurting his feet : we ende our affaires foone enough , when we end them
well enough. Droanes make more hunnie then Bees , and flie much more
haftelie , but they make combes onely
and not honny : fo they that take ex-
cefiue thought , and goe about their
bufineffe with ouermuch folicitude, ordinarilie , neither do much , nor well.

4. Flies difquiet vs not by their
ftrength, but by their number: and great
affaires doe not vexe vs fo much , as a
nomber of affaires of litle valewe ; what
foeuer affaires then befall thee , receaue
them contentedly, with meekenes, and
repofe of fpirit, & endeuour to difpatch
the by due order, one after another , for
yf thou ftriue to doe them all at once,
the ouermuch labour will tyre & werie
thee,& make thee grone vnder the burthen, & difable thee from bringing any
thing to good end.

5. In all thy bufineffe, repofe thy felf
wholly vpõ Gods prouidence, by whofe
onely meanes thy defignements will
                                        growe

growe to a good effect:yet neuerthelesse
for thyne owne part be diligēt, & do thy
endeauour faire and softly, cooperating
with Gods help : & thus doing, beleeue
what successe so euer folowes thy endeauour, is most profitable for thee (yf thou
placest thy confidence in God as thou
shouldest) how euer it seeme good or
bad, according to thy owne particular
iudgemēt. Like as litle childrē who with
one hād hold fast by their father, & with
the other gather strawberries or prim-
roses alōg the hedges: so whilst thou ma-
nagest the affaires of this worlde with
one hand, lay hould with the other vpon
the prouidence of thy heauenly Father:
turning thy self toward him frō time to
time, to see yf thy husbādrie and labours
be pleasaunt vnto him. And take heede
aboue all things, that thou let not goe
his hand, or become vnmindfull of his
protection: for so thou wilt not be able
to goe one only step without falling to
groūd. My meaning is (my Philotheus)
that amidst thy affaires, & cōmon occupations, which require not so earnest at-
tentiō, thou thinck vpō God more then
vpon thy affaires : and when thy affaires
be

be of so great importāce, that to be well done, they require thy whole attention, then also oftentimes thou must reflect vpon God; And as they that saile vpon the sea, to arriue at the desired coast, looke more often vp to heauen, then downe vpon the sea where they saile: doe thou so, and God will work with thee, in thee, and for thee, and all thy labours shalbe secōdēd wïth cōsolations.

---

of Obedience.

CHAPTER II.

1. CHARITIE onelie placeth vs in the hight of perfection, but obedience, chastitie, and pouertie are three excellent instruments to attaine vnto it. Obedience consecrateth our soule, chastitie dedicateth our bodie, pouertie applieth our goods & substance, to the loue, & seruice of almightie God. These be the three branches of the spirituall crosse, which euerie man must beare, all three grounded vpō the fourth vnderbraunche, which is humilitie. I will not say anie thing of these three virtues as they are vowed solemnelie,

nelie, for so they appertaine onelie to
religious persons : nor as they are professed by a simple vowe , for though alwayes a vowe giueth a peculiar valew
and merit vnto all virtues , yet for the
purpose which heere we pretend , it is
not necessarie they should be vowed, so
that they be well obserued. When they
are vowed solemnelie, they place a man
in state of perfection , but to come to
perfection it self, it sufficeth that they be
well obserued : for there is great difference betwixt the state of perfection, &
perfectiō it self ; all bishops & religious
are in the state of perfection, and yet all
attaine not to perfection , as we see but
too too often. Let vs endeuour then,
Philotheus, to practise well these three
virtues , euerie one of vs according to
our vocation : for though they promote vs not to the state of perfection, they
will bring vs to perfection it self , and
we all haue obligation to practise these virtues , though not all after one
fashion.

2. There are two sorts of obediēce· the
one necessarie: the other voluntarie. By
necessarie obediēce, thou must obey thy
eccle-

ecclesiasticall superiours, as the Pope, Archbishops, Bishops, Pastours, and such as are their deputies: thou must obey thy ciuil superiours, to wit, thy Prince, and his magistrats, which he hath established ouer thy countrie: and finally, thou must obey thy domesticall superiours, father and mother, maister and mistresse. This obedience is called necessarie, because no man can exempt him selfe, from the debt and dutie of obeying the aforesayd superiours, whome God hath placed in authoritie, to command and gouerne, eache one according to the charge appointed vnto him ouer vs. Doe then that which they commaund, and that is necessarie obedience: but to doe this more perfectly, their counsailes also, must be followed & their inclinations and desires, so farre as charitie and prudence will permitte thee. Obey them, when they command such things as are agreeable to thine owne will, as to eat, to recreate thy self: for though it seeme no great virtue to obey in these occasions, yet would it be a great vice to disobey in them. Obey them when they

com-

command things that are indifferent in
them selues, or in thy iudgement, as to
weare this, or that habit, to goe this
way, or that way, to sing, or to be silét:
and it wilbe verie commendable obedience. Obey them when they command hard, displeasaunt, and vneasie
things: and it wilbe perfect obedience.

3. Obey I say sweetly without replie,
promptly without delaye, cheerfullie
without repining, and aboue all, obey
louingly, for loue of him, who for our
loue made him self obedient, euen to
the death of the crosse, and who (as *S.*
Bernard sayth) chose rather to lose his
life, then to lose obedience.

4. To learne to obey easilie thy superiours, accustome thy self to condescend and folow the will of thy
equalls, giuing place to their opinions,
when they are nor vicious, or naughtie,
without all strife wrangling or conten-
tion, accommodate thy self willingly
to the desires of thy inferiours, so farre
as reason may permitte, and neuer exercise any imperious commands ouer
them, so long as they be good and
virtuous.

5. It

5. It is a great deceit and errour in vs, to imagin that we would obey more easilie, if we were religious, when we find our selues rebellious to such as God hath placed ouer vs.

6. We call that obedience voluntarie, wher vnto we bind aud oblige our selues by our owne choice, and electiō, and which is not imposed vpon vs by anie other. Men choose not ordinarilie their prince, their bishop, their father or mother, nor manie times men their wiues, nor woemen their husbands: but they choose their ghostlie father, and spirituall directour. Yf then thou choose by vow to obey, (as we sayd aboue, that the holie mother Theresa, besides her obedience solemnelie vowed to the superiour of her order, bound her self by a simple vowe to obey father Gratian) or if without a vowe thou dedicate thy self to the obedience of some guide and gouernour, yet allwaysis this obedience termed voluntarie, because it is grounded, vpon our free will, and depends vpon our owne election.

7. We must obey all our superiours, but

but euerie one in that, in which he hath charge ouer vs : as in that which belongeth to ciuil policie; and publique affaires, we must obey our prince; our prelats in that which belongeth to ecclesiasticall matters; our father, our husband, & our maister in domestical businesse; and our ghostlie father or spirituall directour, in the peculiar guidance of our conscience, and soule.

8. Cause thy ghostlie father, to order dispose, and impose, all the actions of pietie, which thou shouldest exercise, for so they wilbe more excellent, clothed with a double beautie and merit; the one taken from them selues, because they are good of their owne nature and substance; the other taken frō thy obedience to thy directour, in virtue wherof thou doest performe them. Happie are the obedient, for God will neuer suffer them to goe astraye.

Of the necessity of Chastitie.

CHAPTER 12.

1. **C**Hastitie is the lillie of virtues; it maketh mē equall to Angels. Nothing is beautifull but by puritie:

puritie : and the puritie of men, is chaftitie. Chaftitie is called honeftie, and the profeffion therof, honour: it is named, integritie; and the contrarie therof, corruption. In few words, chaftitie hath this excellencie a part, to be iointly, the beautifull and louely virtue of foule and bodie.

2. It is neuer lawfull to receaue any vnchaft delight from our bodies in any fort whatfoeuer, but onely in lawfull marriage : for the fanctitie of that facrement by iuft recompence, repaireth the loffe we receaue in that kind of pleafure. And yet euen in marriage, the honeftie of the intention muft allwayes be kept, that though there be fome indecencie in the delight taken, yet there be always puritie and cleannes, in the intention and will that receaueth it. The chaft hart, is like the mother-pearle, which receaueth no drop of brackish water, but onely the deaw that falleth from heauen : and a chaft hart admitteth no pleafure, but onelie in marriage, which is ordained from heauen : Excepting onelie the lawfull delight of marriage, it is not lawfull fo

much

much as in thought, to entertaine voluntarilie, and deliberatlie, any voluptuous or carnall delight.

3. The firſt degree of this virtue, may be (my Philotheus) to take heed of intertaining any kind of pleaſure, that is prohibited, or forbidden ; as all thoſe, are, which are receaued out of marriage ; and thoſe likewiſe which are taken in marriage, but not according to the rule of marriage. For the ſecond degree, refraine as much as is poſſible, from all vnprofitable and ſuperfluous delights, although lawfull, and permitted. For the third degree, fix not thy affection vpon the pleaſures and delights ordained and commanded in marriage it ſelf, for though it be lawfull to vſe thoſe delights, which are neceſſarie for the end, and inſtitution of matrimonie, yet for all that, we muſt neuer fix our hart thervpon.

4. All perſons and eſtates need this virtue. They that be in widowhood, muſt haue a courageous and ſtrong chaſtitie, to auoide not onlie the preſent or future obiects, and occaſions of delights, but to reſiſt the imagination which

which lawfull pleafures , receaued in
marriage in former times, may breed in
their remembrance , their minds therfore being more fubiect to vncleane
allurements, and vnchaft impreffions.
For which caufe S. Auguftin admireth
the puritie of his deere frind Alypius,
who had whollie defpifed and forgetten
the pleafures of the fleshe , though
tafted by him fometimes in his youth.
And trulie we fee, that when fruites are
not yet tainted with rottenneffe, they
may be wel preferued , fome in ftraw,
fome in fand, & fome in their owne leaues: but being once tainted with a litle
rotte, it is almoft impoffible to preferue
them long, but by confiting or confer-
uing them in honnie and fugar. Euen
fo chaftitie which is not yet violated,
may manie wayes be garded and kept
whole, and vntouched : but being once
corrupted , though but a litle , can not
be preferued , but by an excellent deuotion , which (as I haue oft repeated) is
the honnie and fugar of the mind.

5. Virgins haue need of a merueilous
fimple and tender chaftitie, not fuffring
the touch of anie thing contrarie to
their

their cleannes, but to bannishe without
all delay from their verie thoughts,
all forts of curious conceipts , repre-
fentations, or remembrances of carnall
pleafures : which indeed, deferue not
that men should defire them , fince
Affes , and fwine be more capable of
them, then men. Lett thefe pure and
louely-cleane foules therfore, neuer
doubt, but that chaftitie is incompara-
blie better, more delightfull , & more
honourable, then anie pleafure cótrarie
thervnto. For, as great Saint Hierom
fayth , the deuill endeuoureth violent-
lie, to force virgins to defire the triall
of thefe fleshlie pleafures , prefenting
and painting them to their thoughts,
infinitlie more pleafaunt and delicious,
then indeed they are : which manie times troubleth them much, efteeming
(as this Saint fayth) that to be more fweet, which they haue not as yet
tafted . For as the litle Butterflie,
feeing the flame of a candle , houe-
reth curiouflie about it , to proue
whether it be as fweete , as it is faire ;
and forced with this fantafie, ceafeth
not, till she burne her felfe to death
at the

at the verie firſt triall : ſo theſe young
folk, ſuffer themſelues oft times, to be
ſeaſed with the fond and falſe imagination, which they frame of the pleaſure
of voluptuous flames, that after many
curious thoughts ſpent vpon them, in
ſine they caſt them ſelues vtterly away
in the triall of them ; more ſottiſh and
foolish in this, then the butterflies,
which haue ſome occaſion to imagine
that the flame is ſweet, becauſe it is
beautifull : wheras theſe fond fooles,
knowing that the pleaſures which they
houer about, are indecent, & dishoneſt,
abſtaine not for all that, to proſequute
their beaſtlie and brutish delectation.

6. As for maried folk, though the
common people cannot be perſuaded
therto , yet is the virtue of chaſtitie
moſt neceſſarie to them : for chaſtitie
of marriage, conſiſteth not in abſtai-
ning abſolutly and wholly from carnall
pleaſures, but in being continent, moderate, & temperate in the vſe of them.
Now as this commandement (be angry, but ſinn not) is in my opinion har-
der then this, (be not angry:) which is
rather giuen to auoide anger, then to
rule

rule and gouerne it : so is it farre easier
to keep ones self altogether frō fleshlie
delights, then to keepe due moderation
and temperance in them. True it is, that
the holy licence of marriage, hath a particular force and vertue, to extinguishe
and allay, the heat and fire of concu-
piscence. But the frailtie of them that
enioy this licence, passeth easily from
permission, to dissolutenes, and from
the vse, to abuse. And as we see many
rich men to robbe and spoile, not for
want, but for couetousnesse : so likewise we see many married folk, to exceed in intéperance and lasciuiousnesse,
notwithstanding the lawfull obiects,
wherin they might & should containe
their desires : their vnbridled concupis-
cence being like wild-fire, which runneth scorching and burning heer and
there, without resting in any one place.
It is allways dangerous to take violent
purgations ; for yf one take more then
they should, or yf they be not well
prepared, the poore patient receaueth
much damage thereby: Marriage was
blest, and ordained in part, for a purgation, and remedie against concu-

O   pis-

piscence; and it is, no doubt, a verie good remedie: but yet violent, and consequently somewhat dangerous, yf it be not discreetly applied.

7. Moreouer, the varietie, and chaunge of humane affaires, besides often and long diseases, do many times separate husbands from their wiues: and therfore married folke, do stand in neede of two kinds of chastitie, the one for absolute abstinence from fleshlie delight, when occasions occurring do separate them: the other, for moderation and temperate vse of mariage pleasures, when they liue together. S. Catherin of *Sienna* saw among the damned, very manie soules grieuouslie tormented, for violating the sanctitie of holy marriage; not for the greatnes of the sinne, (as. Saint *Catherin* vnderstood) for murthers, and blasphemies are much more enormous: but becaufe when they vsed these pleasures vnlawfully, they made small conscience of them, and therfore continued the longer in them.

8. Thou seest then that chastitie is necessarie for all sorts of people: *folow peace*

peace with all men (sayth the Apostle)
*and holines, without which no man shall
see God :* Where, by holines, is vnderstood chaftitie, as *S.* Hierom, and *S.*
Chryfoftom obferue. No my Philotheus, none shall fee God without chaftitie ; none shall dwell in his holy tabernacle, that are not pure of hart; and,
as our Sauiour him felf fayth, dogges
and vnchaft shalbe bannished from
thence, and *happie are the pure of hart, for
they shall fee God.*

Aduices how to preferue chaftitie.
CHAPTER 13.

1. **B** E exceeding diligent to withdraw thy felf from all occafions
and baytes of incontinencie ;
for this vice worketh infenfible, and
vnperceaued : and from verie litle be-
ginings, proceeds to great incouenien-
ces. It is allwayes more eafie to auoide
damage before it come, then to redreffe
it when it is happened.

2. Mens bodies are like glaffes,
which cannot be caried together touching

ching one another, without danger of breaking; and like fruicts, which be they neuer so sound and well-seasoned, yet by touching one another, are tainted with rottennesse. Water it self in a vessel, be it neuer so fresh, being once touched by any beast, cannot long time be preserued in his freshnes. Neuer suffer any man (ô Philothee) to touch thee vnciuilly, eyther for myrthe, or for fauour: for though peraduenture chastetie may be preserued in those actions, that are more of lightnes then of malice: yet the puritie and flower of chastitie, receaueth some detriment & losse by them. But to suffer thy self to be touched dishonestly by any, is the vtter ruine and ouerthrow of chastitie.

3. Chastitie dependeth of the soule as of her originall roote, and respecteth the bodie, as the matter about which she worketh. This is the cause that she may leese her self by all the exteriour sences of the bodie, and by the temptations and desires of the soule. It is lasciuiousnesse to behold, to heare, to speak, to smell, or touch any dishonest thing, when the soule obserueth it,

dal-

dallieth in it, and taketh delight and
pleasure therin. Saint Paul in one word
sayth : *Let not fornication be so much as once
named amongst you.* The Bees not only
refuse to touch any carrion, but hate
extremly, and therfore flie hastely,from
all vnsauourie smells proceeding from
it. The sacred spouse in the Canticles
is sayd, to haue her hands full of myrre
that it droppeth downe from her fin-
gers, and myrre preserueth from corruption ; her lippes are coloured with a
blushing vermillion, betokening modestie and shamefastnes in words ; Her
eyes are of Doues,for their puritie ; she
weareth golden earings,as neuer daring
to heare of any vncleannesse;her nose is
cōpared to the cedars of Libanus , that
are incorruptible : such ought to be the
soule of Chrifts seruant, chast, honest,
cleane in hands, lippes, eyes, eares, and
all her bodie.

4. To this purpose will I tell thee
what the ancient father Iohn Cassian
reporteth,as from the mouth of Sainct
Basil the great : who speaking of him
selfe , sayde : *I know not what belongeth
to wemen , yet am I not a Virgin .* For

truly chastitie may be lost as manie wayes, as there be kindes of lasciuiousnesse, and fleshlie delights: which according as they are great or litle, so dee they weaken, wound, or kill it out right. There are certaine particular frindships, and vndiscreet, foolish, sensuall passions, which to speak properlie, do not violate and corrupt chastitie, but yet do greatlie weaken it, and staine the beautifull white of this pure virtue. There are other familiarities and passionate frindships, not onelie indiscreet, but vitious; not onelie fond, but dishonest with all; not onely sensuall, but carnal: and by these chastitie is at least sorelie hurt, and wounded: I say at the least wounded, because it dieth and perisheth altogether, when these dalliances and wanton actions, do cause in the flesh the vttermost effect of voluptuous delight: for then it is lost more vildly, wickedlie, and detestablie, then when it is corrupted by fornication, by adulterie, by incest; since these latter kindes of dishonestie, are onlie sinnes; but the former (as Tertulliã sayth in his booke of chastitie, or

sham-

shamfaftneffe) are certaine monfters of
iniquitie.Now neither Caffiã,nor I my
felf thihck,that S.Bafils words are to be
vnderftood of any fuch filthie diforder,
when he fayd of him felf,that he was no
virgin:but he fayd fo onelie for vnchaft
& voluptuous thoughts, which though
they defiled not his bodie , yet did they
contaminat his foule,of the puritie and
chaftnes wherof , all generous and noble fpirits are exceeding iealous.

5. Haunt not the companie of vnchaft perfons, principallie , if withall
they be shameleffe , and impudent, as
for the moft part they be . For as the
hee Goates,licking the fweete Almond
trees with their tongues,do make them
degenerate into bitter Almonds : fo
thefe wanton foules , infected with the
ftinche of fleshlie lufts, do fcarce fpeak
to anie of either fex ; but they make
them in fome fort, fall from the cleanneffe of their chaftitie : they beare
poifon in theire eyes , and in theire
breath like Bafiliskes . But contrariwife, keep companie with chaft & virtuous people: meditate & read oftē holy things: for the word of God is chaft,
　　　　　O 4　　　and

and maketh them chaſt, that delight
therin : which made Dauid compare it
to the Topace, a pretious ſtone, whoſe
propertie, is to aſſwage the ardour of
concupiſcence.

6. Keepe thy ſelfe allways neere and
cloſe to Ieſus Chriſt crucified : ſpirituallie by meditation:and reallie by holie communion : for as they that lie
vpon the herbe Agnus caſtus, become
them ſelues chaſt : ſo thon reſting and
repoſing thy hart in, and vpon God,
(who is the true chaſt and immaculate
lambe) thou shalt ſoone perceaue thy
ſoule cleanſed from all kind of laſciuiouſneſſe.

Of pouertitie of Spirit, to be obſerued in
riches.   Chap. 14.

1. B Lessed are the poore in Spirit, for theirs is the Kingdom of
heauen: accurſed then be the riche in ſpirit, for the miſerie of hell is
for them; I call him rich in ſpirit, who
hath riches in his ſpirit, or rather hath
his ſpirit whollie buſied and buried in
his

his riches. The Alcyons make their nests no bigger then the palme of a had, and leaue but one litle hole in them, on the vpper side : then do they place them vpon the edge of the sea-shore, and frame it so firme and sound in all parts, that when the waues doe chance to hoise them selues vp, yet the water can neuer get in, but they remaine floting aboue the waues; hauing allwayes as it were, the vpper hand of the sea, euen in the middest of the sea. Thy hart (deare Philotheus) must be in the self same manner, open onlie to heauen ward, and impenetrable, neuer geuing place to riches & transitorie goods; with which if thou chaunce to abound, yet keep thy hart free from doating on them with too much affection : let it in the middest of great wealth, be alway maister of thy wealth, aboue thy riches, not beneath, franck and free out of them, not entangled in them. No, no, lodge not this celestiall spirit of thine, in these base earthlie goods, let it be alwayes ouer them, neuer in them.

2. There is great difference betwixt hauing poison, and being poisoned.

O 5   Al Apo-

Al Apothecaries almoſt, haue poiſon
to vſe at diuers occaſions, but they are
not for all that empoiſoned ; becauſe
they haue not poiſon in their bodies,
but in their shoppes. Euen ſo then
mayſt haue riches, without being empoiſoned at all with them : if thou keep
them in thy bagges, or in thy houſe,
and not in thy hart. To be riche in
deed, and poore in thought, and deſire,
is the greateſt felicitie of a Chriſtian :
for he hath by that meanes, the commoditie of riches for this world, and
the merit of pouertie, for the world to
come.

3. Ah Philotheus, no man will confeſſe him ſelf to be couetous, euerie
one contemneth in words that baſenes
and vilenes of hart : they lay their excuſe vpon the great charge of children
which vrgeth them ; vpon the rule
of wiſdome, which requireth, that
men should diligentlie lay vp meanes
to liue ; they neuer haue too much,
ſome neceſſities are always found out
to gett more. Nay the moſt couetous wretch of all, will not onelie
not confeſſe himſelf to be ſuch, but
                              thincketh

thincketh in his confcience he is not
couetous. No, forfooth, is he not;
for couetoufnes is a monftruous ague,
which maketh it felf fo much more
infenfible, by how much more violent and burning it is. Moyfes faw
that holie fire, which burned in the
bush, and yet confumed it not at all:
but this profane fire, confumeth and
deuoureth the couetous perfon, and
yet burneth him not; nay in the middeft of his heates, and ardour, he boafteth of the cooleft refreshing ayer
that hart could wishe, and efteemeth his infatiable and vnquencheable
drought, to be a naturall and delectable thirft.

4. Yf thou defir long, ardentlie,
and vnquietlie the riches which thou
haft not, it is but a ieft to fay, that
thou defireft not to come by them
vnlawfullie, neither doeft thou leaue to be couetous for all that. He
that defireth a long time, with burning
thirft, and vnquiet wishes, to drinck,
albeit he defire cold water onlie, yet
he giueth fufficient witneffe that he is

trou-

troubled with an ague. O my Philotheus, I know not, I, whether it be a
iuſt deſire, to deſire to haue iuſtlie, that
which another poſſeſſeth iuſtlie : for it
ſeemeth to me, that by ſuch, deſire we
would proffit our ſelues, by the dam-
mage of others. He that iuſtlie poſſeſſeth anie commoditie, hath he not better right to keep it iuſtlie, then we to
deſire to haue it iuſtlie ? And why then
ſtretche we our deſire to his commoditie, to diſpoſſeſſe and depriue him of it ?
Although this could be a iuſt deſire,
verilie it is not charitable, for we our
ſelues would not in anie caſe, that another man ſhould deſire, no not iuſtly, to
haue that, which we doe and will iuſtly
retaine. This was the ſinne of Achab,
who deſired to haue Naboths vinyard
iuſtlie, which Naboth much more
iuſtlie deſired to keepe : Achab deſired
it continuallie, ardentlie, vnquietlie,
and therfore offended God.

5. Expect (my Philotheus) to deſire thy neighbours goods, till he
him ſelfe deſireth to part from them,
for then his deſire will make thy deſire to be not onlie iuſt, but charitable

table also . For I giue thee leaue, to
haue a diligent care, to augment thy
fubftance and wealth , fo that it be
done, not onelie iuftlie , but quietlie
alfo and charitable.

6. Yf thou affect much the goods,
which thou haft not, if thou be much
troubled about them, fetling thy hart,
and bending all thy thoughts to gaine them , and fearing with a feeling
apprehenfion to loofe them, beleeue
me, that thou haft yet the fitte of this
burning ague of auarice. For they that
haue fuch fitts , drinck the water that
is giuen them , with a haftie greedines,and a certain attentiue pleafure,
which healthie men accuftome not to
haue. It is impoffible to take great
pleafure in a thing, but that our affection is much placed vpon it.

7. Yf thou chaunce to fuffer anie
loffe of thy goods , and feele thy hart
clogged with forow, and afflicted therwith : beleeue me, Philotheus. , thou
beareft ouer much affection to them ;
for nothing fo much witneffeth the
loue we beare to a thing which we
haue loft , as the affliction and dif-
                                      conten̄t

content which we shew for the losse.

8. Desire not then with a full deliberate, and earnest desire, the wealth and commoditie, which thou hast not: and setle not thy hart vpon that which alreadie thou hast; discomfort not thy self for the losses which befall thee: and then thou shalt haue some reason to say and beleeue, that being rich in effect, thou art not withstanding poore in affection; that thou art in deed poore in spirit, and consequently, that the kingdom of heauen appertaineth vnto thee.

How to practise true and reall pouerty, remayning notwithstanding reallie riche.

CHAPTER 15.

1. THE painter Parrhasius, represented in his pictures, the people of Athens by a most wittie inuention, painting out their diuerse and variable humours, cholerick, vniust, ynconstant, yncourteous, mercifull,

full, high-minded, proude, humble,
and cowardly: and all this together. But
I (my deare Philotheus, would doe more then all this, for I would put into thy
hart riches and pouertie both at once,
a great care, and a great contempt, of
temporall affaires.

2. Take much more care to make
thy temporall goods profitable; and
gainfull, then worldly men doe. Tell
me, the gardiners of great princes, are
they not more curious, and diligent to
deck and trimme vp the gardens they
haue commended to them in charge,
then yf they were their owne in proprietie? And what is the reason therof?
becaufe without dout they confider
thofe gardens, as Kinges and Princes
gardens, vnto whome they defire to
make themfelues acceptable, by their
good feruice. My Philotheus, the
wealth and poffeffions which we haue,
are none of ours, God hath committed
them vnto our charge to cultiuate
them, and his will is, that we make
them profitable and gainfull: and
therfore we doe him good feruice
when we take care of them. But this
                                    care

care muſt be in vs greater, & conſtan-
ter then worldlings haue of their riches. For their labours are for the loue
of them ſelues, and ours muſt be for
the loue of God. Now as ſelf-loue is
violent, trouble ſome, and haſtie; ſo
the care that we take to ſatisfie this
ſelf-loue, is full of vexation, of an-
guiſhe, and diſquiet; And as the loue
of God is ſweet, peaceable, and quiet:
ſo the care which proceedeth from it,
although it be euen about worldly
goods, is both amiable, ſweet, and gracious. Let vs then haue this gracious
care of preſeruing, yea and of en-
creaſing our temporall commodities,
whenſoeuer any iuſt occaſion ſhall
preſent it ſelfe, and ſo farre foorth,
as our eſtate and condition requireth:
for God will that we doe ſo, for the
loue of him.

3. But take heed that ſelf loue deceaue thee not, for ſome-time it counter-
faiteth ſo craftilie the loue of God, that
thou wouldſt verilie thinck it were
the ſame. Now that it deceaue thee
not; and that this care of thy tempo-
ral goods, turne not into ſecret auarice,

ouer

ouer and aboue that which I sayd in the
chapter going before,we muſt very often practize, a true , reall , and actuall
pouertie,in the middeſt of all the riches
and wealth,that God hath giuen vs.

4. Allwayes then abādon ſome part of
thy goods,beſtowing it vpon the poore
with a willing hart,for to giue away that
which one hath , is to impouerish him
ſelf willinglie,and the more one giueth,
the more poore he becometh. True it is
that God will pay it & rēder it all againe,
not only in the next world , but euen in
this preſent life; (for nothing ſo much
proſpereth our tēporall eſtate,as almes-
giuing) but notwithſtāding,vntill ſuch
time as God doth reſtore & repay that
which thou haſt thus giuē, thou remai-
neſt by ſo much poorer in deed thē thou
waſt. O how holy & rich is that pouertie , which cometh by almes-deeds ?

5. Loue poore folk,& pouertie,for ſo
ſhalt thou becomepoore in deed,becau-
ſe as the holy ſcripture teaceth , *we are
made like the things which we loue.* Loue
makes louers felowes,& equalls ; *who is
weak* (ſayth S.Paul) *with whome I am not
weake?*he might haue ſaid likewiſe:who
is

is poore, with whome I am not poore?
for loue made him like those whome he
loued. Yf then thou loue the poore frō
thy hart, thou shalt be trulie partaker
of their pouertie,& become as poore,as
they. But yf thou loue the poore, witnesse this thy loue,by going ofte amōg
them:be glad to see them in thine owne
house, and visit them in theirs; keep
them companie willingly, reioyce that
theyapproache nigh thee in the church,
in the street,and els where. Be poore in
talking,speaking,and conuersing,cour-
teouslie amonge them : but be riche-
handed, giuing them liberallie of thy
goods,as hauing more abundance.

6. Wilt thou goe one steppe farther,
my Philotheus,cōtent not thy self to be
poore,but procure to be poorer thē the
poore theselues. And how may that be?
The seruant is inferiour to his maister:
be thou then a seruant of the poore:goe
and attend on them in their beds, when
they are sick, I say attend on them, and
serue them with thine owne hands : be
their cooke thy self, and at thine owne
expences, be their landresse, and blea-
cher of their linnen. O Philotheus, this
man-

maner of seruice, is more glorious then
a kingdome. I cannot sufficiently admire the ardent affection , with which
this councell was put in practize by S.
Lewes, one of the greatest kings vnder
the sonne, & I meane, one oft the greatest in all kind of greatnes & excellece.
He waited oft times at the table of the
poore, whome he nourished , & caused
three poore men almost euerie day, to
dine at his owne table , & eat him self
often the reliques of their potage, with
such a loue as the like hath not beene
seene. When he visited the hospitalls of
sick folks (which he did verie often)
he serued them ordinarilie , which
had the most horrible and loathsome
diseases, as lazers, cankers, and such
like : and performed all this seruice
vnto them bare headed , and kneeling
on the ground , considering and res-
pecting in their persons, the *Saueour*
of the world: and cherrishing them
with as tender a loue, as any sweete mother could doe her he child . *Saint*
Elisabeth daughter to the king of Hun-
gary , often times put her self amongst
the poore , and for her recreation,
                                            some-

sometimes would apparell her self like
a poore woman amongst her ladies,
saying vnto them, yf I were poore,thus
would I attire my self. O good God
(Philotheus) how poore were this
Prince and princesse,amidst their royall
riches, and how riche were they, in
this their admirable pouertie!Blessed be
they that be poore in this fort, for vnto
them belongeth the kingdome of heauen. *I was hungry, and you gaue me to eate:*
I was naked and you clothed me; possesse you
the kingdom prepared for you, from the foun-
dation of the world: will the king of the
poore, and of kings, say at his great
doomes day.

7. There is no man but vpon some
occasion, one time or other, shall stand
in need of some commoditie. Sometimes comes a guest whome we ought,
or would entertaine royallie, and for
the present,we haue nothing to receaue
him in good fort withall; Sometime
our best apparell is in one place, and
we our selues in another, where occasion requireth, that we should goe better clothed. It happens another time,
that all the wines of our cellars doe
worke,

worke, and loose their taſt: ſo that there
remaine onely lowe, and greene wines,
for our owne vſe. Another time in a
long iourney, we light vpon ſome cot-
tage to lodge in, where all things are
lacking; wher there is nether table, nor
chaire, nor bed, nor chamber, nor anie
to ſerue vs. To be brief, it is a verie ordinarie thinge, to ſtand oft times in
need of ſome neceſſarie commoditie,
be we otherwiſe neuer ſo rich; well,
this is to be poore in effect, and in verie
deed, when we lack theſe things. Philotheus, reioice in ſuch occaſions, and
accept them with all thy hart, and ſuffer
them cheerfully, for Gods loue.

8. When ſome inconuenience be-
falles that empoueriſheth thee, ether of
a great deale or of a litle, as tempeſt, fire,
inundations, dearth, theeues, proceſſe,
perſecution, or the like, ô then Philotheus is the time indeed; topractize pouertie of ſpirit, receauing with mildnes
this loſſe & diminiſhing of our wealth,
and accommodating our ſelues, patiently and conſtantly, to this vnexpected
empoueriſhement. Eſau preſented him
ſelfe to his father, with his hands all
hairie,

hairie, and so did Iacob likewise : but
because the haire that couered Iacobs
hands, stuck not to his owne skin , but
to his gloues , one might haue taken
away the haire from him without hurting him: but because the haire of Esaus
hands, grew vpon his owne skinne, and
not vpon his gloues , being hairie by
nature , he that would haue endeuoured
to pull of his haire, should haue put him
to paine and torment, and he would haue striued and sweat to defend him self
from fleaing. When our riches cleaue
to our verie soule , if a tempest , if theeues , if a catch pole do but snatch anie
peece from vs , what complaints, what
stirres, what impatience presently shew
we ? But when our riches cleaue but
onely to the care that God would haue
vs take, and do not stick to our hart , if
they seece vs , and despoile vs of them,
we do not fall beside our selues therfore, nor loose the quiet and tranquillitie of mind. This is the difference betwixt beasts, and men as touching their
clothes : for beasts clothes, stick to
their fleshe , and mens apparel, are only
cast about them , so that they may be
put

put of and one at their pleasure, without anie paine or inconuenience.

How to practize richnes of Spirit, in reall pouertie.

CHAPTER 16.

1. **B**Vt if thou chance to be verilie poore in deed, Philotheus, O God, be then poore likewise in spirit : make a virtue of necessitie, and value this precious pearle of pouertie at the high rate and estimation which it deserueth. The lustre therof is not discouered perfectlie in this world, and yet neuer the lesse it is exceeding rich and beautifull.

2. Be patient, because thou art in good companie. Our Lord, and our Ladie, the Apostles, so manie Saināts, both men, and wemen, haue been exceeding poore, though they had meanes to be riche, yet they contemned riches. How manie great worldlinges haue there been, and are, who euen with mightie contradictions and
resistan-

resistance of their frinds, haue endeuo-
ued, and doe intend with incomparable care, to find out holie pouertie, and
enioy her companie in cloisters and
hospitalls? Witnesse S. Alexis, holy Paula, holy Paulinus, S. Angela, and a
thousand others; And behold heere,
Philotheus, holie pouertie more fauourable to thee then to them, she presenteth her self vnto thee of her owne ac-
cord; thou hast mett with her, without
searching painfully after her: embrace
her then as a deare frind of Iesus Christ,
who was borne, who liued, and died in
pouertie, pouertie was his nurse, and his
hostesse all his life.

3. Thy pouertie Philotheus, hath
two great priuiledges, by which she
can make thee riche in merits and de-
sarts. The first is, that she came not vnto thee at thy owne inuiting, or election, but by the only will and choice
of God, who made thee poore, without
any concourse of thy owne will. That
then, which we receaue purely from
Gods holy will, is allway most acceptable vnto him, prouided that we receaue it cheerfully; and for loue and reuerence

rence of his holy will; where there is
leaft of our owne will, there is moft of
Gods pleafure : the fimple and pure
acceptance of Gods will, maketh patience moft excellent, and meritorious.

4.   The fecond priuiledge of thy pouertie is, that it is a pouertie poore in
deed, and in good earneft. Pouertie
that is commended, cherrished, efteemed, fuccoured, affifted, & is not altogether poore, it hath yet fome riches
in it. But pouertie which is defpifed,
efchewed, reuiled, reproached, and
abandoned of all, is pouertie in deed.
Well fuch is ordinarilie the pouertie of
worldlie men, for becaufe they are not
poore by their owne choice, but by
meer neceffitie, men make no great account of their pouertie, and making
no great account of it, their pouertie
is poorer then the pouertie of religious
men : notwithftanding that religious
pouertie, hath a verie great excellencie, and much more recommendable,
by reafon of the vowe and holie intention, for which it was chofen.

5.   Complaine not then (my deare
                    P   Phi.

Philotheus) of thy pouertie. For we
cōplaine not, but of that which displeaseth vs: and yf pouertie displease thee,
thou art no more poore in spirit, but
riche in affection.

6. Be not discōforted, that then thou
art not so well souccoured and assisted,
as is meete and requisite, for in this wat
consisteth the excellence of pouertie. To haue a desire to be poore indeed, and yet not willinge to haue incommoditie, is an ouer-great ambition : for that were to be willing, to
haue the honour of pouertie, and the
commoditie of riches.

7. Be not ashamed to be poore, or
to aske almes for Gods sake. Receaue
with humilitie that, which shalbe giuen
thee, and take the denially meekly and
quietlie. Remember often the voyage,
which our Ladie made into Egypte, to
carie thether her deere childe, and how
much contempte, pouertie, and miserie she was driuen to suffer. If thou liue
thus, thou shalt be most riche amidest
thy pouertie.

Of

Of frindship : and first of fond , and
fruictlesse frindship.

CHAPTER   17.

1. LOVE hath the first and chiefe
place among all the passions of
the soule: it is the king of all the
motions of the hart, it changeth all the
other into it self, and maketh vs alltogether such, as is the thing which we loue:
take heed then, O Philotheus, that thou
loue no bad thing, for then thou thy self
wilt become altogether bad. Now of all
loue, frindship is the most dãgerous; because other loue may be built vpon cõmunication, hardly can one haue frindship with another, without participa-
ting of his qualities and conditions.

2. All loue is not amitie or frindship
for one may loue, and not be beloued,
and thẽ is there loue, and not frindship:
because frindshippe, is a mutuall loue,
and yf the loue be not mutuall, it is nôt
frindshippe. Neither is it enough that
it be mutuall, but the parties that loue
one another, must know and acknowledge the affection that is betweene
them : for yf they know it not, they
P 2   loue

haue loue one to the other, but not friodshippe. There muſt be alſo ſome ſort of communication betwene them, for that is the ground of amitie : and according to the diuerſitie of communications, frindſhippe alſo is diuerſe : & communications are diuerſe, according to the diuerſitie of goods which they do mutually cõmunicate : yf they be falſe, vaine, and forged goods , then is the frindſhippe falſe and forged : yf they be good indeed, thẽ is the frindſhippe true; and the more excellent the goods communicated be, the more excellent is the frindſhippe. The honnie is beſt, that is gathered frõ the bloſſoms of the ſweeteſt and excellenteſt floures : and as there is honie in Heraclea a Prouince of Põtus, which is poiſonous , and maketh them ſenceleſſe that taſt of it , becauſe it is gathered from the venemous hearbe Aconitum ; which groweth in great abundance in that countrie : euen ſo frindſhipp grounded vpon the cõmunication of falſe and vitious things, is altogether falſe and wicked frindshippe.

3. The cõmunication of carnal pleaſures, is a mutuall propenſion & inticement

ment to such delights : which can no
more beare the name of frindshippe a-
mong men, then the self same cōmunicatiō of pleasures among asses & horses.
And yf there were no other cōmunicatiō in marriage, there were also no frindshippe at all: but because beside that cō-
munication of those delights, necessarie
for the procreation of children, there is
also in the estate of marriage, mutuall &
indiuisible cōmunicatiō of life, labour,
goods, affectiōs, & of indissoluble faith
& loyaltie, therefore is the loue of marriage a trew and holy frindshippe.

4 Frindshipp grounded vpō the com-
municatiō of sensuall pleasures , is verie
grosse, & vnworthie the name of frindshippe , as also is that which is founded
vpon friuolous and vaine virtues, which
depend only of the iudgemēt of the sence. I call those pleasures sensuall which
principally & immediatly are receaued
by the operations & actiōs of the exteriour sences of the bodie , as is the beholding of faire beautie, the hearing of
sweet voices, touching daintie bodies,&
the like. I call friuolous virtues, certaine
abilities & vaine qualities, which feeble

P 3   and

and ignorant witts call virtues, and perfections. Harken to the greater part of
maidens, women, & young folk, they
will not faile to terme such a gentleman
wondrons virtuous, and endewed with
great perfections, because he danceth
well, he playeth well at all games, he
goeth decently apparelled, he singeth
wel, he discourseth well, he is of a cour-
tely behaueour. And iesting wits esteeme him most virtuous amongst them,
that is the gteatest scoffer. But as al other
things which depend on the corporall
sences of men, so also these amities,
which belong to thē, are rightly termed
sensuall, vaine, & friuolous, & deserue
rather the name of follie, or fancie, then
of frindshipe and amitie. Such are ordinarilie the amities of youg folke, which
respect and affect a trimme bearde, faire
lock, or goodly tramells of haire, louely
lookes, smiling eyes, gay apparell, idle
behaueour, & fond pratling: frindships
only fitte for the greeue age of those
louers, whose virtue is but yet penn-fea-
thered, & whose iudgemēt is yet in blos-
some: & such amities, as they are slightly
grounded, so they lightlie passe away, &
                                    melt

melt like snow in the sunne.

Of loue, and loue toyes.
CHAPTER 18.

1. WHEN these foolish amities passe among persons of diuerse sex, without pretence of mariage, they be called rightly loue-toyes: for being but certaine abortiue, or vntimely images, or rather shadowes of amitie, they deserue not the name of true loue or frindshippe, for their incoparable vanitie & imperfection. And yet by them are the harts of men & women engaged, chained, and entangled the one with the other in vaine, vpon foolish affections, founded vpon these friuolous communications,& fond delights,of which but euen now I spake. And although these foolish loues do ordinarilie melt, and turne into carnall actions, and filthie lasciuiousnesse: yet that is not the first designe & intention of the persons betwixt whome they passe, for then they would no more be loue-toyes, but manifest and detestable leacherie. Some times manie yeares passe, ere any such

P 4   grosse

groſſe wickedneſſe happen betweene them, that are infected with this follie: and no action wilbe committed directlie contrarie to bodilie chaſtitie : the parties onelie contenting them ſelues to ſteepe their harts, (as it were) in wiſhes, deſires, ſighes, wooing ſpeaches, and ſuch like vanities, and all this for ſondrie motiues and pretenſions.

2. Some haue no other deſigne then onlie to ſatisſie theire harts in giuing and taking loue, folowing their amourous deſires : and theſe take not much conſideration in choice of their loues, but onlie folow the caſt of their owne inclination: ſo that at the firſt encounter of anie obiect pleaſing their humour, neuer examining the inward conditions, or qualities, of the partie, they will out of hand begin this friuolous communication of wanton loue, and thruſt them ſelues ſo farre into thoſe miſerable ſnares, from which afterward they ſhall haue much a doe to deliuer them ſelues. Others ſuffer the ſelues to walke that trade of vanitie, eſteeming it no ſmall glorie, to take & linck harts together by loue : and theſe
persons,

perſons, making election of their loues
for glories ſake, ſet vp their ſnares , and
ſpread their ſayles, in great , eminent,
rare, and illuſtrious places.   Others are
caried away both by theire amourous
inclination , and vaine glorie iointlie:
for though theire hart is alltogether
inclined to loue, yet will they not talke
of it, without ſome aduātage of glorie.
Theſe amities are all naught, fooliſh, &
vaine : naught, becauſe they end and die
at length in the ſinne of the fleſh , and
ſteale away the noble paſſion of loue ,
and conſequentlie, the hart from God,
from the maried wife, & from the huſ-
band, to whome it was due; fooliſhe, becauſe they haue neither reaſon , nor
foundation: vaine, becauſe they yeld no
profit , nor honour, nor contentment :
nay contrarilie, they looſe time, ſtaine
honour, and giue no other pleaſure, but
onely a vaine deſire to hope for they
know not what, and pretēd, they vnderſtand not wherfore ; for it ſeemeth ſtill
to theſe baſe & feeble ſpirits, that there
is I wot not what, to be deſired in the
teſtimonies & ſignes which are ſhewed
them of mutuall loue : but they cannot

tell what it is: so that their defire is end-
leffe, & hath no bound, goinge ftill on-
ward, and vexinge their harts with perpetuall diftafts, iealoufies, fufpicions,
and difquietnes.

3. S. Gregory Nazianzen, writinge
againft vaine wemen, & loue-wantons,
fayth merueilous well of this matter; a
litle parcell of the much, that he directlie fpeaketh againft wemen (but may as
directly be applied againft men) is this
that foloweth : *Thy naturall beautie is fuf-*
ficient for thy husband : but if it be for many
men, like to a nett fpread out for a flock of foo-
lish birds, what will become of it ? he will be
pleasing to thee, that hath pleased him felf in
thy beauty : thou wilt render him glaunce, for
glaunce, one wanton looke for another : foone
after will folow prettie fimles, and often ti-
mes, languishing loue-tearmes shot forth at
randome, for an entrance, or firft begining: but
foone after wilt thou paffe to plaine & mani-
fest idle talke. Take heed ô my prating tongue,
to tell what ufually folowes: yet will I fay this
one truth ; nothinge of all thofe things which
young men and maidens, fay, and do together
in thefe foolish paffetimes, is exempted from
great and ftinginge motions of the flesh ; all
                                        the

the *tricks of wanton loue, are lincked one with another and do folow one another, euen as one peece of iron drawne by the load-stone, draweth diuers other peeces likewise after it.* O how well saith this great and godlie bishope, what doeft thou intend to doe? to make loue? but no bodie maketh Ioue voluntarilie, that doth not receaue it neceffarilie. He that catcheth in this fport, is likewise caught him felf. The hearbe Aproxis receaueth fire fo foone as it commeth neer it : our harts do the like ; fo foone as they fee a hart inflamed with loue for them, they are prefentlie inflamed with loue for it. Well (will another fay) I will take but a litle of this flame of loue. Alas thou deceaueft thy felf, this loue-fire is more actiue then thou imagineft, when thou makeft account to haue receaued but one fparckle therof into thy hart, thou wilt be amazed to fee that in a moment, it will haue feafed vpon thy whole hart, and burnt to afhes all thy refolutions, and turnd thy reputation into fmoke. The wifeman crieth out : *who will haue comp sfion vpon an enchanter, ftung by a ferpeut ?*

I alfo

I also crie after him : O fooles and sen-
celeffe harts, thinck you to charme loue, and tame it as you lift your felues?
you would play and dallie with it, but
it will bite and fting you to the hart : &
what thinck you then will befpoken
of you? euerie one will deferuedly mock
and fcoffe at you, that would needs vn-
tertake to enchaunt loue, that vpó a falfe affurance, would put into your bofome fo dangerous a fnake, which hath
enuenomed your foule, and poifoned
your honour and eftimation.

4. O good God! how miferable a
blindnes is it, to trifle away in this fort,
vpon fo friuolous an aduantage, the
principall iewell of our foule? Philotheus, God careth not for man, but in
regard of his foule: nor for the foule, but
in regard of the will: nor for the will,
but in regard of the excellent acts of
loue. Alas how much want we of that
ftore of loue which we need? the defect
of our loue to God-ward is infinite, and
yet in the meane time, wretches that
we be, we lauish it out and mifpend it
riotoufly vpó vaine & friuolous things,
as if we had enough, and too much to
                                    fpare.

spare, But consider that our great God,
who hath reserued to him self the loue
of the soule, onlie for an acknowledgement of our creation, conseruation, &
redemption : will exact a verie straight
account, for all these foolishe expences
of so pretious riches : if he make so rigourous an examination of idle words,
what will he do of idle, impertinent,
foolish, and pernicious loues?

·5. The Walnutte tree endamageth the
vines and fields where it is planted : for
being so great a tronk, it draweth all the
fat & sappe of the ground where' it groweth, and maketh it afterward vnable
to nourish other plāts: the leaues therof
are so stuffed together, that they make
too large and thick a shadow; and allureth trauailers vnto it, who to beat
downe the nuttes, spoile & tread downe
all round about it. These wanton loues
doe the verie same harme to the soule :
for they do whollie possesse the soule,
& so vehemently draw all the other motions vnto it, that she is not able to employ her powers in any other good work
their entertainments, communicatiōs,
parlies, and amourous toyes, are so frequent,

quent, that all their goldē time, all their
good leasure is spent in them; & finallie
they draw so manie temptations, distractions, suspicions and other such badde
adherents, that the whole hart is tired
& trampled therwith. To be brieffe, these wanton loues doe not onely thrust
out of dores the heauenly loue of God,
but with all bannish the feare and reuerence of his maiestie, and weaken the
spirit, impaire their reputation: they are
in a word the may-game and pastime of
courtes, but the mischief, destruction,
aud pestilence of harts.

Of trew friendship. CHAP. 19.

1. L OVE euerie one (Philotheus)
according as charitie commandeth, & that with as feruēt a loue
as thou canst : but haue frindship onely
with those, with whome thou maist cōmunicate in good and virtuous things:
& the more exquisite the virtues be, in
which this mutuall commnnication is
made, the perfecter will the frindshippe
be , that is grounded theron. Yf the cō-
munication between you , be in sciēces
& learning, the frindship grounded thereon,

reon, is indeed verie commendable: &
more comendable, if the comunication
be in virtues, with prudence, iuftice, and
difcretio. But if the mutuall comunication, be exercifed in the acts of charitie,
deuotion, & true Chriftian perfection,
O God, how pretious & excellent will
this frindship be? it wilbe excellent becaufe it cometh fro God, excellent becaufe it goeth to God, excellet becaufe
it is placed in God, excellent becaufe it
shall laft euerlaftingly with God. How
good is it to loue vpo earth, as they loue
in heaue: to learne to cherish one another in this world, as we shall doe eternallie in the next. I fpeak not heere of
the fimple loue of charitie, for that muft
be borne vnto all men, but of fpirituall
frindshippe, by which two, or three, or
manie foules, do comunicate their de-
uotio, their fpirituall affectios, & make
the felues to be but one fpirit in diuerfe
bodies. Such happie foules may iuftly
fing; *Behold how good a thing it is, and how
plzafaunt for brethren to dwell togeather.* For
the delicious balme of deuotion, di-
ftilleth from one hart to the other,
thorough continuall participation;
in fo

in so much that it may be sayd, that
God hath powred out vpon this frindship, his blessing and life for euer. All
other frindships, are but shadowes in
comparison of this: their bonds be but
chaines of glasse or iette, in comparison of this great bond of holie deuo-
ton, whose lincks are all of gold.

2. Make no other frindship but
this, I meane of those amities, which
thou makest anew heerafter: for thou
must not therfore forsake, or despise
the frindship, and amitie which either
the bond of nature, or the obligation
of fore-passed duties do bind thee vnto
toward thy parents, knisfolks, benefa-
ctours, neighbours, and others.

3. Manie peraduenture will say vnto
thee, that we should haue no kind of
particular frindship or affection, because it distracteth the mind, occupieth
the hart, engendreth enuie and emulation: but they are deceaued in their aduise, for hauing seene in the writings
of manie deuout authours, that particular amities, and excessiue affections,
doe infinit harme vnto religious persons, they imagin therfore, that it is so
with

with the reft of the world. But there is
great difference between both cafes.
For feeing that in a wel ordered mona-
fterie, the common intent and defigne
of all the religious, is to tend to true
deuotion: it is not requifite to make
any particular and priuate communications, of their end, and meanes to attaine vnto it: leaft fearching in particular, for that which is common to them
all, they fall from particularities to par-
tialities. But for thofe which liue in the
world, and defire to embrace true virtue: it is neceffarie to vnite them felues
together, by a holie frindship, to back
and encourage one another, to help, &
fupport them felues naturallie, for the
obtaining of all pietie and goodnes.
And as they that go vpó plaine ground,
need not to be ledd by the hád, though
they which go vpon craggie rocks, or
flipperie wayes, doe hold one by the
other, to walke more fteddilie, and fe-
curely: fo they that be in religion, ftand
in no need of particular frindships, but
they that walk in the flipperie pathes of
the world, muft of neceffitie haue fome
frind or companion thereby, to fuccour

and

and affure one another amongft fo manie daungerous paffages which they are
to go thorough. In the world all afpire
not to the fame end, all are not of one
mind: one muft then doubtleffe withdraw himfelf from fome, and ioine himfelf to other, and fo make frindship according to the pretention of the end
which he intendeth : This particulari-
tie, maketh a partialitie indeed, but a
holie partialitie which maketh no di-
uifion, but only betwixt good and bad,
sheep & goates, bees and drones, which
is a feparation that is moft neceffarie
for our foules.

4. No man can denie, but that our
bleffed Lord with a more fweeter, tender, & particular amitie loued *S.* Iohn,
Lazarus, Martha, and Magdalen, then
he did others of his frinds and acquaintace, for the fcripture teftifieth fo much.
All men know that *S.* Peter tenderlie
loued *S.* Mark & *S.* Petronilla: & *S.* Paul
his Timothee, & *S.* Tecla, *S.* Gregory
Nazianzen boafteth a hundred times, of
the incoparable frindship which he had
with *S.* Bafil the great, & defcribeth it in
this manner: It feemed that in either of
vs there

vs.there was but one foule dwelling in
two bodies : for althoughe you muſt
not beleeue thoſe philoſophers, who
ſayd that al things were in euery thing:
yet of vs two you may beleeue, that we
were both of vs in each one of vs,& one
with in the other: we had both of vs the
ſame pretēſion, to exerciſe virtue, & to
applie all the enterprizes & deſignes of
our life to future hopes, departing in
this manner out of this trāſitory world,
euen before we came to die corpo-
rallie it S. Auguſtin teſtifietht that S.
Ambroſe ſoued S Monica exceedinglie,
for the rare virtues which he marked in
her, & that ſhe likewiſe eſteemed of S.
Ambroſe, as of an Angel of God. But
I am too blame to hold thee ſo lōg in a
matter that is ſo cleere S. Hierom S.
Auguſtin, S. Gregory, S. Bernard, & all
the greateſt & deūouteſt ſeruāts of God,
had moſt particular amities,with outany
breach at al of their perfection. S. Paul
reproaching the ill behaueour of the
Gētils,accuſeth thē,that they were people without al affectiō,to witt, that they
had no true frindſhip. And S.Tho. wirh
al other good Philoſophers cōfeſſe,that
frind-

frindship is an excellent morall virtue: and he and they speak of particular frindship, since they all say that perfect frindshipp cannot be extended to manie persons: so that perfection doth not consist in hauing no particular amitie, but in hauing none but good, virtuous, and holie.

The difference betwixt true and vaine frindship.
CHAPTER 20.

1. **B**Vt now marke an excellent & necessarie aduerticement, my Philotheus; The bonny of Heraclea (of which we spake before) which is so venimous, is like the other which is wholsome, so that there is daunger to take the one for the other, or to mingle them both together; for the goodnes of the one, would not hinder the harme which might come by the other. He must be vpon his garde, that will not be deceaued in these frindships, principallie when they are contracted betwixt persons of diuers sex,

vnder

vnder what pretence ſoeuer: for the diuel oftentimes chaungeth one frindſhip into the other. They beginne by
virtuous loue, but yf they be not verie
warie, fond and idle loue will firſt mingle it ſelf, then ſenſuall loue, and afterward carnall and fleſhly loue. Nay there is daunger in ſpirituall loue, yf one
be not verie diſcreet: though in this it
be more difficultie for the diuel to co-
ſen vs in the change, becauſe the puritie and milk-white cleannes of this loue
diſcouereth verie eaſilie the filth that
ſatan offereth to mingle with it: and
therfore when he enterprizeth to deceaue vs in this, he doeth it more craftilie, and maketh impure affections to
ſlide into vs, almoſt without our notice
or feeling.

2. Thou mayſt diſcerne worldly frindſhip, from holie and virtuous amitie,
as the Heraclæan honnie, is knowne
from the wholſome: the honnie of He-
raclæa is ſweeter to taſt, then the ordinary honnie is, becauſe of the luſcious
iuice of the Aconite, for whence it is
gathered: and ſo worldlie amitie floweth with a ſtreame of honnie words,
bru-

bringeth alwayś abundāce of paſſiona-
te ſpeeches,& affectionate commendations, drawne from beautie, from well
fauourednes, frō graciouś behaueour,
and other ſenſuall qualities : but holie
frindſhip, ſpeaķeth ſimplie, plainlie, &
francklie, & commendeth nothing but
Gods grace & viŕtue, the onely foun-
datiō vpō which herſelfis groūded. The
honnie of Heraclea ſwallowed downe,
cauſeth a dizzineſſe in the heade:& falſe frindſhip breedeth a giddineś in the
mind, making men to ſtaggerin chaſtitie,to ſtūble in deuotion, trāsporting
true and holie affection, to daintie languiſhing lookes, ſenſuall allurements,
diſordered ſighes, pettie cōplaints that
they are not beloued, to alluring geſtures ofloue termes, pourſuite of kiſ-
ſes, & other too familiar and vnciuil fauours,which are aſſured and vndoubted
ſignes of a neer ouerthrow of honeſtie.
But as for holie frindſhip, it hath no
eyes but ſimple, chaſt, & ſhamefaſt: no
entertaniments or embracements, but
ſuch as be pure & francklie offered in
ſight of all men; no ſighes, but forhea-
uen; no fauours, but ſpirituall;no complaints,

plaints, but when God is not loued ; infallible and euident tokens of honeft and chaft loue. The honnie of Heraclea troubleth the fight , and this worldlie frindship blindeth the iudgement , fo that they which be infected therwith, thinck they doe well, when they doe ill, and efteeme their excufes and pretexts to be true and irreprocheable reafons ; they feare the light , and loue darknes. But holie frindship hath a cleere eye fight, and neuer hideth her felf , but appeareth willinglie before honeft perfos. In fine the honnie of Heraclea, leaueth a bitter relish in the mouth : and fo falfe and wanton frindships, turne to carnall wordes, & fleshlie requefts, and, if they receaue the deniall, into iniuries, cauilles, flaunders, fadnes, confufions, iealoufies, which oft times prouoke wildnes & madnes of mind. But chaft & true frindship, is allways alike honeft, mannerlie, amiable, and neuer changeth, but into a perfecter and purer vnion of fpirits, and is a liuelie image of the blefled frindship vfed in heauen.

3. Saint Gregorie Nazianzen fayeth that the crie of the Peacock , when he

she-

sheweth his starrie-wheeled taile, prouoketh the peahennes to lust: when we
see a man play the peacock, deck, and
trimme vp him self, and then come to
parlie and pratle with a woman without
pretence of marriage, without, doubt
it is but to prouoke her to dishonestie,
and a chast woman should stoppe her
eares, to the end she might not heare
this peacoks ill fauoured noise, nor the
voice of this false enchaunter, who
would subtillie enchaunt and charme
her soule: but the woman that harkeneth, ô God, what an ill signe it is, that
the ouerthrow of her reputation is at
hand?

4. Young folke, which vse sweete
lookes, wanton gestures, secret cour-
tings, or speake words which they
would not haue heard or marked by their
fathers, mothers, husbands, wiues, or
spirituall maisters: giue sufficient witnesse, that they deale about other matters, then of honour and conscience.
Our blessed lady was troubled in thought
when she saw an Angel in a mans likenes: because she was all alone, and he
gaue her extraordinarie, though heauenly

nenly praifes. O *Saueour* of the world, puritie feareth an Angel in the shape of a man, and why should not impuritie and frailtie, feare a man, though he come in shape of an Angel, when he praifeth her with humane and fenfuall commendations.

Aduices and remedies againſt naughty
frindships. Chap. 21.

1. BVt what remedie againſt this wicked feminarie of foolish loues, and wanton impurities? As foone as euer thou feeleſt thy felf furprized with this infection, turne thy felf away immediatly, and with an abſolute deteſtation of this vanitie, runne vnto the facred Croſſe of our Sauiour, and take his crowne of thornes to put about thy hart, to the end theſe litle foxes approach no nigher.

2. Take heed of coming vnto any kind of compoſition with this falſe enemie; fay not: I will giue him the hearing, but will do nothing that he shall will me; I will lend mine eares vnto him, but denie him my hart. O no Phi-

Q lo-

Iotheus, for Gods loue be rigorous and
ftiffe in thefe occafions. The hart and
the eare maintaine one another: and as
it is impoffible to ftoppe a ftrong ftrea-
me, that taketh his defcent from a fteep
mountaine: fo it is hard to hinder, that
the loue which entreth into the eare,
make not likewife his entrie into the
hart. Alcmæon fayd, that Goats do
breath by the eares, and not by the no-
fthrills: true it is that Ariftotle denieth
it, and for my part I know nothing
therof: yet this I am affured, that our
hart breatheth by the eare; and that as
it afpireth, and fendeth foorth his thoughts by the mouthe, fo it refpireth and
taketh breath by the eare, by which it
receaueth other mens thoughts. Let vs
then keep our eares diligently from the
ayre of foolish words, leaft it infect our
hart. Harken not then to any kind of
wanton motion or prepofition, vnder
what pretext fo euer it be made, onely in
this cafe it makes no matter, to be vn-
courteous and vnmannerlie.

3. Remember that thou haft vowed
thy hart to God, and facrifized all thy
loue to him, it should then be facriledge

10

to take one dram therof frō him : rather
offer it againe & againe vnto him, by a
thousand hartie resolutions & protesta-
tions; and keeping thy self close within
thē, as Deer within theire thickets, call
vpon God ; he will help thee, his loue
will take thine into his protection, that
thy loue may liue for him only.

4. But yf thou be alreadie ensnared
in the netts of these foolish loues : O
God what difficultie will it be to shift
thy self out ? Present thy self before the
diuine maiestie, acknowledge in his
presence, the greatnes of thy miserie,
frailtie, and vanitie. Then with the greatest force that thy hart is able to make,
detest these loues, which thou hast be-
gunn, abiure the vaine profession, which
thou hast made of them ; renounce all
the promises made or receaued : and
with a firme and resolute will, determine
in thy hart, and resolue thy self, neuer
any more, to enter into these fond di-
sportes, and toyish entertainments of
wanton loue.

5. Yf thou couldst withdraw thy self
from the obiect, it were an excellent
remedie. For as they that haue been

bitten by serpents , cannot easilie be
cured in the presence of them which
haue beene other time hurt with the
same biting : so the person which is bitt
with loue, shall haue much a doe to be
healed of this passion , so long as he is
nigh the other, which is hurt with the
same sting. Chaunge of place is a soueraigne remedie to appease and allay, the
tormenting heats of griefe and loue.
The boy, of whome S. Ambrose , speaketh in his second booke of penance,
hauing made a long voyage , returned
altogether freed and deliuered from his
foolish loues , in which he was before entangled , and became so chaunged , that his fond sweete hart meeting
him , and saying , knowest thou not
me ? I am the same that I was. I marrie
answered he , but I am not the same
that I was : his absence had brought
him , to this fortunate mutation. And
Saint Augustin witnesseth , that to mitigate the grief which he suffered for
the death of his frind, he withdrew him
self from Tagasta , where his frind died,
and came to Carthage.

6. But he that cannot withdraw him
self,

felf, what muft he doe? he muft abfolutely cutt off all particular conuerfation, all fecret familiaritie, all amiable
glaunces of the eyes, all dalliyng fmi-
les, and generally all fort of communications, and baytes, or inticements
which may nourish this fulphurous &
fmokie fire. Or at leaft, yf he be forced
to fpeak and talk with the partie, let
him in a round, rough, and refolute proteftation, declare the eternall and irreuocable diuorcement, that is for euer
fworne between them : I crie as loud
as I can to euerie one that is fallen into
this miferable thraldome of wanton
loue, that he cutt, breake, and rent them
afunder, and not ftand dreaming to vn-
rippe, or vnfewe thefe foolish amities:
they muft cutt, and not ftande to vn-
loofe the knotts, break them I fay, or
cutt them, becaufe cordes, and ftrings
are nothing worth. One muft not be
fparing, or courteous, towards a loue,
which is fo contrarie to the loue of
God.

7. But when I haue broken the
chaine of this infamous bondage, there
will yet remaine vnto me fome fcarres
fome

some marks, and prints of the slauish
chaynes and shackles wherwith I was
bound ; they wilb stick still emprinted
in my feet, that is in my affections. No
my Philotheus, care not, they will not
remaine long yf thou conceaue as great
a detestation of thy sinne, as it deserueth : for so thou shalt neuer be shaken
with any motion , but onely this motion of an extreame horrour of this infamous loue, and of all things that depende of it:and thou shalt remaine free
from all other affection to the obiect
which thou hadst abandoned, sauing
onely the affection of charitie, purely for
Gods cause. But yf for the imperfectió
of thy repentáce, there shall yet remaine
in thy soule any naughtie inclinations:
procure for thy soule a solitarie ermita-
ge,as before I haue taught thee; and retire thy self thether, the oftenest that
thou canst ; and by a thousand iterated
resolutiós of spirit,renounce all thy bad
inclinations, reiect them with all thy
forces ; read holie bookes more then
thou wast woont, goe to confession
oftener, & cómunicate more frequent-
lie : cóferre humblie and plainlie all thy
                                              sug-

suggeftions and temptations,which arriue vnto thy foule in this behalfe, with thy fpirituall maifter, yf thou canft, or at leaft with fome faithfull and prudent frind. And doubt not, but God will fett thee free from all paffions, fo that thou perfeuer faithfully in thy good exercifes.

8. Ah (wilt thou fay vnto me) but will it not be ingratitude, to break fo violently an old frindship? O bleffed ingratitude which maketh vs acceptable vnto God! Nay in the name of God, Philothee, this wilbe no ingratitude, but an infinite benefit,which thou shalt doe to the partie that loues thee: for in breaking thine owne bonds, thou burfteft a funder alfo theirs, in as much they were common to you both: and though at that hower, the other partie feeth not the happines, yet he will acknowledge it foone after,and iointlie with thee, will fing for thankfulnes to almightie God: *O Lord thou haft broken my bonds, I will facrifice to thee a facrifice of praife, and wil call vpon thy holy name.*

Q 4　　　　　*Other*

*Other aduices of the same subiect,
of fond amities.*

Chapter 22.

1. I HAVE yet a note of importance
to giue thee touching this self fame matter. Frindship requireth
great communication betweene frinds,
otherwise it will nether grow, nor continew. It happeneth oftentimes that
iointlie with this communication of
frindship, other communications doe
passe vnseene, and vnfelt from one hart
to another, by a mutuall infusion and
enterchange of affections, inclinations
and impressions. This happeneth especiallie, when we greatlie esteeme of the
partie whome we loue : for then we
open our hart in such sort to his amitie,
that withall, these inclinations and impressions, enter verie easilie altogether,
be they good, or bad. Verelie the Bees
that store vp honnie in Heraclea, doe
search nothing els but honnie, and yet
togeather with the honnie, they suck
vp vnawares, the venemous qualitie of
                                    the

the Aconite, vpon which they make
their haruest.

2. O my Philothee, in this cafe,
practize the wordes which the Saueour of our foules was woont to fay,
as the auncient doctours haue taught
vs : be good bankers, or good exchan-
gers of monie : that is to fay, receaue
not falfe mony with the good, nor bafe
gold with fyne: feparate the good from
the bad, and the vile from that which
is precious. For there is no man almoft,
but hath fome imperfection : and what
reafon is there, to receaue the ftaines
and imperfections of a frind, togeather
with his frindship ? We muft loue him
indeed, notwithftanding his imperfection, but we muft nether loue, nor receiue his imperfection, for frindship requireth comunicatio of good, & not of
ill : wherfore as they that take grauel
out of the riuer Tajo in fpaine, feparate
the golden graines which they find, to
carie with them, and leaue the fand
vpon the shoare : fo in this comunication, euen of good and virtuous frind-
fhip, we muft feparate the gold of virtues, from the fand of imperfections,

and

and receaue thofe, and reiect thefe,
that they enter in no cafe into our foule.

3. S. Gregory Nazianzen recounteth,
that manie louing and admiring S. Bafil
the great, fuffered them felues fo farre to
be caried away with defire of imitating
him, that they fought to folow euen his
outward imperfections, as in his flowe
manner of fpeaking, with an abftract
and penfiue fpirit, in the fashion of his
beard, in his ftraunge manner of gate.
And we fee likewife, husbands, wiues,
children, and frinds, who hauing great
eftimation of their frinds, parents,
husbands, and wiues, do learne either
by condefcendence, or by imitation, a
thoufand fuch like humours, only by
the frequent comunication which they
haue one with another. Yet ought not
this to be done, for euerie one hath
naughtie inclinatiós enow of his owne,
without furcharging himfelf with other
mens faultes: and frindship doth not
onely, not require any fuch matter, but
contrariwife, it bindeth vs to help one
another mutuallie from thefe imperfections. We muft indeed meekly fuffer
our frinds in their imperfectiós, but we
muft

must not throw them into them, and much lesse pull them into our selues. I speak only of imperfections: for as for sinnes, we must neither beare them our selues, nor suffer them in our frinds.

4. It is either a naughtie, or a feeble frindship, to see our frind readie to perish, and not succour him; to see him readie to die of an impostume, & not to dare to launce it with the razor, of correction, so to saue his life: true & liuely amitie, cannot liue amongst sinne. They say the Salamandra, putteth out the fier in which she lieth: and so doth sinne destroy that frindship, wherin it lodgeth: yf it be a sinne that quicklie passeth, frindship will presently bannish it by correction: but yf it be a sinne that abideth and soiourneth in our frinds hart, then frindship soone perisheth, for it cannot subsist but vpō true virtue: and how much lesse then ought we to sinne our selues, for frindships sake. Thy frind is a foe, whē he would induce thee to sinn & he deseruedlie loseth all the priuiledges of frindship, that seeketh to destroy & dāne his frind. Nay it is one of the assured markes of false frindship, to see

it

it kept towards a vitious person, what sort of sinne soeuer it be, yf he whome we loue be vitious, without doubt our amitie is vitious : for since it cannot there be founded in true virtue, needs must it be grounded in some friuolous virtue or sensuall qualitie.

5. Felowship madefor temporall matters among merchants, is but a shadow of true frindship : for it is not made for the loue of men, but for the loue of gaine.

6. Finallie mark these two diuine sentences of the holie Ghost as two sure pillars, vpon which a Christian life is wholly to relie. The one of the wise man : *He that feareth God, shall find good frindship* : the other of the Apostle S. Iames: *The frindship of this world, is enemie to God.*

Of the exercises of exteriour mortification. CHAPTER 23.

1. THE authours that write of planting, and of husbandrie, tell vs that yf one write any word vpon

E

a found almond, and put it againe into
the shell, cloſing and wrapping it vp, &
ſo ſetting it : all the fruict which that
tree produceth, will haue the ſelf ſame
word engrauen vpon it. For my part
Philotheus, I could neuer allow of their
order and method, who to reforme a
man in ſpirituall life, begin with the
outward man, with their geſtures, with
apparell, & with haire. Me thincks the
contrarie order is more naturall, to begin with the interiour : *Be conuerted
vnto me* (ſayd God) *with all your hart.
My child giue me thy hart.* For the hart
being the fountaine of our actions,
they muſt needs be ſuch, as the hart is.
The diuine ſpouſe wooing as it were
the ſoule, *Place me* (ſayth he) *euen as a
ſeale vpon thy hart, euen as a ſeale vpon thy
arme :* For whoſoeuer hath Ieſus Chriſt
engraued and ſealed in his hart, will
quickly haue him in all his exteriour
actions. For this cauſe (my deare Philotheus) I haue deſired aboue all things,
to engraue and imprint in thy hart,
this ſacred word, *Liue Ieſus* : aſſu-
ring my ſelf, that ſo thy life, which
hath his beginning from the hart, as
aa

an almond-tree from its kernell, will
bring foorth all her actions, which are
her fruicts, engraued and superscribed
with that same word of saluation. And
as this sweet Iesus will liue in thy hart,
so will he liue in all thy gesture, and
behaueour, and will appeere in thine
eyes, in thy mouth, in thy hands, and
euen in thy haire, and thou wilt be then
able to say with Saint Paule: *I liue now,
not I; but Christ liueth in me.* To be
brief, he that hath gained the hart of a
man, hath gained the man him self
wholly.

2. But the same hart, by which we
would begin, requireth to be instru-
cted, how it should behaue and gouerne it self in exteriour occasions:
to the end men may not onely see deuotion, but wisdome also, and discretion in it: for this cause I will
lay downe vnto thee, a few brief aduices.

3. Yf thou art able to endure fasting, accustom thy self to fast some
times, beside the fast which holie
Churche enioineth; for so besides the
ordinarie effects of fasting, which are

to

to eleuate the spirit, to tame the
flesh, to practize virtue, to winne
greater recompence in heauen ; it is a
soueraigne meanes, to chaine vp the
deuouring monster of gluttonnie : and
to bridle the sensuall appetite, and
to keepe the bodie subiect and pliable to the lawe of the spirit. And although one fast not with extraordinarie rigour ; yet the enemie feareth vs, when he perceaueth we can
find in our hart to fast something.
Wednesdays, frydays, and saturdays,
are the dayes, in which the auncient Christians did exercise themselues in abstinence : take some of
them therfore to fast in, as much
as thy deuotion, and thy ghostlie
councellours discretion shall councell
thee.

4. I would willinglie say, as holie S.
Hierom sayd to the deuout ladie Læta:
*Long and immoderate fastings do much dis-
please me, especially in those that are yet tender in yeares.* I haue learned by experience, that the litle Asse being wearie
in his iourney, seeketh to go out of
the way : I meane, that young folk
being

being brought low through exceſſe of
faſting , doe fall willinglie to reſt and
delicateneſſe. The Deer runne ill in two
ſeaſons , when they are charged with
ouermuch fat , and when they become
ouer-leane. We are likewiſe moſt ſubiect to tentations , when our bodie is to
much pampered with daintie fare : and
when it is ouer weakened : for the one
exceſſe, maketh it inſolent with eaſe ,
and the other maketh it deſperate with
affliction ; And as we can ſcantlie beare
it , when it is vnweldie through fatnes :
ſo can it not beare vs, when it is enfee-
bled by leanneſſe . The back of this
moderation in faſting, in diſciplininge
in hairclothes , and other auſterities ,
make the beſt yeares of manie to be vnprofitable in the chiefe works of charitie ; (as it did in S. Bernard him ſelf,
who repented that he had vſed ouermuch auſteritie) the more vnreaſona-
blie they afflicted their bodies in their
beginning , the more were they con-
ſtrained in the end to ſpare and fauour
them. Had they not done better, to haue mortified their bodie indifferentlie,
and proportionablie to the offices and
ſabours,

labours, whervnto their ftate obliged them.

5. Fafting and labour both doe turne and fubdue the flefhe. But if the labour which thou art to doe, be necef-farie, or verie profitable to the glorie of God, I had rather thou wouldft fuffer the toile of labour, then of fafting. This is at leaft the intention of holie church; which for labours that are profitable to the feruice of God and our neighbour, difchargeth fuch as are bufied in them, from the faftes otherwife inioyned. It is painfull indeed to faft, but bodilie labour fuffereth this paine in feruing the fick, in vifiting prifoners, hearing confeffions, affifting the defolate, preaching, praying, & in fuch like exercifes: this painfull toile is better then the other; for befides that it weakeneth the bodie as much as fafting, it hath manie more fruicts, and much more defirable. And therfore fpeaking generallie, it is better to preferue more bodilie forces then are precifely needfull, then to weaken them more then one should: for we may allways abate them and pull them downe

when

when we will : but we cannot repare
them allways when we would.

6. Mee thinks we should greatly
reuerence the wordes which our bleffed Saueour fayth vnto his difciples :
Eate that which shalbe fett before you. It is
(as I imagin) a greater virtue to eat
without choice, that which is prefented)vnto thee, be it for thy taft or
no, then to choofe allway the worlt.
For allthough this later kind of mortification, doe feeme more auftere :
the other notwithftanding hath greater refignation ; for therby one renounceth, not onely his owne taft,
but his owne e'action withall ; neither is it a fmall mortification, to
alter a mans taft at euery hand, and
to haue it in fubiection at all occurrences. Moreouer this kind of au-
fteritie, is not fo much marked, nor
troubleth any man with ceremonious
refufals, and exceedinglie befitteth a
ciuil life. To put by one meat, and
take another; to fcrape and lick euery dishe, to find no meffe well
enough dreffed for vs; to vfe cere-
monies at euery morfell : betokeneth
a nice

a nice nature , and too attentiue to the
dishes and platters . I esteeme more
that of S. Bernard , who dranck oile in
steed of water or wine , then yf he had
dronck wormewood of purpose: for it
was a plaine signe, that he thought not
vpon that which he dranck . And in
this carelessnesse of that which one eateth or drincketh , consisteth the perfect practize of this sacred rule of our
Saueour , *Eate that which shalbe sett before
you* . I except notwithstanding such
meats as endamage our health , or
trouble the spirit , as hotte meates
doe to manie men , and such as be
spiced , fumie , and windie; and likewise I except certaine occasions , in
which nature standeth in need to be
recreated , and strengthened , to support some great labour for Gods glorie . A continuall and moderate sobrietie , is better then violent absti-
nences , made at interrupted times,
intermingled with manie recreations
and refreshings.

7. Disciplining the bodie likewise hath
a merueilous efficacie , to stirre vp
in vs a desire of deuotion , when it is
mode-

moderatly vsed. Haire-cloth tameth
the flesh very much, but the ordinarie
vse therof, is neither for married persons, nor delicate complexions, nor
for such as are exercised with painfull
labours. True it is that vpon the principall dayes of penance, one may well vse
it, with aduice of a discreet confessour.

8. Euerie one according to his complexion, must spend as much of the
night to sleep in, as is requisite to make
all the day after profitable. And because the holie scripture in a hundred
places, the examples of Gods Saints,
and naturall reasons, do seriously commend the morning vnto vs, as the best
and most profitable season of all the
daye, and our Lord himself is named
the sunne-rising, and our Ladie is termed *Aurora*, or dawning of the day : I
thinck it is a virtuous fore cast, to take
our rest somwhat timelie, ouer-night,
to awake and arise earlie in the morning ; for that time is most fauourable,
quiet, and fittest for prayer : the verie
Birds doe then inuite vs to our dutie,
and to the seruice of God, to omitte,
that rising in the morning, is a great
helpe

helpe for health and helthfomnefle.

9. ⸱Balaam moūted on his Affe, went
to find out Balaac, but becaufe he had
no good intention, the Angel waited
for him in the way, with a naked fword
in his hand to kill him. The poore Affe
that faw the Angel fo dreadfullie expecting, ftood ftill three fondrie times,
as weerie and tired : wherat Balaam in
rage beat her cruellie with his ftaffe, to
make her go forward : vntill the fillie
beaft, the third time falling downe vnder Balaam of purpofe, miraculoufly
fpake vnto him, faying : *What haue I*
done to thee, for which thou haft beat me now
three feuerall times ? and by and by Balaams
eyes were opened, & he faw the Angell, which
fayd vnto him : wherfore didft thou beat thy
Affe ? yf she had not turned back before me,
I had killed thee , and faued her. Then
Balaam fayd vnto the Angel. Lord I haue
finned, for I knew not , that thou hadſt
placed thy felf in the way againſt me.
Doeft thou fee Philotheus ? Balaam
is the caufe of all this harme, and
he ftriketh and beateth his poore
Affe , that could not doe with all.
The verie fame chaunceth oft' times
in

in our affaires. A woman feeth her hufband, or her child fall fore fick, and prefentlie the runnes to fasting, to haircloth, and to difciplining, as Dauid did in the like cafe. Alas my frind, thou beateft the poore affe, thou afflicteft thy bodie, but it cannot doe with all, nor helpe thy euil; nor can it hinder God from drawing his dreadfull fword against thee. Correct thy hart, which committeth idolatrie with this husband, and fuffereth a thoufand vices in this child, and teacheth it pride, vanitie, and ambition A man perceaueth himfelfe to fall fouly into the finne of luxurie: an inward remorfe of confcience cometh with the fword of the feare of God, to runne him through, and coming to him felf: Ah filthie fleshe (fayth he) ah difloyall carkcas, thou haft betrayed me: and prefently he layeth vpon his flesh, mightie blowes of immoderate fasting, exceffiue difciplining, infupportable hairecloath. O poore foule, yf thy flesh could fpeake as *Balaams* affe did, she would fay vnto thee, wherfore ftrikeft thou

thou me? wretch that thou art, it
is againft thy felf (ô my foule) that
God armeth his vengeance, it is
thou that art guiltie: wherfore doeft
thou leade me to naughtie companie? why doeft thou applye my eyes,
my lippes, and my hands to lafciuiouf-
neffe? wherfore doeft thou bufie me
with vaine and wanton imaginations?
Produce thou good thoughts, and I
shall haue no euil motions: haunt
thou the companie of chaft perfons,
and I shall not be shaken with the batterie of concupifcence. Alas it is thou
that throweft me into the fire, and yet
thou wouldft I should not burne: thou
cafteft fmoke into mine eyes, and
forbiddeft them to be inflamed. And
God doubtleffe in thefe occafions
fayth vnto thee, beate, breake, teare,
and crushe your harts principally;
for it is againft them that my anger
is ftirred vp. To cure the itch or
fcurffe, it is not fo needfull to
washe or bathe the bodie, as to purifie the bloud, and refreshe the liuer:
euen fo to heale vs of our vices,
it is very good to mortifie the flesh,
but

but aboue all it is neceſſarie well to purifie our affections; & refresh our ſoules.
In all, and ouer all, keep this rule, neuer
to vndertake corporall auſterities, but
with aduiſe of our ſpirituall conductour.

Of companie, and ſolitarineſſe.
CHAPTER 24.

1. TO ſeeke companie, and vtterly
to flie from it, are two extrea-
mes to be blamed in ciuil deuotion, which is that wherof I diſcourſe:
for ſhunning all companie, ſauoureth
of diſdaine and contempt of our neighbour: and ſeeking after it, ſmelleth of
idlenes. We are bound to loue our
neighbours as our ſelues, and to ſhew
that we loue him, we muſt not flie from
his companie: and to teſtifie that we
loue our ſelues, we muſt take pleaſure
with our ſelues when we are alone.
Thinck firſt of thy ſelf (ſayth *S.* Bernard)
and then of others. If then no reaſon or
cauſe vrge thee, to enter into anie companie, ſtay in thy ſelf, and conuerſe with
thy

thy owne hart: But yf companie chance
thee, or any iuſt cauſe inuite thee to be
preſent, go thether in Gods name Philotheus, & ſee thy neighbour willingly
and louingly.

2.   They call that euel conuerſation,
which is kept for ſome euil intent: or
when they that keep it, are vitious, in-
diſcreet, and diſſolute: and ſuch we muſt
auoide, as the Bees do vſe to turne away
from a ſwarme of Harnets or Butterflies. For as they that are bitten by
madd Dogges, haue their ſweat, breath,
and ſpittle verie contagious, but principallie daungerous for litle children,
and for thoſe of delicate complexion:
ſo vitious, vnmannerlie, and immodeſt
perſons, cannot be frequented, but with
hazard, and danger, and in eſpeciall by
thoſe, whoſe deuotion is yet but tender
and delicate.

3.   There be ſome kind of conuerſations, profitable for nothing, but for
meere recreation, which are made by a
ſimple turning or abſtracting of our
minds from ſerious affaires: for ſuch,
though a man muſt not be totallie addicted vnto them, yet we may lend them

R   ſo

fo much leafure, as is conuenient for recreation.

4. Other recreations, haue fome honeftie and good refpect for their end:
as are mutuall vifitations, and certaine
affemblies, made to do fome honour
to our neighbour. Touching thefe,
as one should not be fuperftitious in
practizing them, fo one muft not be
vnciuil in contemning them, but fatisfie with modeftie, the obligation, to
efchew equallie the note of lightnes, or
rufticitie.

5. There remaine now the profitable
recreations, fuch as are kept with deuout, and virtuous perfons : O Philothee, it will alway be an exceeding good
turne for thee, to encounter oft times
fuch recreations. The vine planted by
an Oliue-tree, beareth a fat kind of
grape, that fauoureth fomething like
the oliues : and a foule that happeneth
to be in virtuous companie, cannot
choofe but be partaker of their good
qualities. Drones cannot make honnie
alone by them felues, but by the help of
the Bees they make it : it is a great help
for weake foules to exercife deuotion,

to

to conuerse and haunt with vertuous
perfons.

6. In all conuersation and companie, finceritie, fimplicitie, fweetnes, and
modestie, are still to be preferred; There
be fome fo curious, that no one motion they vfe, but is done fo artificiallie, that they make the côpanie weerie;
And as he that would not walk but tel-
ling his fteppes, or neuer would fpeak
but finging, would be tedious to other
men : fo they that euer vfe an artificiall
demeanour, and will do nothing but
in print, trouble the companie in which
they are, and are always fubiect to fome
fpice of prefumption. Let a modest
myrthe for the moft part predominate
in our conuersation. Saint Romuald,
and Saint Anthonie are highlie commended and admired, that notwithstanding all their moft rare aufterities, they had always their countenance pleafant, and their words adorned
with cheerfull alacritie. *Reioice with
them that reioice.* I faye, once againe with the Apostle : *Reioice in our
Lord always, againe I fay, reioice.: Let
your modestie be knowne to all men.*
    R 2   To

To reioice in ourLord, it is needfull the
cause of thy ioye be not onely lawfull,
but honest also : and this I say , because
there are some things that be lawfull,
which yet are not honest : And to the
end that thy modestie may appeer, keepe thy self from all manner of insolen-
cie , for it is alway blame worthie. To
giue one a fall in sport, to begrime anothers face , to pinche one , and such
tricks as these , are fond , foolish and
insolent meriments.

7. Besides the mentall solitude, or
spirituall hermitage wherunto , thou
mayst withdraw thy self, euen amid the
greatest conuersations that are (as I
haue alreadie declared) thou must loue
to be locallie , reallie and in verie deed
solitarie: not to go to the desart or wildernes, as S. Marie of Egypt , Saint
Paul , Saint Anthonie , Arsenius , and
the other fathers of the desart : but to
be sometime in thy garden , or in thy
chamber , or els where , as thou likest
best ; where thou maist withdraw thy
spirit into thy soule , and recreat they
selfe with good thoughts , and holie
considerations , or some spirituall le-
ctur̃e,

ture, according to the example of the great Nazianzen bishop, who speaking of him self sayth : *I walked my self with my self about sunn-setting, and passed the time vpon the sea shore : for I accustomed to vse this recreation , to ease my mind, and to shake of, at least for a litle while, my ordinarie troubles.* And vpon this point he discourseth of the good meditation, which I declared vnto thee in another place ; and according to the example of Saint Ambrose, of whome Saint Augustin recounteth , that him self entring oft times into Saint Ambrose his chamber (for entrance was denied to no man) he beheld him reading in silence ; and expecting sometime, for feare of troubling him, he returned home without speaking a word : thincking that the litle time which remained to this great Pastour, for refreshing and recreating his spirit , after the multitude of his affaires, should in no wise be taken from him. So after the Apostles one day had told our Lord, how they had preached and laboured : *Come* (sayd our Lord) *into the desart, and repose your selues a litle.*

Of

Of decency and handsomnes in attire.

CHAPTER 25.

1. SAINT Paul admonisheth deuout wemen (and the same must be vnderstood of men) to be attired in decent apparell, , clothing them selues with shamefastnes and sobrietie. Now then the decencie of apparell, and other ornaments, depende of their matter, fashion, and cleanlines. Touching cleanlines, it should almost allwayes be a like in our apparel, vpon which as near as may be, we should not permitt anie kind of vncomely foulnes, or slouenrie. Exteriour neatnes ordinarilie signifieth the inward cleannesse of the soule. God him self requireth corporall cleanlynesse, in those that approache nigh his altar, and haue the principall charge and care of deuotion.

2. As for the stuffe, and fashion of attire the comlines, and decencie therof is to be examined and considered according to manie circumstances, of
time,

time , age , estate,companie, occasion.
Men apparell them selues ordinarily
better vpon festiuall dayes , according
to the solemnitie of the feast which is
celebrated. In time of penaunce as in
lent,they rather humble and abase them
selues : at weddings they put on wedding garments , at burialls , moorning
robes ; with princes men sette foorth
them selues according to their estate,
at home they vse themselues more ho-
mely. The married woman may, and
must adorne her self in her housbands
presence , when he desireth it : but yf
she doeth so in his absence , one might
aske her,whose eyes she meant to please
with that particular care? The manner
is to permitte more gallant ornaments
to young maidens : becaufe they may
lawfullie desire to please manie , with
intent honestlie to winne one alone
for holie marriage. Neither is it esteemed amisse that widowes,which pretēd marriage,deck vp themselues hand-
somlie:so that they shew no lightnes or
fondmes in their attire ; for hauing alredie been married , and charged with
gouernement of a familie , and passed

the mourning state of widowhood:
they are held to be, and indeed should
be, of a more ripe and setled iudgement. But as for those which are widdowes indeed, not onely in bodie, but
in hart and purpose, no ornament better becommeth them then humilitie,
modestie and deuotion: for yf they intend to allure men with their brauerie,
they are not true widowes; and yf it
be not their intention to allure men,
why do they vse such instruments? He
that will not receaue guests in his inne,
must pull downe the signe from his lodging. Old folke be always ridiculous,
when they will play tricks of youth:for
these follies are not to be tolerated, but
only in young persons.

3. Be handsome Philotheus, and
suffer nothing about thee to traile vn-
decentlie, or to sitt out of order : we
dishonour them with whome we conuerse, to come into their companie
in vncomelie apparell. But take heed
withal of wantonnesse, curiosities, fooleries, and vanities. As farre as thou
art able, keep thy self always on plaine
simplicities side : for modestie without
dupli-

duplicitie is the greateſt ornament of beautie, and the beſt excuſe for hard-fauour.

4. Saint Peter aduertiſed young wemen eſpecially, that they should not wear their treſſes of their haire curled, frizled, toured, and tormented, as now is the ordinarie faſhion : but yf men should affeƈt ſuch fondnes in their owne locks, they should iuſtlie be ſtiled effeminate perſons. Euen vaine women, giuen to theſe toyes affeƈtiona-tlie, are counted ſcant of chaſtitie, or yf they haue anie, it is not perceiued among ſo manie fooleries. They ſay they haue no ill meaning in it. But I replie (as I haue elſe where ſayd) that the diuel hath enough in it al-ways.

5. I would haue my frind whome I affeƈt, to be apparelled beſt of all the companie : but yet with the leaſt pom-pe and curioſitie ; and, (as they com-monlie ſay) that he were adorned with good cariage, comelines, and worthines. Saint Lewes ſayth in one word, that one should be apparelled according to his calling ; ſo that gra-

R 5   ue

ue and good men might not say: thou
doeſt too much ; nor young perſons
ſay :thou doeſt too litle ; but yf young
heads will not be content with hand-
ſomnes, let 'vs be contented with the
iudgement of the wiſe.

Of talke. And firſt how to ſpeak of God.

CHAPTER 26.

1. **P**HYSICIANS knowe the
health and diſeaſes of a man, by
looking vpon his tongue: and
ſo trulie our words be certaine ſignes
of the qualities of our ſoules. *By thy
words* (ſayth our Saueour) *thou ſhalt
be iuſtified , and by thy words thou ſhalt
be condemned* : we haue our hand ſtill
vpon the ſore that grieueth vs , and
our tongue always in that which delighteth vs.

2. Yf then God delight thee (Philotheus) yf his loue poſſeſſe thee, thou
wilt often talke of him in thy familiar diſcourſes, with thy neighbours,
with thy frinds , with thy houshold
ſer-

feruants. *For the mouth ef the iuſt* will *meditate wiſdome , and his tongue* will *ſpeake iudgement .* As Bees take nothing in their litle mouthes but honnie : ſo should thy tongue be always ſweetned with God , thy lippes should always be ſugered with his praiſes : for ſo they ſay S. Francis was wont to lick his lippes after he had pronounced the holie name of God , drawing therby to his ſoule the greateſt ſweetnes in the world.

3. But ſpeak allwayes of God , as of God , that is reuerentlie , and deuoutlie : not to shew thy ſufficiencie, or to play the eloquent preacher ; but with a ſweet ſpirit of charitie , and humilitie , diſtilling as much as thou mayeſt (as it is ſayd of the ſpouſe in the Canticles) the delicious honnie of deuotion and diuine things , droppe by droppe , ſometimes into the eares of one, ſometimes of another ; and ſtill praying to God in the ſecret of thy hart , that it would pleaſe him to make this heauenlie dewe, pearce to the very hart of them that heare thee.

R 6   4. A

4. Aboue all things performe this Angelicall office, mildlie, and fweetlie, not in manner of correction, but by way of infpirations. For it is wonderfull how powerfullie a louelie and fweet manner of propofing good matters, draweth and allureth the harts of the hearers.

5. Whenfoeuer therfore thou art to fpeak of God, and of deuotion, do it not flightly, by way of common talke, but with attention, and care : which I fay, to take from thee a notable vanitie, that is to be found in manie that make profeffion of deuotion : who at euerie occafion abound in holie and feruourous words, vpon a kind of brauerie, litle minding in hart, that which they fpeak with their mouthes : and after they haue fpoken fuch fpirituall braueries, they imagine them felues to be fuch, as their great words feeme to make boaft; which indeed is nothing fo.

Of cour-

Of courtesie in talk, and due respect of persons. CHAP. 27.

1. YF *any sinneth not in word* (sayth. S. Iames) *he is a perfect man.* Beware thou let not fall any vnseemly word, for although it proceed not from thee with an ill intention , yet they that heare it, may interpret it farre otherwise. An vnseemlie word ouerheard by a weak and feeble hart , spreadeth and enlargeth it self like a droppe of oyle , falling vpon a peece of cloth: and sometime it so seazeth vpon the hart , that it filleth it with a thousand, vncleane thoughts and imaginations; For as the poison, which infecteth the bodie , entreth by the mouth : so the poison which intoxicateth the soule, entreth by the eare : and the tongue which produceth this poison is a murtherer. For although peraduenture the poison which it hath spitte foorth, hath not wrought his effect, because it found the harts of the hearers fortified with some preseruatiue : yet there was no

want

want of malice on his part, to committ
the murther. And let noe man excuse
him self by saying, that he, for his part,
thought no harme: for our Lord, who
knoweth mens thoughts, hath sayd:
*That out of the aboundance of the hart the
mouth speaketh.* And though we thinck
no harme in doing or saying fo, yet
the deuil thincketh a great deale: and
oft times doth secretlie make vse of
those wicked words to wound the hart
of some feeble hearer. They say, such
as haue eaten the hearbe called Ange-
lica, haue allways a sweet pleasaunt
breath: and they that haue honestie
and chastitie (which is the virtue of Angels) in their harts, haue their words
allwayes pure, ciuil, and chast. As for
indecencies and scurrilities, the Apostle will not once haue them named
among vs, assuring vs, that nothing;
*so much corrupteth good manuers, as wicked
talke.*

2. Yf these vnseemly words be vttered cunninglie, with willie conceipts,
or subtil curiositie, then are they farre
more venimous. For as a Dart, the
sharper it is, the more easilie it pier-
ceth

ceth our bodie : so the more sharpe
and wittily that a wanton or vnseemlie word is couched in conuersation,
the deeper it penetrateth into our
harts . And they that esteeme them
selues gallant felowes , for multiplying
such vnseemlie iests in conuersation,
know not indeed wherfore conuersations are ordained ; for they should
be like swarmes of Bees, gathered together , to make honnie of some pleasaunt and virtuous entertainment , and
not like a multitude of Waspes , who
come together to suck some vnsauourie carrion . Yf any bad companion' , speake some misbeseeming
words vnto thee , declare that thine
eares be offended therwith , either
turning thy self to some other matter,
or leauing the companie, or by some
other meanes , which thy prudence and discretion shall dictate vnto
thee.

3. It is one of the woorst conditions
that a man can haue , to be a scoffer.
God himself professeth extreame hatred against this vice,and hath made verie strange punishments alredie therof.

Nothing is so contrarie to charitie, and especiallie to deuotion, as the despising and contemning of our neighbour : but derison and mockerie, is neuer without this contempt, and therfore it is a grieueous sinne : so that the Doctours do say with great reason, that scoffing and flouting, is one of the greatest offences that a man can committ against his neighbour, by words : for other offences are committed alwayes with some respect, and interest of the offender, but this is donne onely of meere dispight and contempt.

4. As for iesting wordes, which be spoken one to another, with modest and cheerfull myrthe, they proceed from a virtue called *Eutrapelia* by the Greeks, which we may call, good conuersation : by which we take an honest and pleasaunt recreation, vpon friuolous occasions, which humane imperfections do offer : onely this we must beware, least from this honest myrthe, we passe to immodest scoffing and flouting. For scoffing, prouoketh to a spightfull kind of laughter, in contempt and disdainfull mockerie of our

neigh-

neighbour : but modeſt ieſting prouoketh to laughter, by a ſimple confidence, and franck familiaritie, ioined with
ſome wittie conceipt, without iniu-
ring anie man.

S. Lewis, when religious perſons
offered to talke with him after meales
of great and high matters : *It is not now*
a time to alledge textes (would he ſay) *but*
to recreat our ſpirits , with ſome merry con-
ceipt, and quodiibeticall queſtion : let euery
man talk decently of what he liſt . Which
this holy king was woont to ſay for the
nobilities ſake, that were then about
him, expecting the fauour of his maie-
ſties amiable conuerſations . But let vs
ſo paſſe our time my Philotheus, in recreation , that we keep for all that , a
certaine perpetuitie of deuotion.

Of rash iudgement .
CHAPTER 28.

1. **I** *VDGE not , that your ſelues be not*
iudged, ſayth the Saueour of our
foules: *condemne not , and you ſhall*
not be condemned . No , ſayth the holy
Apoſtle ; *Iudge not before the time , vntill*

our Lord do come , who *will light the hidden things of darkneſſe* , *and lay open the ſecrets of harts.* O how diſpleaſing be raſhe indgements vnto almightie God! Therfore are the iudgements of the children of men raſhe, and temerarious , becauſe they are not iudges one of another, ſo that in iudging they vſurpe and arrogate to them ſelues the office that is proper and peculiar to our Lord . They be raſhe likewiſe , becauſe the principall malice and wickedneſſe which is in ſinne , dependeth of the intentions and councells of the hart , which is a darke and vnſearcheable dungeon for our eyes . They be raſhe , becauſe euery one hath enough to doe to iudge his owne ſelfe , he neede not vndertake withall to iudge his neighbour. Not to iudge others , and to iudge our ſelues , are two thinges equallie neceſſarie for vs, not to be iudged our ſelues : for as our bleſſed Lord forbiddeth vs the one , ſo his holy Apoſtle inioineth vs the other , ſaying that . *If* we *did iudge our ſelues* , we *ſhould not be iudged* . But ô good God , we doe quite contrarie: that which is forbid vs , we ceaſe not

to doe

to doe , iudging our neighbour at
euerie occafion : and that which is
commanded vs , to iudge our felues , we do not fo much as once
thinck of.

2. The remedies againft this vice of
rafhe iudging , muft be applied according to the diuerfitie of caufes,from
whence rafhe iudgements vfe to proceed . Some men there are of fo fharpe
and fower a condition by nature , that
whatfoeuer they receaue , turnes bitter
in their hatts, chaunging *iudgement* (as
the prophet fayth) *into wormewood , neuer iudging their neighbour , but with rigour and bitterneffe* . Such men haue
great neede of the help of fome fpirituall phyfician , that may teach them
how to vanquish this bitterneffe of hart
which becaufe it is naturall vnto them,
is hardly amended : And though in it
felf it be no finne, but onely an imperfection, yet is it verie daungerous , becaufe it caufeth this vice of rash iudgement to raigne in the hart. Other fome
iudge rashely not for harshenes of condition, but of meere pride , imagining
that by diminishing and fuppreffing
other

other mens honour, they aduaunce and increase their owne, arrogant, and presumptuous spirits, which admire themselues, and place them selues so high in their owne estimation, that they hold all men in comparison of them, to be abiect, base, and of no worth at all : so sayd the fond pharisey in the ghospell, *I am not as other men*. Some there are that haue not in them this manifest pride, but onely of a vaine complacence or delight which they haue in their owne excellence, consider other mens imperfections, to tast (as it were) with more content the contrarie perfections wherwith they presume themselues to be endowed. This self-pleasing conceipt is so secret, and so hard to be perceaued, that vnlesse one haue great insight in diseases of the soule, he can not discouer it : and they themselues that are sick of it, do not know it, vntill it be shewed vnto them. Other there be, that to flatter, and excuse them selues, and to mitigate the remorse of their owne guiltie consciences, gladly iudge other men faultie in the same vice, wherunto they feele themselues to be addicted,

as yf

as yf the multitude of offenders made
their finnes leffe to be blamed. Many
giue themfelues to iudge rashly of
others, onely of a vaine pleafure which
they take, to difcourfe, and prognofti-
cate other mens humours, and beha-
ueours, exercifing their witts, at the
coft of theire neighbours credit and
good name. And yf by mifchaunce they
chaunce to gieffe aright in their iudgement: they wilbe bold thereafter in like
iudgements, that one shall verie hardly
draw them from this follie . Others
iudge of paffion, thincking that beft
which they loue, and that ftark naught
which they hate : fauing in one cafe
onely admirable, yet true, and daylie
experienced; wherin the exceffe of loue
maketh men iudge ill of that which thy
loue ; A monftrous effect, proceeding
allwaies from an impure and fenfuall
loue, troubled and fick with iealoufie,
which as euerie man knoweth, vpon a
bare looke, vpon the leaft fmile in the
word, condemneth the party beloued
of difloyaltie, or adulterie. To conclude, feare, ambition, and other fuch like
defectiue paffions, and difeafes of
the

the minde do ordinarilie contribute toward the breeding of suspicions and
rashe iudgements.

3. But what remedies do we prescribe to this disease? There is an hearbe in
Ethopia, called Ophiusa, the iuice
wherof being drunck, maketh men
imagin, that they see themselues all
enuironed with horrible serpents: so
they that haue swallowed downe pride,
enuie, ambition, & hatred, imagin all
things which they see, to be faultie
and defectiue. These to be healed,
must drinck wine made of palmes,
and these others must drinck as much
as they can of the sacred wine of charitie, and it will purge them of these
naughtie humours, which cause them
to make such rashe and peruerse iudgements. Charitie feareth to meet with
euill, so farre of is she from seeking after it; when she meeteth with it, she
turneth away her face, and maketh as
yf she saw it not; nay at the first noise
of euill, she shutteth her eyes that she
may not see it: & afterward with a holy
simplicitie beleeueth, that it was not
euil, but onely the shadow or likenes of
euill

euill. And yf by no meanes she cā excuse
it, but euidently seeth it to be euill, she
turneth away her sight, & endeuoureth
presently to forget the oughe shape
therof. Charitie is the soueraigne remedie against al euils but especially against
this. All things seeme yealowe to their
eyes that are sick of the iaunders, and
they say, to heale them, they must weare the hearbe Celydonia vnder the plan-
tes of their feet. The sinne of rashe iudgement, is a spirituall iaunders, & make h all things appeere reprehensible to
their eyes that be infected therwith: he
that wilbe cured of it, must applie the
remedies not to his eyes, nor to his vnderstanding, but to his affections, which
are the feet of the soule. Yf thy affectiōs
be mild, & gentle, such will thy iudgement of things be : yf thy affections be
charitable, thy iudgemēt wil also be charitable. I present vnto thee three admirable examples; Isaac had sayde that Rebecca was his sister: Abimelech saw him
playing with her, that is making verie
much of her, & he iudged persently that
she was his wife: a naughtie eye would
rather haue iudged her to haue been
                                         his

his ſtroumpet, or yf she were his ſiſter, that he had been inceſtuous. But Abi- melech, folowed the moſt charitable opinion, that he could gather of ſuch an action. We muſt alway do the like (my Philotheus) as much as is poſſible, in cenſuring our neighbours actions: and yf one action had a hundred faces, we should always caſt our ſight vpõ the faireſt. Our Ladie was great with child, and S. Ioſeph perceaued it well enough; but becauſe on the other ſide he ſaw her to be pure, holy, and of an Angelicall life, he could not beleeue that she came to be with child otherwiſe then became her ſainctitie, in ſo much that he re- ſolued to forſake her ſecretly, and leaue the iudgement of hir innocéce to God, though the appeeraunce of the thing, was a violent argument to make him conceaue an ill opinion of the Virgin, yet would not he iudge her, leaſt he should iudge rashely. And why ſo? be- cauſe (ſayth the ſpirit of God) he was iuſt. A iuſt man, when he can no longer excuſe neither the action, nor the in- tention of him, whome otherwiſe he knoweth to be an honeſt man : yet will

not

not he iudge of the matter, but wipeth the remembrance of it out of his mind, and leaueth it for God to iudge. Nay our bleſſed Sauiour vpon the croſſe, though he could not altogeather excuſe the ſinne of them that crucified him: yet did he diminiſhe the malice of it, alledging their ignorance. When we cannot excuſe the ſinne it ſelf, let vs at leaſt (according to our Lords example) make it worthie of compaſſion, attributing it to the moſt tolerable cauſe we may, as to ignorance or infirmitie.

4. But what? may we neuer iudge of our neighbour? no verely: neuer. It is onely God that iudgeth, euen when malefactours are iudged in publique tribunals True it is, that he vſeth the magiſtrats voice, to make him ſelf the better vnderſtood by vs: they be his interpretours, and ought, to pronounce nothing, but what they haue learned of him, as being his oracles: But yf they doe otherwiſe, folowing their owne paſſions, then it is they indeed that iudge, and conſequently ſhalbe iudged. For men are forbidden, as they are men, to iudge any man.

5. To see or know a thing, is not to iudge or censure it : for iudgement, at least according to the scriptures phrase, presupposeth some true or apparēt controuersie to be ended: and this is the reason of that manner of speeche, in which our Sauiour sayth , that they which beleeue not, are allreadie iudged ; because there is no doubt of their damnation. Is it not lawfull thē to doubt of our neighbour? it is not always vnlawfull , for we are not forbiddē to doubt, but to iudge: yet must we neither doubt nor suspect our neighbour , but when force of reasons, and euident arguments, do constraine : otherwise euen doubts, and suspicions , are rashe and temerarious. Yf some suspicious eye had seen Iaacob kisse Rachel by the well, or Rebecca receaue earings and braceletts at Eliezers hands , being a man vnknowne in that coūtrie: he would doubtlesse haue thought ill , of these two rare paternes of chastitie ; but without sufficient cause or ground; for when the action is indifferent of it self, it is rashe suspicion to draw badde cōsequence from it, vnlesse manie circumstances giue force to the
argu-

argument.It is alfo a rashe iudgemente,
to drawe an argument from the action,
to blame the perfon ; of which we will
by and by fpeak more cleerly.

6. To be brieffe, all men that haue
diligent care of their côfcience, are not
much fubiect to make rashe iudgemêts
of other mens matters. For as Bees in
foggie miftes,or cloudie weather retire
to their hiues,to bufie them felues with
their honny:fo the thoughts of deuout
foules,neuer wander abroade to cenfure
or to marke the doubtfull and fecret
actions or intentions of their neighbour : but leaft they should by marking them , fall in danger of cenfuring
them, they retire them felues by a carefull introuerfion (as fpirituall men call
it) into them felues , there in the clofet of their foules, to view and order
the good refolutions of their owne a-
mendment.

7. It is the part of an idle and vn-
thriftie foule, to bufie her felf in exa-
minge other mens liues : excepted always fuch as haue charge of others , as
well in common wealths , as in pri-
uat families, and communities : for a

S 2   grea

great part of the quiet of their consciences, consisteth in watchinge diligently ouer the consciences of other:
Let such men doe that carefull dutie
with loue and mildnes.: that done, let
them keep them selues with in them
selues, to be at more tranquillitie, and
safer from excesse in this matter.

Of slaunder and back-biting.
CHAPTER 29.

I. **R**ASHE iudgement, breedeth
disquiet, disdaine and contempt
of our neighbours, pride and
self-coceipt, and a hundred other pesti-
lent effects: among which backbiting,
and speaking ill of other men, hath the
first place, as the verie plague of all conuersations. O that I had one of the burning coales of the holy altar, to touch
therwith the lippes' of men, and take
away their iniquities, and cleanse their
sinne: imitating the Seraphin, that purified the mouth of the prophet Esay,
with a coale take from the altar of God:
for he that could bannishe slaunderous
                                              lippes

lippes out of the worlde, would take away one of the greateſt cauſes of ſinne and iniquitie.

2. He that vniuſtlie robbeth his neighbour of his good renowne, beſides the ſinne committed, is bound to repare the domage though differently, according to the diuerſitie of ſlanders vſed : for no man can enter into heauen with other mens goods: and amongſt all exteriour goods, a good name is the moſt pretious. Slaunder is a kind of willfull and perfidious murther : for we haue three liues, one ſpirituall which conſiſteth in the graces of God : another corporall, which cometh frō our ſoule; the third a ciuil or morall life, which conſiſteth in our good name; ſinne robbeth vs of the firſt, death taketh from vs the ſecōd, and an ill tongue depriueth vs of the thirde. Nay a ſlaũderous tongue at one blowe, committeth ordinarilie three ſeuerall murders ; he killeth his owne ſoule, and his that hearkeneth to him, and taketh away the ciuil life of him whome he ſlaũdereth: for as S Bernard ſayth, he that detracteth, and he that harkeneth to the detractour, both of them haue the diuel

vpon them:but the one hath him in his
tongue , and the other in his eare. *They
haue whetted their tongues like serpents* ,
sayth Dauid , speaking of detractours:
for as the serpents tongue is forked,and
double pointed,as Aristotle sayth;so is a
detractours tongue , who at one time
stingeth and poisoneth the eare of him
that heareth him,and the reputation of
him whome he back-biteth.

3. I charge thee therfore(most deare
Philotheus) that thou neuer speak ill of
any man,directlie or indirectlie : neuer
impose false crimes and fained faultes
vpon thy neighbour : neuer discouer
his secret sinnes, nor exaggerate those
that are notorious;neuer interpret in ill
part his good work:neuer denie the virtue & good parts which thou knowest
to be in him,nor dissemble them mali-
tiouslie , nor diminish them enuiously:
for by all these manner of wayes, thou
shalt offend God greeuously : but most
of all by deniyng the truth to the preiudice of thy neighbour , or by accusing
him falselie : for it is a double sinne,of
lying,and robbing thy neighbour both
at once.

4. They

4. They that to speak ill of another, make prefaces of honour, excusing their intentions ; or mingle secret and slie iests , and the prayses which they would seeme to recount of another, are the most venemous and mischieuous detractours of all. I protest (say they) I loue him with my hart, and as for other matters , he is a right honest man : but yet one must tell the troth. I must needs say he did ill to play so treacherous a part. She is a verie vir- tuous maiden (sayth another) but she was ouerreached in such an occasion : and such like diminishing additions, which are most ordinarilie vsed. Seest thou not this flight of theirs ? The archer drawing his bow , draweth likewise the arrow as nigh to him self as he can : but it is onelie to shoot it with greater force. It seemes these felowes do drawe their tongues to the selues , but it is onely to let them ouer- shoot with greater violence, and pierce more profoundlie into the harts of the audience, or côpanie where they talke. Detractiô vttered in a iesting & scoffing manner , is yet more wicked then the

for-

former. Seney (they fay) is not a prefent poifon of it felf, but flowe in working, and eafilie remedied , but being taken with wine it is remedileffe: So fpeaking ill of our neighbours, which would otherwife paffe lightlie in at one eare and out at another (as they fay) ſticketh firmelie in the remembrance of them that heare it, whē it is craftilie couched with fome fubtill & merrie quippe: *They haue* (fayth Dauid) *the venom of afpes vnder their lippes.* The ſtinging of the afpe is allmoſt without any feeling, & his venim at the firſt breedeth a deleɛtable kind of itching, through which the entrailes and hart open them felues , and receaue the poifon, againſt which afterward there is no remedie.

5. Doe not fay, ſuch a one is a dronckard , allthough thou haue feen him dronck:nor, he is an adulterer , though thou haue feen him taken in that finne; nor , that fuch a one is an inceſtuous perfon , becaufe he hath beene once found in that crime : for one onely aɛt giueth not name & title to a thing. The funne ſtood ſtil once in behalf of Iofuas viɛtorie;and loſt his light another time
for

for our Saueours death vpon the crosse:
yet for all that, no man will say that
the sunne is immoueable, or darksome.
Noah was once dronck; and Lot another
time, and withall committed horrible
inceft with his owne daughters;
yet neither the one, nor the other were
drunckardes: nor was the latter an inceftuous
person. So Saint Peter was
not a bloud shedder, though once he
shed bloud: nor a blasphemer, though
once he blasphemed. To beare the name
of a vice or a virtue, one muft haue
frequented the actes therof, and gotten
a habit of it: fo that it is an abufe of
tearmes, to fay, one is cholerick, becaufe
we haue once feene him angrie, or a
theefe, becaufe he hath once ftollen.

6. Although a man haue beene a long
time vitious, yet we incurre daunger of
lying to tearme him a vitious man. Simon
the leaper, called Marie Magdalen
a finner, becaufe she had beene fo not
long before: yet lied he, for she was
then no longer a finner, but a moft holie
and bleffed penitent, and therfore
our Lord himself took vpon him the
defence of her caufe. The prefum-

ptuous pharifey held the humble publi-
can for a finner, peraduenture for an
vniuft oppreffer, a fornicatour, or giuen to fome other hainous vice : but
he was foulie deceaued, for when he
thought fo badlie of him, at that verie time was he iuftified. Alas feinge
the goodnes of God is fo great, that
one moment fuffizeth to obtaine and
receaue his holie grace, what affurance can we haue, that he, who yefterday was a finner, remaineth a finner to
day ? The day paft, muft not iudge
the day prefent : nor the prefent, iudge
the day to come : it is onelie the laft
day, that iudgeth all dayes. Thus we
fee, that we can neuer fay a man is
naught, without probable daunger of
lying : that which we may fay, in cafe
that we muft needs fpeak, is, that he
did fuch a naughtie act, he liued ill
fuch a time, he doth ill for the prefent : but we may drawe no confequence from yefterday, to this day,
nor from this day, to the morrow
folowing.

7. Now though we should be won-
drous carefull, neuer to fpeak ill of
our

our neighbour , yet muſt we take
heed of the other extremitie , into
which ſome do fall , who to auoide
ill ſpeaking , commend and ſpeak well
of vice. Yf thou meete with one that
is indeed a ſlaunderer of his neighbour , doe not ſay , as it were excu-
ſinge his vice , that he ſpeaketh his
minde francklie , and freelie ; Of one
that is notoriouſlie vaine and arro-
gante , ſay not, that he is a gallaunt
courtlie gentleman : dangerous familiarities , muſt not be tearmed plaine
and ſimple dealings ; maske not diſo-
bedience,with the name of zeale ; nor
pride with the name of magnanimitie;
ſtile not laſciuiouſneſſe with the honeſt title of frindship ; No , my deere
Philotheus , thinck not that thou a-
uoideſt the vice of ill-ſpeaking , by
fauouring , flattering , and cheriſhing
other men in their vices : but round-
lie and freelie , ſpeak ill of euill ,
and blame that which is blame-wor-
thie , for in ſo doing we glorifie
God ; ſo it be done with the conditions folowing.

7. To reprehend another mans faultes

and vices lawfullie, it is needfull, that
it be profitable to him of whome wee
fpeake, or to them vnto whome we
fpeake. There be fome, that recite
before maydens, indifcreet priuities of
fuch and fuch, which be manifeftlie
daungerous, others recount, fome mans
diffolute geftures, or wanton fpeeches,
tending manifeftlie to dishoneftie; yf I
should not freelie reprehend this abufe,
or that I should excufe it, thefe tender
young foules who heare it, would take
thereby occafion, to giue them felues
leaue to fay, and to do the like. Their
profit then requireth, that I rebuke
fuch thinges freelie, before I fturre
from the place, vnleffe I may prudentlie
deferre this good office, to doe it with
more deliberation, and leffe intereft of
them, of whome thofe things were recounted, at an other occafion.

8. Moreouer it is requifite, that
in fome fort it belong vnto me to fpeak
of that matter, as when I am one of
the principall of the companie, and
that yf I fpeake not, it would feeme
that I approue their vices : But yf I
be one of the meaner fort, then I muft
not

not vndertake to giue the sentence.

9. But aboue all it is requisite, that I be exact, and warie in my words, and not to vse one too much: as for example, yf I blame the familiaritie of this young man, and that young maide, and call it indiscreet and dangerous; O God (my Philotheus) we must hold the ballance verie euen, that we make not things heauier then they be indeed, allthough it be but the waight of a graine. Yf in the fault I am to speak of, there be but only a bare appeeraunce, I will say no more then so: yf but a simple indiscretion, I will giue it no worse name; yf neither indiscretion, nor probable appeeraunce of ill be in the matter, sauing onely that some malicious spirit may therby take occasion to speak ill, I will say nothing at al, or onely say the same. My tōgue so long as I iudge my neighbour, is like a rasour in a chirurgians hands, that pretends to cut between the sinews and the veines: so the cutt that I make with my tongue in censuring or reprehending my neighbours actions must be so warie, that I launce

no deeper then needs, that I speak neither more nor lesse, then that which the thing it self indeed requireth. And in a word, be carefull to keep this rule, that in reprehending the vice as it deserueth, thou spare the person, in whome it is, as much as discretion and ciuilitie teacheth.

10. True it is, that of infamous and notorious publique sinners, wee may speake more freelie: so that still we declare in our words, the spirit of charitie and compassion, without all arrogancie or presumption, nor taking delight in other folks miseries, which is always an affection proceeding from a base & abiect hart. I except allways those that are denounced to be Gods enemies, and desloyall to his holie churche: for we may and ought in conscience disgrace, and debase all hereticall and schismaticall sectes, and the authours of them: it is charitie to crie against the wolfe, not only when he is among the sheep, but whensoeuer we espie him.

11. Euery one is bold to take so much licence as to censure princes, and speak ill of whole nations, according

to

to the diuerfitie of affections that men
beare them : but thou (my Philotheus)
muft beware alfo of this defect : for befides that God is offended therwith , it
may raife thee vp a thoufand quarrels,
from which thou canft not deliuer thy
felf , without great vnquietnes.

12. When thou chaunceft to heare
any man fpeak ill of another, procure
yf thou canft , to make his accufation
doubtfull : yf thou canft not doe that
iuftlie , endeuour to excufe the intention of the partie cenfured : yf that
cannot be done neither;shew thy compaffion toward his frailtie, cut off the
difcourfe remembring thy felfe , and
bringing the hearers in remembrance;
that yf they haue not offended in that
fort,that they are the more beholding
to the grace of God for the fame, and
withall recall courteoufly the detractour to him felfe : and laftly yf thou
knoweft any good of the partie detra-
cted , endeuour to fet it foorthe.

Other

Other aduices and instructions to be
obserued in talke.

CHAPTER 30.

1. LET our talke be courteous,
franck, sincere, plaine, & faithfull : without double dealing,
subtiltie, or dissembling; for though it
be not good alway to tell the truth in
all matters , and in all occasions : yet is
it neuer lawfull to speak against the
truth . Accustom thy self neuer to lie
wittinglie ; and of set purpose, neither
to excuse thy self, nor for any other
cause, calling alwais to mind, that God
is the God of truth . Yf thou chaunce
to tell a lie , and canst handsomly correct it out of hand , either by recalling
it merily, or by some good explication,
doe it: a true excuse , hath much more
grace and force to giue satisfaction,
then a lie neuer so smoothlie tolde.

2. Though sometime a man may
prudently and discreetly disguise and
couer the truth, by some artificiall colour of speeche , yet must that be vsed
only in matters of importance , when
the

the glorie and seruice of God manifestly requireth it. Excepting onely those
occasions, such artificiall equiuocation
is daungerous, for as holy writt sayeth:
*the holy Ghost dwelleth not in a dissembling
and double spirit*: No cunning is so much
to be desired as simplicitie ; the wisdome of the worlde, and subtilitie of the
fleshe, belong to the children of this
world : but the children of God, walk
plainely, without going awrie, their
hart is free from all doublenes . *He that
walketh simply* (sayth the wiseman) *walketh confidently* . Liyng, double dealing,
& dissembling, are allways signes of a
weak, and base spirit S. Austin had sayd
in the 4. booke of his Confessions,
that his soule, and his frinds soule, were
but one soule ; and that his life was tedious vnto him after the death of his
frind, because he would not liue by
by halfes ; and yet that for the self same
cause he feared to die, least his frind
should die wholly in him. These words
afterward, seemed vnto him too artificiall, and affected, in so much that he
corrected them in the bookes of his
Retractations, censuring them with a
note

note of follie . Seeft thou not Philotheus, what a liuely and delicate feeling,
this holy and pure foule had of curious
painted fpeeches? Surely it is a great ornament of a chriftian foule to be faithfull , plaine , and fincere in talk : I haue
fayd , *I will obferue and keep my wayes ,
that I may not offend in my tongue. Sett (ò
Lord) a watch before my mouth , and a
doore of ftrength and clofenes to shutt my
lippes* , fayth Dauid.

3. It is an aduife of the holy king S.
Lewes, to contrarie or gainfay no man,
vnleffe it were either finne or domage,
to let his words paffe without contradicting them : and by this meanes, a
man may be fure to efcape all quarrels and debates . But when neceffitie
conftraineth to oppofe thy opinion
againft another mans , vfe mildnes ,
warines and dexteritie, not feeking to
vex his fpirit , whome thou gain-
fayeft , nor to confound him : for
nothing is gained by sharpe repre-
henfion , or too much ftomach in
contradicting.

4. The auncient fages highlie commended them that fpake litle , which is
                                         to

to be vnderstood , not of them that
speak few words, but of them that vse
not many needlesse, and vnprofitable
words ; for in this matrer of talk , we
regard not so much the quantitie , as
the qualitie: and in my opinion, we
oughte for to flie both extreams . For
to shew ones self a graue profound doctour, refusing to condescend to familiar talk , vsed in honest recreations,
argueth either some distrust or disdaine. And on the other side , to prate always, and giue neither place nor occasion vnto other men to speak their
pleasure, smelleth either of vainglorie,
or of follie and lightnes.

    5. S. Lewes allowed it not for good
manners, when one is in companie , to
talke to anie man in secret , and in
counsail , principallie at the table:
least he giue some cause to suspect ,
that he speaketh ill of others . *He
that is at table* (sayth he) *in good companie,
and hath any good and merry conceipt to
say , lett him speake, that all the company may heare him : yf it be any
thing of importance, that he would not haue
all men know, let him conceal it altogether,
and*

and tell it no man while *the companie is
not dissolued .*

Of honest and commendable pa-
stimes and recreations .

CHAPTER 31.

I. IT is sometimes necessary to ease
our spirit, and affoord it , and the
bodie also , some kind of recreation. S. Iohn the Euangelist (as the deuout Cassianus reporteth) was vpon a
time found by a huntsman , to haue a
partrige in his hand, and to make much
of it , and play with it for his passetine:
the huntsman demanded wherfore he, a
man of such qualitie , tooke delight in
so low and base a recreation; well (sayd
S. Iohn) and wherfore doest not thou
carie thy bow allways bent ? marrie ,
(quoth the huntsman) least yf it should
be always bent; it would loose his force
and strength , when it should be needfull . Wonder not then at me (replied
the blessed Apostle) yf I cease a litle
from the rigour and attention of my
spirit, to take a litle rest and recreation,
that after this small ease , I may after
employ

employ my self more earneftlie in contemplation of higher matters . It is doubtleffe a great vice to be fo rude and fauage , as nether to allowe ones felf, nor to fuffer any other, to enioy fome kind of lawfull paffetime, & recreation.

2.   To take the ayre , to walke, and talk merrily and louingly together , to play on the lute , and other fuch inftruments, to fing in mufick, to goe a hunting, are recreations fo honeft , that to vfe them well , there needs but ordinarie prudence , which giueth euery thing , due order , place , feafon , and meafure.

3.   Thofe games in which the gaine gotten by them, ferueth for a price and recompence of nimblenes of the bodie or induftrie of the mind , as tennis, baloone , ftoole bale , cheffe , tables , running at the ringe, be of them felues good and lawfull : onely exceffe is to be auoided either in the time employed vpon them, or in the wager that is playde for: yf too much time be fpent in thefe difports, they are no more recreation , but an occupation , not eafing either bodie or mind, but weeriyng the
                                                    one,

one, and dulling the other. After fiue or
six houres spent at cheſſe, who is not altogether weeried in ſpirit with ſo much
attention? To play a whole afternoone
at tennis, is not to recreate the bodie,
but to tire it: Againe if the wager which
is plaid for, be of ouergreat valew, the
affections of the gamſters grow out of
ſquare: & beſides it is an vniuſt and vn-
reaſonable thing, to lay great wagers
vpon ſuch ſlight induſtries, ſo vnprofitable, and ſo litle praiſe-worthie. But
aboue all Philotheus, take heed thou ſet
not thy affection vpō theſe diſports, for
how lawful ſoeuer any recreatiō be, it is
a vice to ſet the hart vpon it : not that
thou ſhouldſt not take pleaſure in ſpor-
tinge, for without pleaſure there can be
no recreation : but that thou ſhouldſt
not ſo place thy hart vpon theſe paſſetimes, as to be allways deſirous of thē,
and not to be content without them.

---

*Of dauncing and ſome other paſſetimes which
are lawfull, but dangerous withall.*

CHAPTER 32.

1. **D**ANCES of their owne nature
be things indifferent, & may be
vſed

vfed either well or ill, but as they are ordinarily vfed, they incline & leane much
to the worffer fide, & confequently are
full of danger & perill. They are vfed by
night, in darkenes, & obfcuritie: & verie eafie it is for the works of darknes,
to flipp into a fubiect, fo apte of it felf
to receaue euil accidents. The greateft
part of the night is fpent in thē, fo that
by late watching, men are faine to fleep
out the mornings, and by confequence,
the meanes to ferue God. In a word, it
is allwais follie to change the day into
night, light into darknes, and good
workes into fond fooleries; Eache one
that cometh to daunce, bringeth with
him his head brimfull of vanitie: and vanitie is fo great a difpofitiō to naughtie
affectiōs, & to dāgerous & reprehēfible
loues, that fuch badde fruicts with great
facilitie, are engēdered in thefe dances.

2. I may fay of dāces (Philotheus,) as
the phyficiās doe of mushroms, or tòad-
ftooles, though manie do eat thē for
dainties, yet (fay they) the beft of thē
are worth nothing: & I fay likewife, that
though dances are much frequēted the
beft of thē are not very good. They that
will

will needs feede on fo vnprofitable a
dishe as mushroms are, procure that
they be excellente well dreſt; yf by no
meanes thou canſt excuse thy felf by
reaſon of the companie in which thou
art from dancing, fee that thy dance
be well ordered. But how muſt it be
well ordered? with modeſtie, feemli-
nes, and an honeſt intention. Eate but
feldome, and in litle quantitie of mushroms (fay the pyſitions) for yf they
be ofttimes eaten, & in great abundance, be they neuer fo well dreſſed, the
quantitie of them becometh venom ih
the ſtomacke. Dance litle at a time, and
verie feldome Philotheus, for otherwiſe thou putteſt thy felf in danger to
affect ouer much this exercife, fo peril-
lous, and apt to brede fuch badd rruiꞓs
in the foule, as we euen now mentioned. Mushroms according to Pliny,
being fpongie, and full of wide pores,
draw vnto them verie eaſilie, all infe-
ꞓion neere them, in fo much that yf
they be nigh ferpents and toades, they
receaue venom from them, which is
the cauſe we call them toadſtooles:
Dancing fports in night-aſſemblies,
                                    do or-

do ordinarilie draw with the these vices
and sinnes, which commonly raigne in
one place, quarrelles, enuie, scoffing,
and wanton loue; and as these exercises
doe open the pores of the bodie that
vseth them, so they open the powers of
the soule, and yf anie serpentine companion, breath into their eares some
wanton or lasciuious word, or some lo-
ue·toy;yf some Basiliske or Cokatrice,
cast an amourous eye, an vnchast looke,the hart thus opend, easilie entertaineth these poisons. O Philotheus,these
impertinent recreations are ordinarilie
dangerous; they dissipate the spirit of
deuotion,weaken the forces,make charitie cold, and stir vp in the soule, a
thousand sortes of euil affections : and
therfore it is , that they are to be vsed
with great discretion.

3. Aboue all , the physicians prescribe, that after mushroms , we should
drinck good wine : and I say, that after
dancinge, it is behouefull to vse good
and holie considerations,to hinder those
dangerous impressions which the vaine
delight taken in dancing may haue left
in our mind.Thinck then; 1. that whist
                                      thou

thou waſt buſied in this idle exerciſe,
manie ſoules did burne in hell fire for
ſinnes committed in dancinge, and by
the occaſion of the time and place, and
cōpanie, and other circunſtances which
dācinge bringeth with it. 2. Many religious, deuout perſōs at that verie time
in the preſence of God, did ſing his heauenly praiſes, & contemplated his diuine goodnes. And how much more happely was their time ſpent in praying, thē
thine in dācing. 3. Whilſt thou dancedſt
merilie, many ſoules deceaſed out of this
world in great anguiſh & dread of conſcience; manie thouſand men & wemen
ſuffered great dolours; diſeaſes, & pangs,
in their beds, in hoſpitals, in the ſtreets,
the goute, the grauell, burning feuers,
canckers, and infinite ſortes of miſeries.
They had thē no reſt, & thou hadſt thē
no cōpaſſion of thē. And thinckſt thou
not that one day perhaps thou ſhalt ſigh
while others dance, as thou haſt now
danced while others ſighe? 4. Our Lord,
our Ladie, the Angels, & Saints, beheld
thee all the while thou dauncedſt, how
deerlie did they pittie thy poore ſoule,
that was buſied in ſo vnprofitable an en-
ter-

tertainment!

5. Alas, while thou wert thus mif-
pending thy goldē leafure, which might
haue been farre better employed, time
paſſed away, and death drewe nigh, and
mocking (as it were) thy indifcreet
paſſetime, inuiteth thee to his dance, in
which theſighes of thy frinds ſhall ſerue
for well tuned vialles, where thou ſhalt
giue but one turne from life to death.
This dance is the true paſſetime of mortal mē, for in it wee paſſe in a moment,
from time to eternitie, of vnſpeakeable
ioyes, or intolerable paines: I haue ſett
thee downe theſe few conſiderations:
God will ſuggeſt many other vnto thee
to the ſame effect, yf thou feare him
truly.

The times to ſport and dance.

CHAPTER 33.

1. **T**O ſport and dāce well and lawfullie, requires that we vſe theſe
delights for recreation of our
minds, and not for any affectiō we beare
to the ſportes them ſelues; that we con-
tinewe them but a ſhort time; not till

we be weeried and dulled therwith; that
we exercife them but feldome, and not
euerie day, for otherwife we turne recreation into an occupation. But in
what occafions may a man vfe dancing
and fportings. The iuft occafions of in-
differente difportes are moft frequent:
occafions of vnlawfull are verie rare, and
fuch games are much more blame worthie and dangerous. But in one word,
the lawfull time and occafió of dancing
and fporting is, when prudence and difcretion telleth thee, that thou mft con-
difcēd to giue cōtentmēt to the honeft
cōpanie, in which thou sbalt be in conuerfation. For difcreet condefcendence
is a braunche of charitie, and maketh
indifferēt things to be meritorious, and
dangerous things, to be tolerable, and
taketh many times malice away from
things that otherwife would be badde,
which is the reafon that games of hazard, which otherwife would be repre-
henfible, are not fo, when iuft condefcendence doth lead vs therunto.

2. I receaued great comfort in hart to
read in the life of bleffed Charles Boro-
mæus, the holy bishop of millan, that he
con-

cōdiſcended vnto the Suiſſers in certain things, in which otherwiſe, he was very ſeuere : and that the bleſſed Ignatius de Loyola, being deſired to play, accepted of it. *S.* Elizabeth of Hungarie, was wonte to ſporte her ſelf, and be preſente at aſſemblies of paſſetime, without hurte of her deuotion: which was ſo deeply rooted in her ſoule, that as the rockes about the lake of Rietta, do increaſe by the waſhing and beating of the waues; ſo her deuotion increaſed among the pōpes & vanities of the court wher vnto her high eſtate expoſed her; Theſe were great fires, and of ſuch propertie, as to increaſe with the wind, wher as litle flames, be ſoone blowne out, yf we carie them not couered.

To be faithful and conſtant in great and ſmall occaſions.

CHAPTER 34.

1. **T**HE ſacred ſpouſe in the canticles ſayth, that his eſpouſe had rauished his hart with one of her eyes, and one haire of her head. Among all the exteriour parts of mans

bodie

bodie none is more noble, for the artificiallnes of the making, or the actiuitie,then is the eye;none more bafe then the haire. The meaning then of the diuine fpoufe is,to giue vs to vnderftād, that he accepteth not onely the great works of deuout perfons, but euen the fmalleft and leaft:and that to ferue him well,and according to his will,is to take great care in greate and litle peeces of feruice,in lowe and in loftie things:and that equallie in both kinds, we may (as it were) robbe him of his hart.

2. Prepare thy felf then (my Philotheus) to fuffer manie great afflictions, yea & martyrdome it felf for our Lord: refolue thy felf to giue vp vnto him, all that which thou efteemeft moft pretious whenfoeuer it pleafeth him to demaund it,father,mother,husband,wife, brother,fifter,childrē, thine owne eyes, and thy life too:thy hart muft be readie to yeld him vp all thefe things at a beck. But as long as his diuine prouidēce fendeth thee no afflictions fo fenfible and heauie,that they require not thine eyes, at leaft giue him thy haire:I meane,fuffer meekly and louinglie litle iniuries,
                                    fmall

fmal offences, & pettie domages, which
daylie happē vnto thee. For by such litle
occasions employed for his loue, thou
shalt winne his hart whollie, and make
it thine owne. The headach, the tooth-
ache, the rheume, a check of thy husbād
or wife, the breaking of a glasse, losse of
a paire of gloues, of a iewell, of a hand-
kerchief, a frumpe or mock patiently
borne, a litle violence offered to thy self
in goinge to bedde soone, and risinge
earlie to serue God, and communicate,
a litle shame sustained for doinge some
actions of deuotion in publique. To be
brieffe, any such slight occasions of patiēce & sufferāce taken & embraced for
the loue of God, do infinitly please his
diuine goodnesse, who for one glasse of
water, hath promised & prepared heauen
to his seruants. And becaufe these occasions offer thē selues euery momēt, they
are great instruments to heape vp spirituall treasures, yf they be well imploied.

3. When I read in the life of *S.* Catherin of Siena, so manie raptes and eleuations of her spirit, so many wise say-
ings, and godly sermons made by her: I
nothing doubt, but that with this faire

T 4   eye

eye of contemplation, she rauished the
hart of her heauenly spouse. And I receaue no leſſe côfort, when I find her in
her fathers kitchin making the fire,tur-
ning the ſpitt, dreſſing meat, kneading
bread,& doinge all the low & baſer offices of the houſe, with a courage full of
louingdelight in her God. And I eſteeme no leſſe the lowlie meditatiôs which
ſhe made in the midſt of thes abieꞒt offices,thê the extaſies and heauêlie viſions
which she had ſo ofté;which peraduenture were giuen vnto her onely for re-
côpence of this humilitie & abieꞒtion.
As for her meditatiôs,they were ſuch as
folowe,when she prepared meat for her
father,she imagined that she prepared it
for our Lord like another martha, and
that her mother was in place of our
bleſſed Ladie,and her brethré in ſteed of
the holie Apoſtles:in this ſort encouraging her mind to ſerue all the court of
heauen,and imploying her ſelf moſt de-
lightfully in ſuch humiliatiôs, becauſe
she knew it was Gods will. I haue ſet
downe this example, (my Philotheus)
that thou mayſt knowe of what importance it is, to direꞒt well all thy aꞒtions,
                                                be

be they neuer so base, to the seruice of
his diuine maiestie.

4. Therfore my counsell is, that thou
imitate that courageous woma whome
the wise king Salomon so highlie commendeth: she sett her hands (as he sayth)
to great, importat, & magnificet things:
and yet disdained not to lay hold on the
spindle and rock. Put thou thy hads to
great things, exercising thy self in prayer
& meditatio, in frequenting the Sacra-
mets, to engeder the loue of God in thy
neighbours, & to stirre vp good inspirations in their soules, and in a word, to do
great & excellet good works according
to thy callinge, forgette not for all that
the rock, and spindle, that is the practize
of lowlie actions, and humble virtues,
which like small flowers growe at the
foote of the crosse, as, to serue the poore,
visit the sick, to haue care of thy family,
with the works belonging therunto, to
vse all profitable diligence, to auoide
idlenes: and amidst all these actions,
enterlace such deuout considerations,
as S. Catherin of Siena did in her mortifications.

5. Great occasions of seruing God,

prefent themfelues but feldome, leffer occafions offer them felues euerie daye: and *he that shalbe trusty in small matters,* (fayth our Saueour) *shalbe established ouer great things.* Doe euerie thing then on the name of God, and euery thing wilbe well done: whether thou eateft or drinckeft, fleepeft, or wakeft, be it in recreation or bufineffe, fo that thou handle thy matters well, and hauing always an eye to Gods pleafure and will, thou shalt profit much before God; dooing all thefe thinges, becaufe that Gods will is that thou doe them.

That we must keep our foule iust and reasonable, in all her actions.

CHAPTER 35.

1. WWE are not men, but through the vfe of reafon : and yet is it a rare thing to find men that are reafonnable indeed : for commonlie felf loue maketh vs fwarue from reafon, conducting vs vnawares, and almoft without our knowledge or feeling, to a thoufand fort of fmal, yet dangerous, vniuft and vnreafonable actios; which

which like the litle foxes in the Canticles, roote vp the fruictfull vines ; for
becaufe they are litle, mē take no great
heed of them : and becaufe they are
many in number, they lett not to doe
harme enough.

2. Thefe things which now I wil reken
are they not vniuft, & againft true reafon ? we accufe our neighbours vpon
euerie light occafion , and excufe our
felues in all things ; wee would fell verie
deer,& buy verie cheape : we defire that
iuftice should be exequuted in another
mans houfe , but mercie and clemencie
in our owne. Our words muft be taken
in good part, and yet we are captious &
cauill precifely at other mens fpeaches.
We would haue our neighbour leaue vs
his goods for our monie: but is it not
more reafonable , that he should keep
his goods,leauing vs our monie? we are
difcontented with him , becaufe he will
not helpe vs to his owne incōmoditie:is
it not more reafon we should reprehēd
our felues , for defiring to hinder his
commoditie ?

3. Yf we affect one kind of exercife,
we difcommend all other:and controlle
T 6   and

and condemne all that displeaseth vs. Yf
any of our inferiours haue no great
good grace in his person or actions, or
that we haue a tooth against him , doe
he what he wil,& doe he it neuer so wel
we take it ill , & neuer cease to contri-
state him, & to be always readie to cha-
lenge him. Contrariwise , yf any be acceptable to vs, & seeme to vs of a good
grace and cariage,he can do nothing so
disorderly but we will excuse it . There
are many virtuous childrẽ whome their
father and mother scarce abide to look
vpon, because of some bodily imperfection : and manie vicious that are their
parents minions , and are cockered vp-
daintelie, onely for some corporall wel
fauourednesse. In all things we preferre
the rich before the poore, allthough
they be neither of better condition,nor
more virtuous:nay we preferre him that
hath the gayest clothes . We will haue
our owne due exactly , but others must
be courteous in demãding their due of
vs;we keep our ranck & place verie precisely, but would haue other men humble & condescend ; we cõplaine easilye
of others, but will heare no complaints
                                             of

of our selues : That litle which wee doe
for other men, seemes in our eye & iudgemente verie muche, but whatsoeuer
seruice or good turne an other mã doth
to vs, it seemes to our sighte in a maner
nothinge. In a worde we are much like
the partridges of Paphlagonia which are
sayde to haue two harts, for to our selues
& in fauour of our owne righte, we haue a harte that is sweete benigne & libe-
ral, but to our neighbour a harde, seuere
& rigerous harte. We haue tow sorts of
ballances, the one to weighe our owne
cõmodities with al aduautage possible,
the other to weighe with all disadaun-
tage what we deliuer to our neighbour.
And as the scripture sayeth, *deceiptful lippes haue spokẽ in hart & hart,* that is to saie
they haue two harts, & two weights, to
receiue a heauye and full weighte, to
deliuer a lighte and skant weighte,
is abhominable before God.

4. Philotheus obserue equallitye & iustice in all thy actiõs ; imagine thy selfe
in thy neighbours place, & him in thyne: & so shallt thou iudge arighte. Whẽ
thou sellest, thinke thy selfe the buyer,
& buyinge, proceede as if thou wert the
seller.

seller, for thus thou wilt be sure to deale
iustly in al the bargaines & cōtracts. All
these inequallityes I confesse are lighte
& binde not to restitution, because we
exceede not the limittes of that rigour
which we may lawfully vse in fauour of
our owne righte: yet notwithstandinge
they are greate defects of reason, & charitie, & consequētly bynde vs to procure
the amendmēte thereof especiallie since the things which we forsake in this
amendment, are but meere trifles. For
what doth a man leese by liuing gen-
tlemanly, nobly, courteously, with a
royall, free and liberall hart.

5. Let this then be thy particular care
Philotheus, to examine thy hart, and see
whether it be so affected towards thy
neighbour, as thou wouldst haue him
affected toward thee, yf thou wert in his
place: for in that stands the triall of true
reason. Traianus the Emperour, being
blamed by his faithfull frinds, for making the imperial maiestie (as it seemed
to thē) too familiar & cōmon: verie well
quoth he, & why should not I shew in
my self being Emperour, such an affection to euerie mā in particular, as I my
                                    self,

felf, yf I were a particular & priuate mā,
would defire to find in my Emperour.

Of defires.   CHAP. 36.

EVERY one knoweth, that he muft
in no fort defire any thing which
is naughtie & vicious: for the defire of euil maketh vs euil. But I fay more
vnto thee, Philotheus, defire not in any
cafe thofe things, which be dāgerous to
the foule, as dancing, gaming, and other
fuch paftimes; nor honours & places of
charge ; no not admirable vifions , nor
heauenly extafies, for al thefe things are
much fubiect to vaine glorie, & deceit.

2. Defire not things which are farre of
frō thee, that cānot come to paffe according to thy defire , but after fome lōng
time; as many doe, who therfore dowee-
rie & diftract their harts vnprofitably, &
put thē felues in dāger of great difquiet.
Yf a yoūg mā defire much to be prouided
of fome great office & charge, beforethe
time be come , to what purpofe ferueth
this defire of his? yf a married womā defireth to be a nunne, to what purpofe? If
I defire to buy the goods of my neighbour, before he defire to fel thē, loofe I
not

not my labour in such a fruitlesse desire? If being sore sick, I desire to preach
or to say masse, or to visit others that
be sick, and performe other exercises
of men that be in perfect health: be not
these vaine desires, since it is not in my
power to bring thē to effect? And yet besides this vanitie of these vnprofitable
desires, they occupie the place of other
better desires which I should haue, to
be patient, resigned, wel mortified, verie obedient, meek, and mild in aduer-
sities, which is the thing that God wills
that I should practize at that time; but
we admitt as fond desires as wemen
great with child, that long for cherries
and strawberies in autumne, and for
freshe grapes, in the springtime.

3. I can not approue in any sort, that
men addicted to one kind of estate and
vocation, should desire any other kind
of life, then that which befitteth their
calling, or busie them selues in exercises, incompatible with their present
condition: for such desires distract the
hart, and altogether destroye the necessarie occupations belonging to his
estate. If I desire the solitarye lyfe of a

Car-

Carthufian, I doe but lofe my tyme, for
thefe defyres occupie the tyme and place of thofe, which I shoulde haue for
the well imploying of my felfe in thinges belonginge to my prefente office.
No furely, I woulde not that men
should be still defyringe better fpiritts,
better witts, better iudgements, for thefe defyres are but vayne, and onely ferue to hinder thofe thoughtes and cares
which euery one should haue of better-
inge thofe parts which God allmightye
hath endued allreadye him withal. No I
would not that one shoulde defyre better meanes to ferue God almightye, then
which allreadie he hath, but that he labour and endeauour to employe thefe
well & profitallie: this in deede is to be
vnderftoode of defyres that, as it were,
still poffeffe the harte, for fimple wishes
if they be not too frequent, doe no
harme or hinderaunce.

4. Defire not further croffes and afflictions, but accordinge as thou hafte
founde thy felfe difpofed and able to
beare thofe which God allmightie hath
allreadye fente thee. If a leffe iniurie we
can not endure without repininge, were it

re it not vayne and foolishe to defyre
martyrdome? About obiects imagina-
rye and fuch thinges as shal neuer come
to paffe, our enemye moueth to greate
and magnanimious defyres, and all to
the ende of euertinge vs from the consideration of thinges prefente, wherein
(how meane foeuer) we mighte exercife
our felues with greate profitte, we imagine combatts with the terrible monfters of Afrique, and in the meane tyme
for wante of care and heede, fuffer
our felues, in effecte to be vanquishte
and flayne, by the poore fnailes that lye
in our waye.

5. Seeke not after temptations, for
that were temeritye and rashnes, but
prepare thy harte to expecte the courageoufly, and to receaue them when God
permittes them to come.

6. Varietye of meates (efpeciallie if
the quantitie be greate) doe allwayes
ouercharge the ftomacke, yea if it be
weake ouerthroweth it. Ouercharge not
thou thy foule with multitude of
thoughts: not worldly, for thefe will be
thy vtter ouerthrowe, nor yet fpirituall,
for they will moleft thee.

7. When

7. When the foule is purged, & difcharged of her ill humours, she feeleth in her felf, an earneft appetite of fpirituall delights, and like a hunger ftarued perfon, fetteth her defire vpon a thoufand forts of exercifes of pietie, of mortificatiō, of penaunce, of humilitie, of charitie and prayer: my Philotheus, it is a good figne to haue fo good an appetite, but cōfider difcreetly whether thou canft well difgeft all that which thou defireft to eate. Then take aduife of thy ghoftly father, which of all thefe many holy defires, may prefently be put in execution, and make thy yttermoft profit of them: And that donne, God wil giue thee other good defires, which thou maift exequute in their time and feafon: and fo thou shalt not loofe thy time in nourishing vnpoffible, and vn profitable defires.

8. Yet my meaning is not, that one should reiect all good defires whatfoeuer: but that one should endeuour difcreetly, to produce and profequute them, euery one in their due order: fo that thefe good purpofes, which cannot prefently haue their effect, be (as it were) locked

locked vp in a corner of our hart, vntill
the time come in which they may be
brought to yſſue and practize . In the
meane ſeaſon , while thoſe deſires expect their time , procure to effectuat
thoſe which be already ripe , and in
their ſeaſon. And this aduiſe is not onely true in ſpirituall deſires , but euen in
wordly purpoſes , in which likewiſe yf
order be not kept , they them ſelues
can neuer liue in quiet and contentment .

Aduertiſments for thoſe which are maried.   C H A P. 37.

1. **M**ARIAGE *is a great Sacra-*
ment, I ſay in Ieſus-Chriſt and in
his churche; it is honourable to all,
amongſt all , and in all : that is , in all the
partes and circumſtances therof ; to all,
becauſe euen the virgins , them ſelues
ought to reuerence it with humilitie:
amongſt all , becauſe it is equallie holy
in rich , and in poore : in all , becauſe
the beginning , the end and intention,
the commodities and profits , the forme and matter of it, all are holie. Marriage

riage is the nurferie of Chriftianitie, which peopleth the earth with faithfull foules, to accomplish the number of the elect in heauen: fo that the conuerfation of all the rights and lawes of the holy eftate of wedlock, is moft necefsarie in the common wealth, as the fpring and fountaine, of all thefe riuers.

2. Would to God that his moft deer Sonne were inuited to all marriages, as he was to the marriage in Cana: for then the pretious wine of blefling and confolation, should neuer want: and yf in ordinarie weddings we find but a litle of that fweet wine, it is becaufe Adonis is inuited to the wedding feaft, in fteed of our Saueour, and Venus in fteed of our Ladie. He that would haue his lambes faire and parti-coloured as Iacobs were, muft imitate his induftrie, and prefent parti-coloured roddes to the ewes when they affemble to conceiue: and he that would enioy a happie fuccefle of his marriage, should always place before his eyes the fanctitie, and excellence of this Sacrament. But alas infteed of thefe, ordinarilie we fee

arriue

arriue a thousand disorders in pastimes, feastinge, and vnseemly talking: and therfore no meruaile, yf the successe of their mariages be disordered.

3. Therefore I exhort all those which are in the holie estate of wedlock, that they loue one another with that mutual loue, which the holy Ghost commendeth so much in the scripture. It is not enough to say to married folk, that they should loue one another with a naturall loue, for so do the Turtle doues: nor with a humane loue, for the verie painims haue wel practised that sort of loue: but I say with the great Apostle: *You that are married, loue your wiues, as Iesus Christ loued his church: and you wiues loue your housbands, as the church loueth her Saviour.* It was God that brought Eue to our first father Adam, and gaue him her for his wife: it is also the self same God, who with his inuisible hand, hath tied the knot of the holie band of your mariage, and hath giuen you power one ouer the other: why then should you not one cherish the other, with a holy, supernaturall, and diuine loue?

4. The

4. The firſt effect of this loue, is the inſeparable vnion of your harts. Two peeces of firre tree glewed togeather, cleaue ſo faſt one to the other, that you may ſooner break the whole peece in any other place, then in that part in which they were glued. But God ioined man to woman in his owne bloud, for which cauſe this vnion is ſo ſtrong, that rather the ſoule ſhould forſake the bodie, then the husband be ſeparated from his wife: and vnderſtand this inſeparable vnion which I ſpeak of, not onely of the bodie, but principallie of the ſoule, and ſincere affection of the hart.

5. The ſecond effect of this loue is inuiolable loyaltie, of the one partie to the other. In old time men vſed to engraue their ſeales vpon the rings which they wore continuallie, as the holie ſcripture it ſelf doth teſtifie: and from this cuſtom of antiquitie may we drawe a fitt interpretation of the ceremonie which holie Church vſeth in the Sacrament of marriage. For the prieſt halowinge the wedding ringe, and giuing it firſt to the man, proteſteth
that

that this holy Sacrament so sealeth and closeth his hart, that neuer after the name or loue of anie other woman, may lawfullie enter into it, so long as she liueth, whome God hath giuen vnto him. And the husband presently putteth the ring vpon his wiues finger, that shee likewise may vnderstand, that her hart is now sealed and shutt vp, from loue or thougth of any other man, so long as he liueth, whome there our *Saucour* giueth vnto her.

6. The third fruit of matrimonial loue, is the lawfull generation, and the carefull education of children. It is an inexplicable honour to you that are maried, that God by his omnipotent power, determining to multiplie reasonnable soules, which might praise him for euer, would make you as it were his feelow-labourers in so worthie a worke, giuing you the priuiledge & honor to engender bodies, into the which he distilles the new created soule, like celestiall dropes into the bodies.

7. Conserue then, you housbands, a tender, constant, and hartie loue towards your wiues; for therefore was the

woman

woman taken from the side of man,
and next his hart, that she should be
beloued of him hartylie and tenderly.
The infirmities of your wiues, corporall or spirituall, must not prouoke you
to any disdaigne or loathing of them,
but rather to a sweet and louely compassion : since God therfore created
them, that depending always on you,
you should therby be more honoured,
& respected ; and that you should haue
them in such sort for your companions
that neuerthelesse you should be their
heads and superiours. And you, ô women, loue your husbands tenderlie &
hartelie, but let your loue be full of respect, and reuerence, for therefore did
God create them of a sex more vigourous and predominant ; therfore did he
ordaine that a woman should be a portion of man, bone of his bone, and
flesh of his flesh ; and that she should be
made of a ribbe of his, and taken from
vnder his arme, to teache her, that she
should be vnder the hand and guiding
of her husband : and holy scripture verie
straightly recommēdeth vnto you this
subiection; which notwithstanding the

V   self

felf fame fcripture maketh fweet and
delectable vnto you ; not onely adui-
fing you to accept therof with loue
and affection , but prefcribing alfo
vnto your husbands , how they should
exercife their authoritie and commaund ouer you, with all patience,
meeknes, and gentle fufferance : *Hou-*
fbands (fayth Saint Peter) *behaue your*
felues difcreetlie towards your wiues, as
weaker veffels , bearing them honour and
refpect.

8. But while I exhort you more
and more to increafe this holy mutuall loue, which you owe one to
another, beware you chaunge it not
into iealoufie. For as wormes breed
ordinarilie in the ripeft and delicateft
apples : fo manie times it happines,
that iealoufie groweth from ardent and
exceffiiue loue, betweene man and
wife , and marreth and corrupteth
the verie pithe and fubftance of the
holie ftate of wedlock, breeding by
litle and litle, troublefome braules,
diffentions, and diuorcements. This
iealoufie hath no place where mutuall
loue is grounded vpon true virtue:
                                and

and therfore it is an infallible marke of a loue, in part at leaſt groſſe and ſenſuall, which hath mette with a weake and inconſtante virtue, and ſubiect to miſtruſt and ſuſpect. And it is a verie vaine boaſtinge of loue, to make it ſeeme greate, by beinge iealous : for iealouſie may well be a ſigne of great and ardent loue, but not of pure, perfect and conſtant amitie : for the perfection of frindſhip and true loue, preſuppoſeth the aſſured foundation of true virtue, and iealouſie preſuppoſeth the vncertaintie of the ſame.

9. Yf you deſire, ô husbandes, that your wiues be faithfull vnto you, giue them a leſſon of this loyaltie by your owne example. *With what face* (ſayth Saint Gregory Naziazen) *can you exact chaſtity of your wiues, when you your ſelues liue vncleanly? how can you require of them, that which you giue them not? Will you haue them chaſt in deed? behaue your ſelues chaſtly: And,* (as Saint Paul ſayth) *let euery man, knowe how to poſſeſſe*

V 2   *his*

his owne veſſel in ſanctification . For yf con-
trary to this doctrine of the Apoſtle , you your
ſelues teach them looſe behauiour , and wan-
ton trickes, no meruail yf you receaue disho-
nour by loſſe of their honeſty : But you (ô
women) whoſe honour and reputation is in-
ſeparably ioined with your honeſtie and
chaſtitie, be iealouſe (in a manner) of this
your glorie , and ſuffer no kind of wan-
tonneſſe , to blemiſh your credit and eſti-
mation .

10. You that deſire to haue the name
and merit of chaſt and worthie matrons, flie all kind of aſſaultes, all manner of courting, be it neuer ſo litle:
ſuffer not any wanton geſtures nigh
you : ſuſpect him , whoſoeuer he
be , that commendeth your beautie,
and good grace : for he that earneſtly praiſeth marchandize which he
is not able to buy, giues a ſhrewd
ſuſpicion , that he meaneth to ſteale
it. But yf iointlie with praiſes of your
beautie, any man diſcommend your
husbands , deteſt him as one that offereth you hainous iniurie ; for it is
euident , that ſuch a one not onely
ſeeketh your ruine and ouerthrow,
but

but accounteth you alredie half ouercome : becaufe we fee ordinarilie,
that the bargaine is half made with
the fecond chap man, when the firft
difpleafeth the merchant. Gentle-
women, as well in time paft, as
now a dayes, weare manie pearles
in their eares, delighted (as Plinie
thought) with the prettie ratling
noife which they make, in touching
one another. Why they wore them I
care not, I thinck verelie Ifaac, that
great feruant and frind of God, fent
pretious earings as the firft pledge
of his loue, to the faire and chaft
Rebecca, as a myfticall ornament
betokening, that the firft part which
a husband should take poffeffion of
in his wife, muft be her eares, which
his wife should loyallie keep onely
for her housbands vfe : to the end
that no fpeech or rumour should enter therin, but onelie the fweet amiable found of honeft and chaft wordes, which are the orient pearls of
the holy ghofpell ; for we muft allways remember that which before I
haue fayd, that our foules are empoi-

foned

ned by the eare, as the bodie by the
mouthe.

11. Loue and loyaltie ioined together, cause a constant and fearlesse
assurance ; and therfore the Saints of
God presupposing this fidelitie, haue
vsed alwais most kind signes and tokens of their mutuall loue : sweet,
and louing fauours , but yet chast
and honest ; tender , and kind harted , but yet sincere , plaine , and
beseeming their graue simplicitie.
So Isaac and Rebecca , the chastest
maried couple of old time , were
seene so louinglie entertaining one
another by a windeowe , that albeit
no offensiue thinge passed betweene
them , yet Abimelech well iudged
therby, that they could not be other
then man and wife . The great
Saint Lewes , as rigourous to his
owne fleshe , as tender in loue to
his wife , was allmost blamed for
too much kindnes ; though in deed
he rather deserued exceeding praise ,
for knowing how to applie his war-
lik and courageous mind , to these small duties , requisite to the
                                      conser-

conſeruation of coniugall loue, for
although theſe pettie demonſtra-
tions , of pure and vnfained affection , bind not the harts of theſe
that loue , yet they approache them
one to another, and ſerue for a kind
of art, to keep mutuall loue in perfection .

12. Saint Monica being with
child of great Saint Auguſtin , dedicated him oftentimes to Chriſtian religion , and to the true ſeruice of Gods glorie : as he himſelf witneſſeth , ſaying that *he had
already taſted the ſalt of God in his mothers wombe*. This is a notable leſſon
for Chriſtian wemen , to offer vp
to God the fruicts of their wom-
bes, euen before they be deliuered
of them, for God accepteth the offe-
rings of a louing and humble ſoule ; and commonly giueth good ſuc-
ceſſe to thoſe holie motions and affections of good mothers at that time : witneſſe Saint Thomas of Aquin,
Saint Andrew of Feſula , and diuers
others . The mother of S. Bernard (a
V 4   wor-

worthie mother of so worthie a child)
so soone as her children were borne,
took them in her armes, and offered them vp to our Lord Iesus Christ:
and from thence foorth, she loued
them with such reuerence, as holy
vessels committed vnto her by God;
which fell out so happilie vnto her,
that in the end they became Saints all
seauen.

13. The children being once borne
into the world, and beginning to haue
the vse of reason, then ought their
parents to haue an especiall care, to
emprint the feare and loue of God
in their tender harts. The good
Queen Blaunche, performed this office excellentlie well in her sonne
king Lewes the Saint; for she would
often times say vnto him, *my dear
child, I had rather farre thou shouldst
dye before mine eyes, then see thee committ one onely mortall sinne*. Which
notable saying remained so engraued in the soule of her royall child,
that, (as he himself was woont to
tell) not one day in all his life past
ouer his head, wherin he did not call
it to

it to remembrance, taking all paines possible to put this diuine doctrine in practize. Races, and generations in our tongue are called houses, and the Hebrewes call generation of children the bwilding vp of a house; for in that sence the scripture sayth, that God builded houses for the midwines of egypt: wherby we learne, that to make a good house, is not to fill it with worldlie treasures, but to bring vp children in the feare of God, and exercise of virtues, wherin no paines nor trauaile is to be spared, for children are the father and mothers glorie. So Saint Monica with great constancie and perseuerance, straue against the badde inclinations of her sonn Saint Augustin: for hauing folowed him by sea and by land, she made him more happily, the child of teares by conuersion of his soule, then he had beene the childe of her bloud, by generation of his bodie.

14. Saint Paul leaueth to wemen the care of their houshold, as their dutie and office: for which cause

V 5   manie

manie are of this opinion , that the
deuotion of the wife, is much more
profitable to her familie , then the
virtue of her husband ; becaufe he,
being not fo ordinarilie within dores,
cannot fo eafilie and continuallie inftruct his folk in virtue : and therfore *Salomon* in his prouerbes , maketh the happines of the whole houf-
hold , to depend of the induftrie and
care of that valourous and courageous woman , whome there he defcribeth.

15. It is written in Genefis , that
Ifaac feeing his wife Rebecca barren,
prayed to God for her , or according
to the Hebrew text , prayed our Lord
ouer againft her ; becaufe he prayed
on one fide of their oratorie , and she
on the other : and the prayer of her
housband made in this manner , was
heard . The greateft and fruictful-
left vnion between man and wife , is
that which is made in deuotion , to
which one should exhort the other
moft earneftlie . Some fruicts for
their fowerneffe are not much worthe , vnleffe they be conferued as quin-
ces;

ces ; others becaufe of their tendernes cannot be long be kept, vnleffe they be preferued , as cherries and aprie-cocks : So wemen should wishe that their husbands were preferued and comfited with the fugar of deuotion; without which man is fower , bittter, and intollerable ; And the husbands should procure that their wiues did ex-cell in deuotion , becaufe without it the woman is fraiie , and fubiect to fall and wither away in virtue. Saint Paul fayth : *that the vnbeleeuing man is fan-ctified by the faithfull* woman *, and the vnbeleeuing* woman *by the faithfull* man: becaufe in this ftraight bond of we-dlock , the one may eafilie draw the other to virtue ; but what a bleffing is it, when the faithfull man and wife, do fanctifie one another in the true feare of God.

16. To conclude the mutuall fup-porting of one another ought to be fo great, that they should neuer be both at once angrie , or moued on the fodaine. Bees cannot reft in pla-ces where ecchoes or redoublings

of voices are heard : nor can the holie Ghoſt certainlie remaine in that houſe, in which ſtrife, and debate, chiding and ſcolding, and redoubled braulings vſe to be. Saint Gregorie Nazianzen witneſſeth, that in his time married perſons, kept the anniuerſarie day of their matrimonie holie and feſtiuall : and I could wiſhe that good cuſtom were put in practize in theſe dayes, ſo that it were not with worldly and ſenſuall demonſtratiõs of exteriour myrth, but that the housband and wife confeſſinge and communicatinge that day, ſhould recõmend vnto God with more then ordinarie feruour, the conſtant quiet of their marriage, renewing their good purpoſes to ſanctifie their ſtate by mutuall loue and loyaltie, taking breath in our Lord, to ſupport the better the charge of their vocation.

Of the honeſtie and chaſtitie of the marriage-bed. CHAP. 38.

THE marriage-bed, ought to be immaculate as the Apoſtle ſaith, that is to ſay, exempt from all vncleañ

cleanlineſſe and profane filthines:ther-
fore was marriage firſt inſtituted and
ordained in the earthly paradiſe, where
vntill that time had neuer been felt any
extraordinarie concupiſcence. There is
ſome likenes between dishoneſt pleaſure, and vnmannerlie eating : for both
of them regard the fleſh, though the
firſt for the brutall heate therof, is ſimplie called carnall. I will declare by the
one, that which I would haue vnderſtood of the other.

1. Eating is ordained, for the conſeruation of them that eate : as then to
eate, preſerue, and nouriſh the bodie,
is abſolutelie good, and commendable : ſo alſo that which is requiſite in
marriage for generation of children, &
multiplication,is good and holie,being
one of the cheefeſt ends of marriage.

2. To eate, not for conſeruation of
life, but for mainteining of mutuall
loue and amitie which we owe one to
another, is a thing verie iuſt and honeſt : and in the ſame ſort, the mutuall
and lawfull ſatisfaction of the parties
ioined in holie marriage, is called by
Saint Paule, debt, and dutie; but ſo
great

great a debt and dutie, that he permitteth neither partie to exempt them
selues from it, without free and
voluntarie consent of the other ; no
not for the exercises of deuotiō (which
is the cause of that which hath been
sayd in the chapter of holy communion) how much lesse then may either
partie exempt them selues from this
debt, for anger, disdaine, or fantasticall pretenses.

3. As they that eate for mutuall
conuersation, doe it freelie, and not
as it were by force, but rather in
outward appeeraunce, at least wise
giue shew of an appetite to their
meate : so the mariage debt should
alway be payed and performed franckly, faithfullie, as it were with hope
and desire of children, albeit for some
occasion there were no subiecte of
such hope.

4. To eate, not for the two former reasons, but only to content
the appetite, is tollerable, but not
commendable : because the onely pleasure of the sensuall appetite, cannot
be a sufficient obiect, to make an
                                    action

action worthie of commendation : yt
is enough that it be tolerable. To
eate not only for our appetite , but
with excesse also and disorderlie, deserueth blame more,or lesse, according as
the excesse is great or litle.

5. The excesse in eating consisteth
not in the quantitie onely , but in the
manner also of eatinge. It is straunge
(my Philotheus) that honnie being so
wholsome, and so proper a food to the
Bees, that yet sometimes they become
sick by it , as when in the spring time
they eat to much of it, it ingendreth in
the the flux of the bellie and sometimes
it killes them without remedie,as when
they are behonnied with it about their
head and wings. Certainlie the act of
marriage,is holie,iust,commendable,&
profitable to common weale : yet notwithstanding in some case it is daungerous ; for sometimes it infecteth the
soule with veniall sinne,as it chaunceth
by a meere and simple excesse ; and
sometime it killeth the soule by mortall sinne , as it falleth out , when
the naturall order appointed for generation of children is peruerted ;
in

in which as one fwarueth more or leffe
from the order of nature , fo are the
finnes more or leffe execrable, but always mortall. For becaufe procreation
of children is the principall end of
marriage , one many neuer lawfullie
depart from the order which it requireth , though for fome accident , it
cannot at that time be performed ; as
it falleth out , when barrenneffe , or
being great which child alreadie , do
hinder the generation. For in thefe
accidents the act of marriage doth not
ceafe to be holie and iuft , fo that the
rules of generation be kept : no accident whatfoeuer being able to preiudice the law , that the principall end of
marriage prefcribeth. The execrable
act committed by Onan in his marriage , was deteftable before God , as
the holie text of the 38. chapter of
Genefis doth teftifie : although certaine hereticks of our dayes , a hundred
times more worthie to be condemned,
then the ancient Cynicks (of whome
Saint Hierom fpeaketh vpon the epi-
ftle to the Hebrues) made God to fay,
that it was the peruerfe intention of
that

that naughtie man which displeased
God : wheras the scripture sayth otherwise , and assureth vs in particular , that
the thinge or act it selfe , was abominable in the sight of God.

6. It is a true mark of a scadle, gree-
die, and beastly mind, to thinck earnestlie of meat, before the time of
repast : much more when after meales
one pawseth and delighteth in the
pleasure he took in eatinge , entertaining it in thought and word, and
reuoluing in his mind the remembrance of the sensuall delight he receaued
in swallowing downe his morsells ; as
they doe, who before dinner haue their
minde on the spitte , and after dinner
in the dishes ; men worthie to be the
skullions of a kitchin , *who mak a God
of their bellie ,* as Saint Paul saith. Those
which be well and mannerlie brought
vp, thinck of the table , but euen when
they are readie to sit downe ; and after
dinner washe their hands and mouthe,
to loose both sauour and smell of that
which they haue eaten. The Elephant
is but a grosse beast , yet most worthie
of all the rest , and which aboundeth
most

most in sense : I will tell you a point
of his honestie : he neuer changeth
his mate , and loueth her tenderlie
whome he hath chosen, with whome notwithstanding he coupleth not,
but from three yeers to three yeares,
and that onelie for fiue dayes , and so
secretlie , that he is neuer seene in the
act : but the sixt day he sheweth him
self abroad againe , and the first thing
he doeth , is to goe directlie to some
riuer and washe his bodie , not willing to returne to his troupe of companions , till he be purified. Be not
these goodlie and honest qualities in
a beast ? by which he teacheth married folk, not to be giuen to much to
sensuall and carnall pleasures , which
according to their vocation they haue exercised : but the vse being passed , to washe their hart and affection
from it , and purge them selues of it,
that afterward with all libertie, and
freedome of mind, they may exercise
other actions more pure and of greater valew . In this aduise consisteth
the perfect practize of that excellent
doctrine of Saint Paul , giuen vnto
the

the Corinthians : *The time is short*
(fayth he) *it remaineth that they who*
haue wiues, be as though they had them
not. For according to Saint Gregorie,
he hath a wife as though he had her
not , who in taking corporall pleafure with her , is not for all that, hindered and difturbed from fpirituall exercifes , and what is fayd of the man,
is to be vnderftood of the woman :
that they that *vfe this* world (fayth the
fame Apoftle) *be as though they vfed it*
not. Let euerie one then vfe this world
according to his calling , but yet in
fuch fort, that he engage not his affection too deeplie therin : but remaine
ftill as free and as readie to ferue God,
as yf they vfed not the world at all.
It is great hurt to a man (fayth Saint
Auftin) to defire the eniqying of
thofe things , which he fhould onely
vfe , and to vfe thofe things which he
fhould onely enioy : we fhould enioy
fpirituall things, and onely vfe corporall things : for when their vfe is turned into enioying, our reafonable foule
is conuerted into a fauage and beaftlie
foule. I thinck I haue fayd all that I
would

would fay, without fpeaking of that, of
which I would not fay.

Inftructions for widdowes.

CHAPTER 39.

SAINT Paule inftructeth all prelats in the perfon of his deere
fcholer Timothie , faying : *Ho-*
nour thofe widowes which are widowes in-
deed. To be a widowe indeed , thefe
things are required.

1. That not onely fhe be a widow
in bodie, but in hart alfo ; that fhe be
refolued with an inuiolable purpofe,
to keep her felf in the eftate of chaft
widowhood. For thofe which are widowes but onely while they expect marriage, are not feparated from hufbands
but onely in refpect of bodily pleafure,
for they be alreadie ioined to them in
hart and will. But yf the true widow, to
confirme her felfe in the ftate of widowhood , will offer vnto God her
bodie, and chaftitie by vowe , fhe fhall
adde a great ornament to her widowhood,

hood , and make her resolution secure.
For since that after her vow she is no
more in her owne power , and cannot
leaue her chastitie without forgoing
her part in paradise ; she wilbe more
zealous of her designement , and suffer
not so much as one litle thought of
marriage to stay in her hart , no not the
space of one onely moment : So that
this sacred vowe, will put a strong bul-
warck between her soule, and all manner of thoughts , that are contrarie to
her holy resolution. Saint Austin coun-
selleth this vow verie earnestlie to a
Christian widow , and the ancient and
learned Origen goeth much farther: for
he exhorteth maried wemen to propose
and vow chastitie of widowhood , in
case their housbands should die before
them : that among the sensuall pleasures which they may haue in their wedlock, they may enioy the merit of chast
widowhood , by this promise and vow
made before hand. The vow maketh
the work more acceptable vnto God,
fortifieth the will to do it more coura-
geously , and giueth to God, not onely
the good works, which are the fruicts
of

of our will , but dedicateth likewife
vnto him our will it felf, as the root
and tree of all our actions. By fimple
chaftitie we lend our bodie to God,
retaining notwithftanding our libertie,
to fubiect it when we lift to fenfuall
pleafure : but by the vowe of chaftitie
we make him an abfolute and irreuocable prefent of our bodie , without
referuing to our felf anie poffibilitie to
goe back from our word ; rendring
our felues happie flaues vnto him,who-
fe bondage is better then all royalties.
As I approue the aduife of thefe two
great perfonages , fo could I wishe,
that thofe foules which are fo happie,
as to folow them , would doe it prudently , holily and foundlie , hauing
well examined their forces , and in-
uoked the grace of God , and taking
the counfell of fome wife and deuout
directour : for fo all will profper the
better.

2. Befides it is neceffarie that the
abrenunciation of fecond marriage,
be made purely and fimplie , to conuert all our affections vnto God more
loyallie , and to make our hart cleaue
vnto

vnto Gods hart on euery fide : for yf the defire to leaue her children rich, or any other worldly refpect, do keep the widow in widowhood, she may deferue praife and commendation perhaps, but not before God : fince in Gods fight nothing is trulie praifeworthy, but that which is done for honour and reuerence of his diuine maieftie.

3. Likewife a true widow muft be voluntarilie abftracted from all prophane contentments : for *the widowe which liueth delicioufly*, fayth *S.* Paule, *is dead in her life time.* She that wilbe a widowe, & yet delights to be courted, embraced, made much of, and takes pleafure in dauncing, and feafting, defiring perfumes, tricking and trimming her felf, is a widow aliue in bodie, but dead in foule. What auaileth it whether the image of Adonis, or prophane loue, which hangeth for a figne before the dore of fleshly delight, be painted with goodlie flowers and plumes round about it, or the face thereof be couered with a nett, or a cypres ? For fo doubtleffe not without much vanitie fome times, black morning apparell ferues,

to make her beautie more apparent :
the widdow hauing made triall of that
wherin women do pleafe men moft,
cafteth more dangerous baites into
their minds. The widow then which
liueth in thefe fond delights, is dead
being aliue, and is nothing els, to
fpeak properlie, but an idoll of widowhood.

4. *The time of pruning is at hand, the
voice of the turtle doue hath been heard in
our land,* faith the holie Ghoft in the
Canticles. All men that will liue deuoutlie, muft prune and shaue away all
worldly fuperfluities : but efpeciallie is
this needfull to true widowes, who like
Turtle doues, come freshelie from bewailing & lamenting the loffe of their
deer husbands. When Noemy returned
from Moab to Bethlehem, the wemen
of the towne, who had knowne her
when she was firft married, fayd one to
another, is not this Noemy? but she
anfwered: call me not Noemy, I pray
you (for Noemy fignifieth comely and
wel-fauoured) but call me Mara, for our
Lord hath filled my foule with bitternes; which she fayd becaufe her husband

band was dead. Euen fo the deuout widowe will neuer be termed or efteemed
faire and beautifull, contenting her felf
to be fuch as it pleafeth God she be.

5. Lampes that are fed with fweet
oyle, caft a fweeter fmell when they are
blowne out: and widowes, whofe liues
were pure and laudable during their
wedlock, powre out a fweeter odour
and virtue of chaftitie, when theire
light (that is their husbands) is put out
and extinguished by death. To loue
their husbands being aliue is an ordinarie thing amongft wemen : but to loue
them fo well, as to take no other after
their death and departure, is a loue
which pertaineth onely to true widowes. To hope in God, fo long as the
husband is a liue, and ferueth for a pillar to fupport his wife, is not a thing
fo rare to be feene: but to hope in God
when she is deftitute of fo great a prop-
pe and ftay of her life, is indeed worthie
of commendations. This is the reafon
that one may with greater facilitie
know in widowhood the perfection of
virtues, then one could haue done in
the ftate of marriage.

X   6. The

6. The widow that hath children which ſtand in need of her aſſiſtance & bringing vp, principallie in matters belonging to their ſoules health, and eſtabliſhing of their courſe of life; cannot, nor ought in anie wiſe abandon them: for the Apoſtle S. Paule ſayth clearlie, that they are obliged to take that care of them, which they them ſelues had before experienced in their fathers and mothers: and that yf anie haue not care of his owne familie, he is worſe then an infidel. But yf her children be in ſtate, that they ſtand no more in need of her guiding, then ſhould ſhe gather to geather all her thoughts, and imploy them whollie to enrich her hart with the pure and holie loue of God.

7. Yf meere conſtraint bind not the conſcience of the widow to outward, affaires, as proceſſes, and ſuch like, I counſel her to auoide them altogether, and to to vſe that order in menaging her affaires, which is moſt peaceable, and recollected, although it ſeeme not ſo gainfull. For the profits gotten by contentions and troubleſome labour, muſt be verie great indeed, to recompence

pence the benefit of a quiet life : befides that wrangling pleas and proceffe
do diftract the hart, and oft times open
a gate to the enemiesofchaftitie: while
to pleafe them , whofe fauour they
need , they are faine manie times to vfe
demeanure and behaueour difpleafing
to God.

8. Prayer muft be the widowes continuall exercife : for she muft now
loue nothing but God : she muft vfe
almoft no words but for Gods fake.
And as the iron which by the prefence
of the Diamant was hindered from folowing the Loadftone, leapes after it
fo foone as the Diamant is remoued
away : fo the chaft widowes hart which
could not eafilie giue it felf wholie to
folowe Gods holie infpirations, during
the life of her husband, should immediatly after his death, runne with ardent
affection after the fweet odours, and
celeftiall perfumes of her Lord , faying
with the facred fpoufe, O Lord , now
that I am all mine owne , receaue me
altogether, *drawe me after thee , and*
I will runne after the fweet fmell of thy
ointments.

8. Vir-

9. Virtues peculiar to Chriſtian widdowes are, perfect modeſtie, neglect of
honors, ranckes, places, titles, and ſuch
like vanities; to ſerue the poore, viſit
the ſick, comfort the afflicted, inſtruct
young maydens, and encline them to
affect pietie and deuotiõ, and in a word
to yeald them ſelues a perfect patterne
all virtues: to the younger woemen,
cleanlines, and honeſt ſimplicitie, muſt
be the two ornaments of theire habits,
humilite and charitie, muſt adorne
theire actions, honeſtie and curteſie,
muſt grace theire ſpeech, modeſtie and
ſhamfaſtnes, muſt beautiſie theire eies,
and Chriſt Ieſus crucified, muſt be the
only loue of their harts. In ſumme,
the true widdowe, is in the Catholique
Church, as it were a freſh ſweete violet
in the month of March, which ſendes
abroad from the flagrant odor of hir
deuotion, an incomparable ſuauitie,
and yet almoſt couers & hides hir ſelfe,
with the great leaues of her humilitie
and voluntarie abiection, betokning
by her dark pale colour, her exerciſes
of mortification: ſhe is vſually found
in freſh coole places, and vnmanured
plots

plots of ground, and will not be bla-
sted with the hott noysome ayre of the
worldes conuersation , the better to
conserue the pleasaunt freshnes of her
soule , against all inordinat heates,
which the desire of riches, of honor,
and dangerous loues, might breede in
her hart. *She shall be blessed,* saith the
holy Apostle , *if she perseuer in this
sort.*

10. I haue many other thinges to
say of this matter , but I haue said
enough, and all , when I said , that
the widdow zealous of the honor of
her estate, reade attentiuely the excellent Epistles, which great Saint Hierom wrote to Furia, Saluia , and all
those other Dames , which were so
happie, as to be the ghostlie children
of that holy Father; for nothing can
be added vnto that which he sayeth,
but only this admonition ; that a true
widdow , should neuer blame those
that marrie the second time , nay
though they marrie , the third, and
fourth time ; for in some cases, God
almightie so disposeth it for his greater
glorie. One must alwayes haue his

eies vpon this doctrin of our holie
forefathers, that nether widdowhood,
nor virginitie, haue any other place
in heauen, but that which true humilitie doth allot and assigne them.

A word or two to Virgins.

CHAPTER 40.

1. **O** VIRGINS, I haue only these
three wordes to say vnto you,
for the rest that is requisit, you
shall find else where. If you intend,
and thinke vpon temporall mariage,
be sure to keepe your first loue, inuio-
lably for your first husband. In my
iudgement, it is egregious cosenage
and deceit, to present in steed of an
entyre, and sound hart, a worne, bru-
sed, and loue vanquisht hart. But if
thy happie lot haue ordayned thee, for
thy chast spirituall Spouse, for whom
thou meanest to preserue perpetually
thy virginitie, good God, how pre-
ciselie, carefully, and tenderlie, ough-
test thou to preserue thy first loue
for

for him, who being puritie it selfe, is delighted with nothing so much as with puritie, to whom are due the first fruites of all thinges, but principally of our loue? Reade *Saint* Hieroms Epistles, there thou shalt finde sufficient precepts and rules, touching this matter. And seeing that thine estate and condition of life, hath made thee subiect to obedience, choose a guide and master, vnder whose conduct and direction, thou maist with greatest sanctitie and integritie, dedicate thy body and soule, to the worship and seruice of almightie God.

THE

THE FOVRTH PART

OF THE INTRODVCTION,
Containing necessary instructions, against those tentations
which are most ordinarily incident, to those that endeuour
to liue spiritually.

That we must not regard the scoffes and
mocking taunts of the children of
this world.

CHAPTER. I.

1. S O soone as the childrē of
this world shall perceaue
that thou resoluest to
lead a spirituall life, they
will discharge vpon thee
as thick as hayle, all their vaine babling
and false surmises. Those that are most
malicious among them, wil calumniat

X   and

and misconstrue thy change attributing
it to dissembling policie, or hypocrisie;
the world frownes vpon him say they,
and because he cannot thriue that way,
he betakes him self to God; thy frinds
will euen break their heads and weery
their tongues to make thee a world of
exhortations , and wise and charitable
admices as they imagin : Thou wilt fale
into some melancholie humour (wil
they say) by this new course of life;thou
wilt leese thy credit and estimation in
the world, and make thy self intolerable
& distastful to all thy acquaintace ;thou
wilt wax olde before thy time, thy domesticall affaires wil go to wrack:a man
must liue in the world , as one in the
world : our saluation may be obtained,
and heauen gained without these mysteries and secrets; and a thousand such like inuentions as these shalt thou heare.

2 My Philotheus, all this councell
of these,is but a fond and vaine pratling.
These men tender neither thy health,
nor wealth , nor honour. *If you were of
the world* (sayth our blessed Sauiour)
*the world would loue that which were his:but
because you are not of the world , therfore the
world*

world hateth you. We haue feene often enough, gentlemen and gay ladies, paſſe many a whole night, nay manie nights together, at cardes, and cheſſe : and is there any attention more melancholy, ſullen, and troubleſom then that ? and yet worldlings that mark it, ſay neuer a word of it, and their frinds neuer trouble them ſelues therfore ; and for meditating but one ſhort hower, or riſing in the morning a litle earlier then ordinarie,to prepare our ſelues to communion : euerie one runnes to the phyſician, as if it were needfull we ſhould be purged from hypochondriac humours, or the iaunders . They wil make no difficultie to ſpend thirtie or fortie nights in dauncing,and no man of them wil complaine of it as of loſſe of time: yet only for watching deuoutly on Chriſtmas night, euery one coffeth next morning, and complaineth of the rheume. VVho feeth not heere that the world is an vniuſt iudge, fauorable and partiall to his owne children,ſharpe and rigourous to the children of God?

2. VVe ſhall neuer be well in peace with the world, vnleſſe, we caſt our ſel-

ues away with it for companie: it is
impoſſible for vs to content it, it is too
much out of ſquare; *For Iohn came nei-*
*ther eating, nor drinking (*ſaith our redeemer*) and they ſay, the diuel is in him: The*
Sonne of man came eating and drincking, and
they ſay, behold a glutton and a wine-bibber.
Moſt true it is, Philotheus, yf we ſhould
condeſcend with the world, and giue
our ſelues a litle, to ieſt, to laugh, to
daunce, and diſport, it would be ſcanda-
lized at vs: yf we do not ſo, it will accuſe vs of hypocriſie or melancholy. Let vs
make our ſelues braue, and the world
will conſtre it to ſome bad end: goe negligently and careleſly attired, and the
world will count vs baſe minded: our
myrth in the worlds eye is diſſolution,
our mortification ſullennes: and looking thus vpon vs with an angrie eye,
we can neuer be acceptable to it . It ag-
grauateth our imperfections, publiſh-
ing them for ſinnes; of our veniall ſinnes it maketh mortall : thoſe which
we committ through frailtie, it ſays we
doe them for malice. Where as *charity is*
benigne (as S. Paul ſayeth) the worlde is
malicious; where charitie thinketh not
ill of

ill of any, the world on the other side
thinketh no good, but alwayes ill: and
not being able to caluniat our actiós, it
will accuse our intentions : so that haue
the poore sheepe hornes or no, be they
white or black ; the wolfe for all that
refuseth noth́to deuoure them, yf he
can.

3. Doe what we can, the world will
still wage warre against vs: yf we be lóg
at Confession, it will wonder what
we are so long about: yf we stay but a
while, it will say we haue not told all,
we haue concealed the worst. It wil
warily spie aud prie into our gestures
and behaueour, and yf it finde out but
one litle word of choler, cast out at vnawares, it wlll protest solemnely, that
we are altogether vnsufferable. If we be
diligent in looking to our affaires, it
termes vs couetous: yf mild and patient,
it calls it meere simplicitie : But as for
the children of the world, their choler
is generositie, their auarice is good husbandrie, their conspiracies are honorable courtesies : thus still the Spiders
marre the poore Bees labours.

4. Let vs therfore giue th́is blind buz-

buzzard leaue (Philotheus) to cry as
long as he lift, and fcreech like a night-
owle to difquiet the birds of the day:
but let vs in our felues be conftant in
our purpofes, and no changelings in our
diffignes: our perfeuerance will cleerly
demonftrate, whether in footh and in
good earneft, we haue facrificed our felues to God, and fetled our felues in the
ranck of thofe, that meaneto liue deuoutly. Comèts, and Planets are almoft
of an equall brightnes in appearaunce;
but comets, or blazing ftarres do quickly vanish away, being ouely certaine firy
vapours, which are in short time confumed; wheras planets, or true ftarres,
haue a perpetuall and euerlafting brightnes. So hypocrifie and true virtue
haue great refembláce in outward shew,
but onemay knowe the one from the o-
ther: becaufe hypocrifie lafteth not lóg,
but vanishelh foone like fmoke, afcending vp a litle way into the ayre; but
true virtu is allway conftant and durable. It is no fmall commoditie, no litle
feouritie, and fortifiyng of the beginning of our deuotion, to fuffer reproaches, and calumniations: for by thofe
meanes

meanes we auoid the dāger of pride, and
valne glorie, which are like the cruell
midwiues of Egypt, appointed by the infernall Pharao, to kill the children of
the Israelits, the very day of their birth.
We are crucified in opiniō of the world,
let the world be crucified in ours: it accounteth vs for fooles, let vs esteeme
the world for mad and sencelesse.

---

*That we must haue continually a good
and manfull courage.*

CHAPITRE 2.

1.   THis light of the day though
it be most beautifull and delectable to our eyes, doth dazel
them not withstanding, after they haue
been shutt vp in long darknes. Before
we be accustomed and familiar with
the inhabitants of any strange countrie,
let them be neuer so courteous and
frindlie, yet we find our selues amongst
them as half amazed. It may be my Philotheus, that after this change of life,
diuers alterations wil arise in thy hart:
and that this great and generall farwell
which thou hast bidden to the follies
X 4   and

and vanities of the world, will ftirre in
thee fome fadnes and difcouragement.
Yf it happen fo, let me winn fo much at
thy hands, as to haue a litle patience: for
it will come to nothing, it is but a litle
aftonifhement which the noueltie of
another life bringeth vnto thee; let that
paffe ouer, and thou fhalt receaue millions of confolations.

2. It will trouble thee in thy beginning (it may be) to forfake that pompe
and glorie, which fooles and mockers
giue thee, accouting thee happie in thy
vanities: but wouldft thou for that vaine eftimation, loofe the euerlafting
glory, which God infalliblie will
giue thee? The fond trifles and paftimes in which thou haft employed
thy fore-paffed yeares, will reprefent
them felues againe to thy hart, to allure it, and to caufe it to come vnto
their fide: but canft thou haue the
hart, to hazard the loffe of bleffed e-
ternitie, for fuch tranfitorie toyes and
pleafures? Beleeue me, Philotheus, yf
thou perfeuer conftantly, ere long
thou wilt feele fuch cordiall fweetnes, fo pleafaunt and delicious, that
                                    thou

thou wilt confesse, that the world
affoordeth nothing else but bitter gaulle, in comparison of that most sweete
and delectable hunny ; and that one
only day of deuotion , is better worth,
then a thousand yeares of worldly delights.

3. I but thou seest, that the mountaine of Christian perfection is exceeding high ; and o my God (sayst thou)
how shall I be able to clime vp so high?
Courage Philotheus, when the litle young bees be ginne to take shape
and forme, we call them grubbes , and
at that time they cannot flie vp and
downe vpon the sweete flowers , nor
on the thymie mountaines , nor litle bushie hilles , to gather honny , but
by litle and litlte, feeding vpon the
honny which their dammes prepare for
them , these litle grubbes or impes,
beginn to haue wings , and to sttengthen them selues , so that after they
flie vp and downe all the countrie
in theire honnie-quest . True it is,
that as yet we be but litle grubbes in
deuotion and that we are not able, to
soare vppe so highe, as our desire

X 5   would

would haue vs , which is euen no
higher, then to the highest top of
Christian perfection ; yet notwithstanding we begin to grow into forme and
fashion , to take some spirituall shape
vpon vs, by good desires and constant
resolutions folowed and secōded by diligent performance, our wings begin to
grow : so that we may well hope one
day to be spirituall Bees, & that we shall
flie freely in searche of the honnie-
sweet pleasures of God : in the meane
time, let vs liue vpon the honny of so
many godly instructions, as ancient deuout persons haue left vnto vs : and let
vs pray vnto God to giue vs the wings
of a doue , that we may not only flie for
the time of this present life , but especially repose our selues in the eternitie
of the life to come.

The

The nature of tentations, and the diffe-
rence between feeling them, and
consenting to them.

CHAPTER 3.

1: I MAGIN a young princesse (my
Philotheus) greatly beloued of
her husband: and that some trai-
trous vilaine to winne her, and defile
her marriage bed, sendeth to her some
infamous pandar, with a loue-message,
to treat with her about his disloyall intent, first this noughtie pandar, pro-
poseth vnto the princesse, the intent of
his maister: secondly the princes taketh
the embassage in good, or euil part:
thirdly she either consenteth, or refuseth. Euen so the diuel, the world, and
the flesh, perceauing the soule of man
espoused to the Sonne of God, do send
their temptations and suggestions vnto
her, by the which first, sinne is propounded vnto her: secondly, she either is delighted, or displeased with the sinfull
motion: and thirdly, she either admit-
      X 6   teth

teth it by confent, or reiecteth and
casteth it away from her: which are in
summe, the three steppes or staires by
which we descend to wickednes, suggestion, or temptation, delight, and
consent. And though these three acts,
are not so manifestly knowne and dis-
cerned in other kinds of sinnes, yet are
they palpablie seene, in all greate and
enormious sinnes.

2. Though the tentation of any sinne
that is, should endure all our life long,
it would not make vs vngratefull to his
diuine maiestie, so that it please vs not,
so that we take no delight in it, nor giue
any consent vnto it. And the reason is,
because in the tentation there passeth
no morall action of ours, but we only
suffer it: and so taking no pleasure in it,
we cã be in no fault for it. S. Paule a lõg
time suffered the tentations of the flesh,
and yet was so far from displeasing God
therefore, that contrarie wise God este-
med him self glorified thereby. The B.
S. Angela de Fulgino, felt such vehemẽt
tentations of the flesh, that she moueth
to compassion when she recounteth
them; great likewise were the temptations

tions which S. Francis , and S. Benet
fuffered,when the one caft him felfe naked into the thornes,and the other into
the fnow,to mitigate them:yet loft they
not for all that , any whit of the grace
of God,but rather augmented it.

3. Thou muft be valiaunt then and
courageous (my Philotheus,(amid tentations, and neuer hold thy felf for vanquished,fo long as thou findeft that the
tētation difpleafeth thee. Obferue well
the difference , between hauing, and
confenting to tentation ; which is , that
we may haue, or feele them, though
they vtterly diflike and difpleafe vs;
but we can neuer confent vnto them,
vnleffe they pleafe vs , fince pleafure
ordinarilie ferueth as a fteppe to confent . Let then the enemies of our
faluation, prefent vnto vs as many
bittes and baites as euer they will ; let
them alway ftand watching at the dore
of our hart to get in; let them make
vs as many offers, and proffers,as they
lift : but yet fo long as we haue a
true purpofe and ftrōg refolution, to take no manner of pleafure in them,
it is not poffible that we shoulde
offend

offend God , no more then the Prince,
husband to the princeſſe before mentioned, can beare her any ill will or diſpleaſure,for the noughtie meſſage ſent
vnto her , yf ſhe haue taken no delight
or pleaſure in it . Yet ther is a difference
betweene the ſoule and this princeſſe,that
the princeſſe hauing once vnderſtood
this dishoneſt errand , may yf ſhe liſt,
driue away the meſſeger and heare him
no more : which is not alwayes in the
power of the ſoule,for ſhe cānot chooſe
but feel the tentation , though it be always in her power not to conſent to it;
for which cauſe,although the tentation
ſhould perſeuer neuer ſo long time, yet
can it not hurt or defile vs, ſo long as it
disliketh and diſpleaſeth vs.

4. But as for the delight which may
folow the temptation , becauſe there are two parts or portions of our ſoule , the one inferiour , and the other ſuperiour ; and the inferiour or ſenſualitie
foloweth not always the ſuperiour , or
reaſonable portion , but keeps houſe
apart (as it were:) it falleth out oft times
that the inferiour part taketh delight in
the tentation without the conſent , nay
                                        againſt

againſt the will of the ſuperiour . This
is the quarrel , and battaile which the
Apoſtle,S. Paule deſcribeth , when he
ſayeth , that his fleſh rebelled againſt
his ſpirit, that there is one law of the
members , or bodie , and another of the
ſpirit, and ſuch other things.

5. Haſt thou not ſeene (Philotheus)
a great burning firebrand, couered with
aſhes and imbers ? when one cometh
ten or twelue houres after to ſeek for fire , he finds but a litle in the middeſt of
the hearth , and ſome times hath much
a doe to find any . Yet there was fire,
there all the while , for other wiſe he
could now haue found none at all : and
with that litle that he found , he may
kindle all the other dead coales and
brád-ends; The ſelf ſame paſſeth in cha-
titie, (which is the ſpirituall fire of our
ſoule) amid many great and violent tentations . For tentation darting her delight into the lower portion , couereth
all the ſoule (as it ſeemeth) with aſhes,
and bringeth the loue of God to ſuch a
ſtraight , as yf it had rome onely (as
men ſay) to ſtand a tiptoe : for it appeareth not at all any where, ſaying only
in the

in the middest of the hart, in the very
bottom and center of the spirit ; and yet
seemeth scarce to be there, and we haue
much a doe to find and perceaue it.
Notwithstanding without all doubt it
remaines there, since how soeuer we feele our selues troubled in soule & bodie,
yet we find in our hart, a setled resolution not to consent to sinne ; not tentation ; and the delight which pleaseth
our outward man, or sensualitie, displeaseth and disliketh the inward, or reasonable will, so that though it be round
about it, like the cenders about the
coale, yet is it not within it: wherby we
may plainly see, that such delight is in-
voluntary, and altogether contrary, to
our will, and can therfore be no sinne
at all.

---

*Two fitt examples of the forsayd
matter.*

Chapter. 4.

1. **I**T concerneth thee so neere to vnderstand this difference well, that
I will not spare to spend a litle
more

more time and difcource to declare it
more at large . That younge man (of
whome S. Hierom fpeaketh in the life
of S. Paule the firft hermit) being
bound with delicat fcarfes of filk, and
lodged in a foft bed , and prouoked by
all forts of lafciuious touches and wanton allurements, by a beautifull harlot,
that lay with him of fet purpofe, to o-
uerthrow his conftant chaftitie : what
ftrange motions of his flesh did he feele? needs muft it be,that his fences were
affaulted with exceffiue delight, and his
imaginatió extremly battailled with the
prefece of thefe voluptuous obiects. Yet
not withftading amógeft fo many troubles, in the middeft of fuch a terrible
ftorme of téptatiós:he teftified fufficiēt-
ly, that his hart was not ouercome , that
his will (though roud about befett with
fuch pleafures) cófented not at all vnto
thē, fince his fpirit perceauing fo generall a rebellion againft it, and hauing no
other part of the bodie at cómandemēt
but the tongue , he bitt it off with his
teeth , & fpitt it in the face of that nau-
ghtiepack , which more cruellie tormē-
ted him with vnlawfull pleafures,thē the
hág -

hang-man could euer haue done with
moſt horrible tourments: for therfore
the tyrant, miſtruſting to ouercome him
by pangs, thought to ſurmount his conſtancy by pleaſures.

2.   The hiſtorie of the battail which
S. Catherin of Siena in like manner ſuffered, is moſt admirable, the ſumme
wherof foloweth. The diuel had permiſſion from God almightie, to aſſault
the chaſtitie of this virgin, with the
greateſt rage that he could, with this
exception, that he ſhould not touche
her. Then did the fiend erect a batterie
of all kind of vnchaſt ſuggeſtiõs againſt
her hart ; and to moue her the more,
coming with his damnable companiõs
in forme of men and wemen, made a
thouſand formes of carnall inticements
in her ſight, adioining words and geſtures moſt dishoneſt and filthie. And
allthough all theſe fleshly engins, were
only exteriourly preſented, neuertheleſſe by miniſtery of the ſences, they
pearced to the verie hart of the diſtreſſed virgin : which (as ſhe her ſelf con-
feſſed) was euen brimfull of theſe dangerous ſuggeſtions, nothing els in her re-
maining

maining free, but only her superiour
will, which was not shaken with all
thefe thunderinge ordenance of lafciuious, and carnall tentations: which
lafted very long, till on a day our Lord
appeared vnto her, and she fayd vnto
him: where wert thou, my fweet Lord,
when my hart was full of fo great darknes, and vncleannes? wherto he anfwered. I was, my deer daughter, in thy
hart. In my hart (replied she) and how
couldeft thou dwell in a hart where
there was fo much vncleanes? or canft
thou that art cleanneffe it felf, abide in
place of dishoneftie? And our Lord anfwered. Tell me, when thefe vncleane
thoughts troubled thee, did they make
thee merrie, or forie? did they produce
in thy hart fweetnes, or bitternes? moft
extreme bitternes and forow, fayd she.
who was it then (fayd our Lord) that
put this exceeding bitternes and forow
in thy hart, but I, that lay there couertly
and hidden in thy foule? Beleeue me
(my daughter) had I not been there prefent, thefe hellishe engins that were
planted round about thy hart, and with
all their batterie could not make one
                                    breach

breach into it , would doubtleſſe haue
ſurprized it and entred at their pleaſure,
they would haue been admitted, and receaued with delight , by conſent of thy
free will , and ſo haue giuen the deaths
wound to thy ſoule . But becauſe I was
within, I armed thy hart with a bitter
diſlike of theſe dishoneſt imaginations,
and placed that ſtrong reſiſtance in thy
ſoule, by which ſhe refuſed the tētation,
as much as ſhe could ; and not being a-
ble as much as ſhe would , conceaued a
vehemēt diſpleaſure and hatred againſt
the tentation, and againſt her ſelfe: and
ſo theſe pangs and afflictions, were verie
méritorious, and a great gaine for thee,
and an exceeding increaſe of thy virtue.

3.   Seeſt thou Philotheus, how this
fire was couered with aſhes in this holy
ſoule? and that the tentation and delight
was alreadie entred into the hart , and
had compaſſed and beſieged the will?
which only aſiſted by her Sauiours grace, reſiſted by a bitter deteſtation of
theſe wicked and lawleſſe pleaſures, all
the batterie that was preſented vnto it,
refuſing alway to giue conſent to the
ſinfull ſuggeſtions , with which it was

fo dāgeroufly and vniuerfally enuironned. O what diftreffe is it to a foule
that loueth God, not fo much as to
knowe whether he be in her or no? Or
wether the heauenly fore of charitie for
which she fighteth, be altogether extinguished in her or no? but this is the
flower and perfection of the heauenly
loue, to make the louer to fuffer and to
fighte for loue, not knowing whether
he haue within him that loue, for which
and by which, he continueth valiantly
fighting.

---

*An encouragement to the foule vexed
with temptation.*
CHAPTER 5.

1. **M**Y Philotheus, God neuer
permitteth thefe vehemēt tētations to arife, but onely a-
gainft fuch foules, which he meanes
to extoll, and promote to the dignitie
of his pure and excellent loue. But
it foloweth not, therfore, that, after
thefe tentations, they shalbe fure to
attaine to this diuiue loue: for it happeneth oft times, that foules which
haue

haue been cōstant in such violent com-
bats, afterward not corresponding with
the heauenly fauours of God, haue been
vanquished and ouerthrowne with verie
smale tentations. This I say, to the end
that yf euer it chaunce to thee to be afflicted with such dreadfull and horrible
tentations, that thou vnderstand therby,
that God fauoureth thee with an extraordinarie signe of his loue, by which he
designeth to exalt thee in his presence,
and make thee great in his familiaritie
and frindship . Yet neuerthelesse , be
thou alway humble and fearfull to offend , not assuring thy self that thou art
able to ouercome the least tētatiōs that
are , after thou hast preuailed against
great ones , sauing onely by continuall
fidelitie and loyaltie towards his maiestie.

2. VVhat temptations so euer then
do arriue vnto thee, and what delight so
euer ensew of that temptation : so long
as thy wil refuseth to giue her consent,
both to the tentation, and to the delight
folowing it , trouble not thy self, God
is not offended with thee. When one falleth into asound , so that there appeer
                                        no more

no more signes of life in him, men
vsually lay their hands on his hart, and at
the least motion that they feele in his
hart, they iudge him yet to retain life,
and by some pretious liquour or resto-
ratiue, make him come againe to him
self, and recall him to his sence and
feeling. So doth it chaunce whē through
the violence of tentations, our soule
seemeth as it were fallen into a sound,
and into an vtter decay of all her spirituall forces, life and motion : but yf we
wil know in what state she is, let vs lay
our hand on our hart; let vs consider yf
the hart and will doe yet retaine their
spirituall motion : that is, yf they do
their endeuour to refuse all consent to
the tentation and delight therof : for so
long as this motion of refusall is with
in our hart, we may be assured, that charitie, the life of our soule, remaineth yet
in vs, and that Iesus Christ our Sauiour
is there present, though hidden, and secretly : so that by vertue of continuall
prayer, and vse of the sacraments, and of
confidence in Gods grace, we shall recouer our forces, and liue a sound, healthie, and delectable life.

How

How tentation and delectation may
be sinne.

CHAPTER 6.

1. THE princesse of whome we
spake right now, could not
hinder the dishonest demaund
made vnto her, because, as we presup-
posed it came to her vnawares, and a-
gainst her will: but yf on the other side,
she should by some wanton glaunces
giue occasion to be requested, by those secret or carelesse tokens, declaring
her self not vnwilling, of rendring loue
to him that should court her: then
doubtlesse were she culpable of the
message it selfe: and though she shew
her self neuer so quaint and coy, she
should for all that, deserue blame and
punishment . So chaunceth it many times, that the very tentation it self is a
sinne in vs, because we our selues willingly are the cause of it, for example . I
know that in gaming I fall easilie to
rage & blasphemie, & that gaming is to
me

me, as it were a tentation to thofe finnes : I finne therfore as often , and as
many times as I play at that game , and
am guiltie of the tentation which thence arifeth. Againe, yf I know certainly
that fuch a conuerfation , is ordinarie a caufe of tentation and fall vnto
me , and yet notwithftanding do willingly go to it, I am acceffarie to al the
tentations which doe enfew from
thence .

2. When the delight which proceedeth from the tentation maye be auoided, it is always finne to receaue it :
according as the pleafure which we receaue, and as the confent which we giue vnto it , is great or litle, long or
fhort in durance : So it is always re-
prehenfible in the young princeffe of
whom we fpake , yf fhe do not onely
harken vnto the lafciuious and difho-
neft demaund , which is made vnto
her: but withal, after that fhe hath heard
it, taketh pleafure in it, entertaining her
thought with fome delight about this
obiect . For although fhe will not
confent to the real execution of the
difloyaltie motioned to her : fhe con-

senteth not withstanding to the mentall appliyng of her hart, to the contentment which she taketh in the naughtie suggestion; And it is allway a dishonest acte, to applie either mind or bodie, vnto any dishonest obiect : nay dishonestie consisteth in such sort in the application of the mind, that without it, the appliyng of the bodie, were no sinne at all.

3. So then, when thou shalt be tempted in any sinne, consider whether thou hast willingly giuen occasion to be so tempted: for then the verie tentation it selfe, putteth thee in state of sinne, by reason of the hazard wherin thou hast wittingly cast thy self, which is to be vnderstood, when thou mightest commodiouslie haue auoided the occasion; and that thou didst foresee, or wert bound to forsee, that in such an occasion, such a temptation would arise. But yf thou hast giuen no occasion at all to the tentation which impugneth thee : it cannot in any sort be imputed vnto thee for a sinne.

4. When

4. When the delight folowing the tētation might baue been shunned,& yet
we eschew it not, there is allwaye some
kind of sinne, according to the litle or
long continuance in it, and according
to the cause of delight takē in it. A woman that hath giuen no occasion to be
courted , but yet taketh pleasure therin , letteth not to be blameworthie ,
though the pleasure which she affected,
haue no other cause or motiue , but
only the courting. For example, yf her
gallant play excellent wel on the lute ,
and she delighteth , not in that he
seeketh her loue, but in the harmonie
& sweetnes of his lute; there is no sinne
in that delight: yet must she not continew long in it, least she easilie passe frō
it,to delight in being wooed. So yf any
bodie prepoūd to me some stratageme
ful of inuētion & cunning,to make me
compasse a full reuenge vpon mine
enemie : yf I take no delight , nor giue
any consent to the desire or purpose of reuenge which is motioned
vnto me , but only in the slight and
subtil art of the engin , or inuention , without doubt I sinne not at all:
                    Y 2   though

though it be not expedient to ftay long
in this delight , for feare leaft by litle ,
and litle , it carie to fome delectation
of the reuenge propofed.

5. We find our felues fometimes
ouertaken and furprized with fome tic-
kling of delight , immediatly after the
tentation is prefented vnto vs , before
we haue well confidered the qualitie
and danger therof : and this delight is
but a fmall veniall finne, though it wax
greater and greater , yf after we perceaue the danger we are in , we ftay, negligently dalliyng , and as it were coping
and cheapning with the delight , whether we should admitt it, or reiect it ;
and yet more , yf we negligently ftay
in it , after we perceaue the perill, without any purpofe at all litle
or great to caft it away out of our hart:
but when as voluntarilie , and of full
purpofe we refolue to take contentment in that delight,that deliberat purpofe is a great finne , yf the obiect of
the delight be verie naught. It is a great
vice in a woman , yf she be willing
in her hart to entertaine naughtie
dishoneft loues , allthough she do
                                    not

not in effect abandon her self to her
louers.

Remedies againſt great and ve-
hement tentations.

Chapter 7.

1.   **A**S ſoone as thou findeſt thy
ſelf in any tentation, doe as
litle children are woont when
they ſee a wolfe or a beare in the field:
for preſently they runne and throwe
themſelues into their father or mothers
armes, or at leaſt wiſe call vpon them
for helpe and ſuccour. Runne thou
in like manner vnto God, crie vpon
his mercie, craue his aſſiſtance, it is
the remedie which our Saueour him
ſelf taught vs ſaying, *pray, leaſt you enter*
into tentation.

2.   Yf neuertheleſſe the tentation
continew, or increaſe, then haſtely runne in ſpirit to the croſſe of our bleſſed
ſaueour Ieſus imagining thou ſeeſt him
hanging theron before thy face, and
embrace the foot of the croſſe vpō thy
knees laying faſt hold vpon it, as vpon

an affured fanctuarie, and proteft that
thou wilt neuer confent to the temptation, aske our Saueour ayde againſt it,
and continew alway this protefting,
that thou wilt neuer giue confent, ſo
long as the temptatió laſteth. But while
thou makeſt theſe earneſt & harty pro-
reſtations, & refuſalls of confent, look
not the tẽptatió in the face, thinck not
on it as nigh as thou cãſt : but look only vpon our bleſſed Lord on the roode:
for yf thou behold & cõſider the tẽpta-
tion, principally when it is vehemẽt, or
carnall, it may shake & vndermine thy
courage, and weaken thy conſtancy
before thou art aware . Diuert thy
thoughts with ſome good and commendable exerciſes, for ſuch occupations, entering, and taking place in thy
hart, will chace away the tentations, &
malicious fuggeſtions, and leaue no
roome in thy hart to be lodged in.

3. The ſound & ſoueraigne remedie
againſt all tentations, be they neuer ſo
great, is to vnfold our conſcience, diſ-
play & lay opé the ſuggeſtiós, feelings,
& affects which ariſe in our minds, to
manifeſt thẽ & their occaſiós to our ſpirituall

ritual directour. For note this well, that
the firſt cŏditiŏ that the diuel would make
with a ſoule whom he would inveigle & deceaue, is to cŏceale the tĕtatiŏ:
as they which would allure any maides
or wemĕ to their vnlawful deſires, at the
verie firſt abourding, warne them to ſay
nothing of their motions & deſires to
their parĕts or housbáds; where as God
on the other ſide in his inſpiratiŏs aboue
& before al things willeth, that we procure them to be examined by our ſuperiours, and conductours of our ſoules.

4. Yf after all this, the tentation obſtinately vex and perſequute vs, we muſt
do nothing els, but ſhew our ſelues
conſtant, and perſeuer in proteſting
from our harts, that we do not, and
will not conſent ; for as maides can
neuer be married, ſo long as they ſay
no : ſo the ſoule, be ſhe neuer ſo much
tormented with tentation, can neuer
be hurt or defiled, ſo long as vnfainedly
ſhe ſayeth no.

5. Diſpute not with thy enemie, diſcourſe not with his ſuggeſtions, anſwer him not one only worde, vnleſſe
it be ſometimes that, which our bleſſed

Lord anſwerd him, and wherwith he confounded him: *Go thy way Sathan, for it is written, The Lord thy God shalt thou adore, and him only shalt thou ſerue.* As a chaſt matron should not anſwer on word, nor look once on the face of that naughtie perſon that ſhould ſolicit her to diſhoneſtie, but cutting of ſhort from his loue-retorick, ſhould preſentlie, and at the ſame inſtant, turne her thoughts and affections towards her housband, and proteſt anew the loyaltie which ſhe oweth vnto him, and neuer ſtay one iont to dallie or parlie, or enterchaunge langaage with the laſciuious ſuiter: ſo the deuout ſoule aſſaulted with any tentation, should by no meanes buſie her ſelf in diſcourcing, or conſidering, or anſwering it, but ſincerely and that inſtantly, turne her thoughts to her Lord Ieſus Chriſt, her deere ſpouſe, and make a new proteſtation and promiſe of loyaltie to him, that ſhe wilbe his only and wholly for euer.

That

That we must diligently resist, euen the least tentations that are.

CHAPTER 8.

1. **A** L L T H O V G H we must fight most carefully against great & violent tentations with an inuincible courage, & the victorie gained against them be exceeding profitable vnto vs : yet peraduenture we may profit more in resisting tentations of leslesser moment: for as great temptations exceed in qualitie, so the lesser infinitly exceed in number, in so much that the conquest of them, may be compared to the victorie ouer the greater and violenter tentations. Wolues & Beares be without all question, more dangerous then flies and gnattes : yet do they not vex and disquiet vs so importunly, nor exercise our patience so often . It is an easie thing to abstaine from murther, but harde to auoide small cholericke passions, & the ordinarie occasions of anger which are presented to vs almost euery moment. It is easie for a man or a woman to refraine frō cōmitting actual

ᵃdulterie, but not fo eafie to abftaine ᶠrom waton lookes, from giuing or re-ceauing loue toyes, frō procuring fond fauours, frō fpeaking & hearing words, of vanitie. It is not verie hard, not to admitt a corriual or companion in loue between housband and wife, and to re-fufe, confent of bodily difloyaltie in that kind, but not fo eafie to keep this difloyaltie from entrie to the hart, and defire. Verie eafie is it for a mā to cōtei-ne himfelf frō ftealing other mēs goods but hard, not fo much as to couet or wifhe them. Eafie is it not to beare falfe witnes in iudgement, but not fo eafie to refraine from lies in cōnuerfation ; verie eafie not to be drunk, but hard to be virtuoufly fober & temperate ; verie eafie not to defire anothers death, but hard not to defire at leaft fome harme and difcōmoditie to him. It is no great difficultie to withhold our felues from defaming our aduerfarie, but hard to withhold difpraifing him. In a word thefe litle temptations of choler, of fuf-pitions, of iealoufie, of enuie, of loue-tricks, of iefts & vanities, of craftie and double dealing, of wanton and vnchaft
                                    thoughts,

thoughts, are things in which the patiéce
and cóstancie of those that are most deuout & resolute in gods seruice, is most
cótinuallie tried and exercised. We must
therefore prepare our selues (my deer
Philotheus) with as great diligence as
may be, to this spirituall cóbat: & assure
our selues, that as manie victories as we
shall winne ouer these petie enemies &
slight tentatiós, so manie pretious gem-
mes shalbe placed in the crowne of glorie, which God prepareth for vs in paradise. Therefore yf we meane to fight va-
liátly against greater tētatiós that besige
vs , we must practize euerie day to resist
& rebutt, these weaker assaults of ordinarie tēptations when they come vpon vs.

Remedies against these lesser tempta-
tions. CHAP. 9.

1. VV E L L then, cócerning these
small tētations of vainglorie, suspition, fretting, iea-
lousie, enuie, loue-fancies, and such like
trashe , which like flies and gnattes do
trouble our eyes , and sometimes bite
and sting vs by the face ; because it is
impossible to be altogether exempted

and freed from their importunitie : the
best resistance that we can make them,
is not to vex our selues for them : for
they cānot hurt vs, though they trouble
vs a litle: so that we be throughly resolued to serue God entirely.

2. Despise then these pettie assaults,
and vouchsafe not so much as to thinck
vpon that which they propose, or would
incline thee vnto: let them buzze about
thine eares as much as they will , and
runne round about thee heer and there
as flies vse to doe, but when they begin
to sting, and make some abode in thy
hart, thē do nothing els but quietlie remoue thē and brush them frō thēce, not
fighting against thē , nor parlying with
them , but producing some contrarie
acts whatsoeuer ; but especially acts of
the loue of God.

3. For yf thou wilt beleeue me, striue
not to eagrelie to oppose manie acts
of the contrarie virtue, to the importunitie of any tentation which thou fee-
lest (for that were to parlie and dispute
with it , which before we forbad thee
to doe) but hauing made an act of the
virtue directly contrarie to the tentation

tion which impugneth thee (yf thou
haft had leafure to furuay the qualitie
of the temptation) take thy recourfe
prefently vnto the hart of Iefus Chrift
crucified, and with an act of feruent
loue to him, kiffe his bleffed feet. This
is the beft meanes to conquer and tame
our enemie as well in litle as in great
tentations; for the loue of God containeth in it felf the perfectios of all other
virtues, and that farre more excellently,
then the virtues them felues do containe them: and therfore is a more foueraigne counter-poifon againft all vices;
And thy foule accuftoming in all tentations, to haue recourfe vnto this vni-
uerfall remedie, need not examin what
particular tentations it fuffereth, but
fimplie feeling her felf troubled with
anie, will find quiet and eafe in this generall refuge: which befides is fo dreadfull and terrible to our ghoftly enemie,
that when he once hath experience, that
all his tentations prouoke vs to this diuine loue of our redeemer, he will
ceafe from battering vs with them.
And thus much concerning leffer temptations : for he that should endeuour

uour to fight with them one by one,
shoud put him self to much care, with
no profit.

How to strengthen our hart against
temptations.   C H A P. 10.

1.   CONSIDER from time to time
what paſſions do raigne in thy
ſoule, and hauing diſcouered
them, begin a manner and courſe of
life cleane oppoſite and contrarie vnto
them in thought, word, and deed. For
example, yf thou find thy ſelf inclined to
the paſſion of ſelf loue and vainglorie:
thinck often vpon the miſerie of this
mortall life of ours ; how bitter theſe
vanities wilbe to our conſcience at the
howre of our death ; how vncomly they
be for a noble and generous hart ; that
they are but trifles, and babies for litle
children to play withall, and ſuch other
conſiderations as theſe. Speak alſo earneſtly and often againſt vainglorie, allthough it ſeeme thou ſpeakeſt againſt
thy will, diſpraiſe it to the vttermoſt of
thy power : for ſo thou ſhalt in a manner

ner engage thy owne reputation to flie from that in deed, which thou fo much condemneft in words : and many times by much fpeaking againft a thing, we moue our felues to hate and defpife it, though at the firft we bare it affection. Exercife works of humilitie and abie-ctió as much as thou canft, euen againft thy owne inclination, for fo thou shalt quickly get a habit of humilitie, and weaken the vice of vainglorie in fuch fort, that when the temptation affaileth thee, thy inclination wilbe now no more able to take part with the temp-tation, and thy foule will haue more ftrength to refift it.

2. Yf thou art inclined to couetouf-neffe, thinck often vpon the extreme follie, and madnes of this vice, which rendreth vs flaues to that droffe which was created to ferue vs ; thinck how at our death we muft leaue all, and that perhaps in the hands of them, that will fcatter it as careleffely, as we had carefully fcraped it together ; and perchaunce in their hands, to whome it wilbe caufe of their vtter ruine and damnation. Speak much againft

aua-

auarice, and praiſe the contempt of
worldlie pelfe. Enforce thy ſelf often
times to giue almes , and to put in vre
the acts of charitie , and works of mercie , and accuſtome ſome times to
omitt ſome occaſions of gaine and
commoditie.

3. So yf thou be ſubiect to the paſſion of idle and carnall loue , thinck
how dangerous a follie it is , as well
to thy ſelf, as to others whome thy fancie may bring to be companions of thy
perills . Conſider what an vnſeemlie
thing it is, to abuſe and (as a man may
ſay) prophane the nobleſt affection
of our ſoule , in ſuch vaine employ-
ments ; how ſubiect this paſſion is to
blame of the wiſer ſort , and how pregnant a token of extreme lightnes of
vnderſtanding. Talk often in praiſe of
chaſt behaueour , let thy diſcources be
ſtill in commendation of cleane and
pure ſoules : and as much as is poſſible,
endeuour to auoide all light behaueour
and all tricks and toyes of fond loue.

4. To be breef, in time of peace and
reſt , that is when the temptations of
thoſe ſinnes to which thou art moſt
                              ſub-

fubiect, do not trouble thee, then exercife all the acts of the contrary virtues thou canft, and yf occasions of doing them, prefent not them felues, find meanes to meet with the occasions, for fo will thy hart be ftrengthened and armed againft future temptations.

Of *vnquietnes of mind.*
CHAPTER II.

I VNQVIETNES is not a fimple and fingle temptation, but a fource and fpring from whence many other temptations take their beginning : I will fpeak a word or two therof. Sadnes is nothing els but a grief and forow of mind, conceiued for fome ill or damage, which is in vs againft our will : whether this euil be outward, as pouertie, ficknes, contempt : or inward, as ignorance, lack of deuotion, repugnance, temptation. For when the foule feeleth her felf charged and burdened with any euil, she is aggreeued therat, and there enters fadnes into her : and prefently she defireth to be deliuered and freed frō it : and not without good

good reason : for euery thing naturally
desireth that which is good, and flieth
from that which is knowen or supposed
to be euil. Yf the soule seek out meanes
to be freed from the euil which oppres-
seth her, and to be rid from the burden
of it for Gods loue, she will seek those
meanes with patience, sweetnes, humilitie, and repose of mind, expecting
her deliuery more from the prouidence
and goodnes of God, then from her
owne industrie, labour, and diligence.
But yf she desire to be eased from her
vexation for self-loue, then will she
torment and weerie, and trouble her
self in seeking the meanes of her ease:
as though it depended more of her
self, then of God. I say not that she
thincketh or iudgeth so, but that she
behaueth her self so carefullie, so ha-
stelie, & so earnestlie, as yf indeed she
thought so. So that yf she meet not
with that which she desireth, presentlie
and out of hand, then falleth she into
great vnquietnes, and impatience ;
by which the former vexation or euil,
not departing from her, but rather
waxing farre worse, she entreth into

an-

anguish, diſtreſſe, faintnes of hart, and loſſe of all courage : ſo that ſhe iudgeth and deemeth her miſerie to be paſt all remedie. Where thou ſeeſt, that ſadnes, which had a iuſt and lawfull beginning grounded vpon rea-ſonable conſiderations, afterward en-gendreth vnquietnes, and vnquiet-neſſe againe, addeth an increaſe of ſadnes, which is exceeding peril-lous.

2. This vnquietnes of mind, is the greateſt ill that can come to the ſou-le, excepting ſinne. For as the ſedi-tions and ciuil diſcords of a common wealth, is the vtter ruine and ouer-throw therof, and maketh it altoge-ther vnable to reſiſt the forraigne in-uader : ſo our hart troubled and diſ-quieted in it ſelf, looſeth all for-ce and abilitie, to defend the virtues which it had purchaſed, and all mea-nes to reſiſt the tentations of the ghoſtlie enemie ; who at that time vſeth all kind of diuices and inuen-tions, knowing that according to the prouerbe it is, good fiſhing in trou-bled water.

3. Vn-

3.   Vnquietnes proceedeth of a inordinate defire to be deliuered from the
euil that one feeleth , or to obtaine the
good that one defireth:and yet nothing
maketh the euil worfe , nor remoueth
the good farther from vs,then doth vnquietnes and vnreafonable haftines.
Birds do remaine faft in the nets and
lime-twigges , becaufe finding them
felues but a litle caught hold of, they
beat and flutter vp and downe fo eagre-
ly,that they are more and more entangled in the fnare. When thou defireft
earneftly to be freed from any euil , or
to obtaine any good ; the firft thing
thou muft doe , is to repofe thy mind,
and quiet thy thoughts and affects from
ouer-haftie pourfuite of thy defire:and
then faire and foftly beginne to pour-
chafe thy wifhe , taking by order, and
one after another the meanes which
thou iudgeft conuenient to the attaining
therof. And when I fay faire and foftly,
I doe not meane flowly and negligetly,
but without poft-haft, without trouble
and vnquietnes:otherwife infteed of attaining to the effect of thy defire, thou
wilt be more entangled in this laby-
rinthe

rinthe of troublſom thoughts , then before.

4. *My ſoule is allway in my hands ô Lord: and I haue not forgotten thy law* ; ſayd Dauid. Examin often euery day , at leaſt morning & euening, whether thy ſoule be in thy hands , or ſome paſſion of vnquietnes hath robbed thee of it. Conſider whether thou haue thy hart at commandement , whether it be not eſcaped and fled away from thee, to ſome vnrulie affection of loue , hatred, enuie , couetouſnes, feare, ioye, ſadnes: and yf it be wandred aſtray , ſeek it out preſently , and bring it back again gentlie to the preſence of God , reſigning it with all thy affections and deſires vnto the obedience and direction of his diuine pleaſure. For as they that feare leaſt they loſe a thing which they loue well , keep it faſt claſped in their hands : ſo in imitation of this great king we ſhould always ſay from our harts : O my God my ſoule is in continuall danger of being loſt , and therefore I carie it always in my hand , and for this diligent care of my ſoule, I haue not forgotten thy holie lawe.

5. Per-

5. Permitt not thy desires, be they neuer so litle, and of neuer so small importance, to disquiet thy mind: for after litle desires, come great ones, and find thy hart more readie and disposed to be troubled and put out of order. When thou perceauest vnquietnes to enter, commend thy self to God, and resolue thy self to doe nothing at all, that thy vehement desire exhorteth, vntill that disquiet be ouerpassed : vnlesse it be some thing that cannot be differred: and then thou must with a gentle an quiet endeuour, withhold the current of thy affection, tempering and moderating it as much as is possible : and after this repose, doe that which is requisite to be done, not as thy desire commandeth, but as reason prescribeth.

9. If thou cast discouer the vnquietnes of thy mind to him that gouerneth thy soule, or at the least to some trustie and deuout frind : doubt not but presently thou shalt find it appeased. For communicating of griefs of our hart, worketh the same effect in the troubled soule, that letting of bloud doth in the bodie of him that is in a cötinuall ague:
                                    and

and this is the remedie of remedies. So
holy king Lewis gaue this councell to
his sonne : If thou feeleft in thy hart
any thing that troubleth thee, tell it
prefently vnto thy confeffour, or vnto
fome good frind, and thou shalt beare
thy greef verie eafily, through the comfort that he will giue thee.

Of fadneffe.   C H A P. 12.

1. SADNES *that is according to God*
(fayth S. Paul) *worketh penaunce
vnto faluation* : *but fadnes of the
world worketh death.* Sorow then and
fadnes, may be good or bad, according
to the fundrie effects which it worketh
in vs. True it is, that it produceth more
naught then good: for it hath but onely
two that are commendable, mercy, and
penaunce ; and fix bad ones : anxietie,
floth, indignation, iealofie, enuie, and
impatience : which caufed the wifeman
to fay. *Sorrow killeth many, and there is no
proffit in it :* becaufe for two profitable
ftreames which flow from the fpring of
fadnes, there are fix other ftark naught,
that runne from the fame head.

2. The

2. The enemie vseth sadnes as a fit disposition to exercise his temptations against the iust; for as he endeuours to make the wicked ioyous and glad in their sinnes; so doth he go about, to make deuout persons, sad and heauie in their good actions. And as he can by no meanes procure euil to be committed, but by making it seeme pleasaunt and delectable, so he cannot withdraw men frō doing that which is good, but by making it appeer distastfull, sad, and displeasing. He taketh delight in sadnes, because he him self is sad and melancholick, and so shalbe eternally: therfore would he haue euery one be like him self in sorow.

3. This preposterous sadnes, troubleth the mind, putteth it into disquiet, assaulteth it with vnreasonable feares, giueth a bitter tast to the sweetest deuotions, dulleth and ouerthroweth the braine, depriueth the soule of resolution, iudgement, and courage. To be short, it is like a hard winter, that cutteth away all the beautie of the field, and swalloweth all liuing creatures: for it bannisheth all sweetnes from the soule,

foule , and lameth her in the vſe of her
powers and faculties. Yf thou chaunce
to-be aſſailed with this daungerous hea-
uineſſe, Philotheus, practize the remedies enſewing.

4. *Is any body ſad* (ſayth S.Iames) *let
him pray.* Prayer is a foueraigne remedie : for it lifteth vp the ſoule vnto God,
who is our onlie ioye and conſolation:
but when thou prayeſt in ſadneſſe and
ſorow, vſe affections and words which
tend to confidence and loue of God,as:
O mercifull father,moſt bountifull and
pitifull God,my ſweet Saueour; O God
of my hart, my ioye, my hope, my deer
ſpouſe, the welbe-loued of my ſoule, &
ſuch like.

5. Striue manfullie againſt the inclinations of ſorowe : allthough all thy
actions and exerciſes , during the time
of this ſad paſſiō, ſeeme vnto thee to be
perfourmed coldlie,heauilie, and ſlack-
lie : omitt them not for all that:for the
enemie who pretendeth to wearie vs
from doing well by ſadneſſe,ſeeing that
notwithſtanding this deuice of his, yet
we folow our woonted exerciſes , and
that being performed againſt all this

Z   repu-

repugnance of heauie paſſiõs, our workes are of greater valew and merit : he
leaueth to afflict vs any more therwith.

6. Sing ſpirituall ſongs ſomtimes ;
for the deuil hath often times left of his
troubleſome operatiõ by ſuch meanes:
witneſſe the bad ſpirit that obſeſſed
Saul, whoſe violence was repreſſed by
Dauids melodious & ſacred Pſalmodie.

7. It is alſo good to diuert our thoughts by externall occupations ; varied
and chaunged as much as we can : that
ſo our mind may be withdrawen from
the ſad obiect, and the ſpirits be hea-
ted and purified, ſadnes being a paſſion of a cold and drie complexion.

8. Exerciſe many externall actions
with feruour, although it be without
guſt or ſpirituall feeling : embracing a
crucifix, and appliyng it ſtraightly to
thy breſt, kiſſing the feet and hands of
it with reuerence, ſtretching thy eyes
and hands vnto heauen, lifting vp thy
voice vnto God by words of loue and
confidence, ſuch as folow : *My welbe-
loued is myne, and I am his : My welbeloued
is vnto me a poſy of myrrhe, he ſhall remaine
betwixt my breaſts. Mine eyes do melt into*
teares

teares vnto thee O my God saying , when wilt thou comfort me ? O Iesus , be Iesus to me: liue sweet Iesus in my soule , and my soule will liue in thee. Who can separate me from the loue of God ? and such like.

9. Moderate disciplines are not amisse. Because this volũtary afflictiõ applied outwardly, obtaineth inward cõsolation frõ God: & the soule feeling paine without, diuerteth her self frõ thincking of those which molest her within. Frequẽting also of the holy cõmunion is an excellẽt cordial: for that heauẽly bread strẽgtheneth the hart, & reioiceth the spirit.

10. Discouer all feelings, affects and suggestiõs which proceed frõ this spirit of sadnes , manifest them sincerely and faithfullie to thy guide and confessour: seek the companie of spirituall persons, and be with thẽ as much as thou canst, during the time of thy sadnes. And last of all, resigne thy self vp to the hands of God , preparing thy self to suffer this heauinesse and sorow patiently, as a iust punishment of thy vaine myrthe and passetimes: and doubt not at all, but that God , after he hath tried thee , will deliuer thee from this euil.

Z 2   *Of*

*Of spirituall and sensible consolations,
and how one must behaue him self
in them.* CHAP. 13.

1. GOD cōtinueth and gouerneth
this great world in a perpetuall
viciſſitude or enterchaunge of
night into day, ſpring into ſommer,
ſommer into autumne, autumne into
winter, and winter into the ſpringtime
againe : & one day is neuer in all things
and points like to another : ſome are
clowdie, ſome bright-ſhining, ſome ray-
nie, ſome drie, ſome windie, ſome ſtill &
louelie. A varietie is this, which giueth
exceeding beautie to the whole world.
The like is with man, who, according
to the ſaying of the auncient ſages, is an
abridgmēt of the world, or another litle
world : for he alſo is neuer in the ſame
eſtate, his life paſſeth like waters ebbing
and flowing in a perpetuall diuerſitie of
motions, which ſome time lift him vp
by hope, ſome time beare him downe
with feare : ſome time carie him to the
right hand with cōſolations, ſome time
waſte him to the left hand with afflictions :

ctions: & nòt one day, no not so much
as one onely hower of all his life, is in
all points like another.

2. This is a necessarie aduertisement
which I set thee downe : we must do
our best to haue a continuall and inuincible indifferencie and equalitie of
hart , amid this wonderfull inequalitie
of occurrences. And albeit all things
do chaunge and turne giddilie round
about vs , yet must we stand stedfastlie
and vnmoueablie, always looking and
aspiring towards our God. Let the ship
take what route it list , let it single
towards east, or weast,north, or south,
what, wind soeuer driueth it , neuer will
the compasse look any other way,but
towards the faire pole-starre. Let all
turne vpside downe , not onlie round
about vs , but euen within vs , let our
soule be sorowfull , or ioyfull, let it be
in peace , or trouble, in sweetnes or
bitternesse , in light, or in darknes, in
tentation,or in repose , in tast , or out
of tast, deuout , or vndeuout , let the
sunne burne and scorche it , or the
deaw moisten and refresh it : yet always
must the point of our hart , our spirit,

Z 3　　　　　our

our superiour will , which is our card or
compasse, look incessauntly,& tend continuallie, towards the loue of God her
Creatour,her Sauiour,& her onely happines and soueraigne good. *Whether we*
liue or dye (sayth the Apostle) *we belong*
to God. And who shalbe able to separate vs
from the loue of God ? nothing shalbe able
to dissolue and vndoe this loue, neither
tribulatiô,nor distresse,nor anguish,nor
death, nor life ;nor present , nor future
dolours,nor the feare of imminent dangers, nor the subtiltie of malicious spirits,nor the sublimitie of consolations,
nor the depth or profunditie of affli-
ctiôs,nor the tendernes, nor drinesse of
hart , nor any other thing shall separate
vs from this holy charitie, founded and
grounded in our *Saueour* Christ Iesus.

3. This absolute and perfect resolution , neuer to forsake God , or abandon his sweet loue , serueth for a coun-
terpoise to our soules, to keep them in
holie indifferencie, amidst the in equalitie & diuersitie of motiôs & chaunges
which the côditiô of this life bringeth.
For as the litle Bees ouertaken with a
storme in the fields, charge them selues
with

with litle grauel-ſtones, to ballaūce thē
ſelues in the ayre, that they may not ſo
eaſilie be caried away by the wind:ſo our
ſoule by a liuely reſolution embracing
the pretious loue of God, continueth
conſtant in the midſt of the inconſtan-
cie and mutabilitie of conſolations and
afflictions, ſpirituall & temporall, interiour and exteriour. But beſides this generall doctrine, wee ſtand in need of
ſome particular documents.

4. Firſt then, I ſay that deuotiō conſiſteth not in that ſame ſweetnes, ſoftnes,
comfort, or ſenſible tendernes of hart,
which moueth vs to teares & ſighes, and
giueth vs a certaine delicious taſt, and a
kind of contēt & ſatisfactiō in our ſpirituall exerciſes. No (my deer Philotheus)
deuotiō, & that māner of tendernes of
hart, is not al one thing. For manie ſoules haue this ſupple qualitie, & thoſe ſenſible conſolations, which for all that let
not to be verie vicious, & conſequently
want the true loue of God, and haue no
true deuotion at all. Saule perſequuting
poor Dauid to the death, who fled from
him into the wildernes of Engaddi, entred all alone ĩnto a vaſt caue, where
                Z 4   Dauid

Dauid and his people lay hidden. Dauid,
who at this occasion might haue killed him a thousand times, spared his life,
and would not so much as put him in
feare: but suffered him to goe foorth
quietly at his pleasure, called after him,
to declare vnto him his innocencie,
and to giue him to vnderstand, that he
had been at his mercie. Well heervpon
what did not Saul to shew that his hart
was mollified towards Dauid ? he called him his childe, fell into plaine weeping, to praise him, to confesse his
meeknes, to pray vnto God for him,
to presage and foretell his future greatnes, and to commend his owne poste-
ritie vnto him. What greater sweetnes,
and tendernes of hart could he make
shew of ? and yet for all that, he had
not chaunged his canckred mind, nor
left of his rancorous intention, but
cõtinued persecuting Dauid as cruellie
as before. Euen so there may be found
many persons, that considering the
goodnes of God, and the dolefull pas-
siõ of our Saueour, doe feele great tendernes of hart, which forceth them to
sigh, to weep, to blesse, ãnd praise God,
and

and giue him thancks verie feelingly, at
least verie sensiblie; in so much that one
would iudge their hart to be seased and
possessed with a mightie deale of deuotion: But when the matter comes to the
proofe, we shall find, that like as short
sodaine shewers of a hot summer, falling in great bigge droppes vpon the
earth and not pearcing it, serue for nothing els but to produce todestooles
and mushroms : Euen so the teares and
tendernes of these men , falling vpon a
vicious hart , and not penetrating it, be
altogeather vnprofitable. For notwithstanding all these great dropps of sensible deuotion , they will not part from
one dodkin of their euel gotten goods,
nor renounce one of all their crooked
and peruerse affections , nor suffer the
least incommoditie of the world for
the seruice of our Saueour , for whose
sake they wept so earnestlie. So that
the good motions which these poore
soules felt , are nothing but spirituall
mushrums ; and are not onelie no true
deuotion, but oftentimes great slights
of the deuil, who nousling them vp
in these false consolations , makes

Z 5   them

them remaine contented and satis-
fied therwith : that so they should
search no farther for true and sound
deuotion , which consisteth in a
prompt , resolute , actiue , and constant will , of putting in execution
that which they know to be agreable
to Gods pleasure . A litle child will
weepe tenderly yf he see his mother
launced when she is let bloud : but
yf his mother at the same time demand an apple , or a paper of comfits which he hath in his hands , he
will by no meanes let it goe from
him , demand it shee neuer so sweetly . Such for the more part are these
tender deuotions, considering the stro-
ke of the speare , which pearced the
hart of our Saueour , we weepe bit-
terlie therfore : And alas (my Philotheus) it is right well donne to be-
waile the sorowfull death and wofull
passion of our father and redeemer,
but why then do we not giue him the
apple which we haue in our hands ,
seeing he asketh it vs so earnestly , to
wit , our hart, the only fruict of loue,
which our deare *Saueour* requesteth
                                    of

of vs ? Wherfore refigne we not vnto
him fo manie pettie affections , delights,& felf-pleafures,which he would
pull out of our hands and cannot , becaufe they be our babies, they be our
comfirs of which we be more fond ,
then defirous of his heauenly grace ?
Ah Philotheus , thefe be babie-loues,
litle childrens frindships,tender indeed,
but feeble , but fantafticall , but frui-
ctleffe, and without effect . Deuotion
then , confifteth not in fuch tender
and fenfible affections , which fometimes proceed of a nature or complexion in it felf foft , fupple, apte
and eafie to receaue any impreffion :
but fometimes of the crafte of the de-
uel , who to bufie vs vnprofitablie
about fuch trash and droguerie ,
ftirreth vp our fantafie to the appre-
fion fit for to receaue fuch motions.

5. Yet thefe felf fame tendre and
fweet affections are manie times good
and profitable , for they prouoke the
appetite of the foule , comfort the
fpirit , and adde to the promptitude
of our deuotion , a kind of iollitie
and cheerfullnes , which maketh our

actions comelie & delightfull, euen in
outward shew & appeerance. Which is
the guſt or taſt that one feeleth in diuine and heauenly matters, of which Dauid exclaimeth : *O Lor how ſweet are thy*
words to my taſt:they are ſweeter then honny
to my mouth. And indeed the leaſt and
meaneſt cōtentment of deuotiō which
we receaue in holy exerciſes , is better
in all reſpects , then the moſt excellent recreations and pleaſures of the
world. The breaſts, and milke, that
is , the fauours of the heauenly ſpouſe , are ſweeter and pleaſaunter to the
ſoule , then the daintieſt and moſt pretious wine of earthly delights. He that
once hath taſted them , eſteemeth all
other comforts, but gaulle and wormewood. As they that hold the hearbe
Scitique in their mouth , taſt ſo pleaſaunt a ſweetnes , that they feele neither hunger nor thirſt for the while :
ſo they, to whome God hath imparted
this celeſtiall Manna of internall conſolations , can neither deſire nor receaue the contentments of the world,
at leaſt to take any pleaſure in them,
or to ſette their affections vpon them.
　　　　　　　　　　　　　　　They

They be tafts giuen before hand, of
the immortall delights which God hath
layd vp in heauen for the foules that
fearche after him : they be the fugred
comfits and carowayes which he giueth
vnto vs as his litle children to allure vs:
they be the cordiall waters which he
prefenteth to ftrengthen them ; and
manie times they be handfels, or pledges of euerlafting felicitie. They fay
that Alexander the great, failing in the
manie fea, difcouered before the reft
of his companions, the land of the
happie Arabia, by the fmell of the
fweet odours which the wind brought with it, and therevpon receaued
him felfe, and gaue great encouragement, to his felow-foldiours : fo oft
times in this mortall life, we receaue
thefe delights and pleafures of deuotion, which no doubt prefent vnto
our memorie, the ioyes and delights
of the happie land of heauen, wherunto we doe all faile and afpire.

6. But thou wilt fay, fince there
are fome fenfible confolations that
be good, and come from God, and
other fome that be vnprofitable, and
per-

pernicious, proceeding either from
nature, or from the enemie, how
shall I diftinguishe the one from the
other, and difcerne the vnprofitable
from thofe that be good. It is a generall rule (my Philotheus) for all the
paffions and affections of our foule,
that we muft know them by their
fruicts : our foules be as it were trees;
affections and paffions be the bowes
and braunches ; works and actions be
the fruicts. It is a good foule, that
feeleth good affections, and the affections are good which bring foorth in
vs great effects of holie actions. Yf
the delights, the tendernes, the confolations which we feele in fpirituall
exercifes, do make vs more humble,
more patient, tractable, charitable,
fuller of cōpaffion towards our neighbour ; more feruent in mortifying our
concupifcence and naughtie inclinations ; more conftant in our good exercifes and refolutions, more meek
and fupple, and pliable to thofe whome we ought to obey ; more fimple and fincere in our liues : then
without all doubt Philotheus, they
                                            are

are from God. But yf thefe delights
haue no fweetnes , fauing onely for
our owne felues , yf they make vs
curious , peeuish , fower , fullen ,
impatient , ftubborne , fierce , pre-
fumptuous , hard-harted towards our
neighbours , yf therefore efteeming
our felues allredie pettie Saints , we
will no more be fubiect to correction nor direction, then deere Philotheus , beware of them , then doubtleffe they be falfe and pernicious
confolations . A good tree cannot
bring foorth any other but good
fruicts.

7. When we receaue thefe delights and comforts in our exercifes
we muft. 1. Firft of all humble our
felues profoundly before allmightie
God : and take heed of faying to our
felues by reafon of thefe fweet comforts : how perfect , how good am I
become ! No Philotheus, not fo, thefe
be good things in deed, but they make
vs neuer the better for hauing them:
for, as I haue fayd, deuotion confifteth
not in them, but let vs faye and thinck
from our harts : O how good is God

to such as hope in him, to the soule
that seeketh after him! He that hath
sugar melting in his mouth, cannot
properlie say that his mouth is sweet,
but that the sugar, which is in his
mouth, is sweet to his mouth: So
though these spirituall delights be verie
good, and that God who imparteth
them to vs, is exceeding good, yet foloweth it not, that he which receaueth
them, is good. 2. Let vs acknowledge
our selues as yet to be litle children, and
that we stand in need of milk: that these
sugred confits be giuen vs, because as
yet our spirit is tender and delicate, and
therfore needeth allurements and baytes, to be drawen with all to the loue of
God. 3. But after that, speaking generallie, and ordinarily, let vs receaue
these graces and fauours humbly, and
reuerently, esteeming them exceeding
pretious, not so much for that they are
in them selues, as that it is the hand of
God whiche powreth them into our
hart. As a louing mother to allure her
child, putteth her owne self the sugred
confits into his mouth one by one,
sweetly smiling, and tenderlie parliyng
with

with him the while: for yf the child had
witt and vfe of his reafon, he would
much more efteeme, his mothers che-
rifhing embraces, then the fweetnes of
the confits, be they neuer fo daintie.
So it is much Philotheus to receaue &
feel in our foules this fweetnes of deuotion : but it is the fweet of all fweetnes
to confider that God, with his louing
and fatherlie hand, putteth them as it
were into our mouth, to our hart, and
foule. 4. Hauing receiued them thus
in humble and reuerent wife, let vs employ them whollie according to the intention of the giuer. And wherfore
think yee, dooth God beftowe thefe
fweet comforts vpon vs ? to make vs
fweet towards euery bodie, and amourous towards him. The mother giues
comfits to her litle child, to make him
kiffe her : let vs likewife kiffe our bleffed Saueour, who maketh much of vs
by thefe confolations : to kiffe our Saueour, is to obey him, to fullfill his
will, to folow his rules and councells:
in a word, to embrace him tenderlie &
louinglie with obedience and loyaltie.
The day therfore in which we shall receaue

ceaue any spirituall consolation , we
must employ most carefullie,and endeuour to spend it diligently in Gods seruice and honour. 5. Beyond all this,we
must from time to time renounce in
our hart all this sweetnes,tendernes,and
consolation , separating our affection
from it as much as we can : protesting,
that albeit we receaue these fauours
humblie , and loue and esteeme them,
because God sendeth them to vs , as it
were dishes and dainties from his owne
table, to prouoke vs the more to his
loue:yet it is not those delights that we
seek and desire , but God him self and
his perfect loue , not the comforts,but
the comforter ; not the sweetnes , but
the sweet Saueour that giues them; not
that tendernes of delight , but him that
is the delight of heauen and earth.
And in this affectuous abrenunciation
of these delights , we must dispose our
selues, to perseuer constant and firme
in the holy loue of God , though in all
our life long we should not tast one
dramme of consolation : and procure vnfainedly, to say as well vpon the
mount of Caluary, as on the mount of
                                      Ta-

Tabor , *O Lord it is good for me to be with thee* , be thou in torments vpon thy croſſe , or be thou in glorie in heauen.
6. To conclude I aduertize thee that yf thou shouldſt chaunce to feele any extraordinarie aboundāce of ſuch conſolations , tendernes , ſweetnes , deuout teares, or ſome vnwoonted thing: that then thou conferre it faithfullie with thy ſpirituall conductour , that he may teache thee how to moderate and behaue thy ſelf therin. For it is written. *Haſt thou found honny ? eate of it but as much as is ſufficient.*

Of dryneſſe and barrenneſſe in our ſpirituall exerciſes.

CHAPTER 14.

1. THvs then muſt thou behaue thy ſelf , as I haue now deſcribed in time of ſpirituall comfort : but alas (Philotheus,) this faire weather will not laſt allwayes : and the time will come , when thou ſhalt be ſo deſtitute , and depriued

of

of all feeling of this deuotion, that thy
soule will seeme vnto thee a fruictlesse
and barren field, or a desart wildernesse,
in which there appeers neither cawsee,
nor pathway to find God, nor auie dewe of grace to moisten and water it,
through excessiue drienes, which thre-
atneth to reduce her altogether to dust.
Alas the poor soule in this case deserues
compassion, and especially when this
desolation is vehement: for at that time
like holy Dauid, she feedeth her self
with sad teares night and day : meane
while the enemie by a thousand suggestions endeuours to driue her to despai-
re, and mocketh her bitterly, saying in
derision, wretche, wher is thy God now
in thy distresse ? by what meanes wilt
thou find him out ? Who shall euer be
able to restore thee the ioye of his
grace ?

2. And what wilt thou doe at that
time Philotheus, consider from what
cause so great a miserie proceedeth: for
oft times, we our selues are the cause of
our owne drienes and desolation, in
the exercises of the spirit. 1. As a carefull mother denies to giue sugar to her
child,

child, when she sees him troubled with
the wormes : so God taketh away his
consolations from vs , when we take
some vaine self-pleasing in them , and
are subiect to the worme of ouer-wea-
ning, to self-conceipt, and opinion of
our owne good progresse in deuotion.
O my God (sayth the psalmist) *It is good
for me that thou hast humbled me* . Yes in
deed, it is verie profitable for me, *for before I was humbled , I did offend thee.* 2.
When we neglect to gather the sweetnes and deliciousnesse of the loue of
God in due time : then in punishment
of our slothfullnesse , he absenteth his
delights from vs . The Israelites in the
desart that gathered not Manna earlie
in the morning , could not find any after the sunne-rising , for then was it all
melted with the heat of the sunne. 3.
We are also sometimes layde in the bed
of sensuall contentment , and transitorie comforts , as the sacred spouse was
in the Canticles , comes me the bride-
grome , and knocketh at the dore of
our hart , and inspireth vs to returne to
our spirituall exercises : but we play the
niggardly chapmen with him , for it
ange-

angeteth vs to leaue of our toyes, and
to separate our selues from our false delights. For this cause the true louer of
our soules goeth his way from vs, and
letteth vs lie as we list: but afterward
when we would faine find him out, we
haue much a doe to meet with him; and
deseruedlie, because we were so vncour-
teous and faithlesse vnto his loue, as to
refuse to folow our exercise for his loue,
and to choose to folow worldly vanities. Ah: then as yet thou hast some
of the branne of Egypt remaining·thou
shalt then haue not a iot.of the heauenly Manna. Bees detest all kind of
artificiall odours : and the sweetnes of
the holy Ghost, cannot agree with the
sophisticated delights of the world.
4. The double dealing, and slights
which thou vsest in confessions, and
spirituall communications with the
conductour and maister of thy soule,
many times is the cause of this drougth
and barrennesse : for yf thou lie to the
holy Ghost, no meruaile yf he withdraw his consolations from thee. Thou
wilt not be simple, plaine, and without guile, as a litle child is : thou
shalt

shalt not then enioy thefe fpirituall comfits, giuen only to Gods litle children.5.Thou art filled and glutted with worldly contentments:no wonder then yf fpirituall delights come not to thy table , or haue no good taft in thy mouth:Doues allreadie filled (fayth the ancient prouerb) do thinck cherries bitter. *He which filled the hungrie with good things* (fayth our bleffed Ladie) *and fent the rich away empty.* They that be rich of wordly vanities, are not capable of fpirituall treafures. 6. Haft thou conferued well and carefully the fruicts of confolations allreadie receaued ? then shalt thou receaue more ftore againe : for to him that hath, more shalbe giuen : and he that hath not (negligently leefing that which he receaued) euen that he hath shalbe taken away from him , he shalbe depriued of the fauours and graces,which were prepared for him , yf he had vfed well the former. The raine quickeneth them plats that be greene,but frō them that be not green, it taketh away altogether all likelyhood of life & growth, for it rotteth them wholly.

3. For

3. For manie fuch caufes doe we loofe comfort in deuotion, and fall into barrennes and drienes of fpirit. Let vs then examin our confcience, and fee whether we can find in vs fuch faultie caufes as thefe. But note, Philotheus, that this examination is not to be made with vnquietneffe of mind, or ouermuch curiofitie, but after thou haft faithfully confidered thy going awrie in this refpect, yf thou find the caufe of the euil in thy felf, giue God thancks, for the harme is half healed, whofe caufe is difcouered. Yf on the other fide, thou find out no caufe in particular, which may feeme vnto thee to haue occafioned this defolation, bufie not thy felf about anie more curious fearche for it, but with all fimplicitie, without examining any more particularities, doe this which I will tell thee.

4. Firft of all humble thy felf reuerently before the eyes of God, acknowledging thy miferie, thy frailtie, the nothing that thou arein thy felf. Alas what am I, when I am left alone to mine owne prouidence? nothing els, O

Lord,

Lord, but a drie barren ground, that
full of gappes and riftes, witnesseth the
drought it suffereth, for want of heauenly dewe: and the wind of tentation
in the mean time doth dissipate it conuerted into fruictlesse dust. 2. Call
vpon God and demaund of him his
spirituall ioye. *Render vnto me, O Lord,
the ioy of thy saluatiou. My father, yf it be
possible, lett this cuppe passe from mee.* Gett
thee away ô thou vnfruictfull Northe-
wind, which driest vp the sappe and iuice of my soule: and come ô prosperous
winds of consolations, and breath gently ouer my poore garden, and then
these good affections wil spread abroad
the odour of their sweetnes 3. Goe to
thy Confessour, open thy hart vnto
him, make him see cleerly all the
plights and corners of thy soule: take
his aduice simplie and humbly: for
God that infinitly loueth obedience,
maketh often times councells taken
from other men, proue verie profitable,
especially giuen by conductours of soules, albeit otherwise there be no great
likelyhood, that they should preuaile: as
he made the waters of Iordan healthfull

A a   to

to Naaman, which Elizeus, without any appearence at all of humane reason, ordained him as a bath for his leprosie.

4. All this being donne, nothing is so profitable, nothing so fruitfull in time of these spirituall desolations, and barrenesse, as not to be ouermuch desirous of being deliuered frō this aggreeuance or calamitie. I say not but that we may simplie and quietlie wishe to be eased of so great a burden: but my meaning is, that we should not too earnestly affect this ease, and freedom from this desolate state of mind: but hartely resigne our soule to the prouidence of God; that so long as it pleaseth him, he may vse our poore seruice, amid these troublesome thornie-brakes, and comfortlesse deserts. Let vs say to God at these times. *O father, yf it be possible, lett this cup passe away from me:* but lett vs with all from our verie harts, adioine the wordes folowinge of our blessed Saueour: *Yet not my will be donne, but thine:* vpon this good resolution let vs rest, and repose. For God seeing vs constantly perseuer in this holy in diffe-

differency, will comfort vs with many graces, and fauours : as when he saw Abraham resolued to depriue him self of his sonne Isaac, he was contented with this his indifferency,& pure resignation, cóforting him with a heauenly vision, & with most admirable benedictions. We must then in al kind of afflictions, as wel corporall as spirituall, in what soeuer distractions, or subtractiós of sensible deuotion happening to vs, with great courage, and resignation always say : *Our Lord gaue me consolations, and our Lord hath taken them from me ; his holy name be blessed.* For persisting in this humilitie and submission, he will restore vnto vs his delicious fauours, as he did vnto Iob, who vsed the aforesayd words constantly and vnfainedly in all his desolations.

5. Finallie my Philotheus, amidst all these sterilities and desolations, let vs not loose courage, but expecting patiétly the returne of spiritual delights, keepe on our iourney, folow our exercises of deuotion, multiplie good works and holy actions: and not being able to present to our spouse, liquid

conserues, present him drie confitures:
for all is one to him, prouided that the
hart which offereth them, be perfectly
resolued to perseuer loyallie in his loue.
When the spring time is faire and pleasaunt, then do the Bees make more honnie, and fewer young impes : for the
good wether fauouring them, they are
so busie in gathering the sappe of sweet
flowers, that they forgett the generation of their young ones. But when
the springtime is troublesome with
gloomie cloudes and windie stormes,
they gett more impes, and lesse honnie
for being not able to flie abroade to
their gathering of honnie, they employ
them selues to multiplie their race, and
people their comonwealthe. So chaunceth it oft times, my Philotheus, that
the soule in the faire weather of spirituall comforts, busieth her self so much
in gathering them together, and suc-
king that heauenlie iuice out of them,
that in the abundance of these daintie
delights, she produceth fewer good wor
kes : and contrariwise amid the bitternesse of clowdie desolations, seeing her
self destituted of those spiritual delights
of de-

of deuotiõ, she multiplieth folid works
of edification fo much more ferioufly,
and aboundeth in fructifiyng of true
virtues of patiēce, humilitie, abiection,
refignation, and abnegation, of all felf-
will and felf loue.

6. It is then a great abufe and errour
of manie, efpeciallie of wemen , to beleeue that the feruice which we doe to
God whithout this pleafant taft, & fenfible delight, & tendernes of hart, is lefle
agreeable to his diuine maieftie: for cleane contrarylie, our actiõs are like vnto
rofes , which though being freſhe and
flourie they haue a better grace & shew,
yet whē they are drie they haue a fweeter odour : fo though our works done
with tendernes of deuotion be more acceptable to vs our felues, to vs I fay, that
confider only our owne delight : yet
when they are exercifed by vs in time of
drinefle and barrenefle of fpirit , then
haue they a goodlier eftimation , and a
better odour in the prefence of God. In
time of defolation , our will carieth vs
(as it were by meer force) to the feruice
of God, & confequently that will muſt
needs be more vigorous and conftant,

then the will which we haue of seruing
god in time of comfort. It is no such
great matter to serue a prince in time
of peace, and in the pompe and pleasures of the courte, but to serue him
constantly in time of trouble and per-
secution, and in warre, that is a true
mark of constancy and loyaltie. Saint
Angela de Fulgino sayth, that of all
prayers, that is most acceptable to god,
which is made by force and meere con-
straint, that is, whereunto we applie
our selues willinglie, not for any tast
or delight which we feele in it, nor by
our owne inclination, but meerly,
purely and onlie to please god: wherto
our will driueth vs, as it were against
our will, forcing and violently repel-
ling the drienesse, and contradictions,
which oppose themselues against it.
The same say I of all sorts of good workes, that the more contradiction we
find in exercising them, be it exteriour,
or interiour, the more are they prized
and esteemed in the court of heauen.
The lesse of our owne particular interest that there is in the poursuite of virtues, the more doth the puritie of the
loue

loue of God shine in it. A litle child wil
eafilie kiffe his mother, when she giueth
him honnie and fugar, but it is a figne of
greater loue, yf he kiffe her after she
hath giuen him wormefeed, or bitter
potions.

---

*The former difcourfe is explained and
confirmed by a notable example.*

CHAPTER 15.

1. TO make this inftruction more
euident and intelligible, I will
recite an excellent peece of the
hiftorie of S. Bernard, in fuch manner
as I find it fet downe in the learned and
iudicious writer therof. He fayth then
in this wife. It is an ordinarie thing, almoft vnto all them that beginne to ferue God, and are not yet experienced in
the fubtraction of grace, nor in fpirituall
viciffitudes or enterchãges of cõfolatiõs
& defolatiõs; that the taft of fenfible deuotion & that fweet acceptable light of
mind, (which maketh them hafte them
felues in the waye of God) being withdrawen from them: they prefently grow
out of breath, and fall into pufillanimitie and fadnes of hart. They that

be of iudgement and vnderſtanding doe
render this reaſon therof : that nature
according to reaſon cannot long endure (as a man might ſay) faſting, & without anie kind of delight or entertainment at all, but needs muſt haue ſome
contentment, either terreſtriall or celeſtiall. But as ſoules lifted vp aboue them
ſelues by taſt and trial of heauenly pleaſures, doe eaſilie renounce the delights
of all ſenſible obiects: ſo when by Gods
diſpoſition and ordinance that ſpirituall
ioy is taken from them, finding them
ſelues alſo on the other ſide depriued of
corporall ſolace, and being not yet ac-
cuſtomed to expect with patience, the
returne and riſing of the true ſunne of
grace, it ſeemeth vnto them that they
are no more in heauen or in earth,
but that they be buried in perpetuall
darknes : So that as litle children
newlie weaned, hauing loſt their mothers dugges they do languiſhe, and
ſigh, and grow froward and troubleſome, principallie to their owne ſelues. This then happened in the voiage
wherof we ſpeake, vnto one of the
troupe, called Geoffrie of Peronne,
　　　　　　　　　　　　　　　　but

but newlie dedicated to the feruice of
God . He being fodainlie become
drie in his deuotions , deftituted of
his woonted confolations , and pof-
feffed with a kind of inward darknes:
began to call to memorie the world,
his frinds , his parents , and the great
meanes that but lately he had left behind him . By which memorie , he
was affaulted with fo cruell a temptation , that not being able to hide it in
his behaueour , one of his truftie
frinds perceaued it , and hauing found
opportunitie , ioined himfelf to him,
and asked him fweetly in fecret : what
meaneth this change Geoffrie ? How
cometh it to paffe , that contrarie
to thy woont , thou art become fo
penfiue and afflicted . Ah my brother
(anfwered Geoffrie with a deep figh)
I fhall neuer more be merrie fo long
as I liue . The other moued with
compaffion at thefe words , with a
fraternall zeale, went and told all this
to their common father *Saint* Bernard : who perceauing the danger,
went into a church there by , to pray
to God for him , and Geoffrie in the

meane while ouerwhelmed with sadnes,
reposing his head vpon a stone , fell fast
a sleepe. But after a litle while , both of
them arose , the one frō prayer with his
request dispatched in the high court of
heauen , the other from sleepe with so
pleasaunt and smiling a countenance,
that his deerfrind meruailing at so great
& sodaine a chaunge, could not refraine
from obiecting vnto him louingly that
which a litle before he had answered
him . Then Geoffrie replied : yf I told
thee before that I should neuer in my
life be ioyfull, now I assure thee, that I
shall neuer in my life be sorowfull.

2. This was the successe of the tēpta-
tion of that deuout personage,& marke
in it (my deer Philotheus) 1. First that
God ordinarilie giueth some fore-tasts
of heauenly ioye , to such as newlie enter into his seruice : so to draw them
from earthlie pleasures, and encourage
thē in the poursuite of the loue of God:
iust as a mother to intice & allure her
litle child to her breasts, layeth honnie
vpon her teats. 2. That notwithstāding
the same good God , which according
to the disposition of his wisdome , taketh

keth from vs this milk and honny of
consolations : to the end that weaning
his children in this manner, they might
learne to eat the drie, but more substan-
tiall bread of liuely and sound deuotion,
exercised by the triall of distast and desolation. 3. That sometimes verie vehement temptations arise amidst these desolate and drie discontentments of ste-
rilitie of spirit: and then it behoueth vs
to resist these temptations côstantly, for
they come not frô god; but withall we
must patiëtly suffer this desolate estate,
of want of spirituall feeling in our deuotions, for god hath ordeined & disposed it for our exercise and merit. 4. That
we must not leese hart & courage amôg
these inward griefs, nor say as this good
geoffrie did , I shall neuer be ioyfull
heerafter : for in the night season, we
must expect the daylights approache ;
Againe in the fairest weather of the spirit, that we câ haue we must not say now
shall I neuer be sad heerafter; No ; for
as the wise man sayes , in time of prosperitie, we must be mindfull of aduer-
sitie , and in our trauailes, hope for rest:
and as well in the one occasion as in the

A a 6   other,

other, we muſt always humble our ſelues. 5. That it is a ſoueraigne remedie
to diſcouer our euel vnto ſome ſpiritual
frind, that may be able to comfort vs.

3. In fine for concluſion of this ſo
neceſſarie aduertiſment, I note, that as
in all other things, ſo in theſe drie ſteri-
lities of our ſpirit, God and the deuil
haue contrarie pretentions. For God
would therby bring vs to puritie of hart,
to a generall renunciatiō of our proper
intereſt in his ſeruice, and to a perfect
depoſing of our owne willes. But the deuil goeth about by the ſame way to lead
vs to puſillanimitie, to abate our courage, to make vs ſteppe a ſide to ſenſible
paſſetimes, and at length to render vs
yrkſome and loathſome to our ſelues, &
others that liue with vs; that ſo deuotiō
may be diminiſhed, and defamed. But
yf thou obſerue diligently theſe leſſons
which I haue giuen thee, thou ſhalt
augment thy perfection in thoſe exerciſes, which thou performeſt in time of
theſe interiour afflictions : wherof one
word more before I make an end.

4. Sometimes theſe diſtaſts, this
drouth and barrennes of ſpirit, doe proceed

ceed from the indifpofitio of our bodie:
as when through too much watching,
labouring, fafting, one findeth him felf
ouerloaden with weerineffe, droufines,
heauines, & fuch like infirmities; which
although they depend of the bodie, yet
lett they not to hinder and trouble the
fpirit, by reafon of the ftraight bond
with which they are tied one to another. In thefe occafiós, we muft allwayes
be mindfull, to produce many acts of
virtue, with our fpirit, or fuperiour will:
for although all our foule feeme to be
ouer layd with fleepe and droufines: yet
the actiós of our fpirit euē in that ftate,
are exceeding acceptable to God. And
we may fay in this cafe with the facred
fpoufe, *I fleep, but my hart watcheth.* And as
I fayd before, though there be leffe delight in this labour of fpirit, yet is there
more virtue and merit. The remedie in
fuch occurrences is, to eafe the bodie
with fome kind of lawfull delight and
recreation. So Saint Francis ordained
that his religious should vfe fuch moderation in their labour, that the burden of them, should not depreffe
and ouerthrow the fpirit. And fince we
                                    haue

haue mentioned S. Francis, let vs remember his example, who was on a time him felf fo vexed and tormented with a profound melancholie, that he could not choofe but declare it in his behaueour. For yf he would conuerfe with his religious he knew not how; if he withdrew him felf, frō their conuerfation, it went worfe with him; abftinence and mortification of his flesh, ouerwhelmed him: and prayer eafed him not at all. And in this fort remained this gloʒious father, the fpace of two yeares, fo that it feemed vnto him, that in a manner, God had forfaken him. But at length after he had fo long and patiently fuffered this rude and vehement tentation, our Saueour in a moment reftored to him the happie tranquillitie and repofe of his fpirit. This haue I fayd, to shew that the greateft and faithfulleft feruants of God, are fubiect vnto thefe aduerfities and afflictions of mind: and that therfore thofe that are leffer in Gods bookes, be not difmayed yf fome times they happen vnto them.

THE

THE FIFTH PART
OF THE INTRODVCTION:
Containing exercises and instructions to renew the soule,
and confirme deuotion.

That we renew euery yeare our good
purposes by the exercises folowing.

CHAPTER I.

HE first & principall poinct
of these exercises, consisteth
in knowing the importance
of them. Our weak & fraile
nature,falleth verie easily frō
her good affectiōs & resolutiōs,through
the bad inclinations of our flesh,which
lie heauie vpon the soule it selfe , and
draw her stil downwards , yf she striue
not oft times to lift vp her self by
manie

maine force of resolution as birds fall
sodainlie to ground, yf they multiplie
not the spreading and wauing of their
wings to mainteine their flight aloft in
the ayre. For this cause, deere Philotheus, thou must very often repeat the
good purposes which thou hast made
to serue God, for feare least neglecting
to doe so, thou tüble downe to thy first
estate, or rather into a farre worse estate.
For spirituall falles haue this propertie,
that they cast vs alway lower, then was
the estate from which we ascended vp
to deuotion.

2. There is no clock, be it neuer so
good, or so well sett, but it must be
wound vp twise a day at least, morning
and euening, and moreouer at least
once a yeare, be taken all in peeces, to
scoure away the rust which it hath gathered, to mend broken peeces, and
repaire such as be worne. Euen so he
that hath a true care of his soule, should
wind it vp to God euening and morning by the foresayd exercises, and besides at diuerse times, make a reuiew of
his estate, and at least once a yeare,
take it downe and consider precisely
all

all the peeces therof, that is, all his
paffions, affections and motions, that
all faults and defects found out, may
out of hand be redreffed. And as the
clockman with fome delicate oyle, an-
nointeth the wheeles, iunctures and
ginnes of his clock, that the motions
may be more eafie, and the whole be
leffe fubiect to ruft; fo the deuout perfon, after he hath in this fort taken
downe his hart to reuiew and renew
it, should annoint it with the facraments of Confeffion, and the holy
Eucharift. This exercife will repaire
thy weather-beaten forces, enflame thy
hart, make thy good purpofes fprout
out a fresh, and thy virtues flourish
anew. The ancient Chriftians diligently practized it vpon the anniuerfa-
rie feaft of our *Saueours* Baptifme, or
Twelf-daye: on which (as witneffeth
Saint Gregory Nazianzen) they renewed thofe profeffions and protefta-
tions, which they made in their chriftening. Let vs doe the like, (my deare
Philotheus) difpofing our felues moft
willinglie, and employing our time
ferioufflie therin. And hauing chofen a
                                      fitt

fitt time, according to the aduice of thy
ghoftly father, retiring thy felf into thy
fpirituall and reall folitude, or wilder-
neffe of deuotion : make two or three
of thefe enfewing meditations, after
the order and methode, which I fet
downe vnto thee in the fecond parte.

---

*Confiderations vpon the benefit which
God doth vnto vs, by calling vs to his
feruice, according to the proteſtation mentioned before.*

CHAPTER 2.

1. **R**VNNE ouer the poinẁs of thy
proteſtation. The firſt is, to reiect and caſt away, deteſt, and
defie for euer, ail kind of mortall finne.
The fecond, to haue dedicated, and
confecrated thy foule, thy hart, and thy
bodie, with all that thou haft, to the
loue and feruice of God : The third;
that yf it should happen vnto thee to
fall into fome naughtie action, that
thou wilt procure immediatlie to rife
                                    agai-

againe by Gods grace. Are not thefe
goodlie, worthie, reafonable, and noble refolutions? Way well in thy foule,
how conformable to the rule of reafon
this thy proteftation is, how iuft, and
how much to be defired, that thou
shouldft fullfill and accomplishe euery
poinct of it.

2. Confider to whome thou haft
made this proteftation: euen to God
him felf. Yf according to reafon, our
word giuen to a man, doe ftraightly
oblige & bind vs, how much more our
word and promife giuen and paffed to
allmightie God? *Ah Lord* (fayd Dauid) *it is to thee that my hart hath pronounced this good word, and I will not
forgett it.*

3. Confider in whofe prefence thou
madeft this proteftation and thou shalt
find, that it was in fight of the whole
courte of heauen. The holie Virgin,
bleffed Saint Iofeph, thy good Angel,
Saint Lewis, all this bleffed companie,
beheld thee, and fighed with fighes of
ioy and contentment at thy words,
and looked vpon thee with eyes of vnfpeakeable loue, when thy hart pro-
ftrated

ſtrated at the feete of our Saueour, conſecrated it ſelf wholly to his ſeruice.
They made a peculiar feaſt and trium-
phe that day of thy entrie into Gods
ſeruice, and they will now make a com-
memoration of that ioyfull feaſt, yf
with a deuqut hart and good courage,
thou reneweſt thy reſolutions.

4.   Conſider by what meanes thou
waſt brought to make this proteſtatió,
and to offer vp theſe great reſolutions.
Ha my Philotheus, how amiable and
fauourable did God ſhew him ſelf vnto
thee at that time ? Tell me, waſt thou
not then drawne vnto it, by the ſweet
inſpirations of the holy Ghoſt ? the
cordes wherwith God drew thy litle
barke vnto this ſecure hauen, were they
not all of loue & charitie ? How deerlie
and daintelie did he allure & intice thee
with his ſugred ſacraments, with holy
lecture, and deuout prayer ? Ah Philotheus, thou waſt a ſleep, & god watched
ouer thee, and had care of thy ſoule, and
had thoughts of peace, and meditations
of loue concerning thee.

5.   Conſider at what time god drew
thee thus happelie vnto him by theſe
holïe

holie purposes. It was in the flower of
thine age. Ah what a felicitie is it to
learne quickly, that which we cannot
know but ouer-late. Saint Auguſtin,
hauing been called to god at thirtie
yeares of his age, cried out : *O ancient*
beauty, how is it, that I knew thee ſo late ?
Alas I ſaw thee before, but I did not conſider
thee till now. And thou maiſt well ſay: O
ancient ſweetnes, why did not I taſt thee
ſooner ? And yet alas, thou deſeruedſt it
not at that time in which it was giuen
thee: therfore acknowledging the great
bountie and grace of god, for calling
thee to him in thy youthe, ſay vnto him
with Dauid : *Thou haſt lightened me, ô God,*
and touched me from my youth, and I will for-
euer pronounce thy mercy. But yf this thy
vocation was in thy older dayes, ô then,
Philotheus, how ineſtimable a benefit
was it, after thou hadſt in ſuch ſort a-
buſed the yeares of thy life paſt, that
god of his goodnes ſhould call thee
before thy death, and ſtay the cour-
rent of thy miſerie, euen at that time, in which yf it had beene conti-
newed, thou hadſt beene miſerable
for euer and euer !

6. Con-

6. Confider the effects which this vocation hath wrought in thee, & I fuppofe thou shalt find change and alteration enough in thy foule, cóparing that which now thou art , with that which thou haft beene. Doeft thou not accoút it a fingular felicitie, to know how to talk familiarlie with God by prayer ? to haue an enflamed affection and burning defire of the loue of God? to haue appeafed, and pacified manie a troublefome paiſion, which before did vex , and torment thee ? to haue auoided many finnes and fcruples of confcience ? And in a word to haue fo often frequented the holy Communion (more then thou wouldft once haue done) fo vniting thy felf to this foueraigne well-fpring of euer-during graces? Ah, thefe be great and ineftimable fauours . We muft way and ponder them with the waightes of the fanctuarie : it is Gods right hand that hath done all this. *The right hand of God* (fayth Dauid) *hath done powerfully , his right hand hath extolled me: I will not dy, but liue ; and will make knowne with hart, word , and deed , the wonders of his goodnes.*

7. Af-

7. After all these considerations, which as thou seest may plentifullie furnish thee with holie and feruent affections : thou must simplie conclude with thancks-geuing, and pray affectionatly for thy good progresse in virtue. And so retire frō prayer with great humilitie and confidence in god: reseruing the enforcing of the resolutiōs, till after the second poinct of this exercise.

The examination of our soule touching her proffiting in deuotion.

CHAPTER 3.

1. THE second poinct of this exercise, is somewhat long, and therfore to practize it, it is not requisite to performe it all at once, but at diuers times : as to take that which concerneth thy misdemeanour towards god for once, that which apperteineth to thy self for another time, that which toucheth thy neighbour for an other, & the examining of thy passions for another. Neither is it requisite or necessary, to doe it all vpō thy knees, but onely the begin-

beginning & ending, which cóprehen-
deth the affections. The other poincts
of the examination , thou must performe profitablie walking , or sitting ,
or best of all in bed , yf thou canst so
remaine without drowsines , or well
awake : but thou must well haue read
them before. Yet it is necessarie to make
an end of all this second poinct in three
dayes , and two nights , at the farthest:
taking eache day & night , some hower
or seasó according as thou best mayest:
for yf it should be done at times farr
distant one from another , it would
loose his force, and would worke but
verie weak and kay-cold impressions
and resolutions.

2.   After euerie point of the examination , note carefully in what thou
findest thy self amended , and in what
thou art defectiue , and what principall
errours or abuses thou hast committed,
that so thou mayst declare thy self the
better to take good councell, and resolution , to comfort thy mind. And although in these dayes of examination,
it be not necessarie to retire thy selfe
totallie from companie and conuersa-
                                                       tion:

tion : yet thou muſt be ſomwhat more
retired thē ordinarie, & principallie towards the euening, that thou mayſt go
to bed earlie, & take that reſt of bodie
and repoſe of mind which is neceſſarie
for theſe exerciſes. And in the day time,
thou muſt vſe verie frequent aſpira-
tions to God, to our Ladie, to the Angells, to all the celeſtiall Hieruſalem:
And all this muſt be done with a louing
hart towards God, & deſirous of perfection. So beginne then this examination well and happelie.

1. Firſt place thy ſelf in the preſence
of God.

2. Inuoke the ayde of the holy choſt,
demaund of him light and cleernes, to
ſee and know well, with S. Auguſtin,
who cried out before God in an humble ſpirit: *O lord let me know thee, and let
me know my ſelfe:* and S. Francis, who
ſweetly asked god ſaying. *Who art thou,
and who am I?* Proteſt that thou doeſt
not purpoſe to marke and note thy aduancement and progreſſe in pietie and
virtue, to reioice therfore in thy ſelf,
but to reioice in God, nor to glorifie
thy ſelf, but to glorifie god, & to giue
Bb   him

him thanckes for it. Protest likewise that
yf thou findest that thou hast not profited nor gone forward at all in deuotion
nay though thou hast recoyled & gone
backward: yet for all that thou wilt not
leese thy courage, nor become any whit
the colder in thy good purposes ,
through faintnes of hart; but that rather
thou wilt more stirre vp thy courage, &
animate thy self to goe more cheerfully
forward in the iourney of deuotion happely enterprized , & that thou wilt the
more profoundlie humble thy self , and
amend thy defaults by the assistance of
Gods grace .

This done, cōsider leasurely & quietly
how thou hast behaued thy self euen till
that presēt power, toward God, towards
thy neighbour, & towards thy selfe.

An examination of the estate of our
soule towards God. Chap. 4.

1. HOw is thy hart affected toward
mortal sinne? hast thou a firme
resolution neuer to committ
any, whatsoeuer should happē vnto thee
therfore ? Hath this resolution and full
purpose, endured cōtinually in thy soule,

le, since thy laſt proteſtation vnto this time? In this reſolution conſiſteth the foundation of ſpirituall life.

2. How findeſt thou thy hart affected towards the commandements of God. Doeſt thou find thē delightful, ſweet acceptable. Ah my deer child, he that hath his mouth in taſt, and a good ſtomak, loueth wholſome meats, and reiecteth the contrarie.

3. How doth thy hart beare it ſelf towards veniall ſinnes? we cannot keep our ſelues ſo pure, but we shall commit ſome now and then: but is there any, to which thou haſt any eſpeciall inclination? or which were worſe, is there any kind of venial ſinne, to which thou beareſt a peculiar affection and delight?

4. How is thy hart affected towards ſpirituall exerciſes? doeſt thou loue them, and eſteeme them? doe they not trouble thee? art thou not out of content and taſt with them? To which of them doeſt thou find thy ſelf moſt inclined? To heare the word of God, to reade it; to talke of it, to meditate it, to aſpire daylie to God, to goe often to confeſſion, to receaue

spirituall inſtructiős, to prepare thy ſelf
duly to the holy Cőmunion, to Cőmu-
nicate frequētly, to bridle thy affectiős:
in theſe and ſuch like acts and exerciſes,
what is there contrarie or repugning to
thy mind? And yf thou find any ſuch
holy exerciſe, to which this hart of thine hath leſſe inclination then it should,
examine the cauſe from whence that
diſguſt ariſeth.

5. How doth thy hart remaine affected towards god him ſelf? Taketh it
pleaſure in the remembrance of god?
feeleth it not a ſweet delight in calling
him to mind? Ah ſayd Dauid, *I haue
thought vpon God, and taken delignt therin.*
Doeſt thou find a certaine promptnes,
redineſſe, and facilitie in thy hart to
loue god, and a particular ſauour in ta-
ſting this his loue? Thy hart, doth it not
recreat it ſelfe to thinke vpon the im-
menſitie, bountie, and maruelous ſwet-
nes of almightie God? If thou chaunce
to thinck vpon God amidſt thy worldly
affaires, and vanities, doth this thought
make place, and winne rome, and ſeaze
vpon thy hart? Doeth it ſeeme to thee
that in ſuch caſes thy hart takes Gods
part,

part, and turnes to his side, and as it were goes before him, to lead him reuerently into the chamber of thy hart?
for there are many soules of this met-
tal in the world.

6. A louing wife, when her housband
comes home from some farre iourney,
so soone as she perceaueth any signe of
his returne, or heareth his voice: what
busines so euer she hath in had, though
she be cõstrained by some forcible consideration to stay her self, yet her hart
cannot be held from looking for her
husband, but abandoneth all other cogitations, to thinck vpon his ioyfull returne. Soules that loue God, doe the
veric same; howsoeuer they be employed, when the remembrance of God
presenteth it self vnto thẽ, they neglect
all thinges else, for ioye that their beloued is returned vnto them; and this is a
verie good signe.

7. How is thy hart affected towards
Iesus Christ, God & man. Takest thou
pleasure in thincking on his life and
death? The Bees delight in their delicious honnie: Waspes and beetles, in ill-
fauoured sauours: so holy soules haue

all their cōtentmēt, placed in our sweet
redeemer Iesus Chrift, with an exceeding tendernes of ardent loue to him:
but such as be vaine, and wicked, plant
their affections altogether vpon vnprofitable vanities.

8. How is thy hart affected towards
our bleſſed Ladie, thy good Angell, the
Sainchts of heauen? Doeſt thou loue,
honour & reuerence them: haſt thou a
ſpeciall truſt in their interceſſion, a reſ-
pect & worship to their images, delight
in their liues: takeſt thou pleaſure to
heare them praiſed?

9. Concerning thy tongue. How
ſpeakeſt thou of God: is it a delight vnto thee to talk and diſcource in his honour, according to thy condition and
abilitie: Doeſt thou loue to ſing hym-
nes to his praiſe and glorie?

10. Concerning workes. Thinck
whether thou haue a true harty deſire of
the outward glorie of God, and to doe
ſomwhat for his honour and worship?
for ſuch as loue God, doe according to
Dauid, loue the ornament of his houſe.

11. Cōſider whether thou haſt left any
affection, or renounced any delight, or
                                    for-

forſook any thing for Gods cauſe? for
it is a great ſigne of true loue, for his
ſake whome we loue, to depriue our
ſelues of any thing. What then haſt
thou in all this time (ſince thy proteſtation) forſaken for the loue of God?

---

*An examination of our eſtate tou-
ching our ſelues.* CHAP. 5.

1. HOw doeſt thou loue thy ſelf,
loueſt thou thy ſelf ouermuch
for the vanities of this world?
For yf it be ſo, thou wilt deſire to dwell
always in the world, with an extraordinarie care to eſtabliſhe thy ſelf heer
vpon earth. But yf thou loue thy ſelf
for heauens ſake then wilt thou deſire,
at leaſt wiſe thou wilt eaſilie conſent,
to depart from hence at the time and
hower, that it ſhall pleaſe our Lord to
call thee.

2. Doeſt thou keepe due order in
the loue of thy ſelf? for there is nothing that marreth vs, but onely the
inordinate loue of our ſelues. As
for well ordered loue, it requires that
Bb 4   we

we loue the foule bitter then the bodie;
that we take more paines to get virtues
then any thing els; that we make more
account of heauenly glorie, then of
bafe and tranfitorie honour? A well ordered hart, will more often fay in it felf:
What will the angels fay yf I thinck, or
doe fuch a thing? thẽ, *what will men fay?*

3. What loue beareft thou to thy
foule? art thou vnwilling and loath to
help it when it is fpirituallie diftempe-
red and difeafed? alas thou oweft this
care and attendance vnto it, to helpe
it thy felf, and procure it to be hol-
pen by other, when paffions doe torment it: and to fet a fide all other
cares, when thy foule ftands in need
of thy care.

4. How doeft thou efteeme of thy
felf before the eyes of God almightie?
to be nothing at all, doubtleffe. But it
is noe great humilitie in a flie, to thinck
her felf nothing in regard of a mountaine; or for a droppe of water, to
efteeme it felf nothing in comparifon of the maine fea: nor for a fpar-
kle of fire, to hold it felf nothing in ref-
pecte of the funne: It is humilitie indeed,

deed, not to preferre our selues before
others, nor to affect, or desire to be
esteemed of, and well liked by others:
How doest thou feele thy self, affected
i i this point?

5. Touching thy tongue: doest thou
not bragge and vaunt of thy self one
way or other? doest thou not flatter
thy self, when thou speakest of thine
owne self?

6. For works & actions. Doest thou
vse to take any pleasure or passetime,
contrarie to thy bodily or spirituall
health? I meane vaine pleasure, vnprofitable recreations, ouer-watching, too
much disordely labour, and such like.

An examination of the estate of our
soule towardes our neighbour.
CHAPTER 6.

1. **T**HE loue between husband,
and wife, ought io be sweete,
quiet, earnest, and constant,
and grounded principallie vpon the ordinance of God, who commandeth it
to be so. And the self same is to be vnderstood, of loue between parents and
their

their children , between vs and out
neighbours, and our frinds , euerie one
in his ranck and degree.

2. But to fpeak in generall. How is
thy hart affected towards thy neighbour ? Doeſt thou loue him from thy
hart,and for gods fake ? To diſcerne
well, whether it be ſo or no, thou muſt
prepoſe and repreſent vnto thy ſelf,
certaine perſons that be troubleſome,
and intractable , for there it is , and
towards ſuch kind of men , where we
exerciſe the virtue of true charitie towards our neighbours : and much more
towards ſuch as haue iniuried vs either
in work or in word. Examin well yf
thy hart be free from paſſion in this
behalf , and whether thou feeleſt not
a contradiction within thee, to loue
anie bodie.

3. Art thou proane to ſpeak ill of thy
neighbour ? and eſpeciallie of ſuch as
loue thee not ? Doeſt thou any harme
to thy neighbour directly , or indire-
ctly ? Though thou haue neuer ſo litle
reaſon or diſcourſe , thou wilt eaſilie
find out thy defects in this point.

An

*An examination of the affections of
our soule.* CHAP. 7.

1. I HAVE extended these poincts
at large, because in the examination of them, consisteth the
knowledge of our spirituall aduancement, or progresse which we haue
made, for as for examining our sinnes,
thats for confessions, and for such as
neuer thinck vpon going forward in
pietie and deuotion.

2. Yet neuerthelesse, we must not labour
to exactlie and curiouslie in examining
euerie one of these articles or interro-
gatories: but fayre and softlie, considering with quiet and repose of mind,
in what estate our hart hath beene in
euerie one of them since our resolution
and protestation, and what notable defects we haue committed therin.

3. But to make a shorter abridgement
of all, we may reduce the whole examination, to the searche and suruay of
our passions: and yf it be tedious and
troublesome, to consider so exactlie
what we haue been: we may in this

manner folowing examine our felues
how we haue behaued our felues.

In our loue towards God, our neighbour, and our felues.

In hatred toward finne in our felues,
and finne in others: for we muft defire the extirpation of the one, and the
other:

In defires of riches, honour, eftimation, paffetimes.

In feare of danger to fall into finne,
and of loffe of goods of this world, for
we may feare the one and the other too
much.

In hope placed more then needs in
the world, in fading creatures: or to
litle in God, and godlie thinges.

In fadnes, yf it were to exceffiue, and
for tranfitorie vanities.

In ioye and gladnes, yf ouermuch
and for vnworthie matters.

To conclude in a worde: what affection
doth predominate thy hart? what paffion doth moft of all poffeffe it? in what
doeft thou principallie goe awrie? for
by paffions of our foule, we may iudge
of our eftate, examining them, and as
it were feeling and tafting them, one
                                    after

after another. As he that is skillfull on
the lute, by touching the diuerse strai-
nes of his instrument, finds which
string is out of tune, and tunes it by
stretching it vp, or letting it downe : so
after we haue as it were touched, and
examined the tune of our passions, of
the loue, hatred, desire, feare, hope, sadnes, or ioye that is in our soule, yf we
find them discording from the tune
which we would strike, and from the
proportionable harmonie of our soule,
which is to be sett to the glorie of God,
we may make them accorde, by bringing them to their due tune and proportion with Gods grace, and by councell and aduice of our ghostly father.

Affections to be exercised after this
examination.   C H A P. 8.

A FTER thou hast duly pondered euery poinct of the examination, and considered at what
stay thou art, and to what thou art
come : then exercise the affects of thy
soule as foloweth.

1. Giue

1. Giue god thancks for that amendment, be it but litle , which thou haft found in thy life , fince thy generall refolution laft made : and acknowledge that it was his only mercie , that caufed it in thee,and and for thee.

2. Humble thy felf reuerently before his maiftie,acknowledging vnfainedly, that yf thou haue not much profited in pietie,it hath been through thine owne default,becaufe thou haft not faithfully, courageoufly,and conftantly anfwered the infpirations , illuftrations, and motions , which he hath often imparted vnto thee in prayer, and by manie other wayes.

3. Promife him fincerely,that thou wilt for euer praife him, for the ineftimable fauours beftowed vpon thee, and efpecially for drawing thee frõ thy bad inclinatiõs by this prefent amendment.

4. Demaund pardon of him for thy ynfaithfulnes & difloyaltie, for not correfponding with his infpirations and graces.

5. Offer him vp thy hart,to the end he may be the fole maifter and Lord of it.

6. Befeech him to make thee faithfullie

fullie accomplishe his will heertafter.

6.   Inuoke the Sainᵈts of heauen, our B. Ladie, thy good Angell, thy patron, Ioſeph, and the reſt to whome thou haſt an eſpeciall deuotion, to helpe thee with their interceſſion.

Conſiderations proper to renew our good purpoſes. C H A P. 9.

1. $\mathbf{T}$ H I S examination being made, and diligentlie conferred with ſome worthie, expert, and ſkillfull guide, to learne the qualitie of thy faults, and the fit remedies for them: beginne thoſe meditations folowing, making one of them euery day, and in it ſpend the ordinarie time which other dayes thou appointedſt to paſſe in thy meditation; with the ſelf ſame method, preparation, and affeᵈtions which thou haſt vſed heertofore in the meditations ſet downe in the firſt part: placing thy ſelf firſt of all in the preſence of God, and then imploring his grace, to eſtablish thee in his holy loue and ſeruice.

The

*The first consideration, of the excellency
of our soule.* CHAP. 10.

1. CONSIDER the nobilitie and
excellēce of thy soule, endewed
with an vnderstanding, which
knoweth not only all this visible worlde, but moreouer vnderstandeth, that
there are inuisible Angels, and a happie
Paradise; that there is a soueraigne God,
vnspeakeable, most good, most mighty;
that there is an eternitie of immortall
spirits : and withall knoweth the meanes how to liue well in this visible
world, and to associate her self with the
angels in heauen, and to attaine to the
familiaritie and frindship of God him
self for euer.

2. Thy soule hath also a free-will,
of a most noble excellencie, which
is able to loue God, and cannot hate
him, considered in him selfe. Loe
what an excellent soule thou hast.
As no corruptible or ill-sauouring
thing can stay the litle Bees, but
onely flowers are their rest, only vpon
them do they setle their flight : so thy
hart

hart can find no repofe , but in God
alone, no creature elfe cã fil or fatisfie it.
Remember hardly & recount with thy
felf , all the deareft and greateft entertainments , wherwith thou haft euer
occupied thy hart, and iudge in good
fadnes , whether they were not all full
of vnquiet, of moleftations, of reftleffe
and ftinging thoughts , importunate
cares, with which thy poore hart was
moft miferably diftract and afflicted.

3. Alas thy hart runneth haftely and
headlong , after the creatures of this
world , thincking it poffible to appeafe
its defires in them : but fo foone as thou
meeteft with them and tafteft them,
thou art as readie to beginn againe as
before : for nothing is able to content
thy hart, God would not permitt that
it should find reft in any place, no more
then the Doue that Noah fent out of
the Arke , that fo it might allways earne
to returne to God , from whence it
came. Ah how admirable is this naturall beautie of thy foule ! and why then
doeft thou endeuour to withhold her
againft her will , to ferue thefe fading
creatures ?

4. Oh

4. Oh my faire and louely soule (mayst thou say) thou canst vnderstand and loue God him self: and wherfore doest thou entertaine thy self in things inferiour to God? thou mayest yf thou wilt, pretend eternitie, wherfore doest thou hunt after moments? This was one of the chiefest complaints of the prodigall child, that wheras he might haue feasted deliciously at his fathers table, he was forced through his owne willfullnesse, to feed at the troughs of his swine. O my soule, thou art capable of God him self: woe be to thee, yf thou rest contented with any thing lesse then God.

Lifte vp thy soule earnestly with this consideration: shew her that she is immortall, and an heire of eternitie, and therefore that she direct her course and courage therto.

The second consideration of the excellency of virtues. CHAP. II.

1. CONSIDER that only virtue and deuotion, can make thy soule to rest content in this world. O what excellent beautie is in them!

them! make a comparison betwixt the
louely virtues, and the hideous vices
that be cōtrarie vnto thē: what sweetnes
is there in patience compared to reuenge? in meeknes in respect of anger and
frowardnes? in humilitie in regard of
pride and ambition? In liberalitie compared to couetousnesse & nigardize? in
charitie compared with enuie? in sobrietie, in respect of intemperancie? virtues haue this excellencie, that they fill
the soule with an incōparable sweetnes
and delight, after she hath practized
them: wheras vices leaue the soule exceedinglie weeried, tyred, and molested.
And why endeuour we not then to obtaine these pleasures, that haue no gall
nor bitternes mingled with them?

2. He that hath but a few vices, is
not content with the delights which
they bring him: and he that hath manie,
is malcontēt with the cumber of them.
He that hath but a few virtues, hath a
great deale of content in them: and
the more his contentment is, the more
his virtues increase.

3. O deuout life how louely art thou,
how honorable, how delectable! thou
                                                    dost

doſt diminiſh tribulations, and aug-
menteſt conſolation : without thee,
euen good is euil, honnie pleaſures are
full of bitter vnquietnes, peace it ſelf is
warre, and trouble, and contradiction.
Ah he that would be acquainted familiarlie with thee, muſt ſtill ſay with the
Samaritan, *O Lord giue me ſome of this wa-*
ter to drinck : an aſpiration much frequented by the holie mother Tereſa,
and Saint Catherin of Genua, although
vpon other occaſions.

The third conſideration of the examples of Sainctes.

CHAPTER 12.

1. CONSIDER the examples of
the ſaincts of all ſorts & orders:
what is it that they haue not
done and ſuffered, to loue God, and be
whollie deuoted and addicted to his
ſeruice ? Look vpon the inuincible
martyrs in their conſtant reſolutions,
what torments haue they not ſuffered
for the maintenance and performance
of their holy purpoſes ? But aboue all
those

those faire and flourishing ladies whiter
then lillies, in puritie, more blushing
then roses in charitie, some at twelue,
others at thirteen, fifteen, twentie, fiue
and twentie yeares of age: consider how
they endured a thousand sorts of mar-
tyrdoms, rather then to renounce their
sacred resolutions, not onely in profession of faith, but also in exercise of
deuotion and pietie: some choosing to
die rather then lose their virginitie:
others rather then they would leaue off
seruing the tormented prisoners, comfort the afflicted, burie the dead,
and such like holy works of Gods
seruice. O good Lord what constancie hath that fraile sex shewed in these occasions!

2. Consider so manie holie confes-
sours, with what valour and magnanimitie did they contemne the world?
How immoueable and vnconquered
were they in their resolutions? nothing in this vniuersall world could
make them forgoe them, they embraced their purposes of sanctitie without
exceptions or reseruations, and went
forward with them, without any te-
dious-

dionſneſſe or faintnes. Good ɢod, what
excellent things doth *S.* Auſtin write
of his holie mother Monica ? with
what courage did she folow her enterprize of ſeruing ɢod, in her marriage, and in her widow-head ? And Saint
Hierom, what rare conſtancie doth he
point out in his deuout Paula, amidſt
ſo great varieties of combrous occurrences.

3. And what is there that we may
not doe, hauing ſuch excellent paternes to folow ? They were fraile mortall men, as we are; they did all for
the ſame ɢod, by the ſame virtues :
why should not we doe the like in
our eſtate and condition; and according to our vocation, for the accom-
pliſhment of our good purpoſe and holie proteſtation ?

---

*The fourth conſideration : of the loue
that Ieſus-Chriſt beareth vnto vs.*

CHAPTER 13.

1. **C**ONSIDER the vnſpeakeable
loue, wherwith Ieſus Chriſt
our

our Lord suffered so much in this
world, and especiallie in the garden of
mount Oliuet, and the bitter place of
mount Caluarie. All that loue of his
was for thy sake: By so manie pangs
and torments, he obtained of God the
father good purposes and holy resolutions for thee: by the same afflictions
did he moreouer purchase all things
els necessarie for thie soule, to mainteine, nourish, strengthen, and bring to
full growthe and perfection, all thy resolutions. O holy resolution, how pretious and noblie borne art thou, being
daughter to such a mother as is the
passiō of our Saueour! O how carefullie
should my soule cherrishe thee, since
thou hast been so deere vnto my sweet
Iesus! Alas, ô Saueour of my soule,
thou diedst vpon the Crosse, to gaine
me my virtuous resolution! ah doe
me the fauour, that I also choose rather to die, then to forget or forgoe
them.

2. Thou seest then (my Philotheus)
it is certaine, that the deere hart of our
Lord Iesus, beheld thy hart from the
tree of the crosse, and there (in a
man-

manner) fell in loue with it; and for
loue of it, obtained for thee all the
good that euer thou hadst, or euer
shalt haue; and amongst all, thefe good
refolutions. Yea (my deer Philotheus)
we may all fay with the prophet Iere-
mie: O my Lord, before my beeing
thou beheldeft me, and calledft me by
my name: for in verie deed, his diuine
goodnes in his mercie, and loue, prepared all the generall, and particular meanes of our faluation, and confequently
all our holie refolutions. Yea without
doubt: As a woman, fo foone as fhe is
with child prepareth her cradle, linnen,
fwathing-bāds, and withall bethincketh
of a nurfe for her child, which fhe ho-
peth to bring foorth, although it be not
yet come into the world: euen fo our
Lord, hauing his goodnes pregnant,
and as it were great with child of thee,
pretending to bring thee foorth to
faluation, and to make thee his daughter and heire, prepared vpon the
holie roode, all that which was neceffarie for thee, thy fpirituall cradle, thy
linnen and fwathing bands, thy nurfe,
and all other meanes neceffarie for thy
                                    falua-

faluation : that is , all the wayes , all the
graces , all the fauours , by which he
conducteth thy foule , and will bring
it at length to perfection.

3. Ah my God , how deeply ought
we to imprint this in our memorie!
Is it poffible , that I haue beene loued,
and fo fweetly beloued by my Saueour,
that euerie fteppe of his life , and euen
euery ftepp that he went to mount
Caluarie , fweating and fainting vnder
his heauie croffe , euen then he went
bethincking him felf of my good , and
of euerie one of thefe litle occafions,
by which he hath draw'n me vnto
him ! And how much then ought we
efteeme , how carefully should we
employe all this to our commoditie!
Ah.how fweet a remembrance is this?
This louing hart of my God , thought
vpon Philotheus, loued him , procured
him a thoufand meanes to faluation :
as though there had been no other
foule in the world , to take care of;
As the funne , shining vpon one fide
of the earth , shineth fo much there,
as yf it gaue no light to anie other
place : in the verie fame manner, did

our Lord take thought and care of all
his children, prouiding for each one of
vs, as though he had not thought vpon
the reſt. *He hath loued me* (ſayth S. Paul)
and hath giuen him ſelf for me. As yf he had
ſayde : for me onelie , altogether as
much as yf he had done nothing for
anie els. *O Philotheus ,* this should be
engraued in thy ſoule , to cherrish
and nourish thy good reſolutions,
which haue beene ſo pretious and
deere to the hart bloud of our bleſſed Saueour.

---

*The fifte conſideration , of the eternall
loue of God toward vs .*

CHAPTER 14.

1. **C**ONSIDER the eternall loue
which almightie God bare vnto
thee: for long before our Lord
Ieſus Chriſt as mā ſuffered for thee vpō
the croſſe : his diuine maieſtie did forecaſt thee in his ſoueraigne goodnes,
and loued thee infinitly . But when
began

began he to beare thee this loue ? euen
when he began to be God . And when
began he to be God ? sure he neuer began to be God, for he hath always been
God , without beginning and without
ending, and so likewise from all eternitie did he loue thee : his loue to thee
neuer had beginning , and therfore did
he from all eternitie prepare the graces
benefits & fauours bestowed vpon thee.
So saith he him self by his prophet : *I*
haue loued thee with a perpetuall charitie ,
therfore haue I drawne thee vnto me , taking
pitie of thee. Amongst other benefits
then which he thought vpon from all
eternitie to giue thee, needs must thou
account thy purposes and resolutions
to serue him.

2. And ô good God, what excellent,
how deere ought these resolutiõs to be
vnto thee, since God hath fore thought,
premeditated and forecast thē from all
eternitie? what should we not suffer rather then to suffer one onelie iott or
title of them to be taken away or dimi-
nished . All the world together must
not make vs forgoe the least of our
good purposes : for all the word toge-

ther, is not worthe one ſoule: and a
ſoule is worth nothing, withour good
reſolutions.

---

*Generall affections ⁓pon the precedent
poincts, or conſiderations, with the
concluſion of this exerciſe.*

CHAPTER 15.

1. O AMIABLE reſolutions! you
are to me the beautiful tree of
life, which my God hath plan-
ted with his owne hand, in the midſt of
my hart: and my redeemer hath watred
with his life dropping bloud to make it
fructifie; rather will I ſuffer a thouſand
deaths thē endure that one of you ſhould
be hindred. No, neither vanitie, nor delights, nor riches, nor ſorowes, nor tribulations, shall euer be able to pull me
from my holie deſignes and purpoſes.

2. Alas ô my Lord, it is thou that haſt
planted this tree of good reſolutions,
and from eternitie kept it in the bo-
ſome of thy fatherlie prouidence, to
place it in the garden of my ſoule: O
how manie ſoules are there, which
haue not beene fauoured in ſo high a
degree:

degree : and how then shall I be able
to humble my self prefoundly enough
vnder thy mercie ?

3. O beautifull and holy refolutions?
If I keep your charitie, you will faue
me eternallie : yf you liue ftill in my
foule, my foule will liue in you ; liue
then for euer ô my good refolutions,
as you were eternally and for euer in
the mercie of my God, liue and remaine eternallie in me, for I will neuer
abandon or forfake you.

4. After thefe affections, thou muft
particularize, and forecaft in efpeciall,
the meanes neceffarie to mainteine
thefe good purpofes : and proteft to
vfe thefe meanes faithfullie, and diligentlie, as are, frequent prayer, often
vfe of the Sacraments, good works
of mercie, amendment of the faults,
which in the fecond point of this exercife thou shalt haue difcouered, cutting off ill cuftoms, and folowing
the councells and aduices, which thy
fpirituall guide shall prefcribe thee.

5. This done, as yf thou hadft taken
breath a while, and refted thy felf
well, proteft againe a thoufand times,

Cc 3   that

that thou meaneſt vnfainedlie to continue in thy reſolutions: And as yf thou
hadſt thy hart , thy ſoule, thy will in thy
hands, dedicate them, conſecrate them,
ſacrifice them to God , with proteſtation that thou wilt neuer aske them
againe , neuer redemaund them , but
leaue them alwais entirely in the hands
of his diuine maieſtie , to folow in all
things his holy ordenance.

6. Pray vnto God that he would whollie renewe thee, and bleſſe this renouation of thy proteſtation and firme reſolution : that he would fortifie thee
and ſtrengthen thee therin: inuoke the
bleſſed Virgin, thy Angell , the Saints,
and eſpeciallie thoſe to whome thou
beareſt particular deuotion.

7 Being thus moued and inflamed by
Gods grace in thy hart , go to the feet
of thy confeſſour, accuſe thy ſelf of the
principall faults committed ſince thy
laſt generall confeſſion : and receaue
the abſolution with the ſelf ſame trace
and effect with which then thou didſt:
and pronounce thy proteſtation before him , ſeale and ſigne it : and
ſo goe againe to vnite thy hart now
rene-

renewed and reformed, to thy Saueour
and Lord , in the holy facrament of
the Eucharift.

Feeling thoughts to be kept in mind
after this exercife .

CHAPTER 16.

1. **T**HE day folowing this renouation of thy hart, and fome
dayes after , it wilbe profitable
to repeat oft times in thy hart to thy
felf & by mouth likewife, thofe ardent
fpeeches which S. Paul , S. Auguftin,
S. Catherin of Genua, and other faints
vfed : I am now no more mine owne
man : whether I liue or die, I am my Saueours altogether : I haue no more in
me thefe cold words , of me, and mine :
my me, is Iefus , and my mine , is to be
wholly Chrifts : O world thou art all
wayes thy felfe : and I likewife he
that haue beene always my felf , but
from hence foorth I wilbe my felf no
longer. No my foule, we wilbe no
longer our felues, as we haue been:

we will haue another hart, another affection , and the world that hath so often
deceaued vs , shall now be deceaued in
vs: for not marking our change but by
litle and litle, he will think vs always to
be Esau , and we will proue Iacob.

2. All these exercises must repose, and
settle in our harts: and whē we lay a side
for the time consideration and meditation, we must enter by litle and by litle,
and not all at a clap into our ordinarie
affaires , for feare least the pretious liquour of our good resolutions, distilled
so diligently out of these cōsiderations,
be not sodainlie ouerturned , and spilt:
it must soke first as it were , and sinck
well into all the partes of our soule,
yet without too much application of
spirit or bodie.

---

*An answer to two obiections , which
may be made against this Introduction.* CHAP, 17.

1. THE world may chaunce to tell
thee, my Philotheus, that these
exercises and aduices are so
manie in number , that he that would
practize

practize thē,had need to applie him self
to nothing els , but let all other affaires
alone.Ah Philotheus , yf in deed we did
nothing els,we should do well enough,
since, so we should doe that,which to
doe, we were placed in this world.
But doest thou not see the decept ?
No doubt yf all these exercises were to
be performed euery day`, they would
busie vs enough, & take vp most of our
time. But it is only required to practize
them euery one in their time and place,
as they come in their turne. How many
lawes are there in the Digestes,& Code
which must be kept and obserued ? but
all men know and vnderstād that theire
obseruāce is required, according to the
occurrences of occasions and actions,
not that one should practize them all
euery day. Otherwise , the holy king
Dauid, practized manie more spirituall
exercises in a day, amidst his waightie
affaires , then I haue heer prescribed. S.
Lewes an admirable king both in peace
and in warre,and that with a wonderfull
care, administred iustice, and managed
affaires of state:was woont to hear two
masses euery day , to say euensong,and
　　　　　C c 5　　　com-

complin with his chaplain , had euerie
day fett time to meditate ; and vifited
hofpitalls verie often:euerie wednefday
côfeffed & difiplined him felfe verie oft;
heard holy fermons, and vfed fpirituall
conferences : and for-all this , neuer
omitted one the leaft occafion of the
publique weale exteriourly offered ,
which he did not moft diligently put
in execution : and his Court was more
gallant , more frequented , more flou-
rifhing , then euer it had been in time
of his predeceffours. Practize then thefe exercifes cheerfully , as I haue pre-
fcribed them : and God will allott vnto
you time, leafure, and ftrength enough
to doe your other affaires : though he
should make the funne for that end to
ftay his courfe , as he did for his feruant
Iofua. We worke enough always, when
God works with vs.

2. The world will fay againe, that almoft throughout all this book I prefuppofe, that my *Philotheus*, hath receaued of God the guifte of mental prayer,
and yet euerie man hath it not : fo that,
this introduction wil not ferue for euery bodie. Tis true, without all doubt,
I pre-

I preſuppoſe it : and it is true too , that euerie man hath not the guiſte of mentall prayer; but it is likewiſe true that almoſt euery man may obtaine that pretious guiſte , euen the moſt rude and vnlearned : ſo that they haue good ſpirituall maiſters and guides , and that they themſelues would vouchſafe to take as much paines in the ſearche of it, as in it ſelf it requires . And yf there be any , that in no ſort nor degree hath this pretious guift (which I thinck can happen but verie ſeldom) a ſage conductour and maiſter, will eaſilie ſupplie that want , by making them to read, or hear read , theſe meditatiõs and conſiderations , with good heed and attention .

Three principall aduices for this introduction .

CHAPTER 18.

1. THE firſt day of euerie mouth, repeate and renew the prote-
Cc 6   ſta-

ftation fet downe in the firft part
at the end of the meditations : and
proteft at all times to haue a will & purpofe to keep euery point of it, faying
with Dauid : *No my God, neuer will I
forget thy iuftification, for in them thou haft
giuen mee life*. And when thou findft any
fpirituall battail in thy foule, take in
hand the felf fame proteftation, and
proftrate in fpirit with all humilitie, pronounce it all from thy hart,
and thou fhalt find great eafe in thy
conflict.

2. Profeffe to all the world, that thou
defireft to be deuout, be not afhamed
of that holy defire and profeffion. I
fay, make profeffion of a true defire
of deuotion, and not, make profeffion of deuotion: blush not to vfe thofe
common and ordinarie actions, which
helpe vs to obtaine the loue of God:
aduow and admitt hardyly, that thou
doeft thy endeuour to meditate, and
thou hadft rather dye then finne mor-
tally. That thou wilt by Gods grace,
frequent the facraments, and folow the
counfels of thy ghoftly father (though
for good confiderations it be not
expe-

expedient to name him). For this
franck and free confeſſion of Gods ſeruice, that wee are with a ſpeciall affection conſecrated and addicted to his
loue: is moſt acceptable to the diuine
maieſtie, who by no meanes alloweth
his ſeruants, to be aſhamed of his croſſe. Beſides, this open profeſſion, cuts
of manie a ſummon, manie an inticement, which the world would make
to the contrarie: and bidds vs to ſtand
vpon our reputation, in the conſtant
pourſuite of deuotion. The philoſophers, openly profeſſed them ſelues to
be philoſophers, that ſo mē might permitt them to liue Philoſophicallie: and
we muſt make our ſelues knowne to
be louers of deuotion and holy exerciſes, that men may lett vs liue deuoutly. Yf any man tell thee, that one
may liue deuoutly without the practize
of theſe exerciſes and aduices: denie it
him not, but anſwer him louingly, that
thy weaknes is ſo great, that thou
ſtandeſt in much more need of helpe,
then other men doe.

3. Laſt of all, I coniure and entreat
thee, my deere Philotheus, by all that
which

which is holie in heauen and earth,
by the baptifme which thou haſt receaued, by the ſweet milk of mercie
which thou haſt ſucked from the breſts
of our Lord Ieſus, by the moſt louing
hart, in which thou placeſt all thy hope
and confidence : Continue and perſeuer in this happie enterprize of ſpirituall life. Our dayes runn on a pace,
death is hand at our gate, *The trompett
foundeth the retreat* (ſayth Saint Gregorie Nazianzen) *lett euery man be
readie, for the iudge is at hand.* Saint
Symphorians mother ſeing him ledd
to martyrdom, cried after him : my
ſonne, my ſonne, remember euerlaſting life, look vp to heauen, and
thinck vpon him that raignes there,
a ſhort end will quickly end the courſe
of this life. I ſay the ſame to thee
(my Philotheus) look vp to heauen,
and leaue it not for this baſe earth;
thinck vpon hell, and caſt not thy
ſelf into that dreadfull gulfe for moments of pleaſures ; remember Ieſus
Chriſt, denie him not for the worlde:
and though the labour of a deuout
life, ſeeme hard vnto thee, ſing merilie

rilie with Saint Frauncis :

Since heauen is for my paines aßignd
Paines are sweet passetimes to my mind.

Liue for euer sweet Iesus, to whome wtih the Father, and holy Ghost, be all honour and glorie, now and alway, and for euer and euer. Amen.

The Errata.

Pag.14.line13.Picaustes, reade, Piraustes. p.17.l.24. many soules, reade, of many soules. p.37.l.23. of riches, reade, of the rich. p.39.l.26.foules, reade, soules. p.68. l.3. were created, reade, we were created. p.91 l.17. infinitle, reade, infinite, p.91.l.19 Certesie, reade, Terresie. p.95.l.11. pight, reade, right. p.120 l.18. of, reade, or. p.135 l.22. forces, reade, species. p.139. l.2. thy, reade, the. p.141.l.20. of, reade, or. p.172. l.12. this, reade, his. p.191.l.22. Consiliat, reade, Conflict. p.235.l.19. perfections, reade, thinges. p.277.l.20. king, reade, kinde. p.337.l.12. and, reade, it. & l.13. it, and. p.344 trade, reade, trace. p.365.l.22. cordes, reade, the cordes. l.376 l.16.back, reade, lack. p 377.l.4. turne, reade, tame. p.405.l.26. word, reade, world. p.21.l.6. part the fourth, fore, reade, fire.

If there be any other faultes escaped, I pray
the getle reader of his curtesie to correct them.

A TABLE OF
THE CHAPTERS.

THE FIRST PART
OF THE INTRODVCTION:
Conteyning aduices and exercises requisite for the cōduct of a soule frō her
very first desire of a deuout life, vntill
she be brought to a full resolution to
embrace it stedfastly in all her actiōs.

The

A Table of the Chapters.

That

A Table

THE SECOND PART
OF THIS INTRODVCTION:
Containing diuers aduices for the
lifting vp of the soule to God by
prayer, and by vse of the Sacraments.

Of the Chapters.

THE THIRD PART
OF THE INTRODVCTION:
Containing ſundrie rules and aduices, concerning the exerciſe of virtues.

A Table

Of

Of the Chapters.

Of de-

A Table

THE FOVRTH PART
OF THE INTRODVCTION:
Containing necessary instructions,
against those tentations which are
most ordinarily incident, to those
that endeuour to liue spiritually.

That

Of the Chapters.

THE FIFTH PART
OF THE INTRODVCTION:
Cōtaining exercises & instructiōs to
renew the soule, & cōfirme deuotion.

A Table of the Chapters.

FINIS.

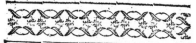

THE COMMVNICATION
OF DOCTOVR THAVLERVS
with a poore beggar, wherein is compre-
hended the example of a perfect man, and
how we should resigne our selues in all
thinges vnto the good pleasure of God.

HERE was on a tyme a greate diuine, who prayed vnto God the space of 8. yeares, that it might be his good pleasure, to direct him to a man, that might instruct and teach him the true way of vertu. And it happened beinge in this desyer, that he heard a voice from heauen, which sayd vnto him, goe vnto such a Church portch, & there thou shalt finde a man that wil instruct thee in the spiritual life. He walking then towards the sayd Church, founde a poore begger, who had his feete filthye and foule, and al naked, whose clothes were not worth a halfe penny; and he saluted him in this sort: God giue you good morrow,
my

my frind. The poore mã anſwered him,
Sir, I do not remember that euer I had
an euil morow. The Doctour ſayd vnto
him ; God giue you a good and hap-
pye life : wherfore ſaye you that? quoth e
the begger vnto him ; for I was neuer
vnhappie. Which the Doctor not vn-
derſtãding, ſayd vnto him againe ; God
bleſſe you my frinde, I pray you ſpeake
a littel more clearlye, for I know not
what you meane. Then the poore beggar anſwered him ; Good maſter Doctour, I ſhall doe it willinglye : you
know you badde mee good morrow,
wher vnto I replyed, that I had neuer
any ill morrow, for when I haue hunger, I prayſe God : if it freeſe, haile,
ſnow, rayne, be it fayre or foule, I giue
prayſe to God ; though I be poore,
miſerable, and deſpiſed of each on, I
giue thankes vnto God. And therfore I
neuer had any euil morow: you did wiſh
vnto mee alſo, a good and happy life ;
wher vnto I made you anſwere, that
I was neuer vnfortunate, becauſe I haue
learnt alwayes to reſigne my ſelfe vnto
the wil of God being certaine that al his
workes cannot be but very good : by
reaſon whereof, al that happeneth vnto
mee

mee by his permiſſion, be it proſpe-
ritye or aduerſitye, ſweete ot ſower, I
receaue it as from his owne hande with
greate ioy and comfort, and therfor I
was neuer vnfortunate, for I neuer de-
ſyred any thinge but the good pleaſure
of God; which the poore man hauinge
ſayde: the Doctor anſwered: but what
would you ſay, my frinde, if God would
damne you? If God would damne mee,
ſayd the poore man, verely if he would
vſe mee ſo hardlye, I haue two armes
to imbrace him; the one whereof is a
profounde humilitye, by the which I
am vnited vnto his holy humanitye:
the other is loue, and charitye, whieh
ioyneth mee vnto his diuinitye, by
which I would imbrace him in ſuch
ſort, that he should be conſtrayned to
deſcende with mee into hel. And I had
rather without compariſon, be in hel
with God, then to be without him in
paradiſe. The Doctor learnt in this
communication, that a trew reſigna-
tion, accompanied with profunde humilitye of hart, is the ſhorteſt waye to
attaine vnto the loue of God. After that
he asked of him againe, from whence
he came? Vnto whom he made anſwere
that

that God had sent him. The Doctor inquired yet of him, where he had found God. I found him, quoth he, so soone as I had renounced and forsaken all creatures. And where didest thou leaue him? replyed the Doctor. I left him, answered the begger, with the pure and cleane hartes, and amongst men of good wille. But who art thou, my frind, quoth the diuine vnto him: The poore man made him answere, that he was a Kinge. And he askinge him where his kingdom was; It is, quoth he, in my soule; for I can so well rule, and gouerne my sences, as wel outward, as inward: that al my affections, and passions do obey vnto reason; which kingdom is without doubte, more excellent, then al the kingdomes of this world. Moreouer the forsayde Doctor demaunded of him, who it was that had brought him vnto so great perfection? It was silence, answered the poore man, and my high and loftye meditations, and the vnion which I had with God. I could take no repose nor cofort in any creature of the world, by meane. whereof, I founde out my God, who wil cofort me world without ende. Amen.